Hollywood Babylon

It's Back!

BY DARWIN PORTER AND DANFORTH PRINCE

BLOOD MOON Productions, Ltd.

HOLLYWOOD BABYLON

IT'S BACK!

Volume One

An Overview of Exhibitionism, Sexuality, and Sin
as Filtered through 85 years of Hollywood Scandal

BLOOD MOON PRODUCTIONS, LTD.
WWW.BLOODMOONPRODUCTIONS.COM

ISBN 978-0-9748118-8-8

Printed in the United States of America
Cover design by Richard Leeds (www.bigwigdesign.com)

Volume One, First Edition, July, 2008

Hollywood ?

"My father called Rita Hayworth a nympho. My mother [murdered on June 22, 1958] wet-nursed dipsomaniacal film stars. My father pointed out the two-way mirrors at the Hollywood Ranch Market and told me they were spy holes to entrap shoplifters and disrupt homosexual assignations. Johnnie Ray was a fruit. Lizabeth Scott was a dyke. All jazz musicians were hopheads. Tom Neal beat Franchot Tone half-dead over a blonde cooze named Barbara Payton. The Algiers Hotel was a glorified 'fuck pad.' A pint-sized Mickey Cohen ran the L.A. rackets from his cell at McNeil Island. Rin Tin Tin was really a girl dog. Lassie was really a boy dog. L.A. was a smog-shrouded netherworld orbiting under a dark star and blinded by the glare of scandal-rag flashbulbs. Every third person was a peeper, a prowler, pederast, poon stalker, panty sniffer, prostitute, pillhead, pothead, or pimp. The other two-thirds of the population were tight-assed squares resisting the urge to peep, prowl, poon stalk, pederastically indulge, pop pills, and panty sniff. This mass of self-denial created a seismic dislocation that skewed L.A. about six degrees off the central axis of planet Earth."

James Ellroy, Author of ***L.A. Confidential***

Rita Hayworth

Tom Cruise.

Johnnie Ray

Lizabeth Scott

Rin-Tin-Tin

Lassie

Psychotic trio: Franchot Tone, Barbara Payton, & Tom Neal

Widow Tied and Slain in Hotel Room

$25 Wkly. & Up. $100 M
HOLLYWOOD ALGIERS HOTEL
445 N. ROSSMORE

Mickey Cohen

WHAT CRITICS ARE SAYING
ABOUT THIS BOOK

"You know, everyone thinks Hollywood is a cesspool of epic proportions today, but please! It's always been that way. And if you love smutty celebrity dirt as much as I do *(and if you don't, what's wrong with you? Ya got morals or something?)*, then have I got a book for you!"

The Hollywood Offender

"Dishing with abandon, the authors spare no one--especially not the dead. Marilyn Monroe had an affair with Ronald Reagan. Marilyn also had a tryst with Joan Crawford but refused to make it an ongoing affair. James Dean showed a disconcerting interest in a 12-year old boy in the early 1950s. Lucille Ball launched herself into show business as a hooker, and her husband Desi Arnaz had a fling with Cesar Romero. Cary Grant had an incestuous relationship with his stepson, Lance Reventlow. And this, by the way, is only the tip of the iceberg."

Rush & Molloy, *The NY Daily News*

"Many of Hollywood's most outrageous secrets remained hidden. Until now. This book will set the graves of Hollywood's cemeteries spinning."

London's *Daily Express*

"This monumentally exhaustive collection of sins, foibles, failings, and sexual adventures is the ultimate guilty pleasure--and publisher Blood Moon pledges that it's merely volume one."

Books to Watch Out For (www.QSyndicate.com)

"The American movie industry is always eager for the spotlight if the close-up is flattering and good for business. But Hollywood may get more than it bargained for with *Hollywood Babylon's* compendium of stories, rumors and myths. Virtually every page features one kind of train wreck or another, usually accompanied by spectacularly lurid photographs. Darwin Porter and Danforth Prince provide a hair-raising list of compromises and strategically granted sexual favors as proof that some stars will do anything for a part. Not even Grace Kelly and Lucille Ball escaped having to get down and dirty on the proverbial casting couch, according to Porter and Prince. Read these pages to learn what Robert Mitchum is said to have taught Marilyn Monroe on the set of *The River of No Return* that would prove useful during her rumored affair with J.F.K. Try as you might, you won't be able to stop turning the pages...In revealing so many facts previously under wraps, this book, in fact, raises the question of how much more remains hidden."

Shelf Awareness / Bookselling News

TABLE OF CONTENTS

Well-Hung Hollywood
The Larger View

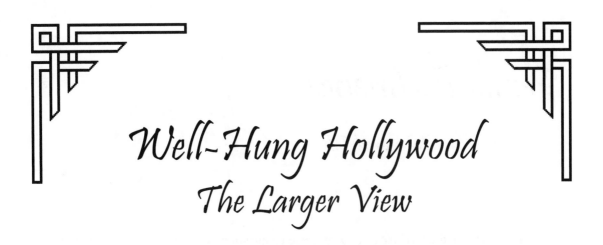

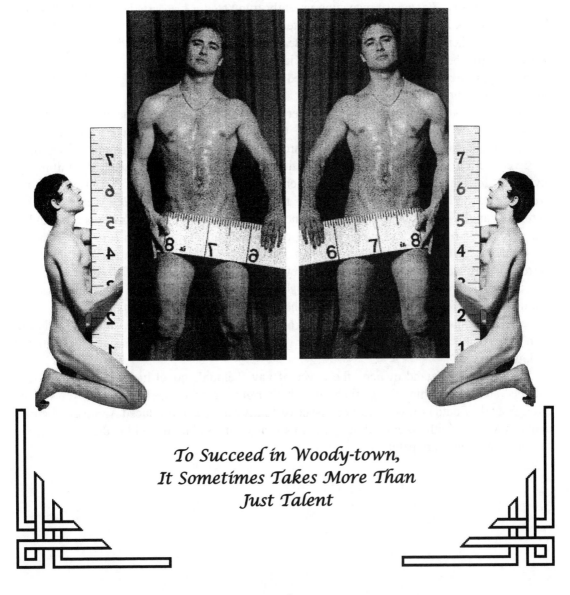

*To Succeed in Woody-town,
It Sometimes Takes More Than
Just Talent*

Penile Pertinence

How the Stars Measured Up

In San Francisco, the *Bay Area Reporter* raised a question decades ago that is still pertinent today – perhaps even more so. "Look all around you and what do you see? The cock consciousness of America is at an all-time high."

The cover of a *Penthouse* magazine urgently trumpeted a lead article in which "Women Talk About Cock Size." An important news item in *Weekly World News* was an exotic dancer's revelation that her erstwhile lover, Warren Beatty, was only average in endowment, but compensated with fabulous technique. Anthony Kiedes, lead singer of the band, "The Red Hot Chili Peppers," appeared on the nationally televised *Saturday Night Live* wearing nothing but tights with a hand appliqué groping his crotch.

And talk about crotch-groping. Remember Mark Wahlberg when he was pop singer Marky Mark? He made crotch-groping part of the foundation of his career. He became far more famous for clutching his taut teenage meat through white BVDs than he was for his singing.

Even the movies, traditional holdouts in the cock-tease department, launched a full monty revolution for males. Remember Richard Gere flapping his dick in the otherwise moribund *Breathless*? John Malkovich maneuvering his meat into a close-up in *The Sheltering Sky?* Tom Berenger dangling his around as the tribal chieftain in *At Play in the Fields of the Lord* and *In Praise of Older Women?* And everyone except John Gielgud showed his in *Prospero's Books*.

Geoff Nasey of *Spy Magazine* said, "Americans have a love/hate relationship with cock. Surrounded by glorifying images of cock, they are nonetheless terrified of it. Americans worship the implied power of cock; advertising shows us cock can fulfill our every physical and emotional need. Yet all those stars who strut that stuff upon a stage wouldn't dare actually show it. Yes, Americans are scared stiff of cock. The fear is implanted early on – why do kids call each other dickheads?" The fear is lifelong. It has fueled political fights over the National Endowment.

To placate newsstand owners, the cover of Fay Weldon's novel had a plain paper band wrapped around it to hide the genitals of – that's right – Michelangelo's *David*. Newsstands throughout the South refused to carry an issue of *Vanity Fair* that reproduced Annie Liebowitz's photo of a nude Keith Haring, although it was nearly impossible to find his dick through the camouflage of his body paint.

Keith Haring (pictured nude on the beach; left), and (right) camouflaged within Annie Liebowitz's notorious body paint photo. Haring (1958-1990) was a pre-eminent artist and social activist who dominated "street culture art" in New York City during the 80s. He first achieved notice with his chalk drawings in the subways of New York. Andy Warhol was the theme of several of Haring's pieces, including "Andy mouse."

The artist's images have become a universally recognized visual language of the 20th century. Openly gay, he died of an HIV-related disease in 1990.

 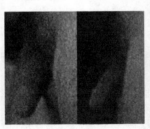 

John Malkovich wasn't embarrassed to show his dick in *The Sheltering Sky* (1990) in which he appeared with **Debra Winger** (see closeup, above left). A double view of his Full Monty appears in all its blurry glory (see above, center).

Was it this shot that got him acclaimed as *Empire Magazine*'s number 70 on its 1995 list of the "100 Sexiest Stars in Film History?" Before devoting his life to acting, Malkovich was a school bus driver, an egg roll salesman, and a house painter.

"You can fake anything in the movies," he claimed, "love, explosions, special effects, horror, and especially sex."

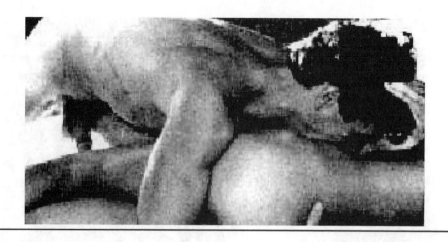

The nude appearances of Chicago born **Tom Berenger** in *In Praise of Older Women* (1978) (photo above) and *At Play in the Fields of the Lord (*1991; photo, bottom left) earned him three stars – the highest rating – from *The Bare Facts*, a printed guide to on-screen nudity.

His most notorious role remains his interpretation of Gary in *Looking for Mr. Goodbar* (1977). "It was such a slimy character with no redeeming qualities. To me it was like playing Charles Manson. I felt dirty."

The Montana Mule & Other Celebrity Cocks

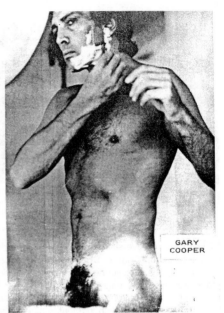

GARY COOPER

The controversial subject of celebrity cocks—and the size thereof—was once only whispered about, perhaps in intimate conversations between Ava Gardner and Lana Turner.

Today, however, the cock size of celebrities, such as the endowment of Colin Farrell, or the lack of endowment of Brad Pitt, are often presented as headline news within gossip columns.

In the mainstream press, *Time* magazine broke the barrier when it ran the size of Hugh Grant's penis—about six inches, maybe slightly less.

Penis size is fair game. After all, the size of a woman's bosom has been routine tabloid fodder for years. Today you no longer have to guess at the identities of the best hung male stars in the *roman à clef* novels of Jackie Collins or in the old paperbacks of Joyce Haber. Nudes of male stars, often posed in their younger days, are in many cases now posted on the web for all to see.

What follows is a survey of the best hung stars of Hollywood's golden age, followed by today's challengers. Call it "Who Was Hung."

By the late 1920s, **Gary Cooper** *(above)* was known as the stud of Hollywood. Seemingly everyone, male or female, had an opinion about him. "I think the men were more interested in him than the women," said Loretta Young. "Cooper found out pretty quick that he could do two things well ... ride a horse and fuck," said Carole Lombard.

"I don't doubt that he had a man occasionally," said Marlene Dietrich, his costar in the 1930s *Morocco*. "They wouldn't leave him alone."

"I've had some big boys in my day," said sultry Mae West, "and Coop ranks up there with the top." What was his secret, aside from the obvious? Coop claimed that it was because he ate a large can of sauerkraut every morning.

Ava Gardner *(left figure in photo, right)* and **Lana Turner** were not only best pals, but they shared some of their lovers, especially if the lover happened to be well hung.

They even married the same man: Musician Artie Shaw, who went on in the wake of those marriages to become the fourth "Mr. Evelyn Keyes."

Some of the men Ava and Lana shared included Robert Taylor, Clark Gable, Richard Burton, Turkish actor Turhan Bey, Peter Lawford, Howard Hughes, Frank Sinatra (who married Ava), Mickey Rooney (who also married Ava), gangster Johnny Stompanato, and the singer Mel Tormé – and the beat goes on.

His mysterious and rugged good looks made Italian-born Valentino the most lusted-after man in the world. The Latin Lover became the silver screen's first and greatest male sex symbol. He took two wives, Jean Acker and Natacha Rambova. From all reports, he never seduced either of them. Both women were lesbians.

Many of his so-called "affairs" were strictly for press consumption, including his dalliance with screen vamp Pola Negri. She, too, was a lesbian. Benefiting from the pleasure of his reported ten inches were the likes of Norman Kerry, matinee idol of the silent screen, actor and icon Sessue Hayakawa—and most definitely Ramon Novarro.

Pola Negri, the silent screen's rival of Gloria Swanson, also romped with Charlie Chaplin. In days of yore, the Little Tramp wasn't so little when he stripped down. He should have been nicknamed The Big Tramp. Chaplin told the size-queen golddigger, Peggy Hopkins Joyce, that his 12-incher was "The Eighth Wonder of the World."

The most controversial actor of the silent screen, and also the most talented, **Charlie Chaplin** (two photos, above) became famous for seducing young girls. What is not widely known, except to a precious few biographers, is that he also liked young boys. "The most beautiful form of life is a very young girl or a lithe young male with a delicate rosebud about to bloom," he once told William Randolph Hearst. "I like to pick the bloom from the flower."

Chaplin's costar in *The Gold Rush* (1925) and second wife, Lita Grey, complained to actress Edna Purviance, "Sometimes Charlie is good for six rounds in one night – almost right in succession, with only a five-minute break in between."

"I learned that about Charlie long before you did," Purviance said.

"Did you ever complain?" Grey asked.

"Yes, I did," Purviance said. "But Charlie told me, 'I'm a stallion – and you'd better get used to it.'"

Mae West (left photo, above), embraces **George Raft**, her costar in *Night After Night* (1932), and formerly, a driver for an important mob boss. Along with Edward G. Robinson, he became the onscreen epitome of a 1930s gangster. Unlike Robinson, Raft was a gangster in real life.

In the right-hand photo, above, **Rudolph Valentino** is pictured with notorious and imperious **Natacha Rambova**, the second of his two lesbian wives,. "He was the dream man to millions of women," said close friend and silent screen star, Mae Murray, who was the duenna of Hollywood's closeted homosexual community. "But you'd catch him in bed at night with Norman Kerry, Sessue Hayakawa, William Boyd, even 'Rae' Bourbon, the female impersonator." Two well-built Italian soldiers in his native Castelleneta, Italy, introduced young Valentino to man/boy love.

After sharing a shower with Chaplin, Orson Welles described the star's genitals as being "like a little peanut." But Welles may have been jealous. Most of Chaplin's sexual partners, who included Lupe Velez, Hedy Lamarr, Marion Davies, and Louise Brooks, agreed with Mae West: "Chaplin was short and his nose was average, but his pecker was really bigtime."

Mae West may never have had an affair with Chaplin, but she did "test" George Raft, Valentino's former roommate. "Raft had the equipment and knew how to use it, but I think he preferred Valentino to me."

Another legendary blonde, Betty Grable, more or less agreed with West. Grable thought that George Raft "was probably a latent homosexual." But he had plenty of female admirers nonetheless, including Lana Turner, Lucille Ball, and Marlene Dietrich. In his early gigolo days, when he was shacked up with Valentino, The Sheik gave him the sexual nickname of "Black Snake." What could "The Great Lover" have meant? Raft reportedly told nightclub owner Texas Guinan, "Rudy and I often perform erotic dances with each other in the nude. It makes us hot and horny. Don't get the wrong idea. I'm the top. He's the bottom."

Lupe Velez never got around to Valentino, but she did manage to seduce Chaplin. He didn't quite do it for her, but she "saw stars" when Gary Cooper mounted her. "*Garree* has the biggest one in town," said that Mexican spitfire. Carole Lombard was more critical.

During 1926, Texas Guinan, "The Queen of the Nightclubs" during the Prohibition Era, earned $700,000 in ten months with her speakeasies – a vast fortune back then. Her clubs were routinely raided by police, but she reopened every time, greeting the Vanderbilts and the Astors with her trademark, "Hello, suckers."

Texas befriended "roomies" George Raft and Rudolph Valentino when they worked as gigolo-dancers in "tea rooms," hustling rich ladies.

Raft once confided to Texas, "I fake a climax with a lady because Rudy wants my offering of joy juice when I return home after a hard night's work. He gets what he wants. I owe it to him. I make him pay all the rent."

The incredibly handsome **Gary Cooper** *(above, center)*, whom Tallulah Bankhead said had "too much beauty and too much cock" – is pictured between two hell-raising screen camps, **Lupe Velez** on the left and the silent screen flapper, **Clara Bow**, on the right. Cooper was just one of dozens of Velez' world-class seductions: she snared everyone from Tom Mix to Errol Flynn, Charlie Chaplin to heavyweight boxing champ Jack Dempsey, Clark Gable, even the father-and-son act Douglas Fairbanks Sr. and Douglas Fairbanks Jr.

Bow lost her virginity to her father, Robert Bow. "My daddy taught me to love dick so much," she once told Cooper, "that I had to milk the bull of every hot man I met," including John Wayne, an entire football team, and even monster man Bela Lugosi, who forever after carried around a nude photograph of her for masturbating in his dressing room. "Clara Bow laid everything but linoleum," claimed gossip maven Louella Parsons.

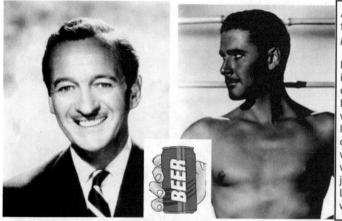

"Gary has it all in front but no ass to push it with."

The bisexual Cooper, whose long list of screwmates included Howard Hughes, Marlene Dietrich, Cary Grant, Carole Lombard, Tallulah Bankhead, and Cecil Beaton, also won the praise of Clara Bow. "Coop's hung like a horse and can go on all night."

That's why he was called "The Montana Mule."

As for "The Aviator" (Howard Hughes), Cooper was but a passing fancy. Hughes dropped Cooper for Randolph Scott. But once Scott introduced Hughes to Cary Grant, the billionaire succumbed. "Cary became Hughes' favorite piece of ass," Joan Crawford said. "Of course, Hughes would fuck a tree, and not just Jean Harlow or Rita Hayworth. Hughes had a lot of experience. William Haines told me his uncle, Rupert, broke him into homosexual love when he was just fifteen years old."

James Bacon, the Hollywood columnist, called Hughes "the great swordsman." Errol Flynn could have testified to that.

Flynn once claimed, "I'm just a goddamned phallic symbol to the world." For verification, one could ask his bottom, Tyrone Power, or else Doris Duke, Rock Hudson, Barbara Hutton, and/or Evita Peron, dictator of Argentina. Flynn often whipped out his erection at parties and used it to bang out such old-fashioned tunes as "You Are My Sunshine" on the nearest piano. Marilyn Monroe saw him perform, but wasn't impressed, calling him "a show-off." Flynn once claimed he'd had sex 14,000 times in his life. "I had a secret. A bit of cocaine on the tip of my penis before intercourse did the trick."

Iron Eyes Cody, in his autobiography, *Portrait of a Hollywood Indian*, once said, "I know of several perfectly sane directors who actually asked to see it, right there on the set. Only too happy to settle any lingering doubts

associated with his masculine dimensions, Errol would publicly unzip and proceed to set the record straight. Regardless of who was present." And once, even in front of the endlessly demure Olivia de Havilland.

Flynn once roomed with actor David Niven. Marlene Dietrich had an affair with Niven and later claimed that "these two womanizers messed around with each other." Niven possessed a "beer can" of a penis according to biographer Graham Lord; and he had a reputation for priapic swordsmanship.

Actress Terry Moore, who has publicly referred to her personal knowledge of Hughes' mighty inches, dated Nicky Hilton after his divorce from Elizabeth Taylor. "He had the absolutely largest penis—wider than a beer can and much longer—I have ever seen," Moore said. "To make love to him was akin to fornicating with a horse."

Tallulah Bankhead once said that she came to Hollywood "just to fuck that divine Gary Cooper." She once told her friend, Estelle Winwood, that if she ever met an actor hung as well as Cooper, she'd marry him. Tallulah was true to her word.

Orson Welles dismissed actor John Emery

Sex kitten **Terry Moore** (photo above) praised Elizabeth Taylor's husband, Nicky Hilton (see previous page) citing his awesome manliness and his gymnastics as a lover. Joan Collins confirmed everything Terry said.

Terry also became involved with the aviator and cinema mogul **Howard Hughes** (left), and lost her virginity to him after a secret "wedding" aboard his yacht. But first he quizzed her about bowel movements. When she didn't remember exactly, he forced her to take laxatives which he carefully supervised.

Tallulah Bankhead's only husband, **John Emery** (left photo, above) wore a "fuck-awful green monstrosity" of a suit when she first met him socially. She wasted no time getting that suit off of him and discovered – in her words – "A handmaiden's wildest fantasy."

"I'm the bigger star," Tallulah told all her gay pals," but John has me beat in one department. His cock is three times bigger than mine."

She allowed gay actor **Vincent Price** (right) a chance to sample the wares of her husband. Vincent told her, "It's the biggest I've ever swallowed, and I've handled some milk bottles."

as a "road company John Barrymore," but he became Tallulah's first and only husband. John and Tallu married on August 31, 1937. Emery said that when he first kissed Tallulah "she damn near knocked my tonsils down my throat."

During their honeymoon in Alabama, while waiting in a rainstorm under an awning at the airport, Tallulah pulled her new husband's trousers down and shouted at her fellow passengers: "How's that for a two-hander, *dah-lings*?"

One morning in New York when gay actor Vincent Price came over to her apartment for breakfast, she invited him into her bedroom, where Emery was still asleep. She pulled down the sheet exposing his nude body. "I married John because he has the biggest cock in Hollywood, and I've had Gary Cooper, so I ought to know."

Knowing that Vincent wanted a taste, she invited him to help himself.

Still half asleep from all the booze they'd consumed the night before, Emery woke up thinking his new wife was giving him a blow-job. He was startled to see it

On his nightclub circuit, singer **Tom Jones** *(upper left)* wore his pants so tight "you could tell what religion he was," said one comedian.

Columnist **James Bacon** *(above right photo, with **Lana Turner**)* claimed that when Forrest Tucker passed out drunk and nude within the locker room at Lakeside Country Club, he'd become a sightseeing attraction. Visitors would parade in just "to get a glimpse of it."

Once, **Milton Berle** *(below, far right)* encountered an actor who had been bragging about his endowment. Berle told the actor, "I bet I've got more than you do." The actor said that he doubted that. A friend, standing next to Berle, said, "Go ahead, Milton, just take out enough to win."

When **Humphrey Bogart** *(above left)* first met **Truman Capote** *(above, right)*, he wrote home to his wife, Lauren Bacall, "At first you can't believe him, he's so odd, and then you want to carry him around with you always."

Stories are still spread about what went on in the little town of Ravello where the film, *Beat the Devil*, was shot. Jennifer Jones, its star, was chased by a tall Italian lesbian. Truman told Tennessee Williams that before the final reel, "I'm going to suck off both Bogie and John Huston."

Back in New York, Tennessee asked Capote, "Did you get your men?"

"Both of them," Capote bragged. "Even Bogie."

"What did they think of male sex?" Tennessee asked.

"They came in my mouth, didn't they?" Capote proclaimed.

was Vincent. "Let him finish," Tallulah called to Emery. "You broke my jaw last night." Like a dutiful husband, Emery obliged. When he'd climaxed in Vincent's mouth, Tallulah said to Vincent, "The weapon is formidable, but I find the shot terribly weak."

Tallulah, Lupe Velez, and Clara Bow were the first actresses to speak out about penis size. The already-mentioned James Bacon was the first newspaper columnist to do so. He was the author of *Hollywood Is a Four-Letter Word.* On the old TV talk show, "The Tomorrow Show," he was bleeped for saying of Forrest Tucker and Milton Berle: "Together they form the Alaskan pipeline." When Berle met Tom Jones, a singer famous for wearing pants so tight they revealed that he was not circumcised, the comedian told the singer: "You want to see a cock, boy. I'll show you a cock." Berle proceeded to whip out 11 inches—and that was limp!

Along came the Forties, an era that tended to either introduce all-new stars such as Frank Sinatra, or recycled 30s stars who were then elevated into positions of greatness, as in the case of Humphrey Bogart.

As Humphrey Bogart once said, "To have a love affair breaks a bond between husband and wife—and even if your partner doesn't know about it, the relationship must be less open, so something very important will never be the same." So what did Bogie

Rat Packers **Dean Martin** *(above, left)*, **Sammy Davis Jr.** *(center)* and **Frank Sinatra** *(right)* eye each other skeptically, but all in good fun – which was to some degree what their notorious lifestyles were all about.

All three entertainers, according to the showgirls of Las Vegas, were exceptionally endowed. Everyone from June Allyson to Marilyn Monroe gave Martin good reports. But not one of his early conquests from Ohio: "He was a bastard. All wine and candlelight, then a pat on the ass in the morning."

The bisexual Davis seduced everyone from porn queen Linda Lovelace *(Deep Throat)* to Peter Lawford, brother-in-law of then-president JFK. Davis admitted to being a Satanist. He painted one of his fingernails red to identify himself to other cult members. "I dabbled around the edge of it for sexual kicks," he confessed.

Sinatra was the leader of the band. It would be easier to draw up a list of actresses he didn't seduce. Included among the more famous of the women he banged were Nancy Davis, Marlene Dietrich, Elizabeth Taylor, and Lana Turner.

"When Sinatra dies, they're giving his zipper to the Smithsonian," claimed Martin.

do? After marrying Lauren Bacall, he continued his longtime affair with his personal assistant, Verita Thompson, who was in charge of his wigs.

Actresses Louise Brooks and Margaret Sullavan reported that Bogie had a skinny cock but that it was very long. So did the not always reliable Truman Capote who worked with Bogie and John Huston on the set of *Beat the Devil* (1952). The author claimed that Bogie told him, "You can suck it but I insist that you spit out the cum. Don't swallow it. Okay?"

Witnesses who included his valet, Marilyn Monroe, Natalie Wood, and Judy Garland all agreed on skinny Frank Sinatra's endowment. "Well, there's only 10 pounds of Frank, but there's 110 pounds of cock," said his wife, Ava Gardner.

Once in Las Vegas, when Sammy Davis Jr. was standing at a urinal beside Rat Pack pal Sinatra, he looked down at his own heavy endowment before checking out what Sinatra was flashing. "If Liberace was here tonight," Davis said to Sinatra, "he'd been singing 'Mad About the Boys.'"

Linda Lovelace, porno star of *Deep Throat*, along with stripper Tempest Storm, Ava Gardner, Kim Novak, and Marilyn Monroe all agreed on one thing: "Sammy might be a midget but not when he dropped trou."

As Kathy McGee, the singer, testified: "He had the sexual stamina of a bull. You couldn't be alone in a room with Sammy for five minutes without giving him a blowjob." In Sammy's case, her choice of animal kingdom images—a bull—was right on target.

Another Rat Packer was Dean Martin.

Three Las Vegas show girls in 1962 confirmed what Jerry Lewis had already said back in the 50s when his then partner and he were taping a radio promo for "At War With the Army." Clowning around, both Martin and Lewis were touting each other's virtues. Lewis accidentally blurted out, "And he has a big cock, too."

Years later call girls pronounced Martin a "terrific and considerate lover," conceding that he had ten inches. The third girl demurred, although admitting that he was great in the sack. "But it felt like more than twelve inches to me."

Other screen queens, including June Allyson, Pier Angeli, Marilyn Monroe, Ann Sheridan, and Lana Turner, also praised Martin's size and performance. Once during Martin's early days, he complained to Lou Costello, part of another comic duo, that he needed a nose job. The closeted comedian lent him the money for some plastic surgery. But Martin spent it with a Jewish doctor who cut off his foreskin instead.

We have to bring back Mae West to comment on the hidden charms of Anthony Quinn,

Dana Andrews (*photo above*) was an amply endowed Hollywood "Bad Boy." He avoided Cesar Romero's passes when they shot *Lucky Cisco Kid* in 1940, but gave in to Gene Tierney during the filming of *Tobacco Road* (1941) – the first of the five films they made together. He seduced many of his leading ladies, including the bisexual Barbara Stanwyck during the making of *Balls of Fire* (1941).

After frequent arrests for drunk driving, he told AA, "My name is Dana Andrews, and I'm an alcoholic."

Linda Darnell, his co-star in *Fallen Angel* (1946), said, "If you can get Dana to sober up, he's a marvelous lover and really knows what to do with what God gave him."

From Mae West to gay director George Cukor, from Ingrid Bergman to Rita Hayworth, all the conquests of **Anthony Quinn** (*photo above*) sang praises about his attentiveness in the sack. "'I want to impregnate every woman in the world,' he once told me," said actress Ruth Warrick (*Citizen Kane*). "I didn't realize 'til later how literally he meant it."

Quinn never had trouble finding a partner. "If there was not a young starlet, or a companionable makeup girl, there was always a lovely local lady to take her place."

"Still waters run deep," said Greer Garson of her *Mrs. Miniver* (1942) costar, **Walter Pidgeon** (*photo above*).

At the time of their first meeting, she told him, "When I first came here from London, I thought I'd arrived in the Babylon-of-the-Pacific."

He assured her that her first impression was right.

The Canadian actor confused her at first, claiming one day he wanted to be a sea captain and on another day that his true goal was to be a singer.

After their on-again, off-again affair, she told Peter Lawford that, "Walter's a better lover than an actor."

although he disdained talk about a man's penis.

"I've never really felt a man's masculinity was in his penis." Or so said Anthony Quinn, one of Hollywood's first male superstars from Mexico (Ramon Novarro was the first). There are many lovely women who would disagree with Quinn's assessment of his penis—namely, Mae West, Ruth Warrick, Ingrid Bergman, Rita Hayworth, Margaret Leighton, Carole Lombard, and at least one male director, George Cukor. "If you like to choke on *mexicano* dick," Cukor told best pal Spencer Tracy, "swing on that pole of Tony Quinn. I got my man. That was something that three pretty boys tried but failed to do—Errol Flynn, Rock Hudson, and Robert Taylor. *Viva Zapata!* Viva Quinn!"

Evelyn Keyes in her autobiography, *Scarlett O'Hara's Younger Sister*, actually complained: "There was simply too much of Tony (yes, there too). Legs and arms too long and miles of male body trying (and succeeding) to invade my limited space."

Cock chronicler Sam Frank told a story he'd heard about Quinn when he was traveling in Rome. A woman and her husband encountered Quinn at a tailor's shop. Since her husband had the same build as Quinn, he offered to stand in for the actor while suit measurements were taken. Later, with her husband's permission, the wife joined Quinn on a tour of Rome.

Frank quotes the woman as saying: "I couldn't take my eyes off the huge bulge in Tony's crotch. As soon as I could, I started feeling him up. He responded by taking me to his hotel room, where I measured his cock and he fucked my brains out. His cock and my husband's were both alike. Both nearly a foot long, both very thick, both gorgeous looking. Later, when I told my husband about the encounter, not only was he not angry, he told me he wished he could have been there to watch and cheer Quinn on. He felt honored—not threatened—that a man of Quinn's stature, size, and sex appeal had made love to me."

Quinn joined a long line of cocksmen in the 1940s. Two of them, Dana Andrews and Walter Pidgeon, appeared in one of the biggest-grossing movies of that decade, Samuel Goldwyn's *The Best Years of Our Lives* (1946).

A pistol packin' mama, **Joan Crawford**, in *Johnny Guitar* (1954), said, "If you go for one brother, chances are you'll go for the other." She spoke from experience, sleeping with **Scott Brady** *(left)* and then his brother, **Lawrence Tierney** *(right)*.

In *Johnny Guitar*, Brady as the "Dancin' Kid" was the bad guy, fought over by a pair of very butch ladies, Joan Crawford and her off-screen nemesis, Mercedes McCambridge. It was Crawford who bagged her man off screen. Not only that, she enjoyed his brother, Lawrence Tierney as well. "Tierney was tougher in bed," Crawford later told her pals. "More so than Brady. Brady went in through the front door while Tierney went 'round the back."

Canadian-born Walter Pidgeon was no *Mrs. Miniver* when he dropped trou. Fatherly in nature, and with a deep, sonorous voice, he was noted as "the biggest cocksman in Hollywood." Just ask Greer Garson. Even Lana Turner sampled his wares during the filming of *The Bad and the Beautiful*. But he turned down Freddie Bartholomew when they shot *Listen, Darling* (1938), together. The child star wanted to pay "homage" to Pidgeon's feet, not his cock. But the actor didn't say no to fellow co-star, Mary Astor, later pronouncing her a "nympho." He also went for fellow player Judy Garland on the set. But she said, "No, Walter, from what I hear you're much too big for me!"

Today, Dana Andrews is almost a forgotten figure, but back in the 1940s he was a household word. When he wasn't drunk, he was a reliable if somewhat wooden actor, who earned immortality when he was cast as the obsessed detective in one of the greatest of all film noirs, *Laura* (1944) starring Gene Tierney. Sometimes directors had to reshoot scenes when Andrews showed "too much basket." Otto Preminger, who directed him in *Laura*, said, "In one scene he looked like it was hanging all the way down to Honolulu." Andrews always refused to wear a jockstrap.

Two *film noir* stars of the 1940s, Scott Brady and Lawrence Tierney, were brothers.

At a restaurant in Greenwich Village in 1960, Anne Bancroft told writers Stanley Haggart and Darwin Porter that "Scott Brady is certainly proud of his equipment." After taking a sip of her drink, she added, "And well he should be!" In 1957 she'd appeared with him in *The Restless Breed*.

When Anne won the Oscar for the 1962 *The Miracle Worker*, she was appearing on stage in New York and couldn't accept it. Joan Crawford, practically knocking down Bette Davis (who'd been nominated for *What Ever Happened to Baby Jane?*), accepted the award for her.

Crawford had already won an Oscar before Anne—in 1945 for *Mildred Pierce*—and she was well aware of the manly endowment of Scott before Anne had the pleasure. Meeting Scott on the set of *Johnny Guitar*, which had been released by Republic Pictures in 1954, Joan came on strong to the handsome young actor, and he quickly succumbed to her vintage charms. She struck out completely with her other co-stars, Sterling Hayden and "that bitch," Mercedes McCambridge, but found Scott a "very competent lover." When another co-star, Ernest Borgnine, put the

When **Joan Crawford**'s lover, Clark Gable, took time off to get his rotting teeth replaced with dentures, she turned to **Franchot Tone** (*extreme left figure in photos above*), whom she later married.

In the hospital, a toothless Gable learned that the suave, sophisticated Tone would be starring with Joan in her next movie, *Sadie McKee* (1934). Gable called Louis B. Mayer and yelled, "It makes me sick that that god-damn fairy is out every night with Joan."

Joan soon discovered why Tone was called "Jawbreaker." She also discovered something else about the bisexual actor: He was what Gable was not. A great lover.

A native of British Columbia, **John Ireland** (*right-hand figure in photos above*) once struggled to eke out a living in New York's Harlem. He found work as a carnival barker before turning to acting. Ireland appeared ill at ease as Joan Crawford's extra-marital fling in *Queen Bee* (1954).

After a romantic close-up with him, she later said, "I thought that I felt the Eiffel Tower rising in that boy's pants."

make on Joan, she looked him up and down and said, "Tell me you're joking!"

One night Joan suggested to Scott that she wanted his brother and fellow actor, Lawrence Tierney, to join them for the weekend. "I want to see if your brother measures up to you." Scott had no trouble arranging such a liaison. Catching "Bad Boy" Tierney during one of the few times he was sober, the actor, who'd once played gangster John Dillinger, measured up to his brother in every way during a hot three-way at Joan's home. Later she told her dear friend and gay actor/decorator, William Haines, "it was like a pair of twin dicks!"

Joan liked to seduce her male co-stars—and some female ones too—but she met her match when she made *Queen Bee*, released by Columbia in 1955. Barry Sullivan might have been the leading male star on the picture, but Joan told Haines that, "My God, John Ireland's got the biggest cock in Hollywood, and I should know. After all, I was married to Franchot Tone, and he was known as 'Jawbreaker.' But John's got him beat." Going to bed with him is the equivalent of giving birth!"

The director, Ronald MacDougall, had a hard time during his direction of the love scenes between Joan and John. "He kept getting a hard-on that looked like a baseball bat," MacDougall is reported to have said.

The beefcake star of many 40s movies was Victor Mature, a bisexual who preferred handsome young men but also seduced a string of actresses, including Alice Faye, Betty Grable, Rita Hayworth, Betty Hutton, Veronica Lake, Gene Tierney, and Lana Turner. Mature often complained that, "I'm tired of being nothing but a male striptease."

When author Gore Vidal saw a nude snapped of Victor Mature lying horizontal in an army cot, he wrote: "If the Nazis had seen that picture, they would have surrendered much sooner."

A picture might be worth a thousand words, but military man David Walsh, today retired, confirms a close encounter with Mature when the teenager was enrolled at the Kentucky Military Institute in 1940.

Returning to Louisville earlier than he anticipated, he checked into the Brown Hotel for a

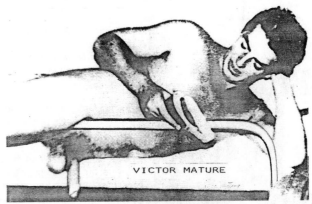

VICTOR MATURE

During his early career, the bisexual actor **Victor Mature** was identified as both "The King of Beefcake" and "A Beautiful Hunk of a Man." On screen, his good looks and massive physique won millions of fans; while after-hours, his large endowment made him "King of the Boudoir."

The son of an Austrian scissors grinder, and Kentucky born and bred, Mature invaded Hollywood. During the shoot of *My Gal Sal* (1942), he fell hard for the titian-haired beauty, Rita Hayworth.

"As far as Victor's love-making is concerned, he's definitely the main course," Rita told gal pal Marlene Dietrich. "After him, all other men are just that quivering Jell-O served for dessert."

The nude on the right was snapped of Victor when he was serving in the Coast Guard.

few days before the school term began.

As he was bending over to pick up his suitcase, he was almost knocked down. Strong arms reached to help him up. He was surprised to discover it was the actor, Victor Mature, also checking into the same hotel. He had just completed filming *One Million B.C.* Victor apologized profusely and asked the 17-year-old what room he was staying in.

About 30 minutes later, Mature knocked on David's door and asked if he could come in. David was gay and only too willing to receive the muscular frame of this actor, with his thick lips, slick wave of hair, and toothy smile. Mature wore an ankle-length velvet bathrobe whose design resembled something that an acrobat might wear as he enters the circus ring. As David soon found out, Mature wore nothing underneath that robe.

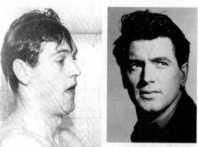

Mature kept feeling David all over, saying "Are you sure I didn't hurt you?" Slowly the actor unbuttoned David's KMI uniform. In no time at all, they were indulged in a wild 69, David almost choking. He still remembers that "magnificent, big, thick, veiny, uncut cock."

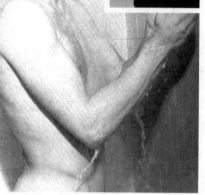

Mature and his boss, Darryl F. Zanuck at 20th Century Fox, often seduced the same women, including Carole Landis and Linda Darnell.

Zanuck told stars who included Marilyn Monroe, Gene Tierney, and Juliette Greco more or less the same

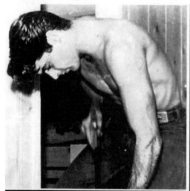

Gay actors **George Nader** (*top photo, above, right*), **Rock Hudson** (*in shower and inset, above*) and **Rory Calhoun** (*top photo, left*) were never afraid of showing their well-developed bodies. Their lovers, mostly male, learned of their endowments and spread the word among Hollywood's size queens.

Nader matched Hudson in looks and was one of his early lovers, but he lacked Hudson's raw sex appeal and spent his life as a friend in the shadows.

Ever since he'd joined the U.S. Navy, Superstar Rock had scores of male lovers, but he also prostituted himself to talent scouts and agents. When the young, handsome, and aspiring actor topped Liberace, the flamboyantly gay singer called his best pal, Merv Griffin. "You've just got to have him. It was the single deepest penetration I've ever experienced, and your mother here has had only the best." Merv responded, "Already been there, done that."

Rory Calhoun once said, "I fucked that ugly Henry Willson to advance my career, but screwed Guy Madison and Marilyn Monroe just for the fun of it.

Producer **Darryl F. Zanuck** (*lower left photo*) virtually shut down 20th Century Fox every afternoon at teatime (4pm) for "a sex break." It was a different star every day. He liked to begin by masturbating his large penis in front of starlets "to get the juices of these broads going."

thing: "You've had nothing until you've had me. I am the biggest and the best. I can go all night and all day." Ava Gardner chimed in, "The only thing bigger than his cigar is his cock, which he's not too shy to show or put into use."

As the stars of the 40s grew bald, fat, and flabby, the 1950s introduced a whole new set of very masculine stars, the prettiest of whom tended to be gay.

George Nader, along with his lover, Mark Miller, became the closest friend of Rock Hudson, and stayed with him throughout his extended days in Hollywood until his death of AIDS in 1985.

Although in a committed relationship with Mark, George made out with Rock on several occasions. Whether Mark knew about this infidelity is not known.

Rock weighed in with ten mighty inches, and Joan Crawford got him too, although Rock later reported to George that "it was a mercy fuck." He also claimed that he gave "mercy fucks" to Liberace, Tyrone Power, and Errol Flynn. "As you know, they were past their prime when I got them, and I screwed them out of respect for what they'd achieved. Personally, right now, you can send over Sal Mineo."

To keep up his reputation as a macho straight, Rock occasionally made it with a woman. Actress Mamie Van Doren found some fast action. She later said, "The boulder his agent named him after must have been a big one. Rock was well endowed."

So was his friend George, who often posed for beefcake photos for his fans. When a publicist saw George in a tight bathing suit, he ordered that the pictures be re-shot. "Too much bulge," he wrote in red marker across the pictures.

Nick Adams *(above)* had the distinction of being the lover of both James Dean and later, Elvis Presley.

In his early days, while rooming with Dean, he hustled older gay men who picked him up in cars along Santa Monica Boulevard.

He told Sal Mineo, another one of his lovers, "I was the highest paid stud on the block, getting fifty dollars a lay when my competition was selling it for five or ten dollars at the most."

Roddy McDowall, a child star in the 40s and a good friend of Hudson's, with whom he also had an affair, was the proud owner of a 10+-inch cock. "It just grew and grew," Hudson said, "once it got started." At gay parties, McDowall often performed auto-fellatio shows for an appreciative audience. Once he and his part-time lover, James Dean, staged "an exhibition."

When *Confidential* was ready to leak Hudson's homosexuality to its millions of readers, agent Henry Willson bartered with them, feeding them the details of Rory Calhoun's prison term instead.

Former jailbird Calhoun once said, "The trouble with Hollywood is that there aren't enough good cocksuckers." He should know. He tested most of them out before finding the perfect bottom in boy beautiful Guy Madison.

Alan Ladd, one of the most closeted of all bisexuals in Hollywood, tested Rory out soon after his arrival. Betty Grable, Lana Turner, and Susan Hayward gave Calhoun an "A" in the bedroom, but Marilyn Monroe flunked him after his performance in the sack with her. Prior to his night with Marilyn, perhaps his agent, the notorious casting couch director Henry Willson, had drained the Los Angeles native dry.

Regardless of how various male and female stars rated their encounters with Calhoun in the bedroom, on one thing all his conquests agreed: Rory Calhoun was one big boy.

The former lumberjack once said that "I learned all I needed to know about sex when I was sent to prison."

Nick Adams gained fame as "The Rebel" on television. Long before that, he was known throughout Hollywood as "the star fucker," bedding everyone from Elvis Presley to Natalie Wood. Nick and James Dean became best pals when they arrived in Hollywood. They had no money to eat or pay the rent, so they hustled their meat on Santa Monica Boulevard.

Partly because of his super-endowment, Nick became the most successful hustler on the boulevard. Closeted actor Jack Palance, one of Hollywood's fiercest villains—he was definitely not a pretty face—understudied for Anthony Quinn on the tour of *A Streetcar Named Desire*. On one drunken night, Palance Outed himself to Quinn. "Nick Adams ruins you for all other hustlers," Palance claimed. "He stretches your rosebud out of shape!"

More lore about other "rosebud stretchers" follows in subsequent chapters of this book.

Rudolph Valentino captured the hearts of millions of women fans around the world – in fact, he was called the most beautiful man of the Silent Screen.

Off screen, and in spite of *faux* romances with the likes of Pola Negri (a lesbian), he was attracted to men. Among others, his lovers included Ramon Novarro.

In the 1920s homosexuals were stereotyped as effeminate degenerates. The well-built athletic and well-hung Valentino was anything but. Above, the Great Lover is shown in a matador's tight-fitting "Suit of Light."

Rudolph Valentino, in one of his most memorable performances, played the matador in *Blood and Sand*, a silent picture from 1922.

Tarzan vs.
Hollywood's Most Seductive Latino

One of the most handsome men ever to grace the silver screen, **Lex Barker** *(above, left)* (1919-1973) is known today for playing Tarzan of the Apes and leading characters inspired by Karl May novels. The son of a wealthy New York stockbroker, he was a direct descendant of Robert Williams, founder of Rhode Island.

His rival in love affairs was **Fernando Lamas** *(above, right)* (1915-1982), hailing from Buenos Aires. In 1951 Lamas signed a contract with MGM and flew to Hollywood to play Latin Lover roles.

Both of these hunks would become embroiled in the love lives of Lana Turner and Arlene Dahl. "A man such as myself should pursue only the most beautiful women in America," said Lamas, who ultimately married MGM's "mermaid," Esther Williams.

Change Partners and Dance

Lex Barker, pictured above with his pal Cheetah, was the tenth official Tarzan of the movies. Although his version of Tarzan never approached the stardom of Johnny Weissmuller, and although Barker made only five Tarzan movies, he remains one of the actors best known for the role.

When movie roles in Hollywood dried up, he sailed to Europe and was cast in Federico Fellini's *La Dolce Vita* (1960), in a short but memorable role as Anita Ekberg's fiancé. Before leaving Europe, he starred in 40 movies and became a box office hit in Germany. Barker died of a heart attack while walking down a New York street to meet his fiancée, actress Karen Kondazian.

"The difference between Latin and American men is that the Latins give you a little more of everything, I think. More headaches, more temper, more tenderness."

Fernando Lamas

"Lex Barker is a streamlined apeman with a personable grin and a torso to make any lion cringe."

The New York Times

"I am a handsome Latin and a wonderful lover. I got into movies because it was a great way to meet broads."

Fernando Lamas

Two proud cocksmen, Lex Barker and Fernando Lamas, shared two very beautiful things in common: Flame-haired Arlene Dahl and blonde bombshell Lana Turner. But whereas Lex Barker and Arlene Dahl actually got married, creating sensational movie mag coverage, Lana and Fernando would never make it to the altar, although at one time or another, they came very close. Both of these hot and highly visible couples vied for coverage in the entertainment media of their day. But within a few years, each the above-mentioned stars decided to change partners and dance.

And as their respective relationships deteriorated, the entertainment media of their day devoted miles of copy to the intrigue.

At the debut of the Eisenhower administration in 1953, Fernando and Lex, although completely differ-

When Lana Turner appeared opposite **Fernando Lamas** *(immediately above)* in *The Merry Widow*, she had to wear heavy bracelets and gloves to cover the scars on her wrists from a recent suicide attempt. She gave her costar the keys to her home and he came and went – "mostly came," as Lana suggestively told gal pal Ava Gardner. Even though Lana had vowed never to marry again, she confided to Ava that "Fernando is going to be my next husband." But when Lana grew tired of the jealous Lamas, Lex Barker – the stud in the loincloth – was waiting to replace him.

ent types, were the two most sought-after lovers in Hollywood. Women whispered about each of their "fabulous endowments."

Fernando, who would father actor Lorenzo Lamas, eventually became known as "The First of the Red Hot Lamas." In the early 1940s he became a movie star in his birthplace, Argentina, where he attracted the attention of Evita Peron. Unknown to the public, and still somewhat of a secret today, they launched a torrid affair.

As their relationship evolved, Fernando learned that Evita had a slight Sapphic streak in her. As Fernando later told Lana Turner, "Evita had the hots for you. You were her role model. She said that if you had surrendered completely, she would have become a lesbian for life."

"I know!" Lana said enigmatically during this pillow talk.

In 1951, MGM imported Lamas, "Argentina's beefsteak," for Latin Lover roles and to give Ricardo Montalban serious competition.

In 1952 Fernando and Lana made a spectacular entrance at the gala of the year, the party that Marion Davies, mistress of William Randolph Hearst, was throwing for gay crooner Johnny Ray. Lana and Fernando were seated at a table with, among others, Esther Williams and Ava Gardner, who were friends from their days together at MGM.

Lana was already on friendly terms with both Esther and Ava—in fact, Ava was her most intimate "gal pal," and Lana was well aware that Ava had already sampled Fernando's charms. But Lana became jealous when Fernando started paying "too much attention" to Esther. Ironically, he would later marry her.

As a means of making Fernando jealous, Lana made some comments about the strikingly handsome Lex, who had entered the room and was surrounded by beautiful women. At the time, Lex was still married to Arlene but they were living apart. "No wonder he was cast as Tarzan," Lana announced to the table, infuriating Fernando. "I bet he has muscle in all the right places."

"It's not a muscle, darling," Ava drunkenly instructed her. "If it was a muscle, it would grow bigger with exercise."

Fernando Lamas and **Lana Turner** *(together in photo, above)* dance "The Merry Widow waltz" in the remake of the silent film which years previously had starred Mae Murray.

Then at the peak of their fame, Lamas and Lana embodied the ultimate in physical beauty. She was particularly attracted to what she saw in his tight pants, and he invited her to sample his wares – "That is, if you can handle it." In real life, Lana was to learn that Lamas was not "the dream prince" he played so well in *The Merry Widow*.

and Fernando Lamas in their Easter

Dressed in their Easter finery in London, **Arlene Dahl and Fernando Lamas** *(together, immediate left)* made a dashing, stunningly beautiful couple. "Being married to Arlene Dahl was very nice at nighttime," Lamas said. "But during the day, it was like being married to Elizabeth Arden."

He also confessed that during their marriage, he had never once seen her without makeup. The elegance and femininity of this star of Norwegian extraction attracted more than Lamas and Barker.

John R. Kennedy went "wild" over her, as did her six husbands.

Born in Rye, New York, into a wealthy family, and a 1938 graduate of the exclusive Phillips Exeter Academy in New Hampshire, Lex had risen to the rank of Major in the U.S. Army during World War II. Blond and blandly handsome, he had earned his place in movie history by becoming the first actor to replace Johnny Weissmuller in the role of Tarzan. When he was tested for loin cloths, the gay boys in Costume spread the word, "Barker is almost the equal of Weissmuller." Lex went on to became lord of the jungle in *Tarzan's Magic Fountain* in 1949.

Two years previously, long before the Wardrobe department formed opinions of their own, the then-famous actress, Paulette Goddard, had already discovered his hidden charms.

Goddard, a bisexual who may—or may not—have been Mrs. Charlie Chaplin, met Lex when he was appearing in an uncredited role as a military officer in *Unconquered,* Cecil B. DeMille's florid and highly melodramatic (and Technicolor) celebration of the American frontier spirit, in 1947. The film also starred her on-again, off-again lover, Gary Cooper.

When not occupied with Gary, Goddard discerned that Lex "was one big boy," as she once taunted actor Burgess Meredith, another of her husbands.

Among her many talents, Goddard was an expert in fellatio. The under-the-table fellatio scene in Warren Beatty's *Shampoo* (1975) was based on an incident in her actual life, when she famously went down on director Anatole Litvak, on her knees under the table at Ciro's night club.

She told actor/producer/*spinmeister* Anderson Lawler, one of Gary Cooper's old flames, that "I put as much enthusiasm into sucking the small pricks—Clark Gable, John Wayne—as I do the big ones—Lex Barker; Gary, of course; Aristotle Onassis, and David Niven."

Breaking from his entourage of admiring women at the Marion Davies party, Lex walked over to the Lamas/Turner table and asked Lana to dance. He ignored Fernando.

As Lex escorted Lana to the center of the floor, he held her in a tight embrace, a style very unlike Fernando and Lana's more courtly dances which had been famously filmed on the set of *The Merry Widow* back in 1952.

"Jungle Boy is fucking her right on the dance floor," an angry Fernando announced at the table. When he could stand it no more, Fernando jumped up from the table and headed for the floor to cut in. He grabbed Lana by the

Arlene Dahl and Lex Barker *(together, above)* enjoy a night on the town. The couple's brief marriage lasted between 1951 and 1952. She went on to marry Fernando Lamas, a marriage that ended in 1960, and which produced another famous actor, Lorenzo Lamas.

Her film career was based on her looks – not her acting. Eventually, she was designated as Sears Roebuck's National Beauty Advisor. But did she really have an affair with Red Skelton, with whom she appeared in a trio of films – most notably *Three Little Words?*

When **Lex Barker** asked **Lana** to dance in front of the jealous eyes of Lamas, it was the beginning of a new love for Lana. Lex held her close and whispered in her ear, "I'm unzipped. Reach inside and see if I've got more than Lamas." Lana must have decided YES because Lamas was out the door that night and Lex was in her bedroom the following evening.

When one critic defined Lana's performance in the film, *The Merry Widow*, "more fizzle than fizz," she encountered him at a party the following week. "Stick a dildo up your ass," she told him. "Which is the only way you'll ever get fucked, you hideous beast."

shoulder, spinning her around. He then turned angrily on Lex, and said, loud enough for everyone on the dance floor to hear, "Why don't you just take her out into the bushes and fuck her?"

Lana was furious. Breaking from the arms of Lex, Lana slapped Fernando's face.

"You fucking cunt!" he yelled back at her, looking as if he were going to strike her. The dance floor grew quiet.

Lana rushed from the room, with Fernando hot on her trail. The ride back to her house on Mapleton Drive was in silence.

Once in the foyer, with the door shut, Fernando slapped Lana so hard her diamond earring shot across the room. As she tried to kick him in the *cojones* with a sequined shoe, he grabbed her right ankle and sent her sprawling onto the marble floor.

With all his fiery temper, he kicked her in her ribs several times before bending over her and pounding her face twice. Screaming, she tried to protect her face from injury. Before he could inflict more damage, he stormed out of the house and into the night.

The following Monday morning, arriving badly bruised at the MGM studio, an angry and distraught Lana put through a call to Benjamin Thau, head of MGM casting. "Benny," she said, "forgive me for interrupting your morning blow-job from Nancy Davis, but get to my dressing room at once."

Lana was referring to the future Mrs. Ronald Reagan, then a starlet at MGM.

Thau came running, finding Lana a "mess of bruises and scratches." She was set to begin filming *Latin Lovers*, starring Fernando and herself.

Lana burst into tears, sharing all the horror of her break-up with Fernando. "He said the vilest things to me anyone has ever said. He told me 'your pussy's been used so much it's gone limp like a wet dish rag. I practically have to jack-off inside you to get an orgasm. You're a lousy lay. You won't even suck cock!'"

Thau knew at once that Fernando was out of the picture. Thau replaced him with Ricardo Montalban.

In the aftermath of his breakup with Lana, Fernando wasted no time and began dating beautiful starlets within less than a week. When he was eventually cast opposite Arlene Dahl in both

The beauty of **Arlene Dahl** *(photo, right)* captivated audiences during her film heyday in the 1950s. "I considered the years in Hollywood nothing but an interim," she later said of her brief movie career.

Before that, at the tender age of 18, she'd been the Rheingold Beer Girl of 1946. In 1962 she posed seminude for *Playboy*, but today she is known mainly as a tabloid astrologer who writes a syndicated column. (It's said to be faithfully read by Nancy Reagan.)

Arlene went on to found a highly successful company that marketed cosmetics and lingerie.

In the pre-Marilyn Monroe days, **Lana Turner** *(photo, left)* was the blonde bombshell of Hollywood. She was the teenage "sweater girl" who, during the 1940s, became a Hollywood superstar.

Her greatest notoriety resulted from a tragic involvement with gangster Johnny Stompanato, who was stabbed to death at her home – either by Cheryl, Lana's daughter (as the former teenager still maintains) or by Lana herself (as Frank Sinatra always privately claimed to friends). Lana searched for love with seven different husbands and countless lovers. She always claimed that the true love of her life was Tyrone Power, but he dumped her. After a request from Howard Hughes and Tyrone Power, Lana agreed to a three-way.

The Diamond Queen and *Sangaree* in 1953, he fell madly in love with her. When her divorce from Lex came through, he became her second husband.

As for Lex, when he heard that Lana and Fernando had broken up, he called Lana. Their affair began on their first date.

In reaction to these marital and boudoir re-organizations, the movie mags went wild. CHANGE PARTNERS AND DANCE was a frequent headline. One reporter wrote, "Ah, *la ronde, la ronde*."

Almost simultaneous with these goings on, when Fernando was cinematically teamed with Esther Williams in *Dangerous When Wet*, also in 1953, he came on to her too. She wisely turned him down. "Come back in ten years. You've got a lot of fucking to do."

Years later, he did come back, marrying Esther on the last day of 1969 and staying hitched until his death from cancer on October 8, 1982.

And indeed, shortly after her breakup with Fernando, Lana and Lex got married, the union lasting from 1953 to 1957. Things came to a crashing end when Lana learned that Lex had repeatedly raped her teenaged lesbian daughter, Cheryl Crane.

During the final year of his marriage to Lana, Lex starred in the strangest movie of his strange career, the "ferociously awful" Cold War campfest, *The Girl in the Kremlin* (1957). In it, Lex is hired by a glamorous European (played by Zsa Zsa Gabor) to track down her twin (also played by Zsa Zsa) who has been living in Greece with a reincarnated Josef Stalin, who has supposedly escaped both death and the Kremlin. In Greece, or so the plot continues, Josef has satisfied his life-long fetish for sexual intimacies with bald women, as played by Natalie Daryll, whose flowing locks have been shaved by the evil Reds.

In the wake of the negative publicity generated by this movie, Lex moved to Europe, and enjoyed a surprising success first in Italian and then in German-language films before his eventual death in New York City in 1973. His fifth and final wife, Maria del Carmen "Tita" Cervera, generated headlines worldwide when she went on to become the fifth and final wife of billion-

After Lamas ended his romance with Lana and Arlene, he married and settled down with MGM swimming star **Esther Williams**, *(photo right)* his costar in *Dangerous When Wet* (1953).

Lamas said, "there was a rumor that I made Esther give up her career when we got married. That's a lie! She was already 'washed up' when we got married." Of her own career, Esther said, "I can't act. I can't sing. I can't dance. My pictures are put together out of scraps they find in the producer's wastebasket."

Before Lamas, Esther dated Jeff Chandler, her costar in *Raw Wind in Eden* (1957). When she ascended the stairs of the home they shared, she found him dressed in drag. After taking in his looks, she commented, "You're too big for polka dots." She then walked out the door, deciding that a cross-dresser was not for her. But Rock Hudson certainly welcomed Jeff.

Paulette Goddard *(left)*, rumored to have been married to Charles Chaplin, had a list of lovers longer than the Brooklyn Bridge, ranging from Gary Cooper to Clark Gable, with an occasional woman on the side. One of these women may have been Marlene Dietrich. Goddard even gave Dietrich some advice: "Every woman needs jewels. They're small, easy to carry, and easy to hide in case the woman has a falling out with the man whom she regards as a keystone in her life."

Goddard had a diverse set of lovers who included musician Artie Shaw. "I don't know why Lana and Ava went for that one," she later said. She also seduced Aristotle Onassis. ("Jackie can have him.") She pronounced John Wayne "The worst lay of my life." David Niven, though, "was among the best, as was (British stage star and acting coach) Constance Collier."

aire patron of the arts, Baron Hans Heinrich von Thyssen-Bornemisza.

* * *

In 1999, more than 40 years after the "change partners and dance" scandal, Esther Williams wrote her provocative memoir, *The Million Dollar Mermaid*. In it she not only Outed a former boyfriend, Jeff Chandler, as a cross-dresser, but revealed to the world that her late husband, Fernando, had indeed been very well hung. But literally hundreds of people, especially beautiful women, already knew that.

Fernando, she went on to reveal, did not like to wear underwear. "This was a twofold conceit," Esther claimed. "The first motivation was to make sure people looked at his crotch. The reason they did, which he spelled out to me in great detail, was that he was 'hung very high.'"

"Somehow, my genitalia have been placed high on my pubic bone," Fernando explained clinically, "so it looks like this thing of mine goes on forever. It's really quite normal, but of course it's very grand if it's erect."

"He talked about his penis as if it were a dear and talented friend with excellent posture, rather than a part of his body," Esther claimed.

Fernando had become legendary for his big basket ever since he appeared opposite the lesbian stage star, Ethel Merman, in 1956. Presented on Broadway, the show was called *Happy Hunting*. Night after night Merman noticed that during her big number most of the audience, especially gay men flocking to the show, seemed to be watching Fernando instead of her.

One evening she sent two spies out into the audience to determine why. Wearing tight pants and already known for his large endowment, even when soft, Fernando had played with himself before appearing on the stage. The play's script called for Merman to engage in a passionate kiss with Fernando. His too tight trousers revealed an enormous erection. That was one of the reasons why Fernando was stealing the show from Merman.

Merman was infuriated and, after the curtain went down, staged one of the loudest shouting matches ever heard on Broadway.

The following night, during their stage kiss, he dispatched his duty with a certain violence and contempt, and then moved downstage and pointedly wiped his mouth. After the curtain fell, that provoked yet another confrontation between the stars. "How dare you insult me like that, you greasy Latin meatball!" Merman shouted at him.

"Kissing you is like kissing a very fat, old, bearded uncle who has bad breath—that and a

MGM's "Million Dollar Mermaid," **Esther Williams** *(right)*, waited patiently until Fernando Lamas "had fucked half the women in Hollywood" (including Lana and Arlene) before she finally snagged her man. At the time of his death, he was still married to the bathing beauty.

Like no one before or since, Esther performed gloriously kitschy water ballets, and always seemed perfectly made up both in and out of the tank.

When Billy Rose asked her to join the San Francisco Aquacade, she found herself swimming with another Tarzan (not Lex Barker). This one was Johnny Weissmuller, who pursued her to no avail.

MGM signed her and had originally planned to star her in *Somewhere I'll Find You* in 1942, but the role went to Lana Turner instead.

Sherman tank," Fernando shouted at her. Except for their lines onstage, she never spoke to him again.

Fernando seemed relieved. He kept kissing Merman on stage but later told friends, "Kissing that dyke is the hardest job I've ever had in show business. Who knows where her mouth has been before coming on? After all, the cow has gone down on half the show gals of Broadway. My God, she's even had Judy Garland."

Fernando was disliked by many other stars, not just Merman. "He was a very beautiful man," Cesar Romero once said. "But very much in love with himself." Perhaps Romero was miffed when Lamas turned down repeated requests for sex. For that, Romero had to go back to his all-time favorite—Desi Arnaz.

One of the most bizarre movies ever made, *The Girl in the Kremlin* (1957, starred **Lex Barker** and the Hungarian diva **Zsa Zsa Gabor** (pictured together, above, Zsa Zsa, alone, circa 1950, below).

The plot claimed that Josef Stalin faked his own death in 1953 and moved to Greece. In a dual role, Zsa Zsa played his nurse and lover as well as her twin sister. Lex Barker was cast as an ex-O.S.S. agent.

The film is best remembered (if at all) for its opening scene that shows Stalin sadistically ordering that a young woman with waist-length hair have her head shaved completely bald.

Ethel Merman (above), the greatest dyke of Broadway and its pre-eminent star of musical comedy, knew how to belt out a song like no one else. Merman once spat in the face of Betty Hutton after Hutton was cast in the screen version of *Annie Ger Your Gun* (1950), Merman's Broadway hit.

At one time, Merman was passionately involved with Jacqueline Susann, a love affair that ended only in anger.

Susann got her revenge in her best-selling novel, *Valley of the Dolls*, by basing the character of the lonely, pathetic, fading Broadway star, "Helen Lawson," on Ethel Merman herself.

Born in Mexico, **Ricardo Montalban** (above) became the rival of Fernando Lamas as Hollywood's Latin Lover, although he is best remembered today for his role of Mr. Roarke in the TV series *Fantasy Island*. Frankly, Lamas had more sex appeal.

After Lamas beat the crap out of Lana, she had Montalban replace her abusive costar in *Latin Lovers* (1953).

When Montalban arrived in Hollywood, the studio wanted to change his name to Ricky Martin.

Each member of the famous foursome – Barker, Lamas, Turner, and Dahl – managed to sleep with at least two other members of that group.

Their success was matched by **Ava Gardner** (above) who managed to seduce her best pal Lana, and have a brief fling with Lamas as well.

Johnny Weissmuller and the Tarzan Yell

Johnny Weissmuller was the greatest swimmer of his era, but he became even more internationally famous as "Tarzan" of the silver screen, a hero to millions.

As the Jungle God created by Edgar Rice Burroughs, Weissmuller appeared in a dozen *Tarzan Adventures* between 1932 and 1948. After retiring from the role, he starred as Jungle Jim, another pulp fiction character that saw him through sixteen thrilling adventures between 1948 and 1955. By the end of that run, the franchise and the allure of both the character and the actor had begun to wear thin.

What his adoring fans didn't know, but what was familiar to dozens of chorus girls and starlets, was that Johnny had a secret need for exhibitionism, which he demonstrated again and again at private parties. And eventually, when he needed money, he took to staging "private shows" for wealthy gay fans.

Johnny Weissmuller

Johnny Weissmuller (1904-1984) arrived on the back lot at MGM where he was fitted for a G-string and asked, "Can you climb a tree?" Elmo Lincoln, the first screen Tarzan, dismissed him as a "sissy." But everybody from Tallulah Bankhead to Joan Crawford praised his manly endowment. So did lesser wannabees, and a gaggle of chorus girls and starlets who consistently rated him 10 on a scale of 1 to 10.

Elmo was wrong. Johnny was no sissy. He was an undefeated swimming champion and a five-time Olympic gold medal winner. He was also a hero in real life, saving the lives of nearly a dozen people after the excursion boat, *Favorite*, capsized in Lake Michigan.

Of all the screen Tarzans, Johnny is more closely identified with the role, even today, than any of his competitors such as Lex Barker. "Me Tarzan, you Jane," became a household joke. In the fading years of the Austro-Hungarian Empire, Johnny came into the world, little knowing that he would become a vine-grappling hero of the jungle.

When he arrived in Hollywood, he was already known as "The World's Most Perfect Male Specimen" because of his fame as a swimmer. He was immediately cast as a Greek Adonis in Paramount's *Glorifying the American Girl*, released in 1929 as one of the first talkies.

He had little hope of being cast in the 1932 film version of Tarzan. After all, Clark Gable wanted the part, and was considered a sure thing. But Gable was not buffed enough to wear a loincloth. The role went to the

The Mexican Spitfire, **Lupe Velez** *(above),* was a tigress in bed, as Johnny Weissmuller soon learned. According to author Floyd Connor, "Lupe's lovemaking was so ferocious that Johnny looked like a wildcat had attacked him. He arrived on the Tarzan set, his magnificent body covered with strawberry-sized hickeys, scratches, and annular bites on his pecs. The studio had to use extensive body makeup before he was ready to shoot."

The battling duo fought both in public and private. "The way to be happy through marriage is to fight once a week, maybe more," said the sultry Velez. "We have two terrible tempers."

28

football star and shot-put record holder, Herman Brix, who would later become Bruce Bennett, playing Joan Crawford's ex-husband in *Mildred Pierce* in 1945. But Brix broke his shoulder, and Johnny won the role by default.

The picture became a big success, and Louis B. Mayer ordered his scriptwriters to come up with other films for his new Tarzan.

For the role, Johnny, appearing opposite Maureen O'Sullivan, gave the most distinctive of all Tarzan yells. It was startling, unmistakable, the greatest jungle "call of the wild" in the history of cinema. Many imitators over the years tried to duplicate the yell, and all of them failed with the possible exception of Carol Burnett.

In New York in 1932, promoting his first Tarzan film, he checked into a small hotel off Broadway that was owned by Marion Davies, mistress of William Randolph Hearst. MGM contract players stayed here. As he walked through the lobby, he spotted the movie star, Lupe Velez, known as "The Mexican Spitfire." She was recovering from a broken heart after Gary Cooper had walked out on her.

She caught sight of his tall, muscled figure, and he certainly noticed her. She was sitting on a couch with her legs up, revealing that she wore no underwear. She later said, "I like all red-blooded men to get a free look."

An hour later, she called his hotel room to introduce herself. She left out that she was the daughter of a streetwalker, who used to peddle Lupe's teenage charms to the highest bidder at the raunchy burlesque house where she worked in Mexico City. She invited him to come and see her Broadway show, *Hot-Cha*, a Ziegfeld production backed by the gangster Dutch Schultz, with whom Lupe was having an affair.

"I wear almost nothing in the show," she said. At that point, she gave her measurements: 37-26-35. "What are your measurements?" she provocatively asked him.

"I stand 6 feet, 3; I weigh 190 pounds, and my waist is 32 inches."

"Any more measurements you care to share, *John-nee*?" she asked.

"Oh, yes, my flexed upper arm measures 14½ inches."

"Do you have anything else that's 14½ inches?" she asked.

"Would you settle for 10½ very thick inches with a foreskin that extends an extra inch?"

"You sound like my kind of guy, Ape Man," she said. "Why don't you haul all those inches up to my suite tonight?"

Over dinner and champagne, she got so drunk she removed her top. Naturally, she wore no brassière. She rotated her left breast in one direction, then rotated that same breast in the oppo-

Weissmuller (above), **Velez** (below)

29

site direction. Weissmuller later confided to gay actor Randolph Scott, "I fell in love with Lupe that night."

He also told Scott that as he was banging her, she became both vocal and articulate, comparing his love-making techniques to her other lovers, especially Gary Cooper. "No one is as good as *Gar-ee* but you're second best, and miles better than Jack Dempsey, Douglas Fairbanks Sr., Errol Flynn, and Clark Gable. Even bigger than Jack Johnson." She was referring to the black heavyweight boxing champion.

From that night on, Lupe and Tarzan were an item, and in time she became his third wife, a tumultuous marriage that ended in divorce in 1939.

When Tarzan and "Spitfire" returned to Hollywood in the autumn of 1932, they set up housekeeping together. In a very short time, they became famous for giving the most notorious parties in Hollywood, most of which turned into orgies before midnight. And as if sex wasn't enough, Lupe staged cockfights at her parties—the kind to which she'd become addicted in Mexico City. She also showed stag movies imported from Tijuana.

The finale to her entertainment came when she pulled up her dress—no panties, of course—and danced in front of her guests. Only a select few were allowed to stick around for some very special entertainment later. Lupe invited a few of her guests, mostly female but with some gay men as well, to a back den. She never asked any man she felt was straight. In the den she told the guests to form a circle around the center of the room. Except for a spotlight shining on the floor, the room was dark.

When the guests were seated, Tarzan suddenly appeared in a loincloth bulging like a tent from the front. Stepping into the spotlight, he dropped the loincloth to share his full erection with the audience, turning around so that everyone could get a full view.

On the floor he began to masturbate, a performance lasting about five minutes until he exploded, his semen shooting out about a foot into the air. Some overeager members of the audience, both male and female, rushed to lick him clean. The applause was deafening.

The performance was such a success that Lupe and Johnny repeated it at numerous other parties. It became the talk of Hollywood, and an invitation to see Lupe dance and Johnny masturbate became the most coveted in town. After 18 months, studio honcho Louis B. Mayer intervened, threatening to fire them based on the morals clause within their respective contracts. Party time came to an end.

After their divorce, both Johnny and Lupe found other loves, but both of them remained promiscuous for years, Lupe conquering men in vast numbers, her best-known suitor being the Mexican actor, Arturo de Córdova, who never really made it as a Latin Lover type with American audiences. They much preferred Gilbert Roland.

Lupe was not faithful to de Córdova for very long, and appeared at Hollywood nightclubs with at least six, sometimes seven or eight, men in tow. It was rumored that after nightclubbing, she'd invite the men back to her house where they drew straws as to which one would go first into her bedchamber.

Johnny was happy to hear that by 1944 Lupe had settled on only one man, a young and classically handsome "French" actor named Harald Ramond. He was in Hollywood hoping to be cast in a screen bio based on the life of Rudolph Valentino.

But on the morning of December 14, Johnny was shocked to read of Lupe's suicide. She had defied her own rule: "I don't believe in loving just one man."

Lupe had became pregnant—presumably by Ramond, but with her record of seductions, how could she really know who the father was?

At one point she confided to a friend that she thought "*Gar-ee* is the father." Even though they had officially broken up, Cooper and Velez continued to spend nights together for years to come.

She asked Ramond to marry her. He not only refused, but ended the relationship, calling her "used goods."

The next morning her maid found her drowned in a toilet bowl where she'd vomited up her overdose of Seconal and the spicy enchiladas with hot sauce she'd consumed the night before. MEXICAN SPITFIRE DIES screamed headlines across the nation.

Even though Ramond appeared at Lupe's open coffin to pay his final respects to both the star and her unborn child, the American public blamed him for Lupe's suicide and turned against him. His hoped-for career in Hollywood films came to an end. It was later revealed that he wasn't French and his name wasn't Ramond. Born in Vienna during the twilight of the Austro-Hungarian Empire, he was originally named Harald Maresch.

In 1948, Johnny appeared in his last major Tarzan movie, *Tarzan and the Mermaids*, with Linda Christian, who would later marry Tyrone Power. It was rumored that Johnny and Linda were having an affair. That same year he developed a new film character, making the first of his *Jungle Jim* movies with Virginia Grey (girlfriend of Clark Gable) and George Reeves, who later became Superman. (In 1959, he was either murdered or committed suicide, depending on which story you want to believe.)

When he'd retired Tarzan, that yell remained lodged in Johnny's brain. By 1979 he was checked into the Country Home and Hospital in Woodland Hills, California, to recuperate after a stroke. Despite his incapacitation, he often woke up fellow inmates with the Tarzan yell in the middle of the night.

Jack Staggs, the hospital's executive director, maneuvered unsuccessfully to have Johnny committed to a mental institution. Only the last-minute intervention of old pal John Wayne prevented Tarzan and his yell from being hauled off in a straitjacket to the loony bin.

The Evolution of Tarzan

The first and ugliest Tarzan, Indiana-born **Elmo Lincoln** *(photo, left)* was featured in *Tarzan of the Apes* in 1918. It became a box office smash, and one of the first films to earn more than a million dollars.

Herman Brix, who later billed himself as **Bruce Bennett** *(right)*, lived up to Burrough's image of a lithe and graceful Tarzan, a sort of "body beautiful" of the jungle. The author later said that Brix was the only actor who presented his creation accurately: i.e., as a sophisticated, polyglot English nobleman.

Lincoln's 52-inch chest made him a heartthrob to post-Victorian women still wearing petticoats and knickers. Edgar Rice Burroughs, who created the character of Tarzan in his novel, envisioned a gracefully athletic Tarzan, and was appalled by Lincoln's "beefy, beastly look."

Brix, not Weissmuller, had been the studio's first choice to play roles eventually awarded to Weissmuller, but Brix suffered a separated shoulder during the filming of a gridiron flick, *Touchdown* in 1931.

Paramount tested pinup boy **Buster Crabbe** (left side, top photo) for the role of Tarzan, but rejected him. "He's just too pretty, too much of a homosexual fantasy," said an MGM casting director. In spite of that, producer Sol Lesser cast Crabbe in an independent production, *Tarzan the Fearless* in 1933. He would later become famous for such sci-fi serials as *Flash Gordon* and *Buck Rogers* (1936-1940).

Oregon-born **Gordon Scott** (right side, top photo) was a massive hulk of muscle, standing 6' 3". In real life, he had fulfilled all those gay porn fantasies--military policeman, fireman, lifeguard, and cowboy. In 1953, two gay talent scouts checked out his 19" biceps and noted a massive bulge in his bikini, and recommended him to Sol Lesser. The producer cast him as the latest Tarzan, marking a rebirth of the jungle character Scott was the most promiscuous of the Tarzans: "Who wouldn't want to fuck Tarzan?"

The tallest of the Tarzans, at 6' 4", a Texan, **Ron Ely** (left side, center photo), became the 15th screen Tarzan when he was cast in the hit TV series *Tarzan* in 1966. Refusing to use a stunt double, he was often injured. Critics noted that Ely, of all the Tarzans, more closely resembled Edgar Rice Burroughs' concept of Tarzan, both in his physique and dialogue. The strikingly handsome Adonis-like Ely said, "The story of Tarzan is beautiful--about an educated man who returns to the environment he knows best--the jungle."

"If Michelangelo were to return to earth, and wanted to sculpt *David II*, he would select **Miles O'Keeffe** (right side, center photo) as his model," said a casting director. "That Tennessee boy has the world's most perfectly sculpted body!" Before playing the lead in *Tarzan, The Ape Man* in 1981, O'Keeffe was an Air Force Academy member, a football player for Mississippi State, and a psychologist for a state prison in Tennessee.

Christopher Lambert (left side, bottom photo), growing up in Switzerland, became a sophisticated man of the world, dating, among others, Princess Stephanie of Monaco. He successfully competed with hundreds of other physiques to win the role in *Greystoke: The Legend of Tarzan, Lord of the Apes* (1984). The movie was a hit with Tarzan buffs, mainly because the script remained faithful to the original story by Burroughs.

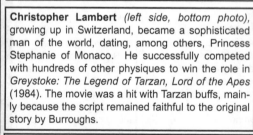

Casper Van Dien (right side, bottom photo) was the shortest of all the Tarzans (5' 9 1/2"), but he was arguably the most beautiful, either stripped or in a tux. To paraphrase Mae West, "Forget the five feet. It's the 9 1/2 inches I want to talk about." Coming from a military family, Van Dien moved to Los Angeles and landed the coveted role as the 20th screen Tarzan in *Tarzan and the Lost City* (1998). His breakthrough roles both came in 1997, when he starred in Paul Verhoeven's masterpiece, *Starship Troopers*, and also portrayed gay icon James Dean in *James Dean: Race with Destiny*. Incidentally, Mark Twain is his great great great-uncle.

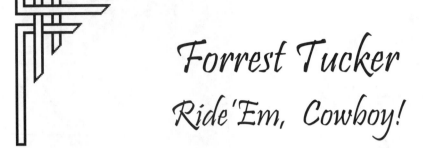

Forrest Tucker
Ride 'Em, Cowboy!

"You're not handsome but your looks are sort of acceptable," said a casting director to **Forrest Tucker** *(above)* for the 1940 film, *The Westerner.* "You might be acceptable to audiences as an outlaw."

This son of Indiana – called "Tuck" by his friends – became one of those rough-and-tough actors who dominated the silver screens of the 1940s and 1950s. He was a hard-drinking womanizer that was considered one of the "biggest" stars in Hollywood, at least in terms of his physical equipment. Women who went to bed with Tuck never stopped talking about it.

Hollywood's Incorrigible Gunslinger

He called it "The Chief," and it was the source of his greatest pride and joy. He also knew how to use his long, thick weapon—and he did so frequently.

Forrest Tucker (1919-1986) was a man's man, hanging out with the likes of John Wayne, who was instrumental in getting him cast in his biggest hit, the 1949 *The Sands of Iwo Jima*.

"Tuck" is known today for his 1958 role as a Southern gent who makes *Auntie Mame* (Rosalind Russell) a rich widow, and for his role in the TV spoof sitcom, *F Troop*, which ran from 1965 to 1967.

The star of many a cowboy movie was so proud of the size of his uncut sex organ that he said his penis—not his hands—should be imbedded in concrete on Hollywood's "Walk of Fame."

Tales of Tuck's appendage began to circulate in the early 1940s when he joined Hollywood's Lakeside Country Club, which over the years boasted such members as Bob Hope, Bing Crosby, Johnny Weissmuller, W.C. Fields, Humphrey Bogart, and Mickey Rooney. Two of Tuck's best pals were Buddy Rogers, the gay

His father died of mustard gas poisoning in World War I, and his mother, Doris, was a tough old broad who'd been a burlesque queen in her youth.

A son of the Depression Era, Tuck came up the hard way, and as a young man, he rode the rails during the 1930s with other hobos, going from town to town and often barely surviving. The hobos robbed people or "stole what wasn't nailed down."

As a thirteen-year old boy, Tuck learned how to make a much-needed quarter. "When I was desperate," he later told his friend, John Wayne, "I knew I could find some cocksucker willing to sample 'The Chief,'" his nickname for his enormous penis.

John Wayne (*left figure in lower left photo*) gave Tuck his big break when he demanded that he be given co-billing with him in the highly successful *The Sands of Iwo Jima* (1949). **Tuck** (*right-hand figure in the same photo*) played a recruit, Private Al Thompson, opposite "The Duke." He and Wayne remained friends for life.

Wayne warned Tuck to be careful when sleeping with Vera Hruba Ralston, the so-called "Queen of Republic Pictures" and one of the worst actresses in the history of Hollywood. Her husband, Herbert J. Yates, was the head honcho at Republic and demanded that she be cast in a string of westerns, often with Wayne or Tuck. A former Olympic ice skater, the Czech born "actress" spoke with a heavy accent.

"If Yates knows you're fucking his wife, he'll cut off your balls," the Duke warned Tuck. Paying no heed, Tuck continued plowing Vera. Apparently, the aging studio honcho never found out about his wife's affair.

husband of Mary Pickford. Tuck called him "Cuz." He was even fonder of the bearish, good-natured Phil Harris, who was married to Alice Faye, remembered as Archie Bunker's dream girl in the TV sitcom, *All in the Family*.

On the Lakeside golf course, a "putt" between Harris and Tuck became the talk of Hollywood. The two stars played golf almost daily. On the 17th hole, Tuck teed off, his ball hitting the green only a foot from the hole. It took Harris three shots to come within four feet of the hole.

Since he was so close to winning, Tuck wanted to declare victory and move on. Harris was adamant, demanding he try the shot. "God damn it, Phil," Tuck shouted in front of a caddie. "Even The Chief can make the fucking hole." Harris reached into his baggy pants and withdrew five $20 bills. "You're on!" Tuck said. He unbuttoned his pants, pulled out his mighty club, fell to a position on his hands and knees above the turf, and scored a perfect bull's eye with his dick swinging.

James Bacon, the Hollywood columnist, wrote that Tuck's big cock was the chief tourist attraction at the Lakeside club. As Tuck lay passed out drunk on the massage table, a stream of members, along with their invited guests, paraded into the locker room for an unveiling. "There was a lifting of the towel," Bacon said, "and a lot of *oohs* and *ahs*."

Friday nights became legendary at Lakeside when all the big names showed up for some heavy drinking, even Clark Gable. Tuck and Weissmuller ("Tarzan") were hanging out at the bar one night, trying to drink one another under the table. Weissmuller boasted that he got pussy at least twice a day from every gal in Hollywood including Tallulah Bankhead and Joan Crawford. Tallulah told him, "You're the kind of man a woman like me must Shanghai and keep under lock and

The antics of **Phil Harris** *(above, left)* and **Tuck** *(above, right)* at North Hollywood's Lakeside Country Club became the stuff of legend. To become a member, at least according to Bing Crosby, "you had to kill a fifth of booze in nine holes." The more notorious members, fabled for their antics at the club, included Wayne himself, Humphrey Bogart, W.C. Fields, Oliver Hardy, and Mickey Rooney. Phil and Tuck would spend their Friday and Saturday nights at the club, "drinking each other under the table."

"Tuck was the only man I've ever met who could drink and raise hell as much as I could," Phil later said.

"The two stateliest homos in England," was how Tuck described **John Gielgud** *(left)* and equally distinguished **Lord Laurence Olivier** *(right)*.

But instead of showing the two actors the respect their professional achievements merited, Tuck mocked them, and in Gielgud's case, even tantalized him with the possibility of greater intimacies. Yet Tuck wasn't a real homophobe, as many thought. He actually showed remarkable sensitivity to the gay lifestyle when he encountered Carl Urbelle.

Two views of Tuck: In *The Music Man* (left, above) and as part of the TV series, *F-Troop*.

key until both of us are entirely spent. Perhaps a leave for ten days!"

Weissmuller said, "Tallulah knew how hot I was. That's not all. I've got the biggest dick in Hollywood."

"So you say," Tuck responded. "I get tail at least three times a day, and sometimes a lot more. And no one—not even Milton Berle—is bigger than The Chief."

Weissmuller challenged Tuck to a duel. It was obvious what the choice of weapons would be. Word spread quickly through the club room, and bets were placed. Since many of the guys had seen Tuck in the locker room, he was the heavy favorite. A coin was tossed to see which man would go first. Johnny Weissmuller lost and had to show and tell. He whipped out a long, thick, uncut penis, and the all-male crowd roared its approval. Gable later told Harris: "I got a case of penis envy. After all, I'm supposed to be the King of Hollywood."

Tuck appraised Weissmuller's hang. "You're right up there with the biggest I've seen. But if you want to see what a man's dick looks like, take a gander at this." He unbuttoned his pants and whipped out The Chief, which was already at half mast. An even louder roar went up from the crowd. As Bill Smith, the Hollywood columnist, later claimed, "It was like a baby's arm holding an apple."

During his four-year run touring with *The Music Man*, Tuck would call all the male gypsies into his dressing room. "I know all the whispering behind my back," he told the wide-eyed men. "So let's get it out in the open once and for all so you can concentrate on your work and not spend all your time looking at my crotch wondering how big it is." He'd lean back in his dressing room chair and open his pants, manipulating his penis to a full erection in front of an admiring audience. After that show, the gypsies filed out, still awed by the private viewing. One slender boy remained behind to tell Tuck, "I'm an unrepentant size queen, and if that thing ever needs lip service . . ."

"Get out!" Tuck shouted.

Tuck wasn't shy about flashing on the other side of the ocean either. At a party for actors in London, he told a companion that he found all English actors "to be a bit swish," an obvious reference to two men he'd just met, Sir John Gielgud and Sir Laurence Olivier. Tuck said he was having a good time at the party but

Tuck became good friends with **Johnny (Tarzan) Weissmuller** *(center figure, above)* at the Lakeside Country Club, although they debated endlessly over who had the largest cock or who had "deflowered" the most virgins.

When Johnny remarried after Lupe Velez, he selected Tuck as his best man. Joan Crawford once told her gay pals, "the two luckiest things that can happen to a gal in Hollywood is to have Tarzan and that Forrest Tucker in her bed."

Pictured with costar **Joan Weldon** above, **Tuck** scored his greatest stage hit in *The Music Man* where he played a fast-talking con man that goes to River City, Iowa, to swindle the town out of its money.

Tuck called the musical "pure corn as corn can get." He performed the show for four years in fifty-eight cities. Tuck did not seduce blue-eyed, chestnut-haired Joan Weldon, who played Marian Paroo in the show, but he was said to have screwed all the other women in the musical. He even met his two future wives while performing, both of whom were more or less "jailbait" at the time. Sheila Forces was only fifteen when she caught Tuck's eyes (she became his fourth wife), and Marilyn Fisk was a somewhat riper nineteen (she became his third wife).

wanted to embarrass the swishes into leaving. "I know how to clear a room," he said.

He mounted a wooden coffee table, unbuttoned as he had at Lakeside, and whipped out "The Chief." "Which one of you English queens has a mouth big enough for this?"

The "swishes" in the party hastily departed, including Olivier and Gielgud. However, Tuck claimed that Gielgud called him at his hotel the following morning and invited him to come to his home for dinner—"and other amusements"—that night. Over the phone, Tuck accepted the invitation but escaped that night with a chorus girl he'd met at the party.

Like most men of his era, Tuck's locker room remarks were often homophobic. In private life, it was a different matter. How else to explain the appearance of a very gay man, Carl Urbelle, into his life? Carl showed up one night in Chicago in 1960 and remained with Tuck until the day he died in 1984 of a brain tumor. From that day on, and in spite of Tuck's marriages and countless girlfriends, Carl was constantly at Tuck's side. "They were bonded at the hip," said John Wayne. "I never understood that damn relationship—and don't wanna."

Tuck called Carl "my man Friday—he does everything for me. Even wipes my ass when I take a shit if I'm too drunk."

Carl massaged Tuck twice daily, even washed out his underwear on the road, and prepared his meals and poured his liquor. He was a virtual slave, his whole world centering around Tuck. It was obvious to all who saw the two men that Carl was madly in love. It was more than love,

The Mexican Spitfire, **Lupe Velez** *(center, above)*, had already married one Tarzan (Johnny Weissmuller), but in *Honolulu Lu*, a 1941 movie, she is teamed with another, **Bruce Bennett** (left figure in the photo, above). The actor had changed his name to Bennett while playing Tarzan, but he was still billed as Herman Brix.

"I had one Tarzan," Lupe said. "Why not another one?" Also appearing in the film was **Tuck** *(above, right)* playing a sailor, Barney. She told her friends, "I thought my biggest thrills would be Gary Cooper and Johnny Weissmuller – that is, until I met Tuck." Three years after making this picture, she committed suicide.

really. He worshipped the star. When not massaging and bathing Tuck, he tended the garden, babysat for Tuck's children, and became an all-around butler and handyman. But his chief job was as Tuck's masseur.

The family denied there was a sexual relationship between the two. But one afternoon in 1964 at a health club at a Sheraton hotel in New York on 49th Street, Tuck and Carl arrived. Carl demurely wore a bathing suit into the steam room but Tuck paraded away naked in front of the clientele of mostly gay actors. When one of the actors asked Tuck if he and Carl were "a thing," Tuck replied, "when I can't get a woman, Carl here might get lucky." He winked at Carl, who beamed at the object of his affection.

(Photo above.) In a tense moment from the 1956 *Stagecoach to Fury*, Tuck confronts **Marie Blanchard**, the voluptuous and exotic-looking *femme fatale* of the 1950s, a California-born actress who excelled at playing ladies of ill repute.

(Photo below.) The Hungarian-born **Eva Bartok** huddles with Tuck at the height of their brief affair. She'd spent several years in a German concentration camp, but eventually married a former Nazi officer, Geza Kovas, in 1941 (it was annulled in 1942).

She told Tuck that her daughter, Deana, born in 1957, had been fathered by Frank Sinatra.

When there were no film offers after the stage version of *The Music Man*, Tuck turned to television. His greatest hit was the zany *F-Troop*, the TV saga of a bumbling cavalry union after the Civil War. It became a favorite of Ronald Reagan's and he and Tuck became close friends. The F-Troopers *(as seen in the photo above)* include a hatted **Forrest Tucker** himself *(upper left)*, **Larry Storch** *(upper right)*, **Ken Berry** *(lower left)*, and "Wrangler Jane" *(lower right)* as played by **Melody Patterson**.

Even though he was aging prematurely, **Tuck** *(large photo and inset photo, above)* a stubborn Irishman, refused to give up his wicked, wicked ways.

(Left) **Tuck** attends the premiere of *Who's Afraid of Virginia Woolf?* with his much shorter third wife, **Marilyn Fisk**, whom he had begun dating when she was still a teenager.

Previously, his co-star in *The Music Man* (Joan Weldon) had said that Tuck, "Just wasn't my type. He really liked fifteen to seventeen year old girls."

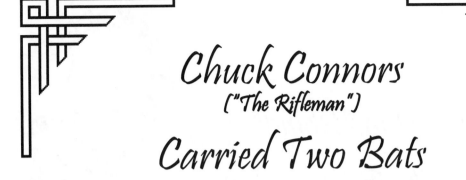

Chuck Connors
("The Rifleman")
Carried Two Bats

Chuck Connors *(above)* in the TV hit *The Rifleman* made fans around the world, playing the immortal character of Lucas McCain.

When the Russian premier, Leonid Brezhnev, visited the Western White House in 1973, his first request was not to meet the U.S. President, but Chuck Connors instead. Coming face to face with the Connors, the Russian dictator gave him a big bear hug which appeared on the front page of some 1,600 papers around the world.

The Man Behind
the Rifle

Chuck Connors, in the words of his biographer, David Fury, was "truly larger than life." He stood 6'5", weighed 215 pounds, and had chest-waist-hips measurements of 45-34-41. But it was a certain 10" measurement that had the horny starlets and gay boys tailing Chuck when he first hit Hollywood. Size queen Mae West, who used to watch his hit TV show, *The Rifleman*, said, "Forget all those other measurements. I'm only interested in the 10 inches."

Born in Brooklyn to parents who had emigrated from Newfoundland, Chuck grew up to become a major athlete in both baseball and basketball. He swung a wild bat both on and off the field. He also became a bit of a "switch-hitter" in his private life as well. In 1946 and 1947 he was a basketball star with the Boston Celtics, later in 1949 becoming a champion baseball player for the Brooklyn Dodgers. In private, he proved he was a home run champion with both women and men, especially women.

In one version of his biography, the claim is made that he broke into movies playing a police captain in the Spencer Tracy/Katharine Hepburn film, *Pat and Mike*, released in 1952. But as porno devotees know, he appeared in a "blue" movie before teaming up with that famous

Long before he became a TV hero to millions, **Chuck Connors** *(both photos, left)* was both a baseball and basketball star. A former team-mate of Jackie Robinson, Chuck made it to the baseball major leagues with both the Brooklyn Dodgers in 1949 and with the Chicago Cubs in 1951. Earlier, in 1946, he had played tough defense with the Rochester Royals of the National Basketball League.

Like Gary Cooper, he liked to walk around nude in his dressing room, but donned pants for this goofy shaving picture. When he was on a shoot, every gay man on the set made up some excuse to visit Connors in his dressing room.

bisexual couple, Tracy & Hepburn.

As a lark and for some big bucks, Chuck was clearly the star of *Hollywood Blue*, released in 1970 as a selection of stag films that featured such other stars as Joan Crawford. All of these films were produced before its stars, both male and female, became famous as "legitimate" actors. *Hollywood Blue* did not go underground, but opened at major film houses on Times Square in New York City. Audiences packed the theater.

"With his mighty endowment, Chuck Connors was quick to get it on with some lucky bottom, and he performed magnificently," wrote one critic for a gay magazine. "Had he not gone on to stardom in films and television, he definitely had the right equipment to make it 'big' (no pun intended) in porno."

Chuck was as straight as his rifle, but not totally adverse to "dropping trou" for a big-time bisexual actor if *The Rifleman* felt it would advance his film career. Aldo Ray, who appeared with him in *Pat and Mike*, told him that he'd "taken it out" for the enjoyment of director George Cukor and a few other powerful men in Hollywood. He suggested that Chuck follow his career-advancing example.

On the set of *Pat and Mike*, Spencer Tracy came on to Chuck strong, and he obliged the aging actor. He did the same thing for another bisexual actor, Burt Lancaster, when they appeared together in *South Sea Woman* in 1953, co-starring Virginia Mayo. That same year he even let Keenan Wynn have a taste in the MGM release, *Code Two*, which starred Ralph Meeker.

When Chuck teamed with Aldo Ray again in Columbia's *Three Stripes in the Sun* (1955), he told his co-star that "the homosexual thing isn't for me. I like women, preferably with big tits."

In spite of that, the bisexual star, Rory Calhoun, who starred with Chuck in MGM's *The Hired Gun* in 1957, told his gay agent, Henry Willson: "Both Vince and I got old Chuck during the shoot—and how good it was." Calhoun, who was also the producer of the film, was referring to Vince Edwards, who went on to greater fame as *Ben Casey* in the hit ABC TV medical drama in 1961.

By the time Chuck teamed up with blonde vixen, Lana Turner, and cross-dressing Jeff Chandler in *Lady Takes A Flyer* in 1958, the tall, square-jawed actor had apparently given up any gay liaisons, even if he'd performed only as "rough trade."

That was good news to Lana Turner, but bad news for Chandler. Chuck turned down repeated requests for sex with Chandler who remained pissed off at him throughout the rest of the shoot.

But whenever he left the set, Chandler tended to do just fine. He usually drove over to Rock Hudson's house at night. Hudson, the handsome hunk, never particularly minded if Chandler wore a dress to dinner. Hudson did, however, tell Chandler that he'd eventually go broke buying dresses, as he preferred

Sammy Davis Jr. (above, left) was a close buddy of **Chuck Connors**. As their girlfriends today still testify, both actors carried "a secret weapon" in their pants.

Here Davis, known as one of the finest gun twirlers in Hollywood, starred with Connors in episode number 131 of *The Rifleman*.

Davis wasn't Connor's favorite singer. When Davis wasn't around, Connors listened to Frank Sinatra and Glenn Miller. "Give me the classics," Connors said. "None of this new shit."

them to be torn and ripped from his body during his nightly "rape."

Regrettably, Hudson lost one of his all-time "best bedmates" when Chandler died of blood poisoning on June 17, 1961.

Vince Edwards, *pictured shirtless above*, played a ruthless murderer and the brother-in-law of Anne Francis in an offbeat Western, *The Hired Gun* in 1957.

Like Connors himself, Edwards had posed for gay porn during his struggling days as an actor. Connors often let closeted bisexuals like Edwards "service" him in his dressing room. But according to agent Henry Willson, Connors was "strictly rough trade."

Cross dressing **Jeff Chandler** (below) learned that Connors did not always drop trou for all of his bisexual costars.

Lana Turner *(above, right)* and **Rory Calhoun** *(below, right)* both got to sample Connors' mighty weapon. Before Lana filmed *Lady Takes a Flyer* with Connors and long before she got to know Connors in the biblical sense, the blonde bombshell dated Rory. The liaison had been arranged by their mutual agent, the very gay king of the casting couch, Henry Willson. Matchmaker Willson ordered Rory to take Lana to the premier of *Spellbound* (1945). He insisted Lana dress all in white to contrast with the dark, sultry looks of Rory.

When Rory both starred in and produced *The Hired Gun* in 1957, he hired Connors as one of the leads. He told fellow player, Vince Edwards, "with Chuck, I took producer's privilege."

Connors *(two photos, each with cowboy hat, this page)*

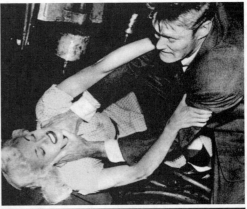

Chuck Connors wasn't always a hero. He could be equally convincing as a villain, as he proved in the 1954 release of *The Human Jungle*. In that film, **Gary Merrill** (aka Mr. Bette Davis, *left figure in left photo, above*) played a policeman. In one scene, Detective Danforth (Merrill) confronts Earl Swados, a smart-ass-punk played by **Connors**, concerning Earl Swados' alleged murder of a woman.

Jan Sterling (Mrs. Paul Douglas; *left figure in right-hand figure, above*) plays a sleazy bar blonde who works at a clip join. As Swados, Connors tracks Sterling down, planning to strangle her to death to prevent her testimony. Luckily, Merrill comes to the rescue just in time.

In the trio of nude or half-nude pictures arranged immediately above, **Aldo Ray** (born Aldo DaRe to an Italian family), a former frogman for the U.S. Navy, went from hairless youth to hirsute chest. In Hollywood, gay director George Cukor fell hard for the young man with the husky frame, thick neck, and raspy voice. Cukor directed him and the bisexual actress, Judy Holliday, in the 1952 *The Marrying Kind*. Cukor sent the rugged hunk to ballet school based on the premise that he walked "too much like a football player."

Cukor suggested to best pal **Spencer Tracy** (pictured with **Katharine Hepburn** on the right) that Ray would "put out to get ahead in Hollywood."

During the filming of *Pat and Mike* (also 1952), Tracy made much use of the actor. As Ray's career declined later in life, he was reduced to appearing in a nonsexual role in a porno film titled *Sweet Savage* (1979). His last film was the campy *Shock 'Em Dead* (1991) in which he appeared with porn star Traci Lords (and Troy Donahue – remember him?).

43

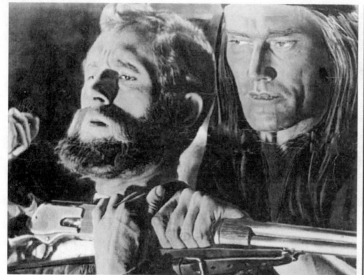

No bullet could kill him. In this scene from the 1962 *Geronimo*, **Connors** *(right figure in photo, left)* as the blue-eyed Geronimo himself puts his rifle to another use. This was a ground-breaking film, offering justice to the famed Apache warrior as he goes on the warpath against the U.S. It posed as a sharp contrast to all those John Wayne Westerns.

Kamala Devi, a beautiful actress from East India, played Connors;' squaw, Teela. She fell in love with Connors off-screen as well, and the couple was married in 1963.

My Favorite Wife (1940) starred Irene Dunne and the male lovers, Cary Grant and Randolph Scott.

Its (less successful) remake, entitled *Move Over, Darling*, released in 1963, starred **Doris Day** *(left)*, **James Garner** *(right)*, and **Chuck Connors** *(center)*. Garner tried to fill Cary Grant's shoes, but fell painfully short. Chuck Connors, however, cast in Randolph Scott's old role, quickly proved himself to be adept at comedy. During the making of *Move Over, Darling*, Connors was in love with his second wife, Kamala Devi, so his off-screen romances were virtually non-existent.

OUR BELOVED FATHER
KEVIN "CHUCK" CONNORS
The Rifleman
APR.10.1921 ✝ NOV.10.1992

Chuck Connors died on November 10, 1992, and was buried at the San Fernando Mission Cemetery. His grave is still visited by fans today. One obit described him as, "lean and squinty-eyed, with a face seemingly carved from solid stone."

His last film, an uninspired one, was called *Salmonberries*. It was released in the U.S. two years after his death – a sad end to an otherwise brilliant career. In *Salmonberries*, Connors appeared opposite k.d. lang who had just recently Outed herself as a lesbian. The film featured lots of lesbianism and female nudity.

John C. Holmes
King of Porn

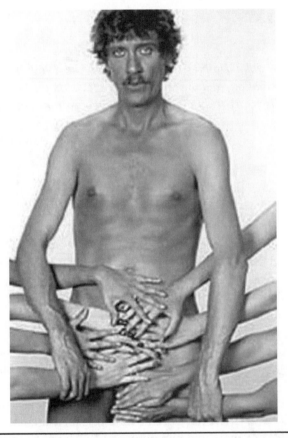

America has produced a roster of near legendary male porn stars. Key players have included Ron Jeremy, Casey Donovan, and Jack Wrangler.

None of them, however, was as big – and we *do* mean big – as **John C. Holmes** *(photo above)*, who gained worldwide popularity playing "Johnny Wadd."

The "little boy with the big dick," as he was called, measured 13 ½ inches and seduced thousands of men and women, both on and off the screen
.

With men, he was "gay for pay," and with certain women (mostly movie stars) he rented himself out as a stud. Some porn critics even called him "a pretty good actor."

Have Penis, Will Travel

"In the world of dicks, John Holmes was the D-Day, the 1969 NASA moon landing, the JFK assassination, and the invention of television all rolled up into one big, giant cock. His penis truly defined a dick generation that came, but hasn't gone yet."

John McAbee

As a boy growing up in rural Pickaway County, Ohio, John Curtis Estes never knew that he would one day be known as "The King of Porn" or "The Sultan of Smut." Born in 1944, he was a Bible student and the son of a religious fanatic mother named Mary.

He did know his real father, a railroad worker, but lived with his stepfather, Edward Holmes, an abusive alcoholic, who gave his name to the stepson he hated. Holmes violently beat John night after night.

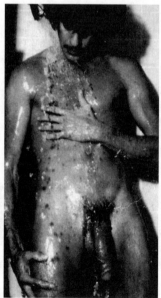

Heeeeeere's Johnny!

When he was sixteen, John ran away from home to join the Army and was stationed in West Germany. There he quickly learned that he was different from most other boys. When he went to take a shower or to use a urinal, gay soldiers followed him. He got used to answering the question: "How big is that thing?" There have been conflicting measurements, but eyewitnesses who measured him put it at 13½" long, 6" thick.

He learned soon enough that his long and enormous penis provided a way to earn extra money. He let soldiers give him blowjobs for only five or ten dollars—after all, the U.S. Army doesn't pay its men big wads of dough.

In 1964, back in the United States, he thumbed his way to Los Angeles. As a hitchhiker, he was often picked up by gay men who took him to a motel for the night. By then his fee had increased to fifty dollars.

In California, he took various odd jobs—taxi driver, door-to-door salesman, even a vat attendant at a Coffee Nips factory. But whenever he ran low of cash, he would go to a cruisy men's room and let his cock hang out of his pants. "In every case, I got an offer as I just stood there smoking a cigarette. One well-dressed older man paid me a hundred dollars, the most I'd ever gotten, for a blow-job," John once said.

While working as an ambulance driver, he met a nurse, Sharon Gebenini, which was around Christmas in 1964. They were married that spring. Unlike the other women who lay in John's future, Sharon was an honest, respectable, morally upright woman who was a virgin until the night of her wedding. As a nurse, she'd seen nude males before and had even given them baths. But on her wedding night "she must have gotten the surprise of a lifetime," a porno producer once said.

Leaving Sharon alone at night, John often visited a card-playing club for men in Gardena, California. One night in the men's room, a photographer stood next to him at a urinal, cruising him. John thought it would be another way to make a quick buck. But the photographer had another idea. "With a dick that big," he told John, "you could make super bucks in porn."

Soon, with deals arranged by the photographer, John was making 8mm loops aimed for gay audiences. Some depicted John masturbating; others showed him getting fellated. In spite of repeated requests, he refused to be filmed "butt-fucking a man," although he later rescinded that.

One day Sharon came home from work to find her husband in the bathroom measuring himself. He told her that he planned to make porno his "life's work." She objected violently, calling porno a "dirty business." After that, she never slept with him again, but stayed married to him for many years to come. "We were more like roommates," she later said, "instead of man and wife."

He was given a check for his first $100 loop, but it bounced. His partner in the film, a beautiful young girl, was given a $50 check that also bounced. From that day on, John jokingly referred to himself as "Johnny Cash," demanding cash for all his performances.

Beginning in 1968 with an uncredited role in *Behind Locked Doors* until his last film in 1987, *The Devil in Mr. Holmes*, John appeared in an estimated 2,274 porn flicks. Nearly all of them were straight, except for those early loops and one final full-length gay porno picture. No

John C. Holmes lets is all hang out *(left photo)*, as he did frequently between 1967 and 1987. During these years, he recorded 2,200 porn flicks, making him the undisputed king of XXX-rated movies. His debut *Johnny Wadd* film was the first porno film to ever gross more than $1 million.

Holmes seduced other famous porn stars such as Marilyn Chambers (both on screen and off) and legendary movie stars such as Rock Hudson.

In Asia, particularly Japan, he was called "Mr. Big." His first Japanese fans, so it is said, thought his penis was fake, refusing to believe that dicks came in that size.

WADD was the name of the most popular male porno character in history. The film *WADD* portrays, fairly accurately, the "Life and Times of John C. Holmes." WADD the documentary explores the many other facets of this pop-culture-icon's life. It spans his childhood in rural Ohio to his death from AIDS. The film unravels many myths that surrounded the star, and bares the darker side of his persona.

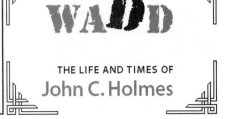

THE LIFE AND TIMES OF
John C. Holmes

other porno star became as well known around the world, and no other performer ever made that many pictures.

John had entered the world of porn at the right moment. Porn films exploded onto the scene in 1969, and there were many legal challenges. But the flood gates had been unleashed, especially after the success of *Deep Throat* in 1972 which made Linda Lovelace a household name. That film made millions, most of the dough going to the mob.

The film, *Johnny Wadd*, released in 1971, launched John into his most successful series. In it, he played a "hard-boiled private dick," the character roughly based on Raymond Chandler's creation of the tough private detective Philip Marlowe. Of course, in the Wadd films, John, playing the role of Marlowe, spent more time in bed with beautiful women that he did solving crime.

In the wild and woolly 70s, especially in New York and Los Angeles, John became a widely sought after attraction at private cocaine parties. He also became the nation's highest paid male whore for wealthy gay men and rich, horny women.

Agent Henry Willson, "The Man Who Invented Rock Hudson," once said, "In the 1970s, John was the playboy of Hollywood, much in demand. Among actresses, especially older ones, it became the thing to sample John's mighty inches. Many big stars—at least big stars of yesterday—wanted him. I fixed him up with Lana Turner, who had been a client of mine. She passed him on to Ava Gardner. Lana or Ava often shared a particularly hot stud. After all, they'd had some of the same lovers or husbands—Artie Shaw, Frank Sinatra. Even sweet June Allyson got in on the act. Unknown to her public, who called her America's Sweetheart, June was actually a nymph. Rock Hudson wanted to sample John, and I set that up. I even hooked up John with my old pal, Liberace, who passed him on to his best pal and fellow queen, Merv Griffin."

Holmes – in a pose he knew so well – prepares to penetrate a porno actress in one of his hundreds of straight films. **Liquid Lips** was among his most successful.

Some actresses refused to work with him because of his massive penis. Others eagerly sought penetration from him, and later claimed he was a "gentle lover." When Liquid Lips hit the screen, it was advertised with a big build-up. JOHN C. HOLMES DARES YOU TO SIT THROUGH THE MOST EROTIC FILM HE'S EVER MADE!

John was paid only $75 for his first Johnny Wadd film, but later was earning $3,000 for a day's work. In the years to come, in addition to the Johnny Wadd series, John would appear with some of porno's top leading ladies, including Marilyn Chambers and even a young, underage Traci Lords.

Regrettably, by the late 70s John had become addicted to cocaine. This began to affect his work, as he found it increasingly difficult to maintain an erection on camera, something he'd never had any trouble doing before.

During the Reagan era, Edward Meese and his "Meese Commission" were on a crusade to shut down the porn industry. Three Johnny Wadd films were brought to the White House to show to President Ronald Reagan. "They made good, clean movies in your day," Meese told Reagan. "*You* made good, clean movies. You won't believe what's showing in America today." Privately, after viewing the films, Reagan told aides that, "I sorta enjoyed them. But I'm glad I didn't have to do scenes like that in my day. Who can measure up to this guy?"

Sharon had had it by 1985, and she filed for divorce. In 1983 John had met Laurie Rose, who became his second wife in 1987. A porn actress, she was known in the industry as the "Anal Sex Queen," appearing under the name of "Misty Dawn."

Late in 1980, when John was becoming increasingly impotent on screen, and spending all his money on drugs, he took to breaking into houses and robbing families when they were away. Over the years he'd turned down offers from producers to do gay porn in color. Desperately in need of cash, he agreed to star in his first full-length porn feature, *The Private Pleasures of John C. Holmes*, in which he played a gay sultan. The film was not released until 1983. For his work, he received the largest check of his life, $500,000. This time he took a check but demanded that it be a cashier's check.

The porno flick became one of the highest grossing gay films of all time, opening at a movie theater in the Times Square neighborhood of New York and playing to a packed audience. Truman Capote was a member of the first-night audience.

The bottom in the film, Joey Yale, had no trouble taking John's many inches. He was a natural and the lover of Fred Halsted, the famous underground filmmaker who'd met Joey at a leather bar in West Hollywood in 1969. Fred had had many years to break Joey in for anal penetration. At the time he met up with John's mighty phallus, Yale had already contracted AIDS. He died three years later of complications in Palm Springs. Soon after, his long-time lover, Halsted, committed suicide.

John was the inspiration for another movie, *Boogie Nights*, in 1997. The star, Burt Reynolds, later called it, "My first porno film." Mark Wahlberg (Marky Mark) was cast as the John Holmes character, Dirk Diggler. In one of the closing scenes, he unzips his pants and shows his mammoth penis to the world. Since "Marky Mark" obviously didn't possess a penis the size of "Johnny Wadd's," a prosthetic penis had to be used for "the dangle shot."

John died of AIDS on March 13, 1988, with his wife, Laura, at his side. He insisted on that. He had a great fear that someone in the hospital would cut off his penis and preserve it in alco-

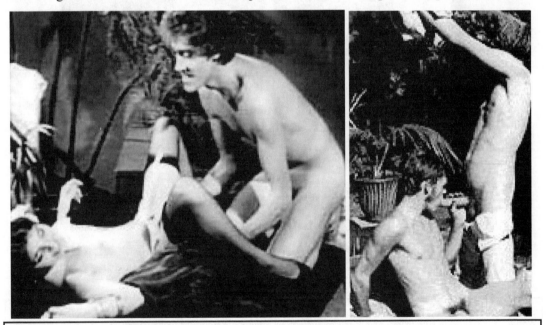

Left photo. **John C. Holmes**, about to enter a porn actress, repeated this scene in hundreds of films. When a writer trying to identify one of Holmes' films from a still shot asked Holmes' if he could name the film, Holmes recognized only himself and failed to come up with the title.

Such was not the case with the right-hand photo, *above*, from Holmes' first full-length gay porn feature, *The Private Pleasures of John C. Holmes* (1983). In this scene, Holmes (right) is fellated by Joey Yale, a young lover of the famous gay underground filmmaker, Fred Halsted. Yale died of AIDS in 1986. Halsted later committed suicide.

hol for future generations to gloat over. He also wanted his body cremated and his ashes tossed into the Atlantic so there would be nothing left of him to preserve. His wishes were carried out.

John was right. There was voyeuristic interest in his penis. One member of the coroner's staff measured his penis in its flaccid state, reporting that it was 8.75 inches long. He also claimed that John's testicles were "the size of a pair of large hen eggs." One private collector, living in the countryside of England, offered £100,000 for John's severed penis. That much money proved irresistible. Before cremation, someone severed both John's penis and his testicles from his body, concealing that act from Laura.

By 1981, John claimed that he'd had sex with 20,000 women since turning 16. That figure is often reduced to 14,000.

John summed up his life this way: "A happy gardener is one with dirty fingernails, and a happy cook is a fat cook. I never get tired of what I do because I'm a sex fiend. I'm very lusty."

Cinematographer Bob Vosse summed up the life of John this way. "What Elvis Presley was to rock 'n' roll, John C. Holmes was to the adult film industry."

Surprisingly, both of the films noted above were based in part on John C. Holmes. *Boogie Nights* (1997) and *Wonderland* (2003) used similar posters to advertise their products – that is, a well-packed pair of jeans.

Boogie Nights, sometimes known as Burt Reynolds' first porn flick, was the odyssey of a young man's adventures in the California porn industry during the 70s and 80s. Mark Wahlberg played Dirk Diggler, a character based on Holmes.

Wonderland, starring Val Kilmer playing John C. Holmes, concentrated more on the famous Wonderland Murders, in which the porn star was implicated (see following essay)

This picture was shot for a movie still, but it evokes the popularity of **John C. Holmes** *(center figure in photo above)* during his offscreen moments. Although hardly a beauty, he was sought out by some of the entertainment industry's most famous stars – male and female – for private performances. In that capacity, he seduced everybody from closeted gay politicians (and their wives) to international society matrons, from East Coast *debutantes* to famous stars in Beverly Hills.

When Holmes first appeared for a porno audition in 1969, he was initially dismissed. "He was just a really skinny kid with an Afro haircut," said porn producer Bill Amerson. Nonetheless, Holmes was ordered into the backroom and told to take his clothes off.

When Amerson entered with a Polaroid camera, he took one look at Holmes and said, **"YOU'RE GONNA BE A STAR!'**

The Wonderland Murders

The Wonderland Murders, sometimes known as the "Laurel Canyon Murders," occurred in Los Angeles in 1981. They were the most grisly Hollywood murders since the death of Sharon Tate and her friends at the hands of Charles Manson and his gang.

In 2003, Hollywood released a rather murky film, *Wonderland*, based on these murders, starring Val Kilmer as John (Johnny Wadd) Holmes opposite Kate Bosworth.

The full story of what happened the night of the murders has never been fully explained; each person connected with the crime obviously told self-serving lies as a means of self-protection. But over the years a scenario has emerged.

When not making money in porn, John positioned himself as a courier, delivering drugs to clients of the so-called "Wonderland Gang." Instead of getting cash for his work, the heavily addicted star accepted cocaine as payment. He was hopelessly hooked on the drug. The "gang" was composed of a notorious quartet known throughout the Laurel Canyon section of Los Angeles.

The gang members, females Joy Audrey and Gold Miller, and men, William R. DeVerell and their leader, Ronald Launius, occupied a rented house at 8763 Wonderland Avenue. Miller and DeVerell were lovers. Neighbors reported strange people arriving at all hours of the day and night. The occupants of the house sold drugs or made drug deals, and ingested a lot

In bearded disguise, **John C. Holmes** is held in custody by a Florida policeman.

Months earlier, Holmes had fled California after dying his hair black and spray-painting his Chevy Malibu battleship gray. A Miami SWAT team, along with two LAPD detectives, broke through the door of a flophouse to find Holmes lying in bed and watching reruns of *Gilligan's Island*. He was extradited to Los Angeles where, in December of 1981, he was formally charged with the Wonderland killings.

(Bottom of this page) Three portraits of a porn king: **John C. Holmes** *(far left)*, the real thing; **Val Kilmer** *(center)* as he appeared in *Wonderland* , and **Mark Wahlberg** *(right)* as he starred in *Boogie Nights*.

Matt Dillon had been the first choice to play Holmes in *Wonderland*, but dropped out at the last minute. The film only required an 18-day shoot and was based on the true story of the infamous "Four-on-a-Floor" Wonderland murders.

Wahlberg initially turned down *Boogie Nights*, thinking it was "another Marky Mark thing." Since Wahlberg could hardly be expected to have a penis the size of Holmes, the director called in a "master of prosthetics."

of the cocaine for their personal use.

John often arrived at their doorstep with the latest stash of drugs. At a meeting, which John attended, the gang, along with two other criminals, David Lind and Tracy McCourt, decided to rob the home of another drug dealer, their "competitor," Eddie Nash.

Nash was famous to the *demimonde* of Los Angeles, as he owned several nightclubs of dubious reputation. John personally liked Nash and often went to his home to buy drugs. But as a means of assuring the flow of drugs, money, and good will from the Wonderland Gang, he agreed to betray Nash by leaving the back door of Nash's house unlocked in anticipation of the robbery of that house by the members of the Wonderland gang.

Early on the morning of June 29, 1981, DeVerell, Launius, and Lind entered Nash's house through the back door. McCourt remained in the getaway car, a stolen Ford Granada. The three men took both Nash and his bodyguard, George DeWitt Diles, by surprise. Nash and Diles were handcuffed, blindfolded, and gagged. The bandits then robbed the house of cash, drugs, and jewelry. Fleeing back to Wonderland, the men split the money but shortchanged John.

In the wake of this robbery, street-savvy Nash suspected that John had betrayed him and been involved in the plot. He ordered Diles to find John and bring him to his home. The bodyguard found John wandering along Hollywood Boulevard. Foolishly, John was wearing a diamond-and-ruby ring stolen from Nash's house.

Back at Nash's home, Nash and Diles tied up John and tortured him until he confessed and identified the burglars. By sheer coincidence and somewhat bizarrely, Scott Thorson, the boyfriend of Liberace, witnessed the beating. He was picking up drugs at Nash's house when John was hauled in for the interrogation and torture.

Three days after the first robbery, on the morning of July 1, unknown assailants entered the house on Wonderland Avenue. John attended the murder party, but did not take part in the actual slayings. Occupying the house at the time were Miller, DeVerell, Launius, and his wife, Susan, and Barbara Richardson. Barbara was there in her capacity as the girlfriend of Lind. The assailants bludgeoned the occupants repeatedly with striated steel pipes, crushing their skulls. Only Susan Launius would survive, the other four dying from the attacks. Susan would live but would suffer brain damage and have no memory of the assault.

Immediately after this bloody and murderous assault, John disappeared for six months, fleeing to Florida. When police finally tracked him down, he was arrested. When he refused to cooperate, fearing he might be killed by Nash's men, the police told him that he would be put on trial for all four murders.

But after months of tireless investigation, the prosecutors assigned to the case failed to accumulate enough evidence, and John was acquitted on June 26, 1982. The authorities, however, were furious and kept John in jail, citing charges of burglary and contempt of court until he was finally released. (In September of 2001, Nash, arraigned on the same charges, entered a plea bargain and received a 4 1/2 -year prison sentence and a $250,000

Holmes was the liaison between a powerful Los Angeles dealer named **Eddie Nash** *(left)* and the household of men and women who lived at 8763 Wonderland Avenue in LA. The house was always open for business, selling virtually any recreational drug ever devised, including coke and heroin, to a steady stream of customers.

Eddie Nash, born Adel Gharib Nasrallah in Palestine, came to Los Angeles to "fulfill an immigrant's dream." It was a dream that quickly turned into a nightmare. His role in the Wonderland murders has never been fully explained.

fine.)

After being released from prison, John found himself "stone broke and with no place to go." Nearing the end of his life, he was on the verge of the most degrading chapter of his existence. The mainstream world, with some exceptions, had little use for him.

Without telling the few friends still left in his life, he decided, in his words, "to place myself on the auction block like a sex slave."

The only takers, as it turned out, would be gay men who wanted a piece of gargantuan meat.

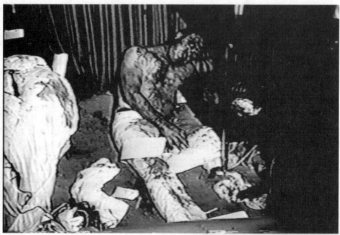

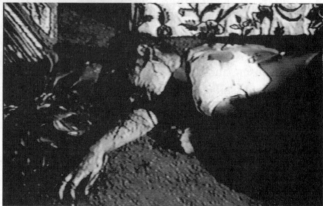

Shortly before 4:00 AM on the morning of July 8, 1981, three – possibly more – intruders broke into the Wonderland house. They carried lead pipes and went from room to room, bashing out the brains of the sleeping occupants. When they departed, four were dead and one was critically wounded. It was the worst Hollywood murder since the Charles Manson gang killed actress Sharon Tate and others.

In the rear bedroom on the first floor, the police – nearly 12 hours after the attack – found the bloody body of Ronald Launius dead on a bed.

Beside him was his horribly mutilated but still breathing wife, Susan. She suffered permanent brain damage, with no memory of the attackers.

In an upstairs bedroom, police found the bodies of **Gold Miller** *(upper left)* and **Robert R. DeVerell** *(lower right)*. None of the investigating officers had ever seen so much blood in a private home. Their chief ordered the police to videotape the murder scene. Although grainy, the tape was later used at the murder trial, marking the first time in U.S. legal history that a video record was admitted as evidence in a murder trial.

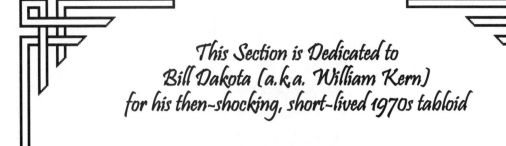

This Section is Dedicated to
Bill Dakota (a.k.a. William Kern)
for his then-shocking, short-lived 1970s tabloid

The Hollywood Star

Bill Dakota's

HOLLYWOOD CONFIDENTIAL STAR

$2.50

PRINTED IN U.S.A.

MOVIE GOSSIP FOR ADULTS

HOLLYWOOD ☆☆☆ STAR

• FEATURING Columnist BILL DAKOTA

TAB HUNTER SAYS I'M HOMOSEXUAL

TAB SEMI RETIRED IN VIRGINIA

Warhol's "Frankenstein" Star Nude

Replicated in the pages that follow is one of the "Ask Dakota" columns that appeared in an early edition of the now-defunct **Hollywood Star.**

Although the answers to the questions (and possibly the questions themselves) are Bill Dakota's, the enhancement of the layout with photos was our idea.

WITH RESPECTS AND IN MEMORY OF

Writing under the pseudonym of "Bill Dakota," William Kern was the editor of an activist magazine, *One,* during the 1960s, and the proprietor of an adult bookstore and owner of Studio D, a gay after hours club in Flint, Michigan. During his tenure in Motown, Kern served four years in prison for gross indecency with a minor, attesting all the while, with much evidence in his favor, that he had been set up.

Several years after his release from prison, he moved to Los Angeles and opened a Coney Island-style restaurant near the corner of Hollywood and Vine.

In 1976, he established **Hollywood Star,** a gossip tabloid published on an erratic schedule that continued on and off for a period of about five years.

Kern wrote much of the magazine himself under the pseudonym "Bill Dakota." Published in a newspaper format (and sold in newsstands), it appeared in 1976, and had stopped publishing by 1981.

Inspired by *Confidential* and other gossip magazines of the 1950s, *Hollywood Star* had a homosexual subtext (Kern's other mid-70s paper was called *Gayboy*) and printed nude photos and sexually oriented gossip with a frankness that had never been seen in gossip magazines. In addition to naming stars who were gay or bisexual, for example, the magazine published lists of male celebrities based on whether they were circumcised.

One issue had a red-letter headline, **"Walt Disney Was Homosexual: Editor Reveals Facts!"** The story included an affidavit from Dakota, attesting that he had been paid to perform a sex act with Disney.

Even serial killer Charles Manson went on record with Dakota about various celebrities that he had been sexually involved with. Included on Manson's list was one of Frank Sinatra's daughters, leading Frank Sinatra to threaten Dakota. Subsequently, Sinatra's threats were published within Dakota's newspaper.

With respects and acknowledgement to Bill Dakota, a pioneering gay journalist, we hereby replicate, this time with photos, one of the "Letterbox" columns that appeared in *Hollywood Star* during its heyday.

Readers Write-In
Or...Dakota's Letterbox

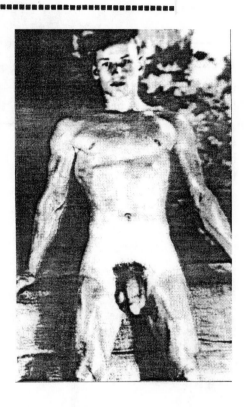

Question:
Who has the biggest cock in Hollywood?

Answer:
Roddy McDowall has the longest. It's long and skinny.

Question:
If Dakota had the choice of making out with any star he wanted to, who would it be?

Answer:
Alain Delon.

Question:
Would you give Alain Delon a blow-job?

Answer:
I'd suck his nose, toes, and everything else....ok?

Question:
Is Mae West a sex change?

Answer:
I was told that Christine Jorgensen said that Mae West was first.

Question:
Did Bill Dakota really piss on James Dean's grave?

Answer:
Yes, in November 1973, at 3am, at Fairmount, Indiana (during a weak moment).

Question:
Does Jan-Michael Vincent have a large cock? In *Buster and Billie*, it looked small.

Answer:
Why all these "cock" questions? Well, in *Buster and Billie*, his cock was in a flaccid state. When it's hard, it's big.

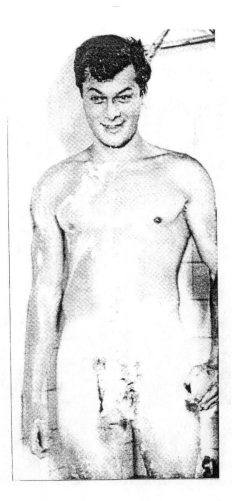

Question:
Does Tony Curtis have a big cock?

Answer:
Maybe I should make a list of who is big and who is small.   No.

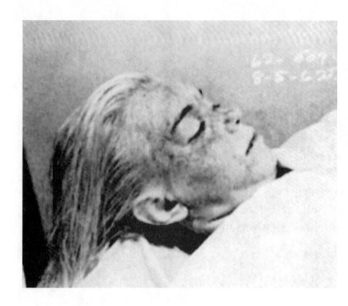

Question:
Do you think Marilyn Monroe was murdered?

Answer:
Yes.

Question:
Has Elvis got a big cock?

Answer:
One of his army buddies says, "No." But a female friend of his says, "Yes."
Colonel Parker isn't talking.

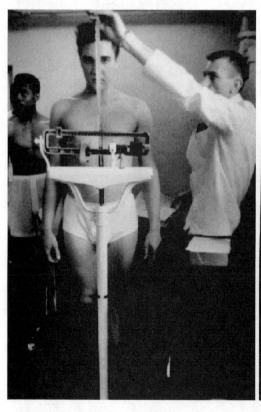
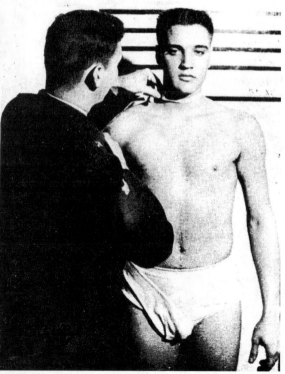

Freddy Frank
and His Monstrous Organ

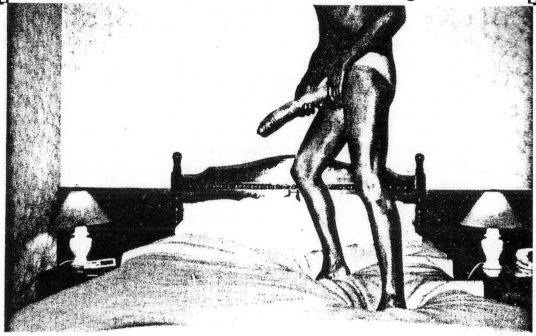

A Size-Inspired Legend
of Golden-Age Hollywood

As a young man, Freddy Frank worked as an extra, mainly on every picture Bud Abbott and Lou Costello made. Costello, who had more than a gay streak in him, was especially intrigued with Freddy's penis.

Costello spread the word that it was "The Eighth Wonder of the World," using the same claim used by Chaplin about his own organ. If any interested party, male or female, on the set of one of Costello's comedies wanted to take a look, Costello, along with Freddy, would retire to his dressing room. Once there, Costello would unbutton Freddy's pants, and with a little hand manipulation, produce an astonishing thirteen inches. Freddy always boasted that when it got fully erect, it was even larger. If anyone needed proof, Costello would take out his tape measure for confirmation.

Freddy was paid way over the scale for an extra for these sideshow performances. Word spread across Hollywood. As a joke, many Hollywood hostesses—not the uptight ones—hired Freddy as a waiter and entertainer at their parties.

A hostess would select one of her guests as the victim, often a newly arrived and morally upright personage from back East. Freddy always arrived for work with his own specially crafted salad bowl, which had a hole in it. He would insert his monster penis through a hole in the side of the bowl, which the hostess would then cover with salad, most often potato. The salad would be offered to an unsuspecting guest. She would dip wooden spoons into the salad bowl only to discover, partially concealed by the mayonnaise, Freddy's penis. To the amusement of the other guests, the woman would usually scream, either in horror or perhaps with fascination.

As news of Freddy's appendage spread, some of the leading ladies of Hollywood hired Freddy for other nocturnal pleasures—not just as a salad man. Iron Eyes Cody, an Italian-American best know for his portrayal of Native American Indians, was well acquainted with Freddy and his conquests. Cody, during an interview with Sam Frank, author of *Sex in the Movies,* was asked for the names of stars who got to know Freddy up close and personal. Iron Eyes responded, "I didn't tell Collin Perry [the writer who penned Cody's autobiography, *My Life as a Hollywood Indian*] and I'm certainly not going to tell you!"

Obviously, judging by his actions on movie sets, Lou Costello wasn't so reticent. In private, to his friends, he revealed the names of some of Freddy's conquests.

The honor list, as noted below, would never have made it past the Hollywood censors:

June Allyson

Mary Astor

Lucille Ball

Tallulah Bankhead

Lynn Bari

Wendy Barrie

Lionel Barrymore (that is not a misprint)

Constance Bennett

Joan Crawford

Paulette Goddard

Betty Grable

Norma Shearer

Ann Sheridan

Lana Turner

Lupe Velez

Cody said that when Freddy and Errol Flynn got drunk enough—which was most of the time—they used to have "stretch-and-measure" contests. Always an inch or two short, Flynn never conceded defeat but blamed his heavy drinking for not stretching as far as Freddy did.

Jockstrap Awards
To Hollywood's Recent Contenders

★

Just ask Lana Turner or Shelley Winters (no, they're dead). Try Ursula Andress, Brigitte Bardot, Lana Wood (sister of Natalie), or even Zsa Zsa Gabor, if she's still around. **Sean Connery** – or James Bond, as we'll always remember him – is the sexiest man on the planet. Kim Basinger claimed he had "a voice that made you melt." The late Ms. Winters herself pronounced him, "The best lay I've ever had, and I went to bed with the mighty John Ireland." When he was a nude model, Connery once said, "The girls always want to sketch me up close – it's so embarrassing."

Who are you kidding, Mr. Bond? You've got nothing to be embarrassed about.

Of his 1973 picture appearance in the film, *Zardoz*, Connery said, "I was clad in nothing but thigh-high red boots, bandoliers, and a red nappy." See picture, above right.

Today's Victors in the Battle of
The Bulge

> *"I like your movies, man. You've got a great penis."*
>
> Val Kilmer

Milton Berle, Gary Cooper, and their many rivals are long gone from today's Hollywood scene. But all is not lost for devotees of large man-meat (i.e., straight women and gay men). There are several candidates out there who get better-than-favorable ratings from their girlfriends (or whatever). Of course, we haven't experienced any close encounters and cannot verify statistics. But there are those who have seen such things up close and personal and have responded with awe.

Admittedly, some of the studs included within this chapter are getting a bit long in the tooth. But like Marilyn's song about diamonds, the human penis hangs on for a long time before it loses its shape. And we sincerely hope that the gents we've singled out have many fine years ahead of them for appropriate use of their God-give appendage.

What follows is a preview, with the full understanding that new challengers arrive in Hollywood every day to take on the old guard.

Johnny Depp, perhaps jokingly, offered to do a cameo in the send-up to his film *Edward Scissorhands*. It was called *Edward Penishands*. Had Depp appeared, it would have been a big box office hit. He's not known as "Donkey Dong" in Hollywood for nothing. Just ask Kate Moss.

Blue-eyed, blond John Schneider was the former Duke of Hazzard. Duke is a good name for it. At least it fit Schneider better than it did John Wayne. Rumor has it that Schneider tops the ruler at nine to ten inches.

Sean Connery once posed in the nude for art studies. One student, Arlene Hector, later said, "The young Sean was magnificent in the nude and certainly lacked nothing 'down there.' In fact, he was the biggest I've ever seen. It made me drop my charcoal pencil."

When Tim Robbins made *Mystic River* with Sean Penn in 2003,

In addition to being a very sexy guy, 6'3" **John Schneider** is a born-again Christian. In 1982 he co-founded with Marie Osmond the Children's Miracle Network. Answering a casting call for *Dukes of Hazzard*, this New York boy showed up with a week's growth of beard and a beer can, claiming he was from Snellville, Georgia. The call was for actors between ages 24 and 30. He was actually 18, but lied in order to obtain his career-making role of Bo Duke. Between 1983 and 1986, he was married to a former Miss America, Tawny Elaine Godin (1983-86). Lucky girl.

insiders in Hollywood facetiously suggested that the film be retitled *The Battle of the Bulge*. Chosen by *Empire* magazine as one of the 100 Sexiest Stars in film history (at a rank of #94) in 1995, Robbins stands 6 feet 4 1/2 inches tall. When he won the Oscar for *Mystic River*, he tied with John Wayne as the tallest actor ever to have won. Those in the know claimed he had Wayne beat by at least five inches in at least one measurement.

It is said that those alleged home videos—that is, if they exist—of Madonna and Sean having sex would make the Paris Hilton sex tapes appear tame. Rumor has it that the Left-Wing actor is heavily endowed. At least that's what a string of tall, leggy blondes have testified. These days, Penn is receiving more press for his political statements than for his performance in the boudoir. Take this remark, for example—"Let's show them we can fire this president and put him in a fucking jail."

Different sentiments were expressed by the lean, strangely handsome James Woods. "I love George Bush right now—and I always have! I'm the only guy in L.A. who voted for him." Utah-born Woods grew up in Rhode Island, the smallest of states. But we understand there's nothing small about him. A former date, who didn't want her name used, said, "His cock is bigger than it should be." Talk about enigmatic pronouncements.

Woods is an actor with strong opinions—and not just about lovable George Bush. When a magazine writer published an unfriendly article about him, he gave his opinion of the writer herself to columnist Michael Musto. "The author is a degenerate scum-sucking pig who instead of sucking dicks on Eighth Avenue, which is where she'll probably end up making her living at two dollars a pop, and she's still getting overpaid, was only setting me up for a muckraking job. She's a fucking pile of unmitigated pus ripped from the ass of a dead dog. I'll let her hang herself by her three tits."

In the early 1950s, **Sean Connery** *(four photos this page)* worked evenings as a bouncer, spending his days training at the Dunedin Amateur Weight Lifting Club in Edinburgh, toning his muscles for London's 1953 Mr. Universe contest, where he represented Scotland. Connery, contestant number 23, filled out his posing pouch admirably, but placed third overall.

Sean was introduced to sex at a very early age. Eight years old, to be exact. "It was a lurid introduction," he said, "and pretty basic. Although I can't remember a particular moment when I lost my virginity, it was a gradual acceptance that I no longer had it." Once, when he was fourteen, while walking down a deserted street in Edinburgh, he was accosted by an older woman wearing a military uniform. She pulled him behind a fence and demanded that he penetrate her. Sean obliged.

Even as a teenager, Sean was surrounded by women. "There's never any trouble getting girls, but it's big trouble getting rid of them."

As if O.J. Simpson didn't have enough troubles, the always outspoken Woods delivered a bombshell in September of 2007 when he appeared on *The Late Late Show* starring Craig Ferguson.

Woods clearly hinted that O.J. once wanted to organize a sexual three-way with him and Nicole Brown Simpson years before he murdered her.

According to Woods, the Simpsons invited him to dinner at a chic restaurant in Palm Springs. As O.J. chatted with Denise Brown, Nicole's sister, Nicole got chummy with Woods, who confided to him that she was "not happy in my marriage."

Later that night, according to Woods, O.J. and Nicole invited him to their hotel suite for a "late-night nightcap." Woods claimed that the intent to establish a short-term *ménage à trois* was very clear, but Woods then went on to say that he didn't take the bait.

Woods might have gone for Nicole, but O.J. was a bit much for him.

Woods went on to say that after that, he received a "Dear Jimmy" letter at his house. Over the "i" in "Jimmy," she'd drawn a heart. "O.J. is out of town," she wrote. "Maybe you would like to get together."

In the same spirit in which he'd turned down the earlier proposal for a three-way, Woods turned down the second proposal for sex alone with Nicole.

On air during the course of Ferguson's *Late Late Show,* an assistant speculated, "What if O.J. had returned home early and caught Woods in bed with Nicole—and without him? It might have been Nicole and Woods that got slashed to death instead of Nicole and Ron Goldman."

Cockfighter, so his more intimate fans tell us, was an apt

A leaner, meaner Sean emerged in the 1960s, no longer as buffed, or as oily, as the *Mr. Universe* contestant of the early 50s.

The women he encountered were quick to form opinions about him. Actress Barbara Carrera found him more attractive without his *toupée*.

Risking the wrath of Lana Turner's then-boyfriend, gangster Johnny Stompanato, Sean made love both on and off the screen to the blonde goddess during the 1958 filming of *Another Time, Another Place.*

"Bond, James Bond." **The Sexiest Man of the Century** – or so thought the editors at *People Magazine* in 1999. That was the same year that Queen Elizabeth knighted him.

In 1962 Sean first starred as Ian Fleming's James Bond, 007, in *Dr. No*, a role that skyrocketed him to international fame. He married his first wife, Diane Cilento, on December 6 of that same year. Three years later he told *Playboy* that he thought it was, "Okay to slap a woman."

That, of course, caused an uproar. Nonetheless, women still flocked to him to get slapped … or whatever.

Johnny Depp *(three photos, above)* might be another of the sexiest men alive, but in the photo *(above, on the left)*, he's hot, hot, hot, playing a transgendered *puta*, incarcerated in a Havana jail, in *Before Night Falls* (2000).

Before settling down, Depp looked more like the image he generated in the center photo, above. A Hollywood "bad boy," he happened to be co-owner of The Viper – the LA nightclub where River Phoenix died of a drug overdose.

Depp's looks have undergone a dramatic transformation over the years, beginning with the sexy teenager look that's visible in the shirtless photo above on the right. The actor evolved into a teen icon in the 80s thanks partly to his appearance in *Private Resort* (1985), a teenage sex comedy. A mention of that flick is often missing from his résumé.

Sean Penn (photos left) was romantically and/or sexually linked with a string of high-profile singers, actresses, and models. Oh, yes, he was also married--first to Madonna, his co-star in *Shanghai Surprise* (1986) and later to Robin Wright, his co-star in *State of Grace* (1990).

Girlfriends on the side included Maria Conchita Alonzo, Valerie Golina, Joyce Hyster, Jewel Kilcher, Elizabeth McGovern (his costar in *Racing with the Moon* (1984), Elle Macpherson, and Pamela Springsteen (his costar in *Fast Times at Ridgemont High* (1982).

Sean is definitely a method actor. Playing the dopey surfer in Ridgemont High, he stubbed out a cigarette on his palm for realism.

name for a 1972 film that starred Ed Begley Jr. "In the battle of the cocks," said one informed source, "Begley would be among the top winners." Another source claims that Begley Jr. owes a debt to his dad for passing on a prized possession. She was referring to Ed Begley, the Academy Award-winning actor with the same name. Junior keeps his father's Oscar at home and proudly displays it.

Begley Senior's Oscar came in 1962 for playing the political boss in Tennessee Williams's *Sweet Bird of Youth*. In that film, the character played by Begley Sr. saw to it that the adorable Paul Newman lost his balls.

Born and reared in Los Angeles, Begley Jr. is tall and blond, an occasional leading man who is much better looking than his father ever was. Junior, however, is not exactly a matinee idol. Although he has snagged male leads, including a star turn in *Meet the Applegates* (1991), he's still considered a second-stringer on casting calls.

Former heartthrob Ryan O'Neal has garnered a lot of bad press in his day, but not for his equipment or his love-making. "He is an incredible lover, totally devoted to giving a woman pleasure," said Joanna Moore, his first wife and mother of his two oldest children.

"A girl should get the best she deserves on her birthday—and he was," said Joan Collins after a birthday spent with the star.

Oona Chaplin (widow of Charlie), Melanie Griffith, Mia Farrow, Anjelica Huston, Bianca Jagger, Ali MacGraw, Linda Ronstadt, Diana Ross, Barbra Streisand, and Liza Minnelli could also offer testimony. Even John Hurt, playing a gay cop in *Partners* in

Chosen by *Empire* Magazine as one of "The 100 Sexiest Stars in Film History," **Tim Robbins** *(above)* showed us how an athlete should dress when he appeared as the dim-witted fastball pitcher, Nuke Laloosh, in *Bull Durham* (1988).

Robbins rarely backs down from his strong left-wing views, even calling George W. Bush a "chicken hawk." He later said he realized that might have a double meaning. His reference was to the president's militarism without actual war service; he didn't mean to suggest that Bush was an older gay man who pursued young dick.

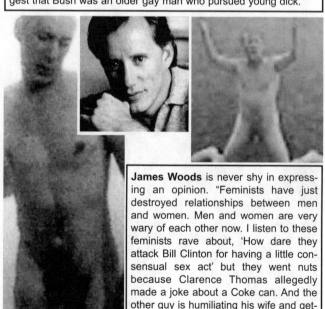

James Woods is never shy in expressing an opinion. "Feminists have just destroyed relationships between men and women. Men and women are very wary of each other now. I listen to these feminists rave about, 'How dare they attack Bill Clinton for having a little consensual sex act' but they went nuts because Clarence Thomas allegedly made a joke about a Coke can. And the other guy is humiliating his wife and getting oral sex while he's talking about Bosnia to a congressman."

1982, lusted after hunky Ryan onscreen.

Mamie van Doren, that Marilyn Monroe clone of the 1950s, claimed that Warren Beatty had a certain sophomoric machismo and made several allusions to the size of his penis. At one time he called her and invited her over. As Mamie quotes him, "I'm sitting here on the balcony, suntanning in the nude, and I'm all hot and sweaty. I've been sitting here greased up with sun-tan oil, thinking of you, and I've worked up this big ——." Madonna was quoted as saying what "Mr. B. packs in his pants is a perfectly wonderful size," but she later admitted that she'd never measured it.

That studly Swede, Dolph Lundgren, actually has a master's degree in chemical engineer-ing and is said to have an I.Q. of 160. "My problem is that people get intimidated by someone big and beautiful like me," he said. "They hate to think I can be smart as well." Lundgren is between 6'4" or maybe even 6'5" in height. He weighs between 230 and 240 pounds. But it's his other measurements we are interested in—reportedly he's a ten-incher. He lived with singer Grace Jones for four years. She told the press that he's the biggest man she'd ever known, and supposedly she knows of such things.

Stories spread that Willem Dafoe had a big wanger when he starred opposite Madonna in the erotic drama, *Body of Evidence* in 1993. In this film, he appeared totally nude. He also gave Madonna cunnilingus in a famous scene in a car park.

Big things come in small pack-ages, or so the rumor goes about Paul Williams, who's been nomi-nated for every possible music award and won at least one of each. Our favorites are "We've Only Just Begun," "Just an Old Fashioned Love Song," and "Rainy Days and Mondays."

When Paul takes off his pants and appears totally nude, he can truthfully say, "Honey, It's Only Just Begun." He once recorded an album, "A Little Bit of Love." It might have been more aptly titled, "A Whole Lot of Love."

Tobey Maguire appears with a question mark on our list of chal-lengers. When he was being fitted for his first Spider Man costume, rumors spread across Hollywood that he required tape to hold "it" in place, so he wouldn't bulge too much. A picture appeared on the Internet revealing him with exces-sively super-size private parts. He was photographed dressed in a Japanese kimono, sitting with his best buddy, Leonardo DiCaprio,

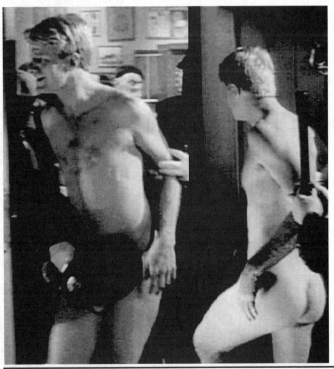

The appealing and affable **Ed Begley Jr**. (two photos above) usually gets praise for his work – except when appearing in a film called *A Mighty Wind* (2003).

A critic for the underground press couldn't resist calling the picture "A Big Fart." Although a vegetarian, he is said to appeal to "big meat eaters" (pun intended).

Streaking in a scene from that film, his private parts are demurely cov-ered but he's not afraid to show his well-shaped ass.

Testimonial from a Swedish Bombshell About
Warren Beatty

Britt Eckland, at the age of twenty-one, married actor Peter Sellers. Her affair with Rod Stewart sparked international tabloid headlines. George Hamilton and Ryan O'Neal were among her other conquests. But her favorite was Warren Beatty, where her "fantasy became reality."

In her words: *"Warren was the most divine lover of all. His libido was as lethal as high octane gas. I had never known such pleasure and passion in my life. Warren could handle women as smoothly as operating an elevator. He knew exactly where to locate the top button. One flick and we were on the way. Nature has sculpted him to perfection and Hollywood might have had a good reason to be eternally grateful. For here, without question, was the quintessential sex symbol."*

No one seems to remember **Sean** (*007, below right*) in shorts doing a handstand in *Dr. No*. But everyone fondly recalls the sexy German bombshell, **Ursula Andress** *(below, left)*, in that white bikini.

The character of James Bond as interpreted by Sean was said to have ushered in the "New Age" of sexual liberation in the 1960s. Sexual liberator or not, Sean did the honorable thing and married his pregnant girlfriend, Diane Cilento, a young Australian actress.

Ryan O'Neal with his costar, **Barbra Streisand** *(immediately above, left photo)*, in *What's Up Doc?* (1972). Streisand's opinion of him? "Yeah, he's good-looking, but no Einstein."

Berry Gordy, record mogul and his competitor at the time for the attention of Diana Ross, said about O'Neal, "Man's got the whitest damn teeth I ever seen in my life."

He's got more than that. Just ask Margaret Trudeau, ex-wife of the former Canadian prime minister. He's definitely a man for the ladies, although homosexual men by the hundreds sent him fan letters after his appearance with Ali MacGraw in *Love Story* (1970). Immediately above, far right, O'Neal plays Cupid

and magician David Blaine.

In the photograph, Maguire sits with his kimono wide open, revealing his penis. The actor charged that the photograph was doctored and denied that his genitalia was that big.

One blogger suggested that instead of a denial, Spider-Man should have issued this statement: "Well, obviously, it's a fake, but it is surprisingly accurate. I cannot tell a lie; I am, in fact, hung like a Budweiser horse. Most of the special-effects budget on Spider-Man was spent digitally erasing my enormous weiner so it didn't frighten people."

Incidentally, our mailbox receives occasional letters from admirers of the male scene in Hollywood, and some of them suggested that Steve Guttenberg, William Petersen, and Kevin Costner should be added to this chapter. As you can see in the photos which follow, those actors richly deserve to be included.

One of the world's great songwriters, **Paul Williams** *(left)* may not look like a Hollywood stud, but rumor says otherwise. He's also a recovering alcoholic. "You know you're an alcoholic when you replace a decade – and that was the 80s for me." Leaving show business temporarily, he became a UCLA Certified Drug Rehabilitation Counselor.

Today Williams is best known for scoring the music for the 1976 version of *A Star Is Born*, starring Barbra Streisand. As a child, he was always moving from one place to another. In schoolyards, he was often ganged up on because of his shorter stature. "New kid," he said, "Smaller – hey, let's whack him."

If Williams had only unzipped, he may have had all those bullies beat.

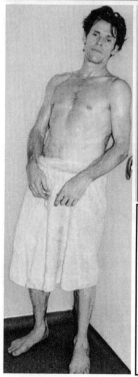

Willem Dafoe *(above)* goes down on **Madonna** in *Body of Evidence* (1993). In this film he appeared totally nude. "Instead of giving Madonna cunnilingus, someone should be performing fellatio on Willem," said a script girl.

He has appeared in erotic dramas, and he's also dared to play Jesus in *The Last Temptation of Christ* (1988; *above, right*). "To this day, I can't believe I was so brazen to think I could pull off the Jesus role."

Is he into kinky sex off-screen? "Weirdness is not my game, " he claims. "I'm just a square boy from Wisconsin."

The big blond Swede, **Dolph Lundgren**, pictured bare ass above and nude with singer **Grace Jones** on the right, may have been the sexiest blond male to ever appear on the 20th century screen. At least that's the opinion of thousands of gay fans who flocked to every movie he ever made. Those same fans were hoping Dolph would beat the shit out of Sylvester Stallone in the 1985 version of *Rocky*.

Stories circulated about Dolph's rumored endowment with an energy which eventually transformed his appendage into something, in the minds of his fans, almost mystical. In 2000, Darwin Porter wrote a novel, *Razzle-Dazzle*, in which Dolph figured as the central heroine's fantasy.

In action pictures, Dolph joined the ranks of Stallone, Schwarzenegger, Steven Seagal, Jean-Claude Van Damme, and Chuck Norris. Some of his characterizations evoked the muscle-bound "Hercules " of the 1950s, Steve Reeves. Incidentally two of the actors mentioned within this paragraph are 100% gay and another was "gay for pay" during his early days as a struggling muscleman.

Films featuring the tall and muscular Swede became wildly popular in Japan. When *Showdown in Little Tokyo* (1991) opened in Japan, Dolph was marketed to the public there as a "ten-foot tall bodybuilder from a country near the North Pole, the son of a bear-trapper who grew up in the harshest northern wilderness known to mankind."

Today, Dolph holds a master's degree in chemical engineering and divides his time between homes in London and Marbella. His deepest darkest secret? He's fond of knitting and once made a "lovely red cardy (cardigan)" for Father Christmas.

Standards of male beauty, at least in films, have changed over the years. Spiderman **Tobey Maguire** *(photos above)* may be a sex symbol for the 21st Century, but he definitely wouldn't have made the grade back in the 1950s heyday of Rock Hudson and Tab Hunter. Tobey and his best pal, Leonardo DiCaprio, often "pork out" between movie shoots. But when the hunky young actor is rehearsing for another *Spiderman* movie, he appears in peak physical perfection.

In 2007, widely broadcast on a blogger's internet site is a version of a photo of the star which was significantly altered from its original version. In the original, Tobey appeared decently and demurely dressed in a Japanese kimono, as were his friends, David Blaine (left) and Leonardo DiCaprio (center). But in the altered and widely distributed inter-net version, Tobey's head was superimposed over the body of a naked guy with a schlong-flopper.

Tobey once revealed to the press that he got the role of Spiderman by going topless to the audition because prior to that, the film's producers weren't convinced that his slight frame was suitable for an action hero on the big screen. But when Tobey showed up and unveiled his yoga-toned pecks *(see above)*, that clinched the deal.

If he had shown more, it would probably have ended the nationwide debate of, **"Just how big is it?"**

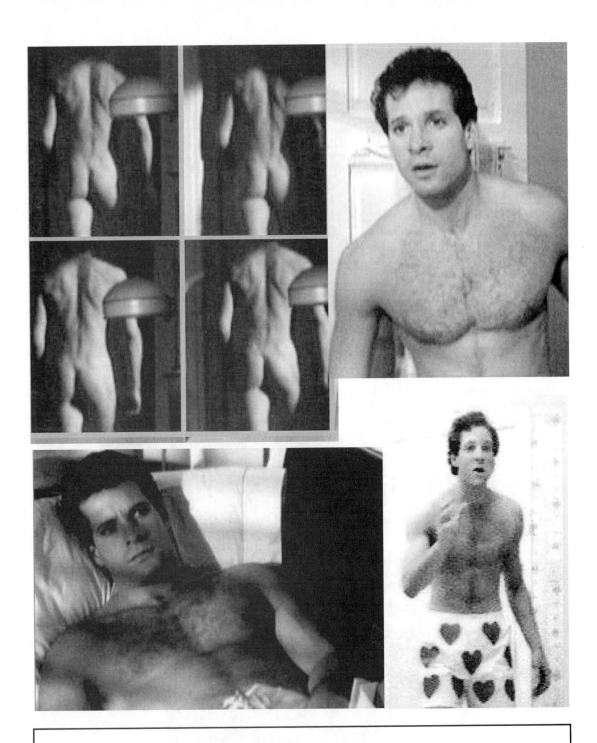

Unlike many other actors, **Steve Guttenberg** had the balls to finally accept, in 2002, the lead role in James Kirkwood's controversial black comedy, *P.S. Your Cat is Dead*. The frank exploration of sexual role playing, centered around homosexuality, had languished on the shelves for a quarter of a century.

Sal Mineo was in rehearsal for the play version when he was murdered.

Guttenberg has always brought comic timing and charm to roles such as *3 Men and a Baby* (1987), as well a great ass *(see above)*. His front part, according to reports, is mighty impressive as well.

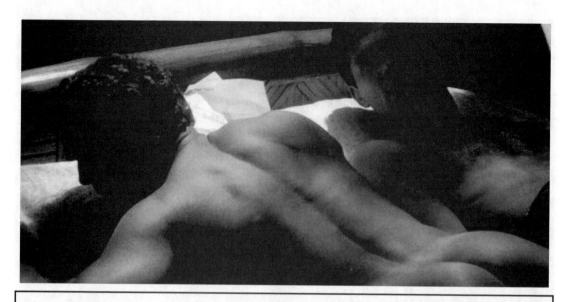

During the peak of his career, Illinois-born actor **William Petersen** wasn't afraid to strip down for sex scenes in movies – even if there was another naked man in the bed. From all reports, he's got nothing to be ashamed of. "When I was younger," he said, "women wanted to sleep with me because of whatever movie or play they saw me in, and for about 15 years I certainly took advantage of that more often than not. Fidelity was hard for me when I was younger, but with maturity, I got to be a mindset of, 'What's with all this running around to get girls?' Now for me it's the old case of, 'Why go out for a hamburger when I've got steak at home?'"

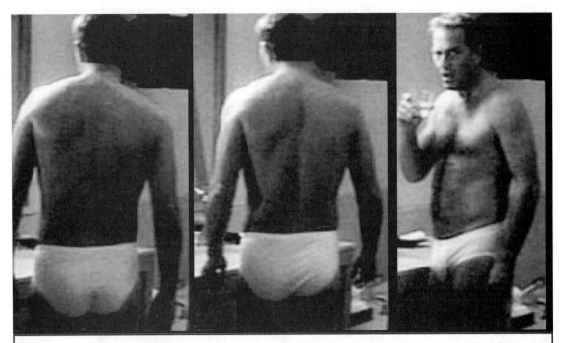

At the age of 18, **Kevin Costner** built his own canoe and paddled down the rivers that Lewis and Clark followed to the Pacific during the early 1800s.

During his high school years, even at the meager height of 5'2", Costner excelled at basketball. Once, on a flight from Mexico to Los Angeles, he sat with bisexual actor Richard Burton, who convinced him to devote his full time to acting. He found work making one soft core sex film (a collector's item today) before he was cast in *The Big Chill* (1983). His scene ended up on the cutting room floor, but he shot to prominence when cast in *Silverado* in 1985. By 1998 he was voted "Most Erotic Male" by the readers of the German magazine *Amica*. His frontal nude scene in *For Love of the Game* (1999) was deleted after being met with wild laughter in test screenings. But from all reports, Costner's endowment is no laughing matter. Far from it. He eventually grew to 6'1".

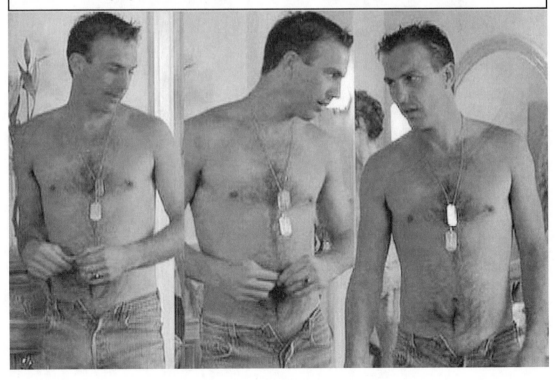

In This Edition of Hollywood Babylon-It's Back,
the Blood Moon Award
for "MOST LOVING COUPLE"
goes to:

Nicole Brown Simpson and O.J.

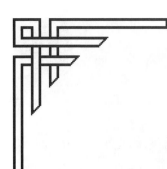

Don Johnson

The Size of It

This son of a Missouri farmer became the male sex symbol of the 1980s when he played the lead role of Sonny Crockett in the hit TV series *Miami Vice*.

In the late 1960s he was in a psychedelic rock band called "The Horses." But it was the fashion-conscious cop series that made him a household word.

He also changed the way young American men dressed, with his thousand-dollar Versace and Hugo Boss suits worn with pastel cotton T-shirts. He drove a Ferrari Testarossa and lived on a 42-foot yacht with his pet alligator, Elvis.

"I'm better than DeNiro,
better than Pacino.
I've got the talent,
they've got the material."

Don Johnson

"I know some people make fun of her nose, but she can smell a phony a mile away."

Don Johnson
on Barbra Streisand

During his brief but torrid romance with **Barbra Streisand** *(above, right)*, **Don Johnson** delivered some zinger quotes to her. "TV actors are bigger than movie actors these days," he claimed. "More people see them, more people recognize them; the salaries in TV are rivaling those in feature films."

He also told her, "I can do whatever I want – I'm rich, I'm famous, and I'm bigger than you."

When the great diva Barbra Streisand met Don Johnson in Aspen in 1986, he was the hottest star in America, at least on TV, playing Detective Sonny Crockett on the hit NBC series, *Miami Vice*. He even set a new style for metrosexuals: rolled-up jacket sleeves and a perpetual five o'clock shadow (although Richard Nixon had already pioneered that kind of beard). A former car thief from Flat Creek, Missouri, Johnson became a nationwide sex symbol in the 1980s with his gravelly voice, dashing good looks, stubble, and wardrobe of assorted pastels.

After that night in Aspen, the romance between "The Diva & the Don"—or Streisand's "Goy Toy," as the press dubbed it—burst into bloom. They were seen on both coasts holding hands in restaurants or at the fights, including the Mike Tyson-Larry Holmes bout in Atlantic City. She claimed, "I've never been so happy before."

When Don met Babs, the macho, boyishly handsome Beau Brummel was "chicken"—that is, eight years younger—and a hell of a lot prettier. A nude rape scene between gay actor Sal Mineo and Johnson in the Los Angeles production of *Fortune and Men's Eyes* had catapulted Johnson to stardom and a film contract. He won both female and gay male hearts in his first

Gay actor **Sal Mineo** *(left figure in photo, left)* rapes a tender, young **Don Johnson** in a scene from the controversial play, *Fortune and Men's Eyes*, a homosexual prison drama produced by, directed by, and starring Mineo.

It opened at the Coronet Theatre in Los Angeles, in 1969. Johnson played the role of Smitty, a young man who became the sexual slave of inmate Rocky. Critic Herbert Whittaker wrote that the play was "the art of washing our dirty linen in the neighbor's yard."

film, *Magic Garden of Stanley Sweetheart* in 1970.

While thoughts of marriage danced through Streisand's head, she recorded a duet with him in 1988, "Till I Loved You," but things weren't going so well. Johnson still had the hots for his first wife, Melanie Griffith whom he had previously divorced. By December, of that same year, the Miami Vicer was slipping an $85,000 diamond engagement ring on Griffith's finger.

For Johnson, it soon became a case of out with the new—in this case, Streisand—and in with the old, Miss Melanie herself.

Although Griffith provided the most obvious reason for Johnson abandoning Streisand, all of Hollywood was abuzz with what may have been the real cause of the rift. Rumors spread that Streisand was demanding that the well-endowed Johnson have his uncircumcised penis "cut" before any marriage ceremony could take place.

Johnson refused, returning to the *shiksas* who made no such demands on his noble tool, which had serviced "literally thousands of women," or so it was said.

Johnson and Griffith would eventually remarry, but love the second time around didn't work out either. There was infidelity. There was drug abuse. And, finally, there was that Pedro Almodóvar heartthrob, sexy Antonio Banderas, who swept Griffith away. Johnson and Griffith divorced again in 1995.

If Streisand did not truly appreciate Johnson "as God made me," groupie and author, Pamela Des Barres, adored the *Miami Vice* star's appendage. She revealed all in her confessional book, *I'm With the Band*.

When she was first invited to his Hollywood bachelor pad, she wondered where "this absurdly beautiful specimen of manhood had been all of my life." When he got around to seducing her, she claimed she could "hardly wait to peel his Jockey shorts down."

She wasn't disappointed. HUGE COCK, she later revealed to the world. "I'm getting off like I haven't in AGES," she exclaimed. His love-making was so intense she compared it to "a searing geyser of adrenaline singeing the roots of my hair, making it impossible for me to stand up, stand still or stand it."

One night he told her, "My dear, do you know

Although **Don Johnson** played a copper on *Miami Vice*, in real life he had several brushes with the law. When he was twelve years old, he was arrested for hotwiring cars and sent to reform school.

Two cast members of *Nash Bridges* (1997) accused him of sexual assault, but both cases were settled out of court with confidential agreements.

In August of 2003, Johnson was stopped by German police, who found and photocopied documents listing transactions totaling $8 billion, but didn't seize them. Later they determined that the documents belonged to someone else. Johnson threatened to take legal action against German customs for causing "irreparable damage" to his reputation.

Groupie **Pamela Des Barres** *(above)* became the symbol of her generation for the freewheelin' rock 'n' roll style of the 60s and 70s.

Of all the groupies who flocked around entertainment-industry figureheads, Pamela became the most famous, laying "bare" the facts about her lovers, including Don Johnson, in her tell-all confession, *I'm With the Band*.

how long it's taken me to *find* you?" But once again that *infant terrible*, as Des Barres called her rival, Melanie Griffith, came back into Johnson's life. The groupie was left with her memories, one of which was "kissing Donnie's perfectly shaped royal ass."

YOUNG LOVE: **Don Johnson** and actress **Melanie Griffith** were just kids when they met, but they were married in January of 1976, a union that hardly lasted until July.

In June of 1989, after experiencing many other partners, the couple remarried. This union lasted until June of 1996.

Madonna, who admitted she wanted to bed **Antonio Banderas** *(right)*, ultimately feared she might be disappointed if she confronted a small cock.

Madonna didn't get this sexy Spanish movie star, but Melanie Griffith did and from the looks of things, it seems she was delighted.

Banderas, of course, became Don Johnson's rival in love for the affections of Melanie. Ultimately Melanie dumped Johnson and settled for this Latin heartthrob, marrying him in May of 1996.

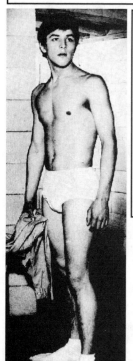

Don Johnson, *depicted left, right, and below*, in all his youthful male beauty, often appeared in films or TV episodes whose titles could easily have symbolized his own life:

Just Legal (best exemplified by the jockey shorts picture on the left); *Soggy Bottom* (*right* as he tans his butt in the desert heat); *Eight is Enough; Hot Dog;* and *Love at First Sight.*

Johnson even appeared as himself in *Porn Star: The Legend of Ron Jeremy* in 2001. However when the bloggers went to work on him, not all TV viewers found his *Miami Vice* character (*see top, right, photo, with cigarette*) so sexy. One female dissenter claimed, "I could never understand why he was supposed to be so handsome."

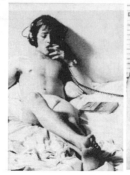

Don Johnson

In homage to the "movieland massacre" that was catalyzed every month beginning in 1952 by *Confidential Magazine*, Blood Moon presents the following features about some female divas--each of them a gay icon--that might have run within the pages of that notorious magazine. It devoted itself unashamedly to sex, scandal, and sensationalism. "No one ever admitted to buying *Confidential*," said Humphrey Bogart. "Everyone always said that the cook or the maid brought it in, but every star in Hollywood read it faithfully."

Its founder, Robert Harrison, was obsessed with anything associated with "homos," sexual intimacy between people of different races, any form of drug addiction, and anything to do with Marlene Dietrich. Harrison was especially fond of detailing her dual-gender love affairs. In those days, the word "lesbian" was rarely, if ever, used, although the phrase "Baritone Babe" frequently crept into headlines.

Long before he became a star, the blond hunk, Tab Hunter, attended an allegedly gay "pajama party" and then had the arrest record which resulted from that documented in print. Rory Calhoun's felony arrest was exposed, as was the fact that Sammy Davis, Jr. dated Ava Gardner, much to Frank Sinatra's rage and chagrin.

Confidential "flamed out" in the late 1950s after reaching a record-breaking readership that exceeded five million. Buried under an avalanche of libel suits, it nonetheless launched a multi-million dollar gossip industry which continues today.

Substitute Zsa Zsa Gabor for Paris Hilton; Lana Turner for Britney Spears, Marilyn Monroe for Jessica Simpson, and Debbie Reynolds and Eddie Fisher for Jennifer Aniston and Brad Pitt--with Angelina Jolie standing in for Elizabeth Taylor. And with that premise in mind, the burning question becomes, "Are Tom Cruise and Katie Holmes a stand-in for 1950s-era Rock Hudson and his then-wife, Phyllis Gates?"

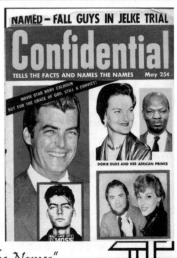

"Confidential Tells the Facts and Names the Names"

Richard Gere, Cindy Crawford, and All Those Rumors

Cindy

...with Richard Gere

The Illinois-born supermodel, cover girl, and actress, Cindy Crawford became a synonym for glamour in the 80s and 90s. As a model, her trademark became a mole on her face, her "beauty mark". As a celebrity endorser, she once hawked chocolates where she "licked off" her own mole.

Her hopes to become a film star more or less bombed in 1995 when she starred in her first movie role, *Fair Game.* Although it cost $50 million to make, it was panned by the critics and took in only $11 million at the box office.

She became the first modern-day supermodel to pose nude for *Playboy.* When she appeared *au naturel* in the October 1998 issue, the magazine became *Playboy's* alltime biggest seller, although its overall effect was nowhere near as shocking as that magazine's inaugural issue featuring Marilyn Monroe.

Eventually, Crawford appeared as number 5 on *Playboy's* list of the 100 Sexiest Stars of the 20th century. In 1997, *Shape* magazine named her number 2 among the most beautiful women in the world, with Demi Moore topping the list.

The most controversial period in Crawford's life was her marriage to Richard Gere (1991-95). During their time together, rumors were rampant that the marriage was a "beard," an attempt to cover up Gere's alleged homosexuality. "Considering the number of women he's been associated with, when does Richard have the time to be gay?" Crawford asked. Her own sexual preference came into question when she graced the cover of *Vanity Fair*, tarted up to shave the lesbian performer k.d. Lang.

After three years of out-of-control gossip, Gere and Crawford paid $30,000 for an ad in *The London Times* in which they declared, " We are heterosexual and monogamous and take our commitment to each other very seriously." Nonetheless, they separated eight months later.

People Magazine named Gere the "Sexiest Man Alive" in 1999, but that didn't stop the rumors, including the most ridiculous of them all. It was falsely alleged that a gerbil became trapped in Gere's anal canal during kinky sex. It was shamelessly reported that a physician was called in to remove the trapped rodent. Reporter Mike Walker of *The National Enquirer* "spent a long time seeking the name of the attending physician that his many doctor informants swore had been there."

Finally, the reporter became convinced that the story of Gere & the Gerbil was an "urban legend."

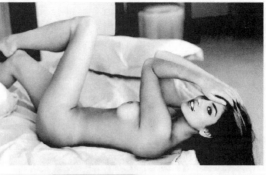

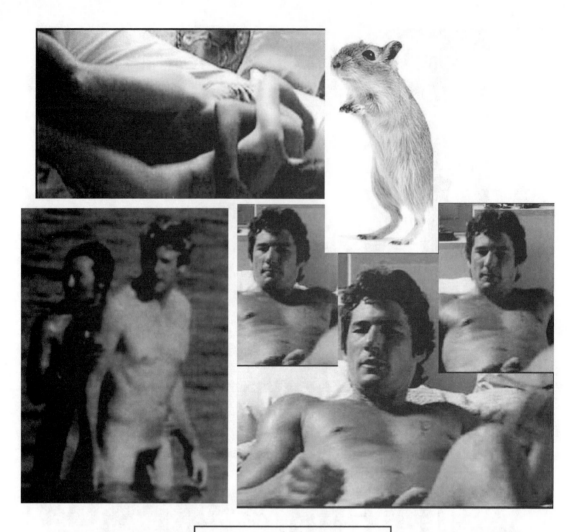

Richard Gere

Joan Crawford's Bisexual Husbands

Involved in bisexual dalliances whose co-participants included both John F. Kennedy and Marilyn Monroe, Joan Crawford blazed a sexual trail across the Hollywood landscape beginning in the 1920s until her last horror film in 1970, when her star finally faded.

Fortunately, she did not live to read the libelous and highly inaccurate portrait which her adopted daughter, Christina, painted of her within her controversial memoir, *Mommie Dearest.* In the 1981 movie version of that memoir, Faye Dunaway did the world's best characterization filmed to date of Crawford.

Joan's first films were "blue movies." Not knowing that she would one day be a fabled, world-renowned movie star, Joan during her flapper days appeared in porno flicks. Her first screen appearance was in a series of stills, designed for display in machines in penny arcades, entitled, *What the Butler Saw.* Actual porno films followed, including *The Plumber* which costarred Harry Green, a distantly remembered name from the silent screen days. Later titles included *Velvet Lips* (guess what that plot was about?), *The Casting Couch, Coming Home,* and *She Shows Him How.* In the *Casting Couch,* Joan (then known as Billie Cassin) is a starlet so eager to get a big break that she strips off her clothes and hops onto a producer's couch, where she delivers a first-class blow job. In the aptly named *Bosom Buddies*, she appears in a topless lesbian romp.

As Billie Cassin, Joan started out as a dancer although a film critic later wrote that "she possessed the terpsichorean grace of a mule".

Despite the tawdriness of her filmmaking debut, *Our Dancing Daughters* (1928) was a nationwide hit, as was *Dance, Fools, Dance* (1931), the first movie she made with Clark Gable. He became her lover, an affair that lasted deep into the 1940s. Crawford later admitted that Gable was a dud as a lover and that during the course of their involvement, she had tried to steer him away from the bedroom as much as possible.

During the course of her busy sex life, Joan sustained affairs with her alltime favorite companion, Barbara Stanwyck, as well as director Dorothy Arzner, Marlene Dietrich, singer Greta Keller, and Marilyn Monroe. Later, she'd seduce a gay actor (Rock Hudson) and a prominent politician (John F. Kennedy).

Three of her husbands were bisexual, including Douglas Fairbanks Jr., Franchot Tone (who demanded she pay homage to his 10 inch shaft), and Phillip Terry, the lover of Robert

Our Dancing Daughters

Taylor. Joan told Terry, who was working with Taylor on the set of *Bataan* (1943), "I had Taylor long before you did. It was no big deal."

Although Dietrich was initially attracted to Crawford, she later turned against her. "That terrible, vulgar woman with the pop eyes beats her children. But what do you expect from that class--a cheap tap dancer."

Later in life, when Joan was accused of using the casting couch as a means of advancing her career, she responded, "Well, it sure as hell beat the hard, cold floor."

Howard Hughes was one of the few men who failed to nab Joan. She told him, " I love homosexuals but not in my bed after midnight." She welcomed Glenn Ford into her bed, as well as both Cary Grant and Spencer Tracy. She found John Wayne disappointing as a lover and Spencer Tracy "too drunk." She admired the appendage swinging from Johnny Weissmuller's legs and found John Garfield "wonderfully aggressive." She gave low marks to Henry Fonda and Kirk Douglas.

Joan's vengeful enemy, Bette Davis, declared loudly and frequently, "She's slept with every male star at MGM except Lassie." But despite her deeply entrenched history as a sexual predator, Joan was still prudish when discussing sex. In ways perhaps influenced by the vocabulary of her past success as a flapper, when a couple fornicated, she said that "they went to

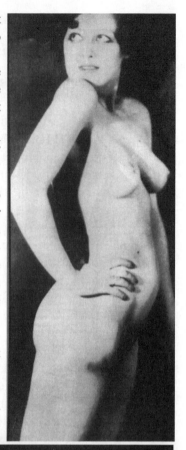

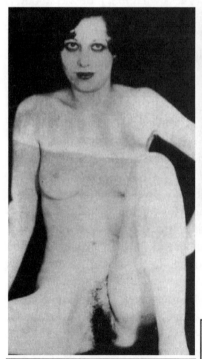

(Two solo photos this page)
Joan during her blue period

Joan's marriage to **Douglas Fairbanks, Jr.** and its associations with Hollywood royalty helped propel her out of the penny arcades. Doug's stepmother, the reclusive, then-faded star of the Silent Screen, Mary Pickford, had yet another reason to loathe Joan: During her divorce from Doug, Jr., Joan got overly friendly with Doug's father (Mary's estranged husband), Douglas Fairbanks, Sr.

heaven," and she referred to a woman's breasts as "ninny pies."

Today, older gay men, although dying off, remain Joan's most devoted fans and keep her memory alive. Most young gay males, however, associate her with wire hangers.

From rags to riches, Joan, in the words of *The New York Times*, "personified the dreams and disappointments of millions of American women."

And so she did.

Robert Montgomery *(left)* with
Joan and **Franchot Tone.**

Joan with **Clark Gable**.

Both Joan and her third husband, **Philip Terry** *(left)* made movies with **Robert Taylor** *(right)* and both of them seduced him offscreen.

What helped perpetuate Joan's feud with Bette Davis? To some extent, it was **Franchot Tone** (above) who takes a smoking break between servicing each of them.

Four photos of **Marlene Dietrich**, pool hall hustler, *Blue Angel* slut, *femme fatale*, and goddess who said, "No way, Adolf."

Joan *(left)* drank Royal Crown with vodka before switching to Pepsi-Cola with vodka. When not consuming beverages, she obsessively changed toilet seats used by estranged lovers or husbands.

As a sex goddess, Bette Davis has drawn mixed reviews, beginning with Humphrey Bogart on the set of her first movie, *Bad Sister*, released in 1931. "That dame is just too fucking uptight. What that bitch needs is a good screw from a guy who knows how to do it." Bogart volunteered to do the filthy deed, and he got turned down. But he was persistent.

Davis turned down the advances of Barbara Stanwyck on the set of *So Big* (1932). When asked privately what she thought of Davis, Stanwyck claimed that, "She's an egotistical little bitch".

Davis might also be called a sex therapist. Her first husband was Harmon Oscar Nelson, nicknamed "Ham." When seeing the rear end of the Oscar, Davis claimed the statue's ass "looked just like my Oscar." The nickname "The Oscars" came from her pronouncement.

Ham had started masturbating as a six-year-old boy and was given to premature ejaculation. Beginning on their honeymoon, Davis began "training sessions" that took eight months before Ham could adequately fulfill his marital duties.

One of her most difficult seductions involved the eccentric billionaire, Howard Hughes. A drunken Davis often told parties--usually with a coterie of gay men attending-- that the aviator failed to achieve orgasm on the first or even the second night of their coupling. On the third night, he was unable to produce an erection to penetrate her. He demanded that she perform fellatio on him, which she agreed to do. "He said if I cursed and swore like a sailor at him, he could shut his eyes and conjure up a vision of me as a handsome young man," Bette claimed.

Hughes was right. According to Davis, he achieved an orgasm that night and for many nights thereafter. "That dyke, Katharine Hepburn, couldn't do that for him--and she's a real boy," Davis told her friends, enjoying their mocking laughter.

The famous feud between Joan Crawford and Bette Davis began when Davis was starring with the bisexual actor, Franchot Tone, in *Dangerous* (1935). After performing fellatio on him, Davis was said to have given him the nickname of "Jawbreaker."

Although Crawford learned some of the details of their affair, she did not initially lash out at Davis, as some biographers have it. Davis claimed instead that "Crawford came on to me. It was only when I rejected her advances that she turned against me. There was more than a little professional jealousy as well. I was a better actress than Crawford, as newspaper critics were fond of printing at the time."

Davis was notoriously successful at seducing directors, some of whom included Anatole Litvak, the husband of Miriam Hopkins. Even more than she hated Joan Crawford, Davis detested Hopkins. When Hopkins heard about Davis' affair with her husband, she said, "Bette Davis is a greedy little girl at a party table. She just has to sample other women's cupcakes."

Not every director was impressed with Davis. Michael Curtiz, who sometimes mixed genders during his insults, called her "A no-good, sexless son of a bitch!"

She was especially well-known for picking up young soldiers at the Hollywood Canteen during World War II. "I hear she screws like a mink," said actor Jack Carson after talking to a U.S. Marine at the Canteen.

Davis could be cruel to some of her sexual conquests. After seducing Henry Fonda, her costar in *Jezebel*, in 1938, she said, "He needs to work out with a sex therapist." In vivid contrast, Davis awarded her "best-in-the-sack" rating to *Jezebel's* director William Wyler; her *Mr. Skeffington* (1944) director, Vincent Sherman, and her *Housewife* costar, George Brent.

During her final years, Davis dated a string of younger men, nearly all of them gay. After knowing a few of them for only a week or so, she'd propose marriage to them but

Humphrey Bogart emotes with Bette in *Bad Sister*

was inevitably turned down. Friends said she was always looking for a replacement for her fourth husband, actor Gary Merrill who had costarred with her in *All About Eve* (1950).

"She never found another Gary," her friend, Olivia de Havilland, was reported to have said. "Not that she didn't search. How sad!"

Husband no. 4, **Gary Merrill** *(left),* and with **Joan Crawford** *(right)* in *What Ever Happened to Baby Jane?*

Barbara Stanwyk tried to get amorous with Bette in the movie, *So Big*.

Bette goes nightclubbing with that premature ejaculator, **Harmon Nelson**

Bette flirts with closeted billionaire recluse **Howard Hughes**

Franchot Tone seduced **Bette** both on and off the screen in *Dangerous.*

,,,with **Henry Fonda** in *Jezebel*

,,,with **Miriam Hopkins** in *The Old Maid*

...and with **Gary Merrill** in *All About Eve*

William Wyler

Vincent Sherman

George Brent

"She can't act; she can't talk—she's terrific," said studio mogul Louis B. Mayer when Ava Gardner's first screen test was shown to him. She seduced men, especially bullfighters and actors, on two continents, and to a much lesser extent, sultry women such as Lana Turner. She temporarily took Richard Burton from her rival, Elizabeth Taylor, and even seduced Robert Taylor when they costarred in *The Bribe* (1949).

Ava later confided in her best "gal pal," Lana, that "Robert and Clark weren't worth messing up your mouth with." Lana, who'd also seduced both men, ranked both Taylor and Clark Gable a "2" on a scale of 1 to 10.

Ava

...with **Robert Taylor** in
The Bribe

...with **Richard Burton** in
The Night of the Iguana

more Ava

Lana Turner

Elizabeth Taylor

Ava & Gable in *The Hucksters*

Titian-haired Rita Hayworth, who immortalized herself in the 1946 film, *Gilda*, lost her virginity to her father, Eduardo Cansino. Her World War II pinup photo was so hot that GIs pasted it on the first atomic bomb to hit Hiroshima in 1945.

The ravishingly beautiful star had a compulsion toward men who victimized her, including her first husband, Edward Judson, who pimped her to lots of men who could further her career. She was also famously married to Orson Welles, who directed her in *The Lady from Shanghai* (1948). In a fit of misogynism, he patterned the film's leading character after Rita, calling her "a lady of ice masquerading as fire."

Rita also married singer Dick Haymes, who used and abused her. But her most notorious marriage was to Prince Aly Khan, the wealthy playboy and son of the Aga Khan, Imam (spiritual leader) of the Shi'a Ismaili Community. "He fell in love with Gilda but married me," Rita later lamented.

She had a fondness for bisexual men, including aviator Howard Hughes, Victor Mature, David Niven, James Stewart (who'd had an affair with Henry Fonda), Robert Mitchum, and Tyrone Power. Peter Lawford, who was more gay than straight, pronounced her "the worst lay in the world." But fellow Latino, Gilbert Roland, claimed that, "A night with Rita is to be transported to pussy heaven. It was the fuck of my life, and I've had the best broads Hollywood can offer. Rita once confessed to me that she got the best head ever—not from a man—but from Marlene Dietrich. When Marlene wanted Rita to return the favor, Rita told her, '*Mañana.*' From what I gather, tomorrow never came."

Once a fan in New York ran up to Rita on Fifth Avenue and accused her of being "a slut." Rita countered, "Put the Blame on Mame," referring to her steamy rendition of this song, which became her signature. "To me, 'Mame' is what 'Over the Rainbow' is to Judy," Rita said.

Raunchy, raucous, and riotous, the "Divine Miss M." got her start working at a Dole pineapple-processing plant in Hawaii. She broke into show business by performing her cabaret act at the famed gay men's bath house, The Continental Baths, in the 70s with Barry Manilow as her accompanist. To show their approval, men tossed their towels at the stage. Despite her career's notorious debut, she often makes disapproving remarks about today's entertainers.

Even though the singer/actress has admitted to some wild times in her younger days, she nonetheless has blasted Britney Spears and Lindsay Lohan, referring to them as "sluts." Midler said she would never have left home without her underwear. The aging Midler has also accused Britney and Christina Aguilera of stealing some of her on- and off-stage accessories. "I broke down the doors for today's pop superstars," Midler claimed. "Because of me, a professional entertainer today is not considered such unless you dress like a *ho*. I opened the door for trashy singers with bad taste and big tits—and don't you forget it, babe."

Midler has always been counted upon to deliver a zinger of a quote. "I married a German. Every night I dress up as Poland, and he invades me." Or . . . "I feel like a million tonight—but one at a time."

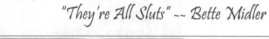
"They're All Sluts" -- Bette Midler

Spears *(left)*; **Aguilera** *(center)*, **and** **Lohan** *(right)*

"If her hips weren't gyrating, she was winching her shoulders or swinging her puzzy pink tits, or making a sucking fish-pucker mouth. Everything about her stated, 'I'm yours--take me.'" Or so stated fellow actress Carroll Baker.

Everyone who ever knew Marilyn--lovers, friends, women, men--has had an opinion about her. Her list of seductions included two U.S. presidents, a pre-presidential Ronald Reagan, and John F. Kennedy, first as a senator and later as president. Her "biggest thrills," she claimed, came in the form of Milton Berle, Dominican playboy Porforio Rubirosa, Frank Sinatra, "jaw-breaker" Franchot Tone, and Darryl F. Zanuck.

During her poverty-stricken early days, she was a streetwalker stalking the side streets adjacent to Sunset Boulevard. She told roommate Shelley Winters that she offered sexual favors just for food. "It might be breakfast if I'm hungry enough in the morning, but often it's a steak dinner with all the trimmings. One good steak dinner can last me for three days."

Marlon Brando, mobster Bugsy Siegel, and Frank Sinatra each got lucky, but Marilyn claimed she turned down many offers, namely Clark Gable ("even though I always had a crush on him"), John Wayne, Vice President Lyndon Johnson (who offered to fly her to his private home in Texas), and gangster Mickey Cohen.

Very few of her affairs were with women, but they notably included such bisexual actresses as Barbara Stanwyck, with whom Marilyn appeared in *Clash by Night* (1952), and Joan Crawford, who turned against Marilyn when she refused to make their brief affair an ongoing event. "Crawford had bad breath," Marilyn told Shelley. "Besides, she wanted to do things to me that no woman should do to another woman, even when making love to her."

Marilyn made one porno film for the aviator and movie producer Howard Hughes. Her "costar" --selected by Hughes-- was 1940s heartthrob Guy Madison. "Hughes wanted to do both of us afterward, but he was much more interested in Guy than in me," Marilyn said.

In spite of reports to the contrary, Marilyn never seduced Albert Einstein, although she stated that he was her all time goal. "I admire his brains," she told Peter Lawford, with whom she did have an affair. President Kennedy had his brother-in-law, Peter, take nude pictures of himself in the bathtub with Marilyn. Those photographs are said to exist somewhere today, but the owner of them isn't selling them.

Marilyn told "big mouth" Shelley that one night after the photo shoot, Peter joined the President and her in bed for a three-way. "Peter had quite a gay streak," she claimed, "and Jack for a thrill, allowed himself to be serviced. I wasn't surprised, having met Jack's gay friend, Lem Billings. He was bonded at the hip with Lem, and Jackie couldn't do anything about it."

Marilyn claimed that while she was in England filming *The Prince and the Showgirl*, (1957), an emissary of Prince Phillip called her for a secret meeting.

...with **Johnny Hyde**

She said, "I knew if I married him I could never be Queen of England. So what was the point?" She did claim that Prince Rainier of Monaco asked her to become the mistress of the principality before he made the same pitch to Grace Kelly.

Marilyn seduced a number of women--but, more to the point, allowed women to seduce her, including stripper Lili St. Cyr, the major rival of the more famous Gypsy Rose Lee.

But Marilyn never got the one woman she wanted in her bed, as she confided to Shelley. "Who might that be?" Shelley asked. "Greta Garbo? She'd go for you. Bette Davis? Your friend Betty Grable? Your idol Lana Turner? Surely not Ava Gardner! She would surely say yes considering her late night tastes."

Dreamboat, Albert Einstein

"None of the above, " Marilyn said. "Miss Jacqueline Kennedy herself."

That ugly runt of a man, Johnny Hyde, helped launch Marilyn's Hollywood career. But he died young. Marilyn didn't miss the sex with Hyde, a chore she actually dreaded, but he was like a father figure to her, and she loved him in her fashion--that is, when she wasn't bedding some movie producer or director like Orson Wells, Nicholas Ray, Elia Kazan, or John Huston. She was heartbroken at Hyde's death. His coffin was placed in the living room of Hyde's home for burial the next day. After his family had gone to bed, Marilyn slipped into the Hyde house.

She told Shelley that she spent the entire night lying on top of Hyde's dead body in the coffin, leaving at five in the morning before the family got up to discover her. "They would surely have called the police," Marilyn later said. "It was my way of saying goodbye to Johnny who had done so much for me."

"I'm glad she died young," said her hairdresser, Sydney Guilaroff, in a shocking statement.

"She could never have stood getting a wrinkle on her face. All she had was her beauty."

Lili St. Cyr

Guy Madison

Jackie Kennedy

Prince Philip and Her Majesty

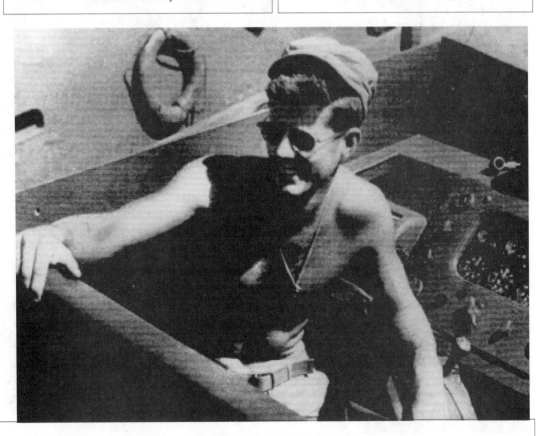

John F. Kennedy in his PT-109

...with **Clark Gable** in
The Misfits

Marilyn didn't just drop trou for anyone. Portrayed below are some of her rejects.

Bugsy Siegel

Lyndon B. Johnson

Mickey Cohen

Joan Crawford

John Wayne

"Dolly is known for two things," said Johnny Cash. "And, oh, yes, she's a pretty good singer too."

This *Steel Magnolia* from *The Best Little Whorehouse in Texas* is intensely private and talented—dynamic yet sexy, and maybe not as innocent as she appears. She brushes off those lesbian rumors and pushes forward with determination with her theme park, Dollywood.

The fourth child of a brood of a dozen, Dolly as a young girl blazed a trail through the Smoky Mountains in her "Coat of Many Colors." Arriving in Nashville with nothing but her guitar and her dreams, she made the world take notice. Dolly never relied just on her big tits. She kept a sense of humor as well. She deflects questions about her sex life when reporters get too nosey.

Q. Have you ever been with a woman?
A. All my life. I love women. My mother was a woman.

She did admit, however, that if she hadn't been born a woman, "I would have been a drag queen."

The Dolly Parton Swim Team

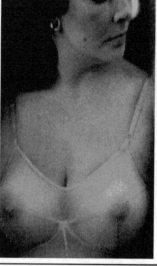

"I guess the world thinks of me as such a scarlet woman. I'm almost purple."
Elizabeth Taylor

"Elizabeth Taylor: Always a bride, never a bridesmaid."
Oscar Levant

"Every man should have the opportunity to sleep with Elizabeth Taylor. At the rate she's going, every man will."
Howard Hughes

Elizabeth Taylor was born in England in 1932 of American parents living there. Her father was a homosexual and her mother a former actress. In Hollywood in 1942 at the age of ten, Elizabeth made her first screen appearance in *There's One Born Every Minute*, but went on to greater fame and glory in MGM's *National Velvet* (1944).

After losing her virginity to her first husband, Nicky Hilton, the big-dicked hotel chain heir, Elizabeth fell into a series of marriages to the likes of Michael Todd (who died in an air crash) and more famously to Richard Burton. (She married and divorced him twice.)

Her list of other lovers is legendary, from Montgomery Clift to Frank Sinatra. Of his new bride, Todd once said, "Lemme tell ya, any minute that this little dame spends out of bed is totally wasted."

She turned down Howard Hughes who offered her $1 million to marry him. She refused his offer, telling him, "I'm not for sale!" even though her parents had aggressively promoted the marriage. No husband appreciated her busts more than Burton, who referred to them as "apocalyptic," claiming they "would topple empires down before they withered."

The last major star to emerge from Hollywood's old-time studio system, violet-eyed Dame Elizabeth has won the Oscar twice and definitely deserves *A Place in the Sun* (1951).

Empire magazine, among many others, named her one of the 100 Sexiest Stars in Film

History. There is still speculation that the insatiable actress is husband or lover hunting. When she headed for the French Riviera at the age of 70, with eight marriages under her belt, she was still on the lookout for love. A pal told the British tabloid, *The Daily Star*, "Liz is always begging her closest friends to fix her up on dates. She's told everyone who she knows to keep an eye out for the perfect gentlemen to wine her, dine her . . . and more!"

...and the husbands

Nicky Hilton

Michael Wilding

Mike Todd

Sen. John Warner

Elizabeth Taylor *(left)* stole **Eddie Fisher** *(center)* from **Debbie Reynolds** *(right)* Fisher was Mike Todd's best friend.

Taylor met **Larry Fortensky**, a truck driver, in rehab. She married him at Neverland with Michael Jackson as Best Man.

Taylor had a reunion with **Richard Burton** (her fifth and sixth husband) only weeks before his death.

Forever defined as "a Marilyn Monroe clone," Mamie Van Doren is a distantly remembered blonde bombshell from the 1950s. Marilyn was once asked if she viewed Mamie as serious competition. "It takes more than a bottle of peroxide for a gal to turn herself into Marilyn Monroe. Men want the real thing."

Despite those put-downs from MM, Mamie's lovers were legendary. She even seduced gay actor Rock Hudson but he prematurely ejaculated before she could guide him inside. Johnny Carson might have disappointed her as a lover, but not so Nicky Hilton (the first Mr. Elizabeth Taylor). "Mamie is a hot number," Nicky said. "She knows how to make a man feel like a man," said this late relative of Paris Hilton.

Referring to Burt Reynolds, Mamie claimed, "High on jive but low on substance." But she approved of Joe Namath. "In my bedroom, Joe proved his ability was just as great off the football field as on it." She also praised Steve McQueen for being "unabashedly wonderful in bed."

Unlike millions of other women, she wasn't attracted to Warren Beatty. "He would often try to interest me in a little casual sex by making allusions to the size of his penis, but I laughed at his advances. It was difficult for me to be interested in him. Most of the time he looked like he had just rolled out of bed and put on yesterday's clothes."

When Joe DiMaggio came to her weeks after burying Marilyn, Mamie confessed that she "did not try to fill the deep void within him. When Joe left I gave him a sisterly kiss and waved him out of the driveway."

Married at the time to Ray Anthony, the bandleader, Mamie did not drop panties for Elvis Presley, even when he hummed "Love Me Tender" in her ear. Later she confessed that "there was a part of me that kicked myself for not succumbing to Elvis's magnetic sexuality."

When they made *Teacher's Pet* together in 1958, Mamie also failed to seduce Clark Gable. He told her, "I'm almost sixty years old, Mamie. Now, that doesn't mean that there's not sex at sixty, but . . . well, if what I read in your eyes is correct, we could end up with big, big problems. Wife problems. Husband problems. But, ma'am, if it wasn't for that, it would surely be a pleasure."

Mamie's Men   The Good & The Bad

Warren Beatty

Johnny Carson

Bo Belinsky

Tony Curtis

Burt Reynolds

Elvis Presley

"Do your best, Mamie, not to fall in love with anyone in government, because after they fuck you--*they* fuck you."

Marilyn Monroe, addressing **Mamie Van Doren**

Rock Hudson

Steve McQueen

Joe Namath

Born in 1893, *The Little Chickadee* wasn't so little. Looking her up and down, Adolph Zukor, Paramount honcho, said, "When I look at that dame's tits, I know what lusty means." Costume designer Edith Head said, "I've seen Mae West without a stitch and she's all woman. No hermaphrodite could have bosoms, well, like two large melons."

West loved boxers, black or white, including Jack Dempsey. For years she kept a nude picture of him over her toilet. She also liked wrestlers and especially men with well-built physiques and endowments. That's why she hired Mickey Hargitay (Mr. Universe) and Steve Cochran for her stage act. She wasn't opposed to what she called "The Music Men" either, namely, Duke Ellington and Oscar Hammerstein II. Of the magician, Harry Houdini, she said, "He didn't escape my trap."

She dated George Raft but finally concluded that, "He liked a boy's rosebud more than my bush." Gangsters gave her a special thrill, especially Benjamin "Bugsy" Siegel. "That mobster knew how to shoot in more ways than one."

When she appeared with Cary Grant, she claimed, "I knew he was a homosexual before he did." She failed to seduce another homosexual, Rock Hudson. Later he said, "She was just plain and simply a sweet old lady who told me marvelous stories about her life." She even told him about the day that Marlene Dietrich tried to seduce her. "I go for men, and then only if they're hung like Anthony Quinn."

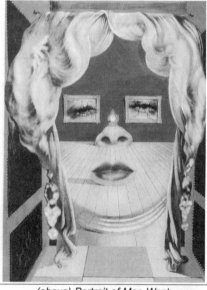

(above) Portrait of Mae West
by Salvador Dalí (1934-5)

Mae Sizes Up Her Men

Jack Dempsey

Steve Cochran

Duke Ellington

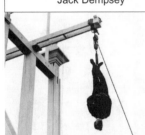

Harry Houdini

George Raft

Bugsy Siegel

Joe Louis

David Niven

(Above left) Stanley Ketchel vs. *(right)* Jack Johnson

Lovers, Gays, Lesbians, and Rivals

Mickey Hargitay with
Jayne Mansfield

...with Cary Grant in *She Done Him Wrong*

...duet with Rock Hudson
at the Academy Awards

Marlene Dietrich

Edith Head (top);
Gary Cooper

with W.C. Fields in *My Little Chickadee*

Marvelous Mae...in *Myra Breckinridge*

When she was a struggling young actress, Shelley Winters roomed with Marilyn Monroe. Rumors still persist on the rare nights they didn't find a date, they took care of each other's needs. A two-time Oscar Winner, Winters is as famous for her movie roles as she is for the men she bedded, including such heavily hung guys as John Ireland, Howard Hughes, Errol Flynn, and Sterling Hayden, as well as the more modestly endowed— Burt Lancaster, Clark Gable, and Marlon Brando.

Sean Connery was one of her all-time favorite lays. "He makes a woman feel sexual chemistry," she said of him. "To be his leading lady today, I'd lose 50 pounds and get my face lifted. As a matter of fact, I'd get everything lifted." Winters became known for being outspoken. "I desperately needed to get fucked," she once told her director when she flew cross country one weekend while she was on location for a film. Why she couldn't get laid on the West Coast remains a mystery. Where was her lover Anthony Quinn?

Frank Sinatra called her a "bowlegged bitch of a Brooklyn blonde," and women have had other comments. Marlene Dietrich, referring to Winters' weight gain in later life, said, "It is surprising what some people will let happen to themselves. Shelley Winters is a prime example."

Winters and Monroe remained "best gal pals" for life. In 1955 Winters told Monroe, "I'm fucking Adlai Stevenson, and he's going to become President of the United States, beating the hell out of Ike."

A few months later Monroe told Winters, "I'm fucking Senator John F. Kennedy, and he told me that by no later than 1960 he was going to become the president of the United States, unlike your friend Adlai. He's also prettier than Adlai."

"Bullshit!" Winters replied. "If Kennedy ever becomes president, I'll spend three hours a day eating out your asshole."

It is not known if Monroe ever held Winters to that rosebud promise.

Adlai Stevenson at the U.N.

Sean Connery

In September of 2007, Pamela Anderson and Denise Richards were offered $1 million to pose nude together for *Playboy*. Both of these blondes have disrobed for *Playboy* in days of yore, but Hugh Hefner wanted Richards and Anderson to pose as a team. Anderson posed nude for *Playboy* a record 12 times, Richards stripping only once (December, 2004). This former fashion model has appeared on several "Sexiest Women" lists.

Denise with Eve Cambell in *Wild Things*

In 2002 she disastrously married actor Charlie Sheen, with whom she appeared in *Scary Movie 3*. The couple has two daughters. But March of 2005 found her filing for divorce from Sheen, who is alleged to have cheated on her during their ill-fated marriage. Richards even sought a restraining order against Sheen, citing alleged death threats against her. She also charged in court that her husband visited prostitutes and was addicted to porno that featured "very young girls." She further claimed that he frequently viewed gay pornography featuring "very young men who did not look like adults."

In a court document, Richards also claimed that Sheen sent pictures of his "erect penis" to nearly three dozen women on sex sites. "I'd love to give it to you any time," Sheen wrote to one woman under the screen name of mrjonze55.

Sheen denied these allegations, even that he had an "abnormal fascination with Nicole Simpson's death." As for her on-screen life, the actress claimed that "doing love scenes is always awkward. I mean, it's just not a normal thing to go to work and lay in bed with your co-worker." Richards is known to get furious at how she is portrayed on the Internet and on screen.

In 2002 the former Bond girl claimed that her film bosses digitally enlarged her backside on promotional posters for her comedy, *Undercover Brother*. "What in hell did they do to my ass?" she asked when seeing ads for the film. The star claimed that she had approved a different photograph. "They twisted the art around. That's not my ass. It's a computer." She's also furious about fake nude pictures of her on the web. "I don't appreciate these pictures. They are just sick."

Denise Richards alone (left photo) and with Charlie Sheen (center and right photo)

112

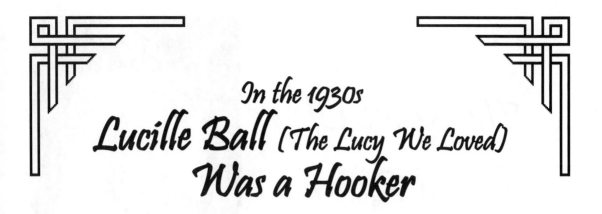

In the 1930s
Lucille Ball (The Lucy We Loved)
Was a Hooker

A Mini-biography of Lucille Ball
Tell Us That It Isn't So!

"Love! I was always falling in love," said **Lucille Ball**. The most famous woman in the history of TV wasn't exactly what she appeared to be on *I Love Lucy*. Gritty, feisty, abrasive, intelligent, and edgy, Lucille lived through the heady years of 1930s show business as a chorus girl. But her wild runaway years as a star-struck teen have been kept largely concealed from her adoring public.

Here is the ultimate close-up of this extraordinary redhead, who worked her way up from starving hooker/model to B-film stardom--and ultimately, became a world-renowned comedienne.

The Secret Life of Lucy Ricardo

She looked like a two-dollar whore who had been badly beaten by her pimp. She had a black eye, her hair was hanging down in her face, and her skintight dress was coming apart at the seams."

Desi Arnaz,
remembering his first glimpse of Lucy

When **Lucille** first landed in Hollywood, the studio didn't quite know what to do with her, other than make an attempt to turn her into a glamour girl – a role that she never quite fit. She kept her mouth shut in most photos to hide her crooked teeth. As a contract player, she was forced to pose for every cheesecake shot the studio requested. "Am I ever going to succeed?" she'd endlessly inquire of anyone at the studio willing to listen – including complete strangers. "I need to make money."

"You ain't got what it takes, gal," said her rival, Betty Grable, pulling up her dress to reveal the world's shapeliest gams.

What Desi Arnaz didn't know was that Lucille Ball was dressed for her part in *Dance, Girl, Dance* (1940) in which she had been cast as "Bubbles." She'd just had a fight on screen with the star of the movie, Maureen O'Hara. Lucille was having a hard enough time playing the part, but off screen she had to battle to keep film's lesbian director, Dorothy Arzner, "out of my drawers," as Lucille so colorfully put it.

The next time Desi saw Lucille, she was beautifully dressed and made up. He later claimed that he fell in love with her at first sight. But that was not the case with Lucille. She claimed it took her all of five minutes to fall for this handsome, charismatic Cuban band leader.

Lucille Désirée Ball is an iconic American comedian and the star of the landmark 1950s sitcom, *I Love Lucy*. The glamour girl of the 1930s and 1940s became a charter member of the Television Hall of Fame.

She was married to her co-star, Desi Arnaz (1940-

During her earliest modeling days in New York, **Lucille** worked as a model for Hattie Carnegie, owner of a woman's clothing salon. Carnegie felt that Lucille resembled Constance Bennett, the movie star – translucent skin, blue eyes, reed thinness. The only difference was Lucille's red hair. She was forced to peroxide it.

1960). But make no mistake about it, Lucille and Desi had nothing in common with the characters they played on TV, Ricky and Lucy Ricardo.

Born in 1911 in Jamestown, New York, the daughter of a telephone lineman for Ma Bell, she went to Montana at an early age, living in Anaconda, before moving on to Wyandotte, Michigan, and eventually returning to Jamestown. Her father had contracted typhoid fever and died in February of 1915.

Stacked up against the big-breasted glamour-girls of her day, **Lucille** came in a distant second. Nonetheless, Bugsy Berkeley saw talent behind Lucille's steely determination. A fellow actress, Kay Harvey, gave her a harsh critique: "In those days, Lucille, even if she was a Goldwyn Girl, was actually a plain Jane with nondescript brown hair. She had no legs, no breasts, only a high energy drive."

Lucille became sexually active at an early age when Johnny DeVita, a local hoodlum, seduced her. She was only 14 in 1925 when she shocked Jamestown by bobbing her hair and hanging out with DeVita, who was a ripe, experienced 21. Lucille later remembered him as looking like "John Travolta in *Grease*, but a gangster version." A gambler and rum runner (across the Canadian border), DeVita was proud that he'd taken Lucille's virginity. But the next year she said goodbye to him. With $50 sewn into her underwear, she headed for New York and acting school.

At the John Murray Anderson School for Dramatic Arts, Lucille encountered fellow pupil Bette Davis. After seeing her perform, Davis informed the shy Lucille: "You have no future as a performer." It was back to Jamestown High and Johnny DeVita but not for long.

New York was in her blood, and Jamestown and DeVita weren't all that enthralling, so Lucille struck out again for Manhattan. She remembered arriving in time to see the Empire State Building undergoing completion.

Getting a Broadway gig became almost impossible for her, and when the Depression descended, it was hopeless. Lucille was determined to break into show business at all costs.

Meeting with Earl Carroll's show girls, she was befriended by a teenage *femme fatale* who informed Lucille how she could make extra money on the side. At first Lucille resisted but soon she was going out with a different escort every night. As a chorine on Broadway making the rounds, she adopted the stage name of Diane Belmont because it sounded more dramatic. But she told her johns that her name was "Montana."

"At least you get a square meal even if you have to put up with some action later in the evening with these Stage Door Johnnies," Lucille later told her "gal pal," Ginger Rogers in Hollywood.

"I was determined to advance my career even if it meant sleeping with every guy from the stage door guardian to the director."

Lucille always credited Lela Rogers, the mother of Ginger Rogers, in urging her to the casting couch. Encountering Lela at a rehearsal one day, the woman asked Lucille, "Do you want to be a star in two years?"

"I'd love it," Lucille said. "The dream of my life."

"Then fuck every director on Broadway," Lela advised.

"If that's what I have to do, I'll go there."

Unknown to Lela at the time, that was what "Montana" (her alternate persona) was already doing. After speaking with Lela, Lucille made a change in her dating patterns. To her wealthy, high-class escorts, she began calling herself Diana Belmont. Montana was the name she reserved for the five-dollar johns.

Getting a role on Broadway was proving more and more difficult. She did get a chorus job in the third road show company of Ziegfeld's *Rio Rita*. But she was much too skinny and not big busted like the more endowed competition. Finally, the stage manager, Stanley Sharpe, fired her. "Go back to the ranch, Montana. Maybe you can make it as a cowgal."

It was back to Jamestown and back to DeVita's bed. After a few months, she would grow restless and head back to Manhattan again. At one point she remembered having only four cents in her pocketbook when the New York subway cost five cents. But there was always a man willing to stake her to five or ten dollars and a meal—"The experience was awful, humiliating," she later recalled to friends, "but some of the guys were nice, family-type men, willing to cheat a bit on their wives with a glamorous chorus gal."

"Two broken down old broads" was the phrase Wilson Hicks, former photo editor of *Life* magazine, used to describe **Lucille** (left) and **Ginger Rogers** (right) in this photo. Lucille and Ginger had been good friends since the 1930s. When they came together for a reunion, the ultra-conservative Ginger was horrified to learn that Lucille had posed in the nude. "I was never at ease wearing too little," Ginger said, "much less nothing at all. I would never have made it on the screen today."

Modeling hats or modeling topless, to break into show business, a girl's gotta do what a girl's gotta do. Photographers criticized Lucille's "boyish figure," but she desperately needed the money.

At the time the pictures immediately above were taken, she was surviving on tomato soup made from catsup

She found most of the choreographers were gay but occasionally she encountered a straight one and would get a chorus job in such musicals as *Step Lively*. "But even though I slept with the bastard, he fired me after only a week."

She hated "singing for my supper" and sometimes went for weeks without turning tricks. "But then I would be starving to death," she said. "When a young girl isn't eating, she'll do a lot of things. I didn't have much of a figure at the time—but that didn't matter to the johns, 'cause I told them I was fourteen and they liked them young."

She decided to try out as a coat model because "that would cover my missing figure." To her surprise, she got jobs as a model, alternating between chorus work and the casting couch.

She posed for artists and photographers, sometimes in the nude. For one bare-breasted assignment, she got fifty dollars—the most she'd ever been paid.

Her biggest modeling assignment came at Hattie Carnegie's chic salon at 42 East 49th

Street, off Park Avenue. Hattie suggested to Lucille that she'd get better jobs if she dyed her hair blonde. Hattie was right. Lucille's salary rose to $35 a week.

The dye job worked and at seventeen Lucille became the youngest model ever employed by Hattie. The salon owner felt that with Lucille's blonde hair she resembled the svelte movie goddess, Constance Bennett, who was pulling in $30,000 a week in Hollywood, an astonishing salary in those days. Constance and her sister, Joan Bennett, also an actress, were Hattie's best customers. Lucille would always model for them whenever they came into the salon.

Constance Bennett *(left photo, above)* and her sister, **Joan Bennett** *(right photo, above)*, were the daughters of stage actor Richard Bennett.

They were the most beautiful sisters ever to appear on the screen. Their lives only marginally touched Lucille's. She found the popular sisters to be haughty, and she plotted revenge.

At the time, Lucille could not even imagine that one day in Hollywood she'd be competing for the same men with these two glamorous women. Surely these two movie star sisters never knew that the frightened teenage girl modeling clothes for them would ever be viewed as a serious rival for a Hollywood hunk.

One day while modeling at Hattie's salon, Lucille collapsed on the runway. There have been many conflicting stories about this event in her life, and over the years Lucille has contradicted previous tales. Allegedly, she'd succumbed to a crippling rheumatoid arthritis. The doctor who examined her warned that "you might not walk for many years."

Lucille claimed that she was taken back to Jamestown where she was virtually crippled for 2½ years. If indeed Lucille had rheumatoid arthritis, it was not likely to go away, as it did in Lucille's case. Perhaps she had rheumatic fever instead, the symptoms of which were relieved by a new sulfa drug.

There are other stories that Lucille wasn't paralyzed at all during this time and that she was living in an apartment subsidized by DeVita. It was also rumored among Jamestown friends that she underwent an abortion at this time. One story that won't go away is that Lucille was riding in a car one night when her hoodlum boyfriend pulled out a gun and shot an innocent young boy—"just for the fun of it." Whatever the truth, it may never be known as all eyewitnesses are now dead. Even Desi told friends that he thought "Lucy was always covering up something in her life—and maybe she got sick too. Who knows? She never gave me a straight answer as many times as I asked her."

Back in New York, Lucille resumed her modeling career at Hattie's, appearing again in front of Constance Bennett who had just stolen a title and the husband of Gloria Swanson. She introduced Lucille to the Marquis de la Falaise.

While his new wife was in the dressing room changing into a gown, the Marquis got Lucille's telephone number. That night he pleaded sick and couldn't take Constance to a premiere. Lucille came to his hotel suite for an hour, and he slipped her a hundred dollar bill, a high price in those days for sex. Lucille would later recall that the sleazy European aristocrat told her, "Don't be astonished—Constance has a lot more where that came from."

At night Lucille frequented speakeasies with the man of her

Trophy boy, **Le Marquis de la Falaise**, with Gloria Swanson, circa 1924. She married him, and so did Constance Bennett. But it was Lucille he turned to for sex.

choice—often a lowlife—but by the afternoon of the next day she was often seen better dressed at a polo club with a richer, more refined escort. She was known as "a gal about town," and it was said that her telephone number was passed around a lot.

Somewhere along the way, Lucille developed a passion for playboy Pat DeCicco. Married to a famous Hollywood actress and nightclub owner, Thelma Todd, he secretly dated Lucille. Todd was found dead on December 16, 1935, perhaps a victim of mob boss Lucky Luciano when she refused to transform her club into a front for his gambling operations.

DiCicco would later become a pimp for Howard Hughes. Whenever he wanted to, The Aviator would sodomize DeCicco, much to his pain and humiliation.

DiCicco later married the heiress, Gloria Vanderbilt, who pronounced him a hustler. Ironically, she too became involved romantically with Hughes.

Lucille remembered DiCicco with fondness, finding him "a fascinating escort, full of both humor and sophistication." She told girlfriends such as Ginger Rogers that "Pat taught me tricks in bed he must have learned in a Shanghai brothel."

Hugh Sinclair, an actor from London working on Broadway, said "Lucille was one of the most popular models in town. She had a sense of humor. America was in a Depression, but she always seemed to have money. She even had an elegant apartment being paid for by some wealthy married man. I know she was dating Sailing P. Baruch, Jr., a nephew of the famous financier Bernard Baruch." Sailing was president of Baruch Brothers & Company, an investment house. He died young at the age of 53 in 1956.

"Somehow," Sinclair said, "Lucille managed to satisfy Baruch and manage several boyfriends as well. She was also seen with this photographer, Arthur O'Neill, a cousin of the Vanderbilt family."

It's a wedding day for playboy **Pat DiCiccio**, a pimp for Howard Hughes, and **Gloria Vanderbilt**. Lucille got to sample DiCiccio's wares long before the heiress got a chance at them.

During her days as a model, Lucille fell hard for an English photographer, Roger Furse. Tall, dark, and handsome, he wore a Van Dyck beard and was also a commercial artist. She met him when he was only 25.

Descended from the theatrical families of Kemble and Siddons, Furse later gained professional recognition by designing sets and costumes for Laurence Olivier's stage and film productions.

He worked with Lucille on her make-up, camera angles, and clothing. "With him, I got rid of that Girl from Buffalo look," Lucille later said. "The sex wasn't bad either." Jamestown was near Buffalo, and her family often went there to shop for clothing.

One year she didn't have a cent to her name, but the following year she became known as a soft touch along Broadway. During the most severe depths of the Depression, she was lending one-hundred dollar bills to friends. Rumors spread at the time that she was a gun moll, and a future lover, George Raft, who had mob connections,

Sir Laurence Olivier, playing Hamlet, in a costume designed by Roger Furse. Lucille found the British designer's eyes "exotic and big – in fact, he had a big everything."

insisted that these stories were true. One rumor spread that a jealous gangster had one of his henchmen attempt to shoot her while she was taking a bath at the Kimberly Hotel.

Sinclair himself said that while dancing with her at a club in Harlem, "Lucille grabbed his arm and fled with him into the night. She'd seen a gangster come into the room. Indeed she was right to run. Just minutes after we left the club, that gangster shot dead one of the patrons and escaped."

After her picture was posted all over the country as the Chesterfield Cigarette Girl, Lucille seemed to have more and more money and better heeled admirers. In the ad, she wore a blue chiffon dress with a matching picture hat. She was posed with two Russian wolfhounds. The ad was sensational and from it derived her first nationwide fame.

Sinclair later claimed that "things were heating up for Lucille in New York at one point. She was said to have double-crossed one of her gangster lovers, and had to get out of town." But, first she needed a job in California. An opportunity arose when she answered a "cattle call" from Samuel Goldwyn, who was producing *Roman Scandals* in Hollywood, starring Eddie Cantor. She met Goldwyn's right-hand man, James Mulvey.

In *Roman Scandals*, Lucille played a slave girl figure in **Eddie Cantor**'s *(above, left)* dreams. She only appeared in the manically energetic bug-eyed comedian's dreams on film, not in real life. A chorus girl who had had a one-night stand with Cantor once told Lucille, "Honey, you didn't miss anything. There's not enough there to mess up your mouth with."

In the movie, one scene of which is depicted below, the chorus girls – who included Lucille – were chained to the wall in the "No More Love" number. They were actually nude, and the number was filmed at night when no studio bosses were around.

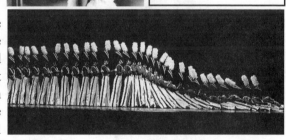

But the audition was to be before Russell Markert, who is known today as the founder and long-time choreographer of The Rockettes at New York's Radio City Music Hall. Lucille was bewildered to see at least fifty "better stacked" models and chorus girls trying out for the part, each delectably clad in a skimpy bathing suit.

Hoping to stand out and also hoping that Markert had a sense of humor, Lucille wet pieces of red crepe paper and stuck them all over her arms and face. When Markert got around to her, he looked astonished. His jaw dropped and then he burst into laughter.

He asked Lucille out that night, promising her $125 a week for a six-week run in Hollywood. Of course, bedding him was part of the deal. Many of The Rockettes later recalled that Markert wanted a blow-job early in the evening, followed by heavier action in the early morning hours.

From all reports, Lucille was only too happy to make him happy. "He didn't inspire me, but I gave it my best shot," she later said.

Within three days, Lucille was on the train to Hollywood with the other Goldwyn Girls. She told friends in New York that she was leaving all her New York boyfriends behind. "Why not?" she asked. "Hollywood has the most beautiful men in the world, and I bet I can have my pick."

DuBarry Was a Lady (1943), in which she played a tongue-in-check interpretation of an imperial French courtesan, was **Lucille's** all-time glamour role.

MGM stylist Sydney Guilaroff styled her hair for the film, dying it flaming red. That color, of course, later became her trademark. Ann Southern was set to play the role of May Daly (Madame du Barry) but discovered that she was pregnant just before filming started. Lucille was cast instead.

She feared she would not be able to follow in the footsteps of Ethel Merman and the acclaim won in the Broadway version by Cole Porter, but she created a sensation in high powdered wigs and hoopskirts. As the film revealed, the entire scenario was a dream of Red Skelton in which he became King Louis XV after he'd been slipped a Mickey Finn.

During the filming of *Du Barry*, Lucille fretted about Desi's prolonged absence on the road, as word came back to her that he was having numerous affairs. Back at Culver City, Desi tested in front of MGM mogul Louis B. Mayer, who summoned Lana Turner to his office. "Hold her in your arms and kiss her passionately," Mayer told Desi. After Desi obliged, Mayer ordered Judy Garland in for the same treatment. "Good to see you're not a fag," Mayer told Desi. "I'll hire you as a Latin lover type."

Lucy's Early Hollywood Adventures

In her day, Lucille Ball would seduce many sexy, handsome, desirable men. But one afternoon in a candid conversation with Marilyn Monroe, the blonde goddess told Lucille—and she agreed—that on the way to stardom there are a "lot of piggies you have to sleep with as well."

On the set of *Roman Scandals*, Eddie Cantor didn't even make a pass at Lucille. In fact, he detested her eyebrows, finding them too shaggy. Lucille shaved them off, and they never grew back. When she met Samuel Goldwyn, he chased her around his desk, trying to seduce her. She didn't let him, although later she wondered why. "I slept with every other producer. Why not dear old Sammy boy?"

Instead of Goldwyn, Lucille told friends, "I much prefer going to bed with Fred Kohlmar." She was referring to Goldwyn's personal assistant, who was also the casting director. "I don't really like his body, but I sure like his job," she said.

While under contract to Goldwyn, Lucille appeared in ten films, all in unbilled parts. She even renewed her acquaintance with Constance Bennett. The blonde goddess claimed she didn't remember Lucille modeling those clothes for her at Hattie's in New York. Lucille felt humiliated.

Constance did introduce her to the co-star of the picture she was making at the time, Franchot Tone, who had the male lead in *Moulin Rouge* (1934). After one night with this smooth-talking,

When **Lucille** appeared in *Roman Scandals* (photo above) with Eddie Cantor, Lucille became known on the set as "Lady Godiva." Completely nude, she rode a beautiful brown horse up and down the set, with a long blonde wig floating around her shoulders. "She rode that poor, tired horse back and forth before the cameras while we were being lighted for a shot," said Kay Harvey. "She accidentally almost crushed a chorus girl who fell under the horse's hooves."

sophisticated seducer, Lucille told Constance, "Now I know why his nickname is Jawbreaker."

On the set of *Bottoms Up* (1934), Lucille had a one-night stand with Spencer Tracy, the star of the picture. She even met the doomed Thelma Todd, who was aware that she'd seduced her husband, Pat DeCicco. "Welcome to him," said Todd. "I'm divorcing the son of a bitch."

Reunited with Constance again on the set of *The Affairs of Cellini* (1934), Constance remembered Lucille this time. She then warned her that Fredric March, the picture's star, would try to seduce her. Lucille later admitted, "I let him have his fun." She was surprised, however, when one of the other stars of the picture, Fay Wray, made a pass at her. "If only King Kong had known that he was holding a secret lesbian in his paw," a giggling Lucille told Constance the following day.

Kid Millions (1934) brought her back with Eddie Cantor again, who didn't even remember his role in ruining her eyebrows for life.

The one friend she made in those days was George Raft, who was becoming famous for playing gangster roles. In real life, he was the front man on the West Coast for the mob back east. On the lot making *The Bowery* (1933) for Darryl Zanuck, Raft was in his late 30s and cut a striking figure with his dark, brooding Italian looks.

He was in the thick of an affair with wise-cracking Carole Lombard, who was at the time divorcing William Powell. Raft and Lombard were later cast in a musical, *Bolero* (1934), and Lucille often visited them on the set. Here she met an old-time vaudevillian named William Frawley. Only 46 at the time, he looked older. Of course, he would eventually become Ethel's Fred Mertz on the *I Love Lucy* show.

With Raft involved with Lombard, Lucille fell for his bodyguard, Mack Grey. "Your boy, Mack, doesn't have a pretty face, but when he strips down he could have any woman in Hollywood he wants," Lucille told Raft. The closeted bisexual had already coerced Grey into his bed on more than one occasion, so she fed him information he knew all too well.

Above, **William Powell** with **Carole Lombard**, in happier times. Before their separation, both took up with Jean Harlow and Clark Gable.

Below, **Lombard** and her then current lover, **George Raft**, danced in *Bolero* in 1934.

Lucille let three men (*above, from left to right*) **Franchot Tone, Spencer Tracy,** and **Fredric March,** score, but she turned down *King Kong's* **Fay Wray** (*above, far right*) when the actress made a lesbian pass.

Tone was a bisexual, and Tracy mostly homosexual (using Katharine Hepburn as a "beard"). But March was strictly a ladies' man. Fay Wray had romances with guys, but preferred the ladies.

Grey, who rose from the back streets of Brooklyn, was nicknamed "The Killer" by Lombard. She was well aware of the gangster associations of the men she and Lucille were dating. In fact, Grey had been secretly accused on several occasions as being Raft's "hit man," so Lombard's nickname was chillingly apt.

Seen driving around Hollywood in "mob limousines," Lucille once again endured being labeled as a gun moll, which did little to advance her film career.

Grey might do a dirty deed for Raft and the mob, but Lucille found him a considerate gentleman. On the night of August 27, 1936, they showed up as a "loving couple" at the Cocoanut Grove, the most popular nightclub of its day. Lucille was spotted chatting with Gail Patrick, Margaret Sullavan, and Ann Southern (a future rival in TV comedy). Later Lucille became so amorous at table with Grey that the manager came over to her and sarcastically said, "Why don't you two rent a room?"

Grey apparently told too many stories to his boss, Raft, about how great Lucille was in bed. Raft decided to try her out for himself. At first Lucille resisted, and he couldn't understand why. "C'mon," he told her, "I'm irresistible. Even Mae West says so."

Finally, Lucille confessed why she kept turning him down. "Tallulah Bankhead says she got gonorrhea from you," Lucille told Raft. "She told me her weight went down to just seventy pounds by the time she checked out of the hospital. She also laughed hysterically when she confided that coming down with a bad case of V.D. hadn't really taught her a lesson. She claimed she went right back to her 'bad girl' ways."

"But that was so long ago, and I'm completely cured now," Raft assured her. He finally won her over, and she went to bed with him. Later she told Grey, "Now I know why Valentino nicknamed your boss Black Snake."

Rudolph Valentino and George Raft had been lovers and roommates when they worked as dancing gigolos during their early days in New York.

Raft always carried around a roll of hundred dollar bills. One night when Lucille complained to him that she was flat broke and behind in her rent, he lent her a hundred. Years later when she was rich and heard that he was heavily in debt, she sent him the hundred, and even offered to pay interest, but he wouldn't hear of it and returned the bill to her.

Lucille remained friends with Raft. "He never listened to my career advice," she once said. "As a man, he thought he knew more than I did." Lucille read three scripts that Raft turned down, and urged him to star in each of them. After thinking it over, Raft decided to reject *High Sierra, Maltese Falcon,* and *Casablanca,* the roles going, of course, to Humphrey Bogart. When Raft encountered Lucille at a nightclub in Hollywood in 1946, he said, "If only I had listened to mama."

Both Raft and Lucille went on to other loves, but she still remembered her good times with him. When he died of leukemia at the age of 85 on November 25, 1980, Lucille paid a secret visit to the mortuary where his body lay in state. To her surprise she discovered that Raft and his long-ago

Tallulah Bankhead *(above, right)* warned Lucille not to take up with the gangster/actor **George Raft** *(above, left).* But "Black Snake" (his nickname) conquered Lucille's fears.

On one occasion, when Raft got mad at Lucille, he broke into her home and cut up all of her clothing with a pair of tailor scissors. He'd pulled the same stunt with another girlfriend, actress Marjorie King, in New York.

lover, Mae West—the two stars of the 1932 *Night After Night*—"were having a posthumous reunion," in her words. West had died only two days before, and her body was resting in peace beside that of Raft's.

In the 1930s, no matter how torrid the affair, Lucille did not confine her attentions to just one boyfriend.

Later in life, she recalled her affair with the famous author, S.N. Behrman. "Marilyn Monroe had her Arthur Miller; I had my Behrman."

She claimed she met Behrman by accident . . . literally. It was a rainy afternoon—Lucille didn't remember where—and he was coming out of a building. He slipped on the pavement and fell, his glasses bouncing into the street where they were run over by a taxicab. Since he was near-sighted, he appealed to her to help him. She didn't know who he was at the time of her first meeting.

Taking him to a coffee shop, she learned over coffee and a grilled cheese sandwich that he had just written *Queen Christina* for Greta Garbo. She was duly impressed and wanted to know more about him.

He was more than willing to tell her that he was one of Broadway's leading authors of "high comedy," writing for such stars as Katharine Cornell, Ina Claire, and Jane Cowl, even for the acting team of Alfred Lunt and Lynn Fontanne. Lucille later admitted that she hoped he might write a high comedy for her because she'd grown tired of her silly walk-ons.

She drove Behrman back to his home and, when he invited her to stay over, she did. She visited him frequently after that until one day she encountered her first pre-Desi Latin lover. His name was Gilbert Roland, and it was love at first sight.

Born in Mexico, he grew up wanting to become a bullfighter. But when all the girls told him he was handsome enough to become a film star, he moved to Los Angeles to break into the movies, beginning with a bit part in *The Lady Who Lied* in 1925. He was billed by his real name of Luis de Alonso.

The leading female stars of that day, including Norma Talmadge, heard of his charm and "bedside manner," and were in

"My God, now I've seen everything," Lucille told one of her best pals, Ann Miller, after writer **S.N. Behman** *(above)* seduced her.

"When he was a baby, his mother had the skin on the head of his penis clipped. Now it's all raw and exposed to the world. It's a bit repulsive but fascinating in a morbid kind of way. Sexual mutilation."

Mexican actor **Gilbert Roland** *(two photos, left)* was always aware of his good looks. In his maturity *(far left)*, he said, "I was devastatingly handsome, but as a young man just escaping boyhood, I was more beautiful than any girl." George Cukor directed both Gilbert and **Constance Bennett** in *Our Betters* (1933).

When Cukor encountered Lucille, she said, "Amigo told me that I was much better in bed than that bitch, Constance, and I believe him." Lucille had previously dubbed Gilbert "Amigo," a nickname that stuck.

hot pursuit of him. Soon he was seducing "legends," including Clara Bow, who whipped him in *Call Her Savage* (1932), and Mae West for whom he performed gigolo duties both on and off the screen during the filming of *She Done Him Wrong* (1933).

Around the time Constance met Lucille, she'd appeared with Roland in *Our Betters* in 1933. Their love affair was on again, off again. At one time both Lucille and Constance were competing for the affections of Roland. It wasn't until Lucille met Desi that Constance finally won. She married Roland in 1940, a union that lasted for five troubled years.

Roland always maintained a soft spot for Lucille, and would sometimes stop over for the night when Desi was on the road with his band and shacking up with showgirls.

After all those junk movies with Goldwyn, Lucille moved to "Poverty Row," signing a contract with Columbia, a B-picture studio run by the dreadful mogul, Harry Cohn.

Cohn was called "the Jewish Howard Hughes," and was the most secretive of Hollywood bosses. Before arriving on the lot, Lucille was told that Cohn was ruthless and mean-spirited and that every female under contract would have to submit to him. It was part of the deal: if you signed with Columbia, you had to have sex with Cohn.

Lucille signed a term contract for a salary of $75 a week. Cohn ordered that she be cast in two-reel comedies made by the Three Stooges. She'd been on the lot for ten days before she was summoned to Cohn's office.

She'd been told how crude Cohn was. But even for a Broadway veteran of the casting couch, Lucille was a bit stunned by his approach. After she'd entered the office and had been ordered to take a seat, Cohn got up from behind his desk and approached her. He unbuttoned his pants and pulled out a circumcised penis. "Suck it, bitch!" he commanded. Wanting to succeed in Hollywood, Lucille dutifully did her duty, as Marilyn Monroe would do in an equivalent scene in years to come.

A Bostonian, Benny Rubin, is hardly a household name today, but he can still be seen on reruns of *I Love Lucy*. Long before they actually worked together, they'd had a brief fling. Born in 1899, Rubin made his first film appearance in the 1928 *Daisies Won't Yell* and worked in movies until as late as 1979. He died of a heart attack, in Los Angeles on July 15, 1986, and Lucille sent flowers.

He'd been a show business veteran for some seven decades, known as a comedian, character actor, and dialectician. Lucille once jokingly said, "The only difference between Desi and Benny when they took off their shorts was a tiny

Lucille claimed that Columbia chieftain, **Harry Cohn** *(above, right),* "was crude, uneducated, as foul as a big fart, and on his best day, merely abrasive."

"I kiss the feet of talent," Cohn told Lucille. "In your case, I'll merely fuck your much used pussy. And don't forget one thing: I don't have an ulcer. I give them."

Lucille shot back, "So you're the head of the studio? I guess that's better than being a pimp!"

"The It Girl" and *"The Flapper of the 20s,"* **Clara Bow** *(with whip, above),* was still trying to hold onto her stardom when she made the talkie, *Call Her Savage,* for which she was paid $125,000. Clara succeeded at whipping **Gilbert Roland** in the film, but he tamed her off screen. "He has one inch less than Gary [Cooper] but he has more ass to push it in with," she told actress Louise Brooks.

After her seduction of Gilbert, **Mae West** *(above)* proclaimed, "That boy is the exception to most Mexicans, and I'm talking down below."

125

piece of skin."

Lucille and Rubin added a footnote in Hollywood history one night in San Francisco when they attended a performance at the Club Bal Tabarin. Lucille was dating Rubin at the time, hoping he could use his influence at RKO to get her better parts. He was a leading talent scout for the studio at the time, hardly realizing that his date would one day own the studio.

Lucille was impressed with "a tap-dancing babe and wise-cracking chorus girl" by the name of Ann Miller. She was so impressed with Miller's machine gun taps that she urged Rubin to get her a screen test at RKO. "Pussy whipped," as Rubin described himself, he ultimately agreed, and "sugar baby" got her first contract with a big Hollywood studio.

By 1940 Miller was appearing in *Too Many Girls* with Lucille Ball and Desi Arnaz.

In spite of Lucille's agreeing to have sex with him, Harry Cohn dropped her after three months when her contract expired. "Cocksuckers like Ball are a dime a dozen," he said.

In 1948 Cohn wanted her back on the Columbia lot to appear in *Pink Lady*, a film that never got off the ground. Actually, he wanted her for the film version of *Born Yesterday* but rejected her in favor of a bigger name, Rita Hayworth, another actress he'd forced to have sex with him. In the end both Rita and Lucille lost out to Judy Holliday, who went on to win an Oscar for her interpretation of the role.

Lucille signed a three-picture deal with Cohn at $85,000 apiece, including *Miss Grant Takes Richmond*, starring opposite William Holden with whom she had a brief fling.

In 1951 Cohn offered her a trashy part in *The Magic Carpet* (1951). He expected her to turn it down, which would save him the $85,000 he owed her for a final picture. Knowing what his scheme was, she called his bluff, claiming "It's a wonderful part." Cohn was forced to go through with the film, knowing that Lucille's fee would consume most of the budget.

Comedian, character actor, dialectician, and by the time he died in 1986, **Benny Rubin** *(above)* was a veteran of almost 70 years in show business. He also had a brief fling with Lucille.

"I gave him a few mercy fucks," she later told Ann Miller. "I thought the bastard would get me better parts. Oh, well."

One of Lucille's best friends and her co-star in *Too Many Girls*, the tap-dancing **Ann Miller** always claimed that the reason she never became as big a star as Judy Garland was because "I refused to sleep with any of my producers." She forgot to mention that she'd had an affair with MGM's director, Louis B. Mayer.

Janet Leigh, noting that Miller could ramble on about every subject in the universe, said: "No one knows what will pop out of her mouth, Annie least of all. Perhaps I should have said, 'No one knows what will pop into her mouth.'"

Janet was referring to the diverse lovers Ann Miller entertained. They included Conrad Hilton and Randolph Churchill, son of the British prime minister. Cowboy star Gene Autry told Miller that she was, "The first gal I ever kissed on the screen."

"Since we've gone this far," Miller said, "let's cap the day with you mounting my saddle."

126

Lucille told her friends, "Cohn once fucked me, and now I'm fucking him!"

With her commitments at Columbia finished, Lucille landed at RKO in 1935. And although they awarded her a contract, it was based on a cut in pay, amounting to only $50 a week. "I keep going down, down," she told Ginger Rogers. "Pretty soon I'll be working for ten bucks a picture."

Producer Pandro S. Berman cast Lucille in a small part as a Parisian mannequin in ostrich feathers in *Roberta* (1935), with Irene Dunne, Fred Astaire, and her friend, Ginger.

Berman took notice of his new contract player. Lucille noted that he was making a big star out of Katharine Hepburn. Perhaps, she reasoned, he could do the same for her. In all, Berman would produce 14 films with Hepburn. Lucille was thrilled when Berman was promoted to chief of all studio production at RKO in 1937. She found him "gruff, irascible, and a darkly handsome dynamo."

Although married to Viola Newman, Berman began meeting Lucille at his hideaway near RKO. Soon everyone on the lot knew they were an item, and the staff treated her with great respect, not wanting to anger "the boy wonder."

Even though he was sleeping with her, he kept her in limited roles. Where Lucille was concerned, Berman didn't seem overly jealous. In fact, he wanted her to be seen dating other men, hoping that this would keep his wife from finding out about his affair. "To Pan," as Ginger called him, "Lucille was just a hot piece of ass. He was smitten with her in the beginning but it was all about sex—not love. The trouble was, Lucille wanted to get married, and she began to 'try out' suitable candidates. She knew there was no future with Pan."

Berman was later accused of using Lucille as a virtual hooker, ordering her to date RKO's financial backers coming in from the East. But Ginger always claimed that going out with these rich men was Lucille's idea, and Berman agreed to set it up, since he wanted word to get around that she was dating plenty of men.

Although details are scarce, it appears that Lucille slept with a number of these men from New York, but turned quite a few down. Bernie Kahn, a stockholder, claimed he seduced

When he was a young executive for MGM at RKO, **Pandro S. Berman** *(left photo, above)* was often compared to MGM's resident boy genius, Irving Thalberg. Lucille hoped he would make her a dramatic star, but he ended up pimping her out to the studio's "moneybags" from back East. When Lucille made *Miss Grant Takes Richmond* with **William Holden** *(above, right)*, her film career was sliding. There were predictions that she'd be washed up within a year.

Holden's love-making renewed her security. She said, "He was the only man that I'd seriously consider leaving Desi for, but he didn't ask me." Her pronouncement was not completely accurate. There were other men that had her dreaming of a divorce and the fresh peal of new wedding bells.

Lucille on the night he took her to the Cocoanut Grove. "I didn't force her, but she went along with it. In my hotel suite, she pulled off all her clothes and went about having sex with me as if duty bound. It wasn't much fun for me, and I had a hard time maintaining an erection because of her indifference."

To reward Lucille for entertaining so many of RKO's important clients, Berman cast her in *Stage Door* (1937), with an all-star cast that included Katharine Hepburn, Ginger Rogers, Gail Patrick, and Lucille's new friend, Ann Miller.

Berman and Lucille eventually went their separate ways, though he came back into her life in 1954 to produce *The Long Long Trailer* for MGM. In the film she co-starred

All dolled up, **Milton Berle** *(left-hand figure in bottom photo)* meets a very skeptical **Desi Arnaz**, but cigar-smoking Lucille seems to go along with the gag.

Berle was called "the first great drag queen of television." He's pictured *(top right)* with his powerful Jewish mother who tried to dominate his life. On the right, Berle appears in drag again as Cleopatra. As one critic noted, "Uncle Miltie made a far better Serpent of the Nile on TV than Tallulah Bankhead did on the stage."

with Desi Arnaz, both of them playing newlyweds getting used to life in (guess what?) a trailer.

Ann Miller once told Lucille that while making *Stage Door*, "Katharine Hepburn came on to me real strong. She was impressed with my long legs, I think." Miller also claimed that during the making of Frank Capra's *You Can't Take It With You* (1938), "Jean Arthur tried to seduce me."

Miller once said that "I never slept with any of the producers," and she cited that as the reason she never became a top star. Perhaps she forgot about Louis B. Mayer, or else, as the head of MGM, maybe she didn't classify him as a producer.

Lucille agreed that it was a mistake *not* to sleep with producers. "When I start getting a little flabby, I'm going to become a producer myself—and that way I can command any man I want to come join me in bed."

"Good thinking, gal," Miller said.

At RKO, Lucille met a young contract player who was appearing in *New Faces of 1937*. It was Milton Berle. When he first encountered Lucille, "She was in a pair of white slacks, and I'd never seen a woman in white slacks before. Only Robert Taylor wore them. I asked her out. We danced at the Trocadero. Back at her place, when I took off my underwear, she ran screaming into the bathroom, locking herself inside. It took me two hours to persuade her to come out. I promised I'd be gentle with her."

She later joked to Bob Hope that "seeing wasn't believing."

Lucille later confessed that a romance with the man who became known as "Uncle Miltie" was impossible because of his domineering mother who was always around. A frustrated wannabe actress herself, Sarah Gloantz Berlinger was the quintessential stage mother, and Lucille detested her.

She later confided to Ginger Rogers that Berle once told her that an actor challenged him saying he didn't believe stories that he was that exceptionally endowed. "Go ahead, Milton," an unnamed friend said to Berle. "Just take out enough to win!"

Lucille's rival at RKO, Betty Grable, once said, "They say the two best hung men in Hollywood are Forrest Tucker and Milton Berle. What a shame. It's never the handsome ones. The bigger they are, the homelier."

Berle apparently was the first person to talk to Lucille about the new medium of television, a medium that both of them would dominate for years. The world knows that Berle launched *The Milton Berle Show* in 1948 when many Americans didn't have sets. What is less known is that he was the first entertainer ever to appear on TV in an experimental broadcast—in 1929.

In 1947, there were only 17 TV stations in the U.S., broadcasting to 136,000 sets. Partly because of Berle's success, by the end of 1948 there were 50 stations broadcasting to 750,000 sets.

Berle agreed to appear on the monthly Lucille Ball-Desi Arnaz show in 1959, the first show of the 1959-60 season. NBC agreed to Berle's appearance on CBS provided

When Lucille married her second husband, Gary Morton, she told friends, "It was only because of Broderick and Paul. They taught me that ugly men are often the best lovers." She was referring to actors **Broderick Crawford** *(above, left)* and **Paul Douglas** *(right)*.

129

Lucille and Desi would appear on Berle's show. Airing on September 25, 1959, and called *Milton Berle Hides Out at the Ricardos*, Berle appeared disguised in drag as Ethel's dear friend, Mildred. He later told Lucille, "For me, drag is another way to get laughs. My drag is too gay to be gay!"

In July of 2000, two years before his death, Berle sued OUT magazine and Century 21 Real Estate for running the 1959 picture of him in Carmen Miranda drag in one of their ads. The caption read: OUR TEAM OF FRIENDLY PROFESSIONALS KNOW HOW TO CATER TO ROYALTY. AFTER ALL, EVERY QUEEN DESERVES A CASTLE.

In his lawsuit, Berle cited a violation of privacy and defamation, claiming that every "reasonable person looking at the ad would think he was a homosexual." According to the prostitutes of Polly Adler's famous whorehouse in New York City, Berle was "very straight and very big," although the madam heard that he'd once had a brief roll in the hay with Bob Hope in their younger, more sexually experimental days.

Lucille once said that her biggest laugh once came when Berle introduced her at the Friars Club. He announced to the rowdy audience that he would wear kid gloves and have a silken tongue when he honored Lucille. "So here she is—Lucille Testicle!"

Lucille always claimed that she never liked pretty boys and proof of that came when she started having affairs with both Broderick Crawford and Paul Douglas. "Even though she was trying to get Broderick to marry her," Ann Miller once said, "she was often arranging two dates in one night with both of them—but never at the same time, of course."

Douglas had come to Hollywood to break into films in the late 1930s, but it would be 1949 before he got his big break in Joseph L. Mankiewicz's *A Letter to Three Wives*, playing Linda Darnell's husband. Lucille called him a "likable lug," and in time would pronounce him a cross between William Bendix and Wallace Beery. She also said he "was great sex—missionary position, nothing too experimental."

Lucille found it a "hoot" that Douglas turned down the role of Harry Brock in *Born Yesterday*, which brought screen immortality to her other lover, Broderick Crawford. In memory of times gone by, Lucille offered Douglas work which included his appearance for an episode in 1959 on *The Lucy-Desi Comedy Hour*.

Crawford is mainly known today for his machine-gun delivery of dialogue in *Born Yesterday* in 1950, in which he co-starred with the bisexual actress Judy Holliday, who beat out Bette Davis (*All About Eve)* and Gloria Swanson (*Sunset Blvd.)* to win the Oscar.

In 1949 Broderick Crawford won the Oscar for his leading role in *All the King's Men*, his character based on the spectacularly corrupt Louisiana governor Huey Long. In a disappointing 2006 remake, Sean Penn's portrayal of the Huey Long role which Crawford had originally made famous was generally viewed as unsuccessful.

Lucille much preferred

Actor **Broderick Crawford** *(above photos, left and right)*, pictured with **Lucille** *(center figure above)*, was the burly son of Helen Broderick, that matronly figure in so many Astaire-Rogers movies from the 30s. He took a tough attitude toward women. "Every now and then, a man has to beat the shit out of his woman. First, to show her who's boss. Second to show the bitch who clanks the balls in the family. Lucille always fucks better when I slap her around a bit. She loves it and begs me to marry her every night."

Broderick Crawford to Douglas, and at one point begged him to marry her. The burly, brutish actor went so far as to buy her an engagement ring.

"At the last minute," Lucille said, "I chickened out and didn't go rolling down the aisle with him. It wouldn't have worked out because he was drunk most of the time. But we had some really fine rolls in the hay. That was one man who really knew what to do with a woman when he was sober, which wasn't all that often."

During their dating, Crawford was known to the Los Angeles police department as "Old 502," the California radio code for drunken driving. He was notorious for driving under the influence of alcohol. A policeman tried to arrest Crawford and take him to the station one night, but Lucille talked the cop out of it, promising she'd drive him home.

Hollywood insiders said that Crawford was just a "beard," covering up her secret affair with Berman. In a private talk with author Darwin Porter in Barcelona in the 1960s, Crawford denied this. "Lucille and I almost went to the altar. But she broke it off when her affair with Gene Markey heated up. I'd given her an engagement ring but the bitch refused to return it. For that, I gave her a black eye."

"With Broderick and Paul," Lucille told Gene Markey, another one of her lovers, "it's like getting the same fuck twice. They have almost identical equipment and plow the same way. It's amazing. Only difference is, Paul likes to keep his tongue in your mouth all during the screw. You end up swallowing a quart of spit—or drowning. Take your choice!"

After dumping Douglas and Crawford, Lucille took up with Markey, and would entertain the idea of marrying him. This Hollywood writer and raconteur had been a Rear Admiral and was known in Hollywood for his talent in attracting beautiful women.

Having just emerged from a five-year marriage (1932-1937) to Joan Bennett, he was looking around for another trophy wife. He liked to marry movie stars, but told his cronies that Lucille "wasn't big enough a name for me." He married two other trophy wives, including Hedy Lamarr (1939-1941) and Myrna Loy (1946-50), though these two women had each had extensive lesbian involvements.

The Beast and his Beauties. The big question in Hollywood was: What did the pudgy and relatively plain **Gene Markey** have that so deeply fascinated some of the greatest beauties of Hollywood? Lucille fell big for this former Admiral in the U.S. Navy.

His final and most successful marriage was to **Lucille Parker Wright** (top photo), the widow of the owner of Calumet Farm, the most famous horse-racing stable in Kentucky. He also married **Joan Bennett** (center right) as well as **Myrna Loy** (third row, left) and **Hedy Lamarr** (third row, right).

While married to Loy, Markey also tried to rescue actress **Carol Landis** (seen in a champagne toast below) from the brink of disaster. But it was too late. She committed suicide with Seconal in 1948, mourning the end of her torrid affair with Rex Harrison.

131

Lucille found it a "riot" that she was dating Joan Bennett's husband throughout the final year of her failed marriage. "I used to model clothes for Joan and her bitch sister, Constance," Lucille told Markey.

Markey is best known today for producing that circa 1937 late-show favorite, *Wee Willie Winkie*, starring Shirley Temple. He finally got it right when he married Lucille Parker Wright in 1952, staying wed until his death in 1980. She owned Calumet Farm, the most famous horse-racing stable in Kentucky. By marrying her, Markey became part of America's premier racing dynasty. Perhaps to show off, he invited Lucille and Desi to Kentucky.

He once told Desi, "I love racing horses more than I do fucking movie stars." His sexual orientation is listed as straight, although on one drunken night he admitted to his best friend, John Wayne, that "Douglas Fairbanks—Junior, that is—and I did a little sexual experimenting."

Years later, when Lucille encountered Joan Bennett at a Hollywood party, the fading star told her: "by the time you took up with my husband, we were sleeping in separate bedrooms. I don't know what I saw in the son of a bitch. Maybe he had some hidden talent he showed you—and not me. Besides, I've found Walter Wanger."

Old jealousies aside, both Joan and Lucille laughed about their auditions for the role of Scarlett O'Hara in *Gone With the Wind*, which they both lost to Vivien Leigh. "In the case of Vivien, it was type-casting," Bennett told Lucille. "A bitch cast as a bitch."

A few months later Lucille was saddened when a gunshot in 1951 brought a screeching halt to Joan's movie stardom. While she and her agent, Jennings Lang, sat in a parked car outside Marlon Brando's apartment, Joan's jealous husband, Walter Wanger, showed up with a pistol. He accused Lang of being a home-wrecker and shot him in the testicles. Deballed, Jennings survived, but Wanger served 100 days in a minimum security prison. Regrettably the studios, blaming Joan, blacklisted her. She told the press, "It was almost like I pulled the trigger myself."

In 1940, Lucille was flattered that "the great Orson Welles," fresh from his success in *Citizen Kane*, wanted her to play in his latest film *The Smiler With a Knife*. Unknown to Lucille, Orson had first asked Carole Lombard and then Rosalind Russell, both of whom had declined.

When Lucille demanded to know why Welles was impressed with her as an actress, he "blamed" the German producer Eric Pommer, who claimed that "Lucille combines the traits of Jean Harlow and Mae West while remaining herself." Welles had also been impressed by Lucille's performance in *Dance, Girl, Dance*.

RKO, which held Lucille's contract, said no to Welles. Word was out that "Ball doesn't have what it takes to carry the leading lady role." Finally, the RKO suits rejected the entire film "for political reasons."

While Welles was still in negotiation with Lucille, he took her to a roadside motel where he planned to seduce her. Perhaps because of too much booze, Welles couldn't get it up for her. He warned her not to spread any stories that he was a homosexual. "There are too many stories out there like that," he said. "From my earliest years, I was the Lillie Langtry of the older homosexual set. Everyone wanted me. I always seduce actors

After the release of *Citizen Kane*, **Orson Welles** was proclaimed a "boy genius." Previously, he'd caused havoc with his broadcast of H.G. Wells' *War of the Worlds*. Terrified radio listeners, not knowing that it was a dramatization, feared that the Maritians had landed.

Producer Erich Pommer convinced Welles that he could turn Lucille into one of the biggest stars in pictures, "a combination of Mae West and Jean Harlow."

and make them fall in love with me. That way, I get a better performance out of them like I did with Joseph Cotten in *Kane*."

Although he couldn't get it up for Lucille that night, Welles managed admirably with the likes of Marlene Dietrich, Judy Garland, Marilyn Monroe, and many of the prostitutes in many of the brothels in Shanghai and Singapore. Occasionally, he'd try a man for a change, including actor John Houseman.

Later in life Welles attempted to make a deal with Lucille's Desilu Productions. Desi and his wife agreed to back a TV series of his adaptations of classic stories. But the Welles' pilot, John Collier's *Fountain of Youth*, was not picked up by the networks.

In 1937, Lucille launched her longest-running pre-Arnaz affair with the Boston-born Alexander Hall, a noted director of light comedies since 1932. He'd divorced Lola Lane the year before, and is best known today for that charming fantasy, *Here Comes Mr. Jordan*, released in 1941.

Born in 1894, he was older than Lucille, and she was impressed that he'd made his stage debut at the age of four. Lucille was a much experienced 26 when she took up with this 43-year-old director.

Hall was not known as a nice man, and he and Lucille had knock-out, drag-out fights. "She was just rehearsing for her marriage to Desi," Ann Miller said. Rumor had it that on a weekend visit to Hall's ranch, Lucille fired a gun at him, wounding him. He was rushed to the nearest hospital, where he claimed some hunter had accidentally shot him in the arm.

Hall liked to show off Lucille in front of his friends, and it is said that she learned many tricks from his show business cronies, which she would later use in her *I Love Lucy* series. On weekends she hung out with George Burns, Gracie Allen, Charles Ruggles, Fred Allen, Buster Keaton, Arthur Treacher, and Eddie Sedgwick who'd directed *The Keystone Kops*. Even though she learned old vaudeville tricks from this clan, Lucille told them that the way to stardom for her would be through dramatic roles, claiming she

Lucille's most unlikely candidate for romance was director **Alexander Hall** *(above, left)* Hall was known for turning out sophisticated comedies such as *My Sister Eileen* with **Rosalind Russell** *(shown with **Hall** in right-hand photo, above)*).

Lucille's love affair began late in 1937 when she was 26 years old – Hall, a riper 43, had been twice divorced. He was enjoying success for having directed Shirley Temple in *Little Miss Marker*. Author Kathleen Brady said that the director's "slicked back hair and his pouchy eyes gave him the face of a disengaged owl." Garson Kanin suggested that Lucille was dating Hall just to advance her career. "The man was a beast. He okayed one script that had a black man spitting in another's face. When I protested, Hall said, 'What in the hell do you mean? It's nigger to nigger, isn't it?'"

Not all of Lucille's attempts at glamour were successful. She protested her treatment at RKO, saying she found the roles worthless and shallow. When told she was set to appear opposite the Marx Brothers in *Room Service*, she simply yawned. In *Dance, Girl Dance* Lucille told lesbian director Dorothy Arzner that she would not strip down to her underwear even if the censors allowed it.

didn't have the right timing to become a comedienne.

She spent most weekends at Hall's 75-acre turkey ranch in the Simi Valley, and often tended barbecue. During weeknights Lucille was dating other men, though still officially engaged to Hall.

It wasn't just men who occupied her time. From 1938 onward, beginning with *Go Chase Yourself*, co-starring Joe Penner, she became "Queen of the Bs," taking the title from Fay Wray. Occasionally, she'd get an A-list movie, but often she was cast with the likes of Jack Oakie in such flicks as *The Affairs of Annabel* (1938).

Lucille still wanted to get married, and she continued to date and have her flings, but, as she told Ginger, she was still "looking for the love of my life—when I see him, I'll know him at once."

Screwing Around
in Golden Age Hollywood

Lucille Ball had a love/hate relationship with the handsome hunk, **Victor Mature** *(right figure, above)*, and enjoyed friendly relationships with **James Stewart** *(below, left)* and **Henry Fonda** *(below, right)*. Her best pal *(below, center)* was **Ginger Rogers**.

Because Victor was involved with Rita Hayworth at the time he met Lucille, he didn't appreciate her charms. However one day on the set, he found her crying. "I'm always a sucker for a lady in tears," he later said. She broke down and told him that because of Desi's constant cheating, her marriage wasn't going well. In the days to come, Victor offered her the chance to, "make love to a real man." Lucille accepted his offer.

Making Hay with Jimmy, Hank, George, Victor, Brian, etc.

During a Barbara Walters interview, Jane Fonda claimed that her father, Henry Fonda, had once been "deeply in love" with Lucille Ball. There is no evidence to support that claim. Quite the contrary.

In her pre-Desi days, Lucille often double-dated with her best pal, Ginger Rogers. One night, their respective beaus were "roomies," James Stewart and Henry Fonda. They lived in Brentwood just as they had roomed together in their poorer days in New York. Ginger got James, leaving Lucille stuck with Henry.

Henry cooked dinner for the stars while Ginger in the living room taught James and Lucille how to dance the carioca. Lucille remembered that, "I ended up doing the dishes." After dinner, the stars headed for Cocoanut Grove at the Ambassador Hotel to dance to Freddy Martin's band, later going for a hamburger at Barney's Beanery on Santa Monica Boulevard. Here they ate under a misspelled sign that read NO FAGOTS ALLOWED.

The date lasted until dawn when Fonda looked at Lucille's nighttime makeup in the morning sunlight and said, "Yuk!" He later claimed, "Shit, if I hadn't said that they might have named the studio Henrylu instead of Desilu."

The romance between Henry and Lucille came to an end that night, although Ginger got lucky. Leaving Lucille to get home on her own, she headed back to Brentwood with James and Henry.

Once there, she disappeared into James' bedroom. The next morning, Ginger had already left for the studio before James emerged to join Henry for breakfast. There, James gleefully informed Henry, "I lost my cherry last night."

Henry looked skeptically at his friend. "You can't lose what you don't have. Remember all the others? Marlene Dietrich? The abortion? For all I know, you lost your cherry to me. Remember?"

This interchange between these two friends was later reported to their mutual friend, director Josh Logan.

Lucille discussed Henry with her former lover, Broderick Crawford, who had known both Henry and James during

The Big Street paired **Lucille Ball** with **Henry Fonda** in this Damon Runyon thriller-packed story of Broadway. She replaced Merle Oberon, whom the producers felt lacked box office clout.

Desi showed up on the set and, in front of all the cast, accused his wife of "sucking Fonda's dick." She slapped her husband and ran to seek solace from (of all people) Charles Laughton. "Forget Desi, at least for the moment," he said. "Play the hell out of this woman. She's the bitchiest bitch ever – and don't soften it." She didn't, and gave her best performance yet.

"George Sanders is a polished seducer," Lucille told Ginger Rogers. "Desi has more passion and enthusiasm, but George has more boudoir skill." Lucille learned that he acted "only for the money, and I don't give a God damn what part they offer me. All my roles are stupid anyway."

Lucille gushed that George was like an "English duke – great intelligence, fabulous manners, and he knows how to flatter a woman and make her feel she's the czarina of all Russia. His eyes are both gray and green and you can lose yourself in them." In spite of his attention, he spanked her one night like a naughty little girl, and sent her back home to Desi. Too bad Desi wasn't at home.

their struggling days in New York. Crawford claimed that in the 1930s the two actors had been lovers. A future lover of Lucille's, George Sanders, proclaimed that "Fonda is a Don Juan homosexual who has to prove himself with one woman after another."

When Henry heard that, he retaliated, accusing Sanders of having a gay affair with Tyrone Power.

Lucille was later to appear with Henry in *The Big Street* in 1942, which critics labeled "a poor man's *Of Human Bondage*." But there were no fireworks between the two of them.

On the set of *Seven Days' Leave* (1942), her next picture, she co-starred with hunky Victor Mature. He was seriously pissed off at Lucille because he had wanted his current girlfriend, Rita Hayworth, to play the role. Vengefully, he deliberately set out to sabotage her every scene.

In one love scene where their bodies were pressed together, he slipped out his huge cock to dangle between them. Suddenly aware of what was happening, she ran screaming to her dressing room. She later was very sarcastic about his manhood. "He's got the size all right, and I pity not only Rita Hayworth but the pretty young boys he also screws."

In a final *adieu* to each other, Henry and Lucille reunited for their last film, *Yours, Mine and Ours*, released by United Artists in 1968. It was a comedy dealing with a widower and his children. "During the entire shoot of the film, Henry locked himself away in his dressing room with his crewel work like an old queen," Lucille said. "I don't think he was ever known as a lover—at least that's what Margaret Sullavan claimed—but that boy sure knew how to do embroidery."

James fully understood that there were no fireworks between his friend Henry and Lucille, but he remained friends with the redhead nevertheless. During his filming of *Destry Rides Again* in 1939, co-starring Marlene Dietrich, he introduced Lucille to his movie character's nemesis, a role played by Brian Donlevy, an Irishman.

When **Lucille** made *Seven Days Leave* with **Victor Mature** in 1942, one critic claimed she was "nearly as beautiful as the rugged, dimpled, eye-rolling Mature himself."

Once Victor belatedly discovered Lucille's charms, it was hard to get him out of her dressing room to continue the afternoon's shoot. In the film's re-release in 2005, one sharp-tongued critic claimed, "Mature even sings with someone else's baritone. It's like seeing Glenn Close and Sylvester Stallone in a remake of *High Society*...or maybe even Johnny Weissmuller and Betty Grable in an imitation of *The Philadelphia Story*.

When **Rita Hayworth** teamed up with **Victor Mature**, she said, "When he talks his voice goes through you like a pound of cocaine! Oh, what a beautiful hunk of a man."

On the set of *My Gal Sal* for Fox, their kiss in a love scene went on and on, long after the director had yelled cut. Soon the movie mags caught up with their romance.

She told the tough guy actor that when she went to see his first film, a 1923 silent called *Jamestown*, she had mistakenly thought it was about her hometown in New York State. Donlevy laughed and gave her a big hug. Over coffee that same day, he told her that he hated playing villains on the screen. "I'm very sensitive. I want to be a poet." (His collected poems, entitled *Leaves in the Wine*, issued under his *nom de plume* Porter Down, were eventually published in the 1940s.)

Lucille and Donlevy disappeared for a week together after his work on Destry was finished. According to James, who relayed the news to Ginger and Henry, they ran away together for an off-the-record stay in Riverside.

Back in Hollywood, when Lucille encountered James again, she said, "It was great, but the first and only time I'll go away with him again. Your friend comes onto a woman like he'd been locked up in jail for ten years."

A remake of the 1932 Tom Mix Western, *Destry Rides Again*, starred **Brian Donlevy** (above, left) and **James Stewart** with **Marlene Dietrich** (above, right).

Dietrich and Stewart were more passionate off screen than on screen. Their first night of unprotected sex led to Marlene's abortion. Lucille let Dietrich have Stewart while she pursued Brian Donlevy, whose private life was more colorful than anything he ever played on screen. At 14 years old, he was part of a corps of American troops invading Mexico in pursuit of Pancho Villa, and in WWI he was a pilot with the Lafayette Escadrille – a unit of the French Air Force.

By the time an aging **Lucille Ball** encountered an aging **Henry Fonda** on the set of *Yours, Mine and Ours* (1968), all thoughts of their disastrous 1940s romance were but a forgotten memory.

Based loosely on the stories of Frank and Helen Beardsley's autobiographical book, *Who Gets the Drumstick?*, the film took great liberties. At Desilu Productions, Lucille called in screenwriters Madelyn Pugh and Bob Carroll to write several *I Love Lucy* style stunts into the script. The comedy dealt with a widow and her children teaming up with a widower and his children. Fonda warned her on the first day of the shoot, "I hate children. Keep the brats at bay."

Lucy Meets Ricky

To a naïve American public during the 1950s, Lucy and Ricky Ricardo exemplified domestic bliss.

In real life, the actual **Lucille Ball** and **Desi Arnaz** *(pictured together, above)* were quite different. "He was like Jekyll and Hyde," recalled Lucille bitterly. "He drank and gambled, and he went around with other women … and in some cases men as well. It was always the same – booze, broads, and Cesar Romero. But Desi's nature is destructive. When he builds something, the bigger he builds it, the more he wants to break it down. That is the scenario of his life."

While filming *Too Many Girls* in 1940 for RKO, Lucille met Desi Arnaz. The rest is history, as Lucille herself said many times in the years to come. As a team, with their *I Love Lucy* series in the 1950s, they became the most successful man/woman act in the history of television. According to Ann Miller, after their first night together, Lucy reported: "It was the best sex I've ever had in my life, and probably will be the best sex I will ever have."

Miller delivered this information during a question-and-answer session after a performance of *Sugar Babies* in New York, based on having also appeared with Lucy and Desi in the above-mentioned *Too Many Girls.*

The year she met him, Lucille and Desi were married at the Byram River Beagle Club in Connecticut. But she filed for divorce in 1944, but before it was finalized, they reconciled and stayed married until 1960. At the time she said, "Desi was the great love of my life. I will miss him until the day I die. But I don't regret divorcing him. I just couldn't take it anymore."

She was referring to his constant womanizing, especially with showgirls. Soon after they were married, he was said to have taken on all the girls in Polly Adler's famous bordello in New York City. Word was leaked to Lucille, who, back in Hollywood, had begun to drink heavily.

She was shocked to hear that he said, "I don't take out other broads—I take out hookers."

She also learned about sexual involvements he'd had with men.

Finally, Lucille despaired that Desi would ever become a proper husband. "I don't believe he ever intended to settle down and become a good, steady, faithful husband," Lucille said later in life.

During the weeks he was on the road, and unknown to the general public, Lucille took a string of lovers of her own.

"What's good for the goose is even *better* for the gander," she was fond of saying.

When Lucille and Desi formed Desilu Studios, their *I Love Lucy* series dominated weekly TV ratings in the United States for most of its ten-year run (October 15, 1951, to September 24, 1961). They became the biggest stars in the nation, at long

In the 1930s, a blonde **Lucille Ball** *(left photo, above)* could be convincing as a gun moll – and well she should. With her lover, George Raft, she was a gun moll in real life as well. On the right, the "happy couple's" perfect life was exposed as a lie to *Confidential* magazine's four million readers when it ran a cover story reading: DOES DESI REALLY LOVE LUCY?

The magazine accurately called **Desi** *(center figure in photos, above)* a "duck-out daddy who has proved himself as an artist at philandering as well as acting. Arnaz has sprinkled his affections all over Los Angeles for a number of years and quite a bit of it has been bestowed on vice dollies who were paid handsomely for loving Desi briefly but, presumably, as effectively as Lucy."

last dominating the A-list in Hollywood. They would also produce two children, Lucie Désirée Arnaz and Desi Arnaz Jr.

In 1953, to her horror, Lucille faced glaring headlines: SAY IT ISN'T SO—OUR BELOVED LUCY A COMMIE PINKO?

As strange as it may seem today, Lucille had registered to vote in the Communist Party primary in the election of 1936. It was at the insistence of her socialist grandfather. In 1953, she was subpoenaed to appear before the House Committee on Un-American Activities. The headlines were damaging.

In Episode 68 of *I Love Lucy*, *The Girls Go Into Business*, the studio audience booed her. Desi came out to save the day. "The only thing red about Lucy is her hair, and even that's not legitimate." His warm presence and humor won out. When he brought Lucille out, the audience cheered.

After she and Desi bought RKO from Howard Hughes, she became the first woman in television to be head of a production company, Desilu, the company she'd formed with Desi.

Desilu produced several other popular shows, notably *The Untouchables*. In Miami, Florida, Desi's best friend had been Al (Sonny) Capone Jr., son of the fabled gangster. Capone Jr. later sued Desi—unsuccessfully, that is—for one million dollars over *The Untouchables*, violently objecting to how his father was portrayed.

On May 4, 1960, just two months after filming the final episode of *The Lucy-Desi Comedy Hour*, Lucille filed for divorce. When she divorced Desi, she bought out his share of the studio.

REGISTERED RED IN '36: LUCILLE

Star Denies She Voted Commie

On March 19, 1936, **Lucille** gave in to her socialist grandfather and went to downtown Los Angeles where she registered as a Communist. "I remember feeling quite bad about the whole thing, " she later recalled. "I wasn't really a Communist – far from it. In fact, I'd become a capitalist later in life. I felt my being registered a Communist wouldn't matter if I didn't bother to vote."

In 1952, however, she was called before the dreaded House Committee on Un-American Activities, which at the time was terrorizing Hollywood and destroying careers. The committee seemed to accept her explanation that she'd registered as a Communist to please her late grandfather – but that she didn't vote in that year's presidential elections.

But 17 months later she faced renewed investigations and became the target of right-wing hatred. Desi intervened in her behalf to win back the public support, claiming, "We despise everything about communism. Lucy is as American as Barney Baruch and Ike Eisenhower. And by the way, we both voted for Eisenhower. So, ladies and gentlemen, don't judge too soon."

At one point, **Fred Ball** *(with Lucy in photo, right)* was hired as Desi's road manager.

Lucille mistakenly thought the presence of her brother would make Desi cut down on his womanizing. But whether Fred was with him or not, Desi continued to chase wine, wild women, and song, even gambling away his band's entire payroll during a two-week engagement in Las Vegas.

Desi considered playing Elliott Ness himself in Desilu's hit TV series, *The Untouchables*, but decided against it. Instead, he offered it to gay actor Van Johnson, who demanded too much money. Finally, he settled on the very handsome **Robert Stack** *(photo, left)*.

Lucille had objections to the show, abhorring the violence. Reportedly, she was also jealous of the buxom blonde, Barbara Nichols, who appeared on it frequently. But what made Lucille really furious was when Desi signed the right-wing columnist Walter Winchell for the series.

"He tried to destroy my career by linking me with Communism. How could you hire him, you bastard?"

Desiderio Arnaz de Acha III was born on March 2, 1917, in Santiago, Cuba, where his father was the mayor. His mother, Dolores, was nicknamed "Lolita" and hailed as "one of the ten most beautiful women in Latin America."

At the age of 16, Desi owned his own car, his own boat, and a stable of horses. He also had several notches on his belt from having visited the local whorehouse every Saturday night.

"The world was my oyster," he later recalled. "When I wanted something, I took it – especially if it were a hot puta selling it for the equivalent of two Yankee dollars."

He found he could sing ("a bit ") and play the guitar ("better"), and decided to break into show business. At the Roney Plaza Hotel in Miami Beach, he had a hit in a number called "Babalu." He was hired by bandleader Xavier Cugat, king of Latin dance music, for a role as the vocalist with Cugat's orchestra.

In the upper right, **Desi** in military uniform poses with his bride, **Lucille**. Staff Sgr. Arnaz was, in the words of Lucille, "screwing everybody at Birmingham Hospital near Van Nuys (California) where he was assigned to the U.S. Army Medical Corps. Below, **Desi carries Lucille** across the threshold of their suite while honeymooning in Greenwich, Connecticut, in 1940.

"My friends gave the marriage six months," Lucille later said. "I gave it six weeks." Desi seemed amazed that two such different people from different backgrounds and different parts of the world would get married in the first place. "Our differences were part of the attraction," he said, "but also the reason for so many of our big brawls, arguments, and endless problems. She wanted to tame me, and I was a Tomcat in heat."

Linking the names of Desi and Lucille, **Desilu Productions** *(photo above)* was purchased for $6 million – in spite of the fact that Lucille and Desi had only $500,000 in available cash. After filming a scene with Tallulah Bankhead, Lucille was told she and Desi now owned RKO.

Drinking champagne, she made her first request. She wanted to see the miniature gorilla used to depict King Kong.

Her next request involved visiting the sound stage of the old Selznick studio where, as a rain-soaked hopeful, she'd auditioned for the role of Scarlett O'Hara in *Gone With the Wind*.

Her next demand was that she be given the dressing room of Ginger Rogers, which the dancing star had occupied during her reign as Queen of RKO.

An Aging Lucy Says "Down with Love"

Left-leaning First Lady, **Eleanor Roosevelt** *(above, right)*, never thought Lucille was a Communist. "Worse has been said about me," Mrs. Roosevelt told Lucille upon meeting her. "You do the nation a great service by making all people laugh, even Republicans."

Mrs. Roosevelt may or may not have known about Lucille's brief fling with her son, Elliot Roosevelt, one Sunday afternoon during a boating party at Balboa Beach. While Desi was "sleeping one off," Lucille and the late president's son checked into a local motel under an assumed name. The manager later said, "I knew who they were – they were not Mr. and Mrs. John Smith – and they occupied the room for just one hour."

"The Battle of the Hats" was staged by **Lucille** *(left)* and gossip maven, **Hedda Hopper**, the egomaniacal right-wing columnist. Hedda by this time had "forgiven" Lucille for registering as a Communist.

When Lucille filed for a formal separation from Desi, she called Hedda. "I'm sure our separation will come as no surprise to you. You've been hinting at it for months. I can't control Desi. He does what he wants and who he wants."

As Lucy Ricardo *(right)*, **Lucille** had more or less abandoned her attempt "to be a glamour puss. Let's face it, comedy is my calling. No one ever accused me of being Lana Turner, and I completely failed to take over those Betty Grable roles in the 1930s."

143

The Jamestown Hussy

The young woman who had been known in Jamestown as the town hussy acquired so many lovers over the years that she once told Vivian Vance, "All their faces have become a blur. Desi was the only one who ever meant anything. The others came and went so fast I hardly knew them."

That might have been an overstatement, since some of her involvements were more memorable. An example is Franchot Tone, to whom she became sexually linked in the 1930s, and again when they co-starred in *Her Husband's Affairs* (1947). After the heat of her passions had cooled, she had only praise for Robert Mitchum and William Holden, but detested Ray Milland, who once propositioned her.

She starred with Bob Hope in *Sorrowful Jones* in 1949 and *Fancy Pants* in 1950, but she always claimed there was nothing between them. "Once we kissed, but burst into hysterical laughter and decided to forget the whole thing," she told Vivian Vance.

Occasionally she got serious, as she did in 1947 when she co-starred with George Sanders in *Lured*. An actor born of British parents in St. Petersburg, Russia, he entered show business as a chorus boy in London. His career highlight didn't come until 1950 when he won the Best Supporting Actor Oscar for his portrayal of the theater critic, Addison De Witt, in *All About Eve*, starring Bette Davis.

Before his suicide outside Barcelona in 1972, his deep voice and Continental charm momentarily fascinated Lucille. In time she seemed proud to be included among the list of famous women Sanders had seduced, whose rosters included the tobacco heiress Doris Duke (then the richest woman on the planet), Dolores Del Rio, Hedy Lamarr, Gene Tierney, and Marilyn Monroe.

He once said, "I don't like nightclubs, and I don't

like women. They bore me." Years later, Lucille claimed that "George Sanders had the best legs of any man in Hollywood. He was among the fellows what Betty Grable, that bitch, was among women." To our knowledge, Lucille never commented on his penis, either its performance or its size.

Although she was married to Desi at the time, Lucille fell hard for Sanders. She told associates that he was the "best looking, most charming and brilliant man she'd ever met." Later, she denied ever having an affair with him, but Zsa Zsa wasn't so sure. After she'd divorced Conrad Hilton and married Sanders, she picked up the phone at her house one day and eavesdropped on her new husband's private conversation. She recognized Lucille's voice: "What in the fuck are you hooked up with that Hilton woman? What a bitch! What a golddigger! You know I love you. She's completely wrong for you!"

In *Lured*, Lucille was paid $75,000 to play an American dancer in London. In the film she acted as a decoy for a murderer in the foggy streets of London. Desi was jealous of her making the movie because Sanders was known as a skilled seducer of women.

Desi had also been jealous of George Brent, a famous "lady-killer" with whom Lucille had worked in *Lover Come Back* (1946). With Sanders, Desi had much to be jealous about, but not with Brent.

For reasons of his own, George Brent apparently chose not to add Lucille to his list of "conquered women," a roster that included Loretta Young, Diana Barrymore,

George Brent's *(left photo above)* third wife, Ann Sheridan, had already warned Lucille about George Brent's sexual equipment, citing it as the cause of their divorce. "Brent bent," she said, explaining why their marriage in 1942 only lasted a year.

At a party, **Sammy Davis Jr**. *(center, above)* told Lucille that, "You can't possibly know what sexual pleasure is until you've tried it with a black man." She did not accept his offer, but asked why one of his fingernails was painted bright red. "I practice Satanism," he said. "The red nail is how we Satanists identify ourselves to each other. Actually, I'm not really into it. I dabble around the edges of it for sexual kicks."

Like his former lover, Nancy Davis (Reagan), **Peter Lawford** *(right photo above)* was adept at oral sex, as Lucille quickly learned. So did dozens of starlets, Venice Beach Bunnies, L.A. coeds, $50-dollar-a-night hookers, young callboys, older male hustlers, and male extras and studio messengers at MGM.

BALLING HOPE. In front of a camera, **Lucille Ball** and **Bob Hope**, her costar in *Critics Choice,* were the best of friends. Privately they were jealous of each other.

"He's got such a nice guy image in public," Lucille privately said, "Off camera, he's a whoremonger. My God, he even ended up having an affair with that blonde slut, Barbara Payton. I hear she's giving it away for five dollars a night these days." Lucille agreed with Groucho Marx when he said, "Hope's not a comedian. He just translates what others write for him."

Hope admitted that he and Lucille "never had a romance – nothing after hours."

He told Bing Crosby, "I couldn't get it up for her if I've had to. And I've known Lucy through five shades of red." Actually, he stole that line from Jack Warner.

Greta Garbo, Olivia de Havilland, and the great Bette Davis. Brent soured on Lucille when she rejected his request to box with her. He claimed "Garbo and I used to put on boxing gloves and spar with each other in her backyard. Why not you?"

"Indeed," Lucille said, "Why not?" She turned and walked away from Brent. "Imagine Ann Sheridan going for that?" she later said.

When Lucille was featured in the Warner Brothers film *Critic's Choice* in 1962, co-starring Bob Hope, many famous people wanted to visit the set, including Peter Lawford, who was married at the time to Patricia Kennedy, sister of President John F. Kennedy. The producers of the film gave the president's sister a bit part.

Although on the brink of her fifty-first birthday, Lawford seemed attracted to Lucille. Sammy Davis Jr. felt that he merely wanted to throw Lucille "a mercy fuck," hoping that she'd get work for him at Desilu.

Whatever his motive, Lawford showed up one night at Lucille's house when her husband at the time, Gary Morton, was away, performing as a stand-up comic at the Shamrock Hilton in Houston. Lucille later confided to Vivian Vance, "I don't think Peter was getting it up at the time. He was too drunk and drugged. But he sure did give the best head in Hollywood."

Eventually, toward the end of her life, Lucille seemed to give up on men completely. "No one, but no one, will ever replace Desi."

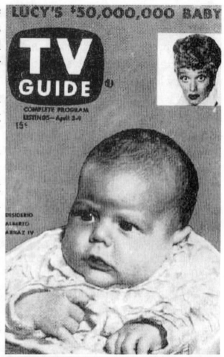

LUCY'S $50,000,000 BABY

TV GUIDE

COMPLETE PROGRAM
LISTINGS—April 3-9
15¢

DESIDERIO
ALBERTO
ARNAZ IV

When Lucille and Desi gave birth to two children, Lucie (July 17, 1951) and Desi Jr. (July 19, 1953), they became America's most famous parents. Lucie was born right before her mother's 40th birthday. When the baby started coming out feet first, Lucille's doctors quickly performed a cesarean. Both Lucille and Desi had wanted a boy so much that before the birth of their next child, Desi instructed his writers to "give Ricky Ricardo a boy," even before he knew the sex of his second child.

When **Desi Jr.** *(photo, above)* was shown to Lucille, she said, "His nose is so turned up he'll drown when it rains." When he did grow up, Desi Jr. pursued drink, drugs, and older women. One day Lucille packed her son's bags and deposited them on the front lawn of one older woman with whom her son was having an affair. It was Mother's Day. When a teenage Desi Jr. had an affair with Patty Duke, Lucille threatened to charge the actress with statutory rape.

146

Lucille at Twilight

Two New Sitcoms, a New Man, & a New Marriage

When **Lucille Ball** married **Gary Morton,** love the second time around wasn't much more passionate, but the marriage (if not made in heaven) at least wasn't a journey on the road to hell.

A product of the Borscht Belt resorts of New York's Catskills mountains, Morton was a stand-up comic who made a living as an opening act for major artists who included Tony Bennett.

"He was a fourth rate, warmed-over Milton Berle," said Sammy Davis Jr. "But I liked the fucker. He had a certain charm and didn't seem to mind being called 'Mr. Lucille Ball.'" Morton had a few claims to fame other than being the stepfather of Lucie and Desi Arnaz Jr. He was also the ex-brother-in-law of Judith Campbell Exner, the most notorious of the many mistresses of President John F. Kennedy.

In 1961, Lucille returned to Broadway to star in *Wildcat*. There she met her second and final husband, a Borscht Belt stand-up comic 12 years her junior. He was Gary Morton, not a pretty face, but she stayed married to him until the end.

The comedian was no Desi Arnaz, and Lucille entered into the marriage with little of the passion she'd had for "my Cuban."

Morton, her new husband, became executive producer of *Here's Lucy* (1968-74) and was co-executive producer of her ill-fated 1986 series, *Life With Lucy.*

He met Lucille on a blind date at New York's Copacabana nightclub. At first he infuriated her with his indifference to her celebrity, but he eventually won her over with his charm.

Although Lucille had no plans for a remarriage, she found Morton "uncomplicated, good, sweet, hip, funny, and he appreciated a home, not just the trappings."

Lucille's friends were almost equally divided about Morton, one man calling him "a horse's neck." Others said he loved Lucille and worked hard to become an executive.

Morton survived Lucille by about a decade, living until the age of 74 and dying in Palm

Springs on March 30, 1999, of lung cancer. He was married at the time to Susie McAllister, but he will be forever known as "Mr. Lucille Ball."

In 1962, Lucille launched her own TV series, *The Lucy Show*, starring her old sidekick, Vivian Vance. Arnaz was out, but Gale Gordon played the long-suffering male. The plot got tiring, but the show ran for 12 years, at one point being the highest rated show on TV.

But by 1986 Lucille's luck had run out when she launched yet another sitcom, *Life With Lucy*. It was both a critical and a commercial flop, and ABC canceled it after two months. Lucille plunged into a serious depression from which she never really recovered. She hit the bottle more and more until at times she was too drunk to appear in public.

Right after taping *Password* on December 2, 1986, Lucille was told that her beloved Desi had died at the age of sixty-nine. She burst into tears. Driven back to her home, all she could say was, "He was a good father." She kept repeating that. Never could she say, "He was a great husband."

After all these years she'd remained his friend, and she had spoken to him briefly while he lay in his hospital bed dying of cancer. She may have been the last person on earth he spoke to.

In May of 1988, she suffered a stroke, becoming partially paralyzed. She had only months to live herself.

Right before her death, she underwent eight hours of surgery, after having been diagnosed as having a dissecting aortic aneurysm. Death came at 5:17am on April 6, 1989, ending one of the greatest success stories in the history of American show business.

On July 6, 1989, Lucille was posthumously awarded the Presidential Medal of Freedom by President George H.W. Bush.

According to legend, Lucille's last words were, "Once in his life, every man is entitled to fall madly in love with a gorgeous redhead."

The Ricardos and the Mertzes (left photo, above) from left to right: **Vivian Vance, Desi Arnaz, William Frawley,** and **Lucille Ball**. All was not happy behind the scenes of the TV cameras. Frawley detested Vance, calling her "that dried-up old cunt." She claimed her on-screen husband was "old enough to play my grandfather." Frawley called Desi "that Cuban heel," and Lucille's singing as a "shovel of shit on a baked Alaska." As Vance later recalled, "To him (Frawley), Lucy and I were brass-bound bitches."

During his long association with Lucille, character actor **Gale Gordon** (*far right figure, above*) always played the curmudgeon, having appeared in various episodes of her series for a period that lasted more than two decades beginning in 1962.

Lucille made her final appearance with her old sidekick, **Vivian Vance** (above) in 1977 on the CBS special, "Lucy Calls the President."

Vance was known for having made these quotes:

"I'm going to learn to love that bitch."
(After meeting Lucille on the set of in 1951)

"Champagne for everyone"
(Shouted after learning of the death of her former costar, William Frawley, in 1966)

Desi paid her an opening salary of $280 a week for the first season of *I Love Lucy*. Vance died in California on August 17, 1979 of breast and bone cancer.

Lucille turned down the script of the hokey *The Star* in 1952, after Joan Crawford and Claudette Colbert had each previously rejected it. "I refuse to play an aging has-been who was big in the 1940s but has now fallen on bad days."

Right, she's pictured at 77 years old at her last public appearance before her death in April of 1989. She was extremely nervous about the way she photographed. Nevertheless, Lucille refused to submit to plastic surgery to have the bags under her eyes removed.

Lucille grew up in a working class family, in a modest house (*pictured above, left*) in Jamestown, New York. That house in western New York State was part of a smoke-covered factory town, and her family barely managed to scrape by.

After becoming one of the richest and most successful entertainers in history, Lucille could afford palatial digs in Beverly Hills (*pictured above, right*). She was a practical decorator, preferring Formica tabletops, nylon carpeting, white vinyl upholstery, and artificial flowers. But she stored her rickety old furniture in case she fell on bad days and needed it again.

Lucille's surprised expression above was from a segment of *I Love Lucy*. But bloggers went to work and Photoshopped the picture. The final product shows why she was surprised: In the *faux* picture, she's being sodomized.

Peace at last came to "The Great Redhead" when she was cremated and buried on May 8, 1989.

Her ashes in Forest Lawn Memorial Park in Hollywood Hills were interred with the bodies of her parents, but she lives eternally on film with her fictional family of Ricky, Fred and Ethel.

Lucy and Marilyn Gossip about Bob Mitchum

Is **Lucille**, *(pictured above)*, actually showing her surprise at **Robert Mitchum**'s *(pictured below)* favorite form of sex?

"Carrot top had never really been fucked like it should be done, until I did the dirty deed," Mitchum once proclaimed to John Huston. It was hardly a secret among Hollywood starlets that Mitchum was "anal retentive."

Speaking of carrots, famous gossip columnist Mike Connolly had spies stationed everywhere--including within Hollywood hospitals. One night, through a nurse informer, he learned that Mitchum had had an emergency operation to remove a large carrot from his rectum. In Connolly's column the next day, he wrote: "Bob Mitchum underwent minor surgery and went on a protein diet."

Lucille met the handsome, sleepy-eyed hunk Robert Mitchum when he was shooting *Thirty Seconds Over Tokyo* on the Metro lot in 1944. Director Mervyn LeRoy introduced them, and they ate together in the commissary. He seemed fascinated by her and she seemed turned on by his cool charm. She later told LeRoy that "Bob is the most masculine man I've ever met."

"I've seen you around," Mitchum said on first meeting Lucille. "I've been dying to find out something that has really bothered me."

"Yes, I know. Desi is fucking every showgal in America."

"No, it's not that. I want to find out if you're a real redhead all over."

LeRoy later described their romance as casual and short-term,

River of No Return (1954) started out as a cheap B Western but mushroomed into a big production directed by Otto Preminger and starring **Marilyn Monroe** and **Robert Mitchum** *(together in left photo, above)*. It was shot at scenic locales which included Jasper, Wyoming and Banff Springs, near Lake Louise in western Canada.

Holding Marilyn in his arms, Mitchum found her over-articulating. Apparently her "smelly surrogate mother," Natasha Lytess, had suggested this. "She looked like she was doing an imitation of a fish," he told Preminger. He slapped her on the ass and told her to act like a human being. He later became more familiar with her famous ass.

Many infamous stories arose from the making of this film, including one promulgated by Preminger – that Marilyn requested a *ménage à trois* with her costars, Mitchum and Rory Calhoun. According to Preminger, Mitchum "fucked Marilyn in the ass while Calhoun plowed into Mr. Beefcake."

One night, Marilyn called Mitchum from her hotel suite claiming that she was lying in bed nude with "the hots for you." Drinking since three o'clock that afternoon, he visited her suite. Later, he told Preminger that "I whipped it out and pissed all over her."

In *River of No Return*, **Marilyn** *(right photo, above)* played a woman of dubious reputation, a frontier saloon singer in the year 1875.

involving at the most no more than three separate trysts. During the peak of their involvement, he ran into Lucille in the commissary one day and asked her, "What do you think of our boy, Bob?"

"He's a real pain in the ass," she said enigmatically.

"It was only years later that I found out what Lucille meant," LeRoy said. "Ava Gardner told me that Bob liked to go in through the rear door. Apparently, Desi is strictly a front door kind of guy, and Lucille had never had it that way before."

Mitchum faded from her life until the spring of 1957, when he came to her for advice on launching his album of calypso vocals for Capitol Records. The album was called "Robert Mitchum—Calypso Is Like So!" He also wanted to sing on one of her specials.

She later said that she told him bluntly, "You're no Harry Belafonte."

When Lucille met Marilyn Monroe, they bonded temporarily one drunken evening by talking about Hollywood studs and searching to see if they'd shared a lover in common. Mitchum was at the top of their list. Marilyn had made *River of No Return* with him in 1954.

She claimed that "Bob brags" about how he used to share a locker with her first husband, James Doughtery. Both men at the time were working as sheet-metal workers at Lockheed Aircraft.

"Bob gives interviews about how he used to go dancing with me and my husband in the war years," Marilyn told Lucille. "Actually, I never met him in those days. The closest he came to knowing me was when Jim showed him a nude picture of me he'd taken when I was a teenager standing by the garden gate. And Bob sometimes ate the baloney sandwiches I packed for Jim's lunch."

Marilyn also told Lucille that Jim went out and got drunk one night with Mitchum. "If Jim is to be believed, Bob came on to him. Around midnight he told my husband that he was a real cute Irishman, and he'd like to plug his ass. Jim told him, 'I don't go that route, not with Norma Jean waiting at the house for me.' Jim said he sorta avoided Bob after that and no longer shared a locker with him."

Close friends of Mitchum's knew that he'd had a number of homosexual encounters during his wild and woolly days as a young man on the road. In Hollywood, he once "rented himself out" to gay actor Clifton Webb.

Marilyn also confessed that on the set of *River of No Return*, and knowing Mitchum's interest in anal sex, she approached him one day with a book on sexuality. She asked Mitchum to explain to her what the author meant by anal eroticism.

Mitchum might have suspected that James Dougherty, her former husband, had told her about his long-ago attempt at seduction. But regardless, Mitchum behaved like a gen-

During the making of *River of No Return*, **Marilyn** kept a copy of this picture immediately above, taped to her dressing room mirror. She told Mitchum it was her favorite photograph. "I thought I looked very gay in it," she said.

When Joe DiMaggio arrived, he ripped the picture off the mirror and slapped her so hard makeup could not conceal the damage for filming the next morning. He told her, "I refuse to have a wife who's nothing but a glamorous piece of meat!"

Before he went fishing the next day, DiMaggio warned Calhoun and Mitchum, "If I find either of you has been fucking my wife, I'll cut your dicks off while you're sleeping!"

Robert Mitchum blew his chance to work with director **John Huston** *(right)* and Marilyn Monroe on *The Misfits* and also his opportunity to masturbate Huston's pet monkey. The actor did, however, work with Huston in *Heaven Knows, Mr. Allison* (1957).

Huston later recalled, "Bob devoted more effort to trying to seduce Deborah Kerr than he did to his on-screen characterization." Mitchum cursed the role when he learned that Huston had actually wanted Marlon Brando for the part. "Second fiddle to Brando – fuck that!"

The film dealt with a nun (played by Kerr) stranded on an island with Mitchum, a rough marine. Huston feared censorship problems and invited Jack Vizzard, a censor for the Legion of Decency, down to Trinidad where the film was being shot. Kerr, Huston and Mitchum decided to play a joke on Vizzard. With no film in the camera, Huston directed a scene in front of the censor in which Mitchum put one hand down the front of Kerr's dress to feel her tit and another up her skirt to fondle her vagina.

"Cut! Cut! Cut!" Vizzard screamed. "Print it!" Huston yelled before turning to Vizzard. "This scene is tame. In the original version I shot, Mitchum actually took out his whopper and showed it hard to Sister Deborah."

tleman and agreed to break her in to the finer points of anal sex. Marilyn went on to appraise Bob as an expert at "back door entry."

Marilyn claimed that she was going through a particularly debilitating period of menstruation at the time and had willingly submitted. "I found it a bit of a turn-on and was glad Bob broke me in. It came in handy with later lovers."

Marilyn could have been referring to President John F. Kennedy, who told friends that "I'm never through with a woman until I've had her three ways."

But before wiggling away, she delivered one final appraisal, noting that "Bob should watch that bad breath. And as you probably already know, he's a lousy kisser."

Lucille was never to see Marilyn again and was saddened to learn about her suicide (or murder?) on August 5, 1962. Lucille weighed in with those in *tout* Hollywood who claimed that Marilyn's death was a homicide.

As for Bob Mitchum, she was surprised, years after their inaugural fling, when he called her and said that he considered her "the most savvy woman in show business" and that he wanted her career advice. She knew he wasn't trying to rekindle their romance from World War II. He expressed his regrets at having turned down the role of "the last cowboy," in *The Misfits,* which subsequently went to Clark Gable. Released in 1961, *The Misfits* is best remembered as a somewhat tepid movie best known for having showcased the last film appearances of both Clark and Marilyn.

"I think it would have been a great part for you," Lucille told him. "It would also have been a great learning experience."

"Yes, I think it would have been," Mitchum said. "And we'd have had some laughs too."

"What about?" she asked.

"Huston has this pet monkey," Mitchum said. "He likes to take him out drinking. When everybody's drunk and crazy enough, Huston likes to masturbate the monkey in front of friends. Ol' John and I would have had fun boozing all night and and jerking off that damn monkey."

Desi Arnaz and His Gay Caballero

As Latin lovers, Ricardo Montalban and Fernando Lamas heated up the screen. But whenever a director wanted a gay Latin lover, he cast **Cesar Romero** *(above)*. "I was never stereotyped as just a Latin lover in any case because I played so many parts in pictures, " Romero said. "I was more of a character actor than a straight leading man." He paused. "No pun intended."

"I did many kinds of characters – Hindus, Indians, Italians. There were very few pictures where I ended up with the girl." And as an aside, he added, "Not that I would know what to do with one."

In a career that spanned 60 years, tall, suave, and sophisticated Cesar Romero (1907-1994) blazed across the screen. In the 1930s he played a Latin lover in seemingly countless musicals and romantic comedies. In a series of low-budget westerns, he became that rogue bandit, "The Cisco Kid." To the generation growing up in the 1960s, he was the green-haired, white-faced cackling villain, The Joker, of *Batman* (1966) on television.

Like Desi, Cesar was born of Cuban parents—not in Havana, but in New York, where, as he grew into maturity, he became a ballroom dancer. The year 1927 found him on Broadway in *Lady Do*. Hollywood beckoned, and he arrived there in 1933 to perform in *The Shadow Laughs*. He's still seen on the late show with Shirley Temple in *Wee Willie Winkie* (1937). In the 1930s, Hollywood columnists labeled Romero as "the new Valentino."

The Cisco Kid series, including *The Gay Caballero* in 1940, was a hit in the United States but practically caused riots south of the border. Romero played the Kid from 1939 until 1941. In his book, *They Went Thataway*, author James Horwitz wrote: "Romero was no cowboy, but one of those Brill-Creamed Latin Lover types, and played the Kid as a smarmy dandy and fop, while Chris Pin-Martin's Pancho (the Kid's sidekick) was a gutbucket slob. Latin American

sensibilities were offended by this unlikely duo. An international incident nearly occurred. Diplomatic cables few back and forth between Latin America and the State Department. The Cisco Kid, as portrayed by Romero, was, so to speak, queering America's south-of-the-border foreign policy. Darryl F. Zanuck at Fox was more or less ordered by Washington to change Cisco's style or stop making the pictures. He decided to drop the series altogether."

In World War II, Romero left to serve in the Coast Guard. One man who served with him later said, "If one of the guys wanted a great blow-job, they went to call on Romero."

Most of his conquests were unknown men. For some odd reason, he seemed to especially like gas station attendants, and cute, smart, feisty young men. One of his conquests, Nick Carbone, a tax auditor now living in a suburb of Harrisburg, Pennsylvania, remembers him with fondness and a certain alarm. "There we were, sometime in the 70s, making out in a car somewhere in Los Angeles, with the police banging on the window, and Cesar screaming at them and daring them to arrest him. He was a loud and radical kind of bugger... totally Out and completely unafraid of being identified as gay."

Occasionally, Cesar went after a famous star. He was especially taken with the beauty of Tyrone Power, with whom he appeared in the Technicolor historical epic, *The Captain from Castile* (1947). As the director, Henry King, once said, "Ty gave it away to almost any Topman who propositioned him."

Today, if you search the web, you can find all sorts of outrageous statements, including the assertion that Lucille decided to dump Desi when she caught him fucking Romero. She may have caught her husband fucking Romero, but that was not the reason for the divorce.

She tolerated Romero and was well aware of the actor's crush on her husband as

Immediately above, from left to right, a hit-and-miss roll-call of **Cesar's** lovers and wannabes:

Vincente Minnelli, Tyrone Power, Lorenz Hart, and **Desi Arnaz.** (Desi, incidentally, said "yes" to Romero but "no" to director Minnelli.)

And although Tyrone Power said "yes" to Romero, Romero later, somewhat unchivalrously, confided: "That was no major accomplishment. That dear boy, Ty, said yes to anybody who asked."

Desi told Romero that he, too had once had an affair with the American lyricist, Lorenz Hart.

Desi also claimed that he was once invited to stage a solo sexual exhibition in front of Hart and his two best friends, Monty Woolley and Clifton Webb: These gay men wanted to snap candid shots of Desi masturbating.

Cesar Romero as the Cisco Kid

THE GAY CABALLERO

Cesar ROMERO

AS THE CISCO KID

Sheila Robert Chris-Pin
RYAN STERLING MARTIN

Janet Edmund Jacqueline
BEECHER McDONALD DALYA

A 20th CENTURY-FOX PICTURE

Cesar Romero offended nearly every Latino when he starred as *The Cisco Kid* in the 1940s. His crime? Being ... well... too gay, even though that slang term for homosexuality had not yet come into general usage.

In his early days, many of Romero's costars didn't know he was gay, so he got propositioned by Alice Faye, Betty Grable, and Carmen Miranda. Romero later revealed, however, that Miranda was "mostly lez oriented." He also claimed that, "Grable and I often sucked off the same stage hand and truck drivers. Some guys claimed she was better at it than I was, but others said that I was the true Queen of Fellatio."

156

early as 1940. She considered it a harmless diversion on Desi's part, and preferable to "taking on five whores a night—one by one."

In an interview with Boze Hadleigh published in *Hollywood Gays*, Romero admitted that he'd had sex with Desi. Romero claimed that Desi "knew he was pretty irresistible, and he knew about me. I guess he could see it in the eyes. One day Desi said to me, 'All right, we both know what you want. Let's get it over with.' We did."

What Romero didn't confess to the reporter, but what Lucille found out about, was that the affair lasted for eight years. Reportedly, it was a one-sided affair. Desi would allow himself to be fellated, or else he'd sodomize Romero, who would have to resort to masturbation for his own relief.

Romero suggested that over the years, Desi allowed other gays to fellate him as well, including his co-star on Broadway, Richard Kollmar, husband of the famous columnist, Dorothy Kilgallen. When Desi was appearing on Broadway in *Too Many Girls*, he reportedly had an affair with one of the co-authors, Lorenz Hart, the homosexual lyricist.

Lucille later claimed that when Vincente Minnelli (father of Liza) had directed them in *The Long, Long Trailer* in 1954, he came on sexually to Desi, who rejected him. "Why not?" Minnelli is reported to have said. "Are you saving it for Cesar Romero?"

With hair the color of stainless steel, Romero became a seemingly permanent fixture on the Hollywood scene, living a long life. In 1968 *TV Guide* dubbed him "one of the most beautiful men in the world."

Ironically, Romero eventually evolved into a favorite escort of Lucille herself. Knowing he was gay, she considered him a safe choice, as did Joan Crawford and Carmen Miranda. In later life, he escorted aging actresses such as Ginger Rogers and Jane Wyman to various media and social events.

Wyman told friends that "Cesar is a far better escort than Ronnie was. Cesar pays attention to the lady, but Ronnie ended up in some corner talking politics to some guys all night." She was referring, of course, to her former husband, Ronald Reagan. Near the end of his long career. Romero had appeared as Wyman's love interest in the soap opera, *Falcon Crest*, playing Peter Stavros from 1985 to 1987.

He was a "beard" for actresses involved in off-the-record romances. After an event in a public place, he would drop off the actress with her male or female lover before departing for a night in the arms of his current male hunk, which, much to Romero's sorrow, no longer included Desi. By 1948, Desi had told Romero: "Let's cut out all this shit but remain friends."

Cesar Romero *(photos this page, top and bottom)* usually talked candidly about his sexual conquests with men.

"The all-time love of Lucille Ball's life was Desi Arnaz. Lucy and I had something in common. The all-time love of my life was Desi Arnaz as well."

"In my day, and in addition to Desi, I got to suck off some of the most beautiful men of my era – Tyrone Power, John Payne, George Montgomery, Scott Brady, and Gary Cooper."

"Do I have any regrets? Yes, that I didn't get to suck off some additional fantasies of mine – Lex Barker, Johnny Weissmuller, Sterling Hayden, Steve Cockran, John Derek, Errol Flynn, and Robert Taylor."

As the "Clown of Crime," **Cesar Romero** *(above)* as The Joker reached a new and younger audience, a generation that knew nothing of his past as a Latin lover or as The Cisco Kid.

Romero played the clown with green hair and a white face, and as a thorn in Batman's side. He was a wild card, but refused to shave off his mustache. If you look closely, you will see makeup merely painted over it.

"I had enormous fun playing The Joker on *Batman*," Romero claimed. "I ended up doing something like 20 episodes of *Batman*, as well as the full-length film version. There was certainly nothing hard about that assignment. Even the makeup sessions weren't too bad. It took about an hour and a half to put the full makeup on, including the green wig. I didn't mind it at all."

Cesar Romero *(above photo, left)* was a frequent escort of aging **Jane Wyman**, the first Mrs. Ronald Reagan. He joked with her about his sexual conquests and even encouraged her "in our mutually shared obsession with young men. How could I dare chastise Jane for falling for younger men when I'd done the same thing every night of my life?"

He did warn her not to develop too strong a crush on Rock Hudson when they made the film *Magnificent Obsession* together. "I have a better chance of winning Rock's affection than you do, darling," he told Wyman, who at the time, didn't know Hudson was gay.

The queen of New York gossip columnists, **Dorothy Kilgallen**, pictured *(left)* with her husband, **Richard Kollmar**, were seen in the early 1950s lifting glasses while listening to jazz pianist Nicky DeFrances.

Kilgallen was well aware of her husband's flings with other people, both men and women. He told her all about his affairs, including a brief fling with Desi Arnaz and a longer involvement with cult film goddess Liz Renay.

Kilgallen told friends, "I demanded loyalty from Dick – not fidelity."

Gay, Holy, and Closeted
POPE PAUL VI

In the words of the Italian periodical, *L'Espresso*, **Pope Paul VI** *(photo above)* had a certain "waywardness" involving homosexual acts he was said to have performed on Italian actors, including the most famous one of the 20th century. So prevalent are stories of the homosexuality of Paul VI that the charges remain a great wall to hurdle by those who seek his canonization.

In his report on Paul VI's alleged homosexuality, Dr. Marian T. Horvat wrote: "It is especially painful to report that the moral integrity of one of the Sovereign Pontiffs was marred by serious reports of homosexuality. For Catholics who love and defend the Papacy, the revelation that homosexuality could have penetrated the highest cupola of the church is particularly sorrowful."

Doin' the Vatican Rag:

When Should "His Holiness" be addressed as "His Majesty, The Queen?"

Recent studies have suggested that a large percentage of Roman Catholic priests are homosexual, which comes as news to nobody. And some devoutly faithful Catholics are aware, historically speaking, that some of the Popes presiding over the Vatican have been gay as well.

It's even known, at least to thousands, that Pope Paul VI (1897-1978) was gay as a goose. He and New York's Cardinal Spellman (known as "Nellie" Spellman in the Vatican and the friend of many a New York hustler) reportedly had a "gay old time" when he visited Pope Paul in Rome. Before Spellman checked in, a papal assistant warned the Swiss guard that they should "wear clean underwear" while entertaining the holy man from New York.

Pope Paul VI began his papal reign on June 21, 1963, a few months before John F. Kennedy was assassinated in Dallas. He died on August 6, 1978 at the Castel Gandolfo, in the hills outside Rome, at the age of 80.

His "achievements" were dubious. Defined by historians as a caretaker at best, with little or no flair for substantive reform, he's best known as the sponsor of the papal encyclical *Humanoe Vitoe,* which was published in July of 1968. In it, perhaps as a response to the development of the first contraceptive pill and the modernization of many modern Catholics' definition of the numbers of children they felt they wanted and could afford, he reaffirmed the Catholic Church's traditional condemnation of artificial birth control. His lack of flexibility shocked many modern Catholics, especially in America, effectively positioning the official Catholic church into a mindset more akin to the Middle Ages than the

age of Sputnik. Perhaps, as his detractors have said, he wasn't really able to understand the procreational angst of modern-day straight people.

Except for the inevitable rumors, the secret life of Pope Paul VI was kept hush-hush during his lifetime. In recent years, however, some leading Italian publications have published "scoops." Foremost among them was the respected Milan-based periodical, *L'Espresso*, which revealed that the Pope was being blackmailed because of his sexual preference during the period he occupied the papal throne. Essentially the same charges were subsequently published in the newspaper *Il Giornale*, on January 27, 2006, the same year that gay rumors whirled around the head of the present Pope, Joseph Ratzinger (aka Benedict XVI) and his handsome airplane pilot, now the Pope's personal assistant.

The French author, Roger Peyrefitte, in an interview in the Italian magazine, *Tempo*, not only charged that Paul VI was a homosexual but that he had a boyfriend who "was a certain movie star." These revelations sent the tabloid writers spinning. Who was that movie star?

It was **Marcello Mastroianni**, the suave, sophisticated heartthrob who often appeared in films opposite Sophia Loren. Paul VI was born in 1897, Marcello in 1924. Surely the star wasn't attracted to the Pope physically, but as a good Italian Catholic, Marcello "accommodated" his prelate's wishes, sources close to the actor have claimed. Federico Fellini once said that "Snaporaz (i.e., Mastroianni) and I have one sexual habit in common: Both of us can only make love if we keep our socks on during the act itself—black socks, that is." Perhaps that came from watching too many 1930s porno movies.

Fellini always called Marcello "Snaporaz," a nickname he applied to him after he'd cast him in *La Dolce Vita* in 1960.

Fellini claimed that his friend Marcello merely closed his eyes while the fully clothed Pope performed an act of fellatio on him. "I'm sure Snaporaz thought of Ursula Andress, Catherine Deneuve, or even Faye Dunaway when the Pope did the dirty deed," Fellini told Tennessee Williams and Anna Magnani in Rome.

Marcello once said that "lovemaking is often an ordeal." Was he thinking of the Pope when he made that statement? He also told Dick Cavett, "I'm not a great fucker." Evidently, to satis-

Franco Bellegrandi (*above, left*), the *camariero di spada e cappa* (honorary chamberlain) of Paul VI was an insider at the Vatican during the reign of Paul VI. He later reported on who he saw coming and going from the papal apartments. In the center is **Paul VI** (*above, center*) as he wanted to be remembered, blessing little children. Actor **Marcello Mastroianni** (*above, right*) shared "dark secrets" about the Pope to directors Federico Fellini and Luchino Visconti.

fy the Pope, he didn't have to be.

Marcello's relationship with the Pope continued for many years—very secretively, of course.

Marcello wasn't the Pope's only love interest. Apparently, the prelate was partial to actors. Franco Bellegrandi, the *camariero di spada e cappa* (honorary chamberlain) of his Holiness during Paul VI's reign, and a member of the Vatican Noble Guard, claimed that when the Pope was Archbishop of Milan he was caught by the police one night wearing civilian clothes "and in not so laudable company." Actually, for many years the future Pope was said to have had a special friendship with a red-haired actor named Paul (last name not known). Bellegrandi also reported that after Paul VI assumed the throne, a member of the Vatican's security force told him that "this favorite of Montini [a reference to Paul VI's birth name, Giovanni Battista Enrico Antonio Maria Montini] was allowed to come and go freely in the pontifical apartments. The young man was often seen taking the papal elevator at night."

Bellegrandi further charged that during the Pope's reign, he "appointed homosexuals to positions of prestige and responsibility close to the papacy. This plague infested, transformed, and devastated the Vatican during his time."

The author went on to describe how the men appointed by the Pope later brought in their respective favorites, whom he described as "effeminate young men wearing elegant uniforms and make-up on their faces."

Maybe the clues lay in that hat, those slippers, that art collection, and some of most rococo set designs in the history of the world. Indeed, collectively they were perhaps a bit much...

In 1995, in *El Mundo*, a respected publication that's widely regarded as Spain's newspaper of record, Spanish author Pepe Rodrigues charged that it was "common knowledge" in the inner circles of the church that "there were not only many homosexual bishops but also a great homosexual Pope."

His final charge was that this massive homosexual infiltration into the Catholic church, at home and abroad, eventually led to a crisis, parts of which have been very publicly played out in secular courts around North America and, to a lesser extent, the world. "This explains in part the immense complacency from the highest cupola regarding homosexuality among ecclesiastics," said Bellegrandi.

If Pope Paul VI was indeed a practicing homosexual, he had many role models to follow among his predecessors. They included Julius III (1550-55), a patron of Michelangelo. Before he became Pope, Cardinal Giovanni Maria del Monte fell in love with a 15-year-old ragamuffin named Innocenzo. Shortly after his designation as Pope, Julius elevated this child-man to the role of cardinal and designated him as his "chief diplomatic and political agent."

The last of the High Renaissance popes, **Julius III** *(above, left)* was a gay old blade, and catalyst of some of the most destructive homosexual scandals ever to be associated with the papacy. Note his coat-of-arms *(above, center)* and *(above, right)* a commemorative stamp the Vatican recently issued in his honor.

During his tenure as pope (1550-1555), he elevated both of his lovers (Innocenzo and Bertuccino) as well as several other handsome teenage boys to the rank of cardinal. He would bring these "cardinals" together for orgies, where he'd watch as his charges sodomized each other. Cardinal della Casa's celebrated poem, "In Praise of Sodomy," was dedicated to Julius III.

On the cover of *Time (far right)* or bestowing a papal blessing, **Paul VI** was a lackluster Pope of dubious achievements.

Shortly after he assumed the papacy, Paul VI was threatened by blackmail. A freemason pressured him to do away with the church's condemnations of those who asked to be cremated, which the Pope did. If he hadn't the freemason claimed he'd reveal details of a secret rendezvous the Pope, then Archbishop of Milan, had had with his actor friend in a hotel in Sion in the Valais region of Switzerland. The charges, with "indisputable evidence," were made public in Paris months later.

La Dolce Vita

When he wasn't involved in trysts with the Pope, which he did not seek or want but went along with anyway, **Marcello Mastroianni** was becoming a major star in Italy and around the world. In these photos above, he is pictured (clockwise from the upper left) with the American movie star, **Faye Dunaway,** with whom he was said to have had an affair. In the top center photo, he is observing the antics of his favorite director **Federico Fellini**. On the upper far right, he stands dripping wet in Rome's Trevi Fountain with **Anita Ekberg** in 1960 in the Fellini film that made both actors stars, *La Dolce Vita*. **Marcello in sunglasses** *(center left)* was his favorite photo of himself. In the lower center he is pictured with film director **Luchino Visconti**. The buxom **Anita** *(lower left)* thrilled us in that fountain again, in the movie on the lower right that became a legend.

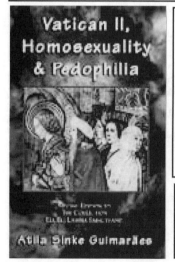

(Right) Two Catholics and a Quaker pose for the camera, each with revelations of scandal awaiting them in their futures. **John F. Kennedy** on the left stands with **Francis Cardinal Spellman** *(center)*, whom the Vatican hierarchy secretly mocked, calling him "Nellie Spellman."

The staunch Quaker on the right is, of course, **Richard Nixon** himself.

(Left) In Atila Sinke Guimarães' controversial book, *Vatican II, Homosexuality and Pedophilia,* the charge is made that homosexuality and pedophilia are so firmly entrenched within the Catholic church today that for the Vatican to punish guilty parties would be tantamount to gravely damaging itself.

164

How Sir Winston Got "Musical" with Ivor Novello

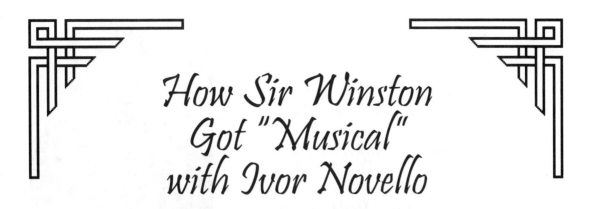

The story of a middle-aged Winston Churchill seducing a handsome youth, Ivor Novello *(two photos above, right)*, is so old it's new again. It's never been made clear whether the "tantalizing" (in Noel Coward's words) Novello seduced The Great Man – or whether The Great Man seduced Novello.

As Churchill *(two photos above, left, and two photos below)* related to best-selling author W. Somerset Maugham, his seduction of Novello was "motivated more by intellectual curiosity than desire." Novello's biographer, Paul Webb, revealed that Churchill's wife, Clementine, had a "morbid fascination with Ivor" and found him "irresistible," although she seemed more of an awestruck fan than a woman bent on seduction.

An Early Adventure of a Curious Sir Winston

never
never
never
give
up

It was 1911. A rising politician during the heyday of the British Empire, Winston Churchill had recently married the beautiful Clementine Hozier. The year before he'd been appointed Home Secretary. A big future in politics was predicted for him.

His good friend was W. Somerset Maugham, a homosexual author whose *Of Human Bondage* and other novels would make him a household word. Churchill and Maugham attended weekend parties that summer at a country mansion at Stoke Poges, near Windsor. The two figures, both of whom were destined for monumental careers, felt at ease with each other and often shared personal details about their private lives.

Maugham was also on familiar conversational terms with Sir Winston's mother, the scandalous American beauty, Lady Randolph Churchill (Jennie), who told him indiscreet stories. One day, Maugham decided to query Churchill about one of his mother's revelations. "Jennie told me that when you were much younger, you had a number of affairs with other men. That true?"

"A bloody lie," Churchill said. "You know my darling mother never tells the truth if a lie would make a better story."

Young Winston *(top photo)* coined the World War I slogan: NEVER NEVER NEVER GIVE UP! He displayed the same tenacity when he stood, almost alone, against Hitler's Nazi Blitzkrieg in yet another world war.

Despite their differences in sexual preferences, author W. Somerset Maugham *(immediately above)* retained his life-long friendship with Churchill. They often shared secrets of a sexual nature over many glasses of good brandy.

The scandalous American beauty, Lady Randolph Churchill (called Jennie), is pictured with her sons, Jack (left) and Winston (right).

The "girl from Brooklyn" *(pictured solo, far right)* was hailed as "the most fascinating and desirable woman of her age."

"So you never knew another man?"

"I didn't say that," Churchill said. "And in fact, I have a certain intellectual curiosity. I wanted to know what sex with a man was like. So I selected the handsomest man in England and seduced him. It was the only time for me."

"Who might that lover have been?" Maugham asked. "The Prince of Wales, no doubt."

"Ivor Novello."

"What was the experience like?"

"Musical."

In those days "musical" was a euphemism for gay. Churchill provided no further details, but the next time Maugham encountered Novello, who by that time had evolved into one of the leading actors of Britain, he asked for all the dirt.

"All of that happened years ago, when I was about 18, and Sir Winston was in his 30s. He buggered me for fifteen—maybe twenty—minutes and he's got the biggest cock of any politician in Britain," Novello confessed. "Not that I've sampled them all. He liked it so much he buggered me again the next morning and then he went down on me. He was great in the saddle but a lousy cocksucker."

Maugham was able to learn how the actor, who in his 30s was celebrated as one of the most handsome men in Europe, had, many years previously, as a late teenager, originally met Churchill. At the time, Novello was the *protégé* and sometimes lover of Edward Marsh, Churchill's private secretary.

It all started after Churchill's mother, Jennie, invited the supremely talented and charming then-eighteen-year-old to her elegant home for dinner. There the teenager met Jennie's 37-year-old son, Winston.

After dinner, members of the dinner party gathered around the piano, Churchill requesting that Ivor play his favorite music hall ditties, some of which dated back to the 1880s. The politician seemed enchanted, but later, Britain's future Home Secretary seemed disappointed when Ivor didn't know the music hall song, "You'd Be Far Better Off in a Home." As the evening progressed, and as their friendship blossomed, Churchill invited Ivor into the library for a brandy. Ivor later claimed, as related by Maugham, that he wasn't surprised when Churchill invited him to spend the night in his bedroom.

Although he's almost forgotten today, Ivor Novello was once the most successful British theater composer of his day and the biggest entertainer in the British Isles, his fame and talent even greater than that of his chief rival, Noel Coward. A prolific playwright, Novello also became a successful silent movie star. But what made him a household word occurred at the age of 21, thanks to his authorship of the popular wartime song, "Keep the

Ivor Novello was one of the most successful British theater composers of his day. His rival, Noel Coward, once said, "There are two perfect things in the world – my mind and Ivor's profile." A household name at 21 thanks to his wartime song, "Keep the Home Fires Burning," Novello dominated British musical theater between 1935 and 1951.

Ivor and actress **Lili Elsie** as they appeared together in *The Truth Game* in London's West End in 1928. A forgotten figure today, Elsie achieved her greatest fame when she appeared in the hit musical, *The Merry Widow,* on the London stage, a role immortalized on the silent screen by dingbat Mae Murray. Ivor first met his idol, Elsie, at (of all places) 10 Downing Street when the prime minister's daughter, Elizabeth Asquith, invited both of them to tea.

Home Fires Burning." The song became the unofficial anthem of the Allies during World War I and made Novello a millionaire. Later he would compose a string of musicals that dominated the West End in London between 1935 and his death in March of 1951—an astonishing span that incorporated many different eras of taste, history, and politics.

Before the end of World War I, Novello met a handsome young actor, Bobbie Andrews, and they became lovers for life. But in spite of that alliance, Novello often turned to others to enliven his sex life.

Insofar as we know, Churchill never seduced the Prince of Wales. But Novello did.

In 1936, years after Novello's drunken fling with Churchill, shortly after the Prince of Wales (by then, known as King Edward VIII) abandoned his throne to "marry the woman I love," Novello joked to friends, "He's really abdicating for me, darlings. Not that I really want him. It's so much more exciting to bugger Tyrone Power and Clifton Webb than His Majesty."

Portraits of Churchill as a young politician *(above left)*, and as a wartime prime minister in 1940, pictured in front of 10 Downing Street.

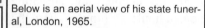

Below is an aerial view of his state funeral, London, 1965.

Fey and fetching in a flowery hat, Ivor appears *(above, left)* in a 1908 school production. School mates kidded that he should have been born a girl since he was "too pretty to be a boy." Ivor is pictured *(above, right)* in tights, as he appeared in 1926 with veteran diva Constance Collier. Collier would eventually emigrate to Hollywood, where she became an intimate companion of Katharine Hepburn.

The Prince of Wales, a closeted homosexual *(left)*, also had an affair with Novello. In the center is the much-married American socialite, Wallis Simpson, for whom the king abandoned his throne. He was virtually pushed off the throne by his nemesis, British Prime Minister Stanley Baldwin *(right)*.

Whatever Happened to
Judy Garland's Body?
(Fan Worship and Necrophilia in New York)

One of Judy's last photographs (above) was taken at London's Heathrow airport on May 21, 1969, about a month before her death.

She was known as "the world's greatest entertainer." With her massive talent, and because of the millions she had earned for MGM, "Dorothy" should have had an enchanted life. Instead, in a life punctuated with heartbreak and disaster, she died owing more than $4 million.

Hollywood's first true diva--the reigning queen of musicals during the 1940s--Judy Garland died tragically of a drug overdose at the age of 47.

At least that's what was reported in the newspapers. Her body was stored in a temporary crypt for more than a year because no money was available to transfer her to a final resting place. What happened to that body during that period is still the subject of lurid speculation.

Weep No More My Lady

The marriage of Peter Lawford to actress Deborah Gould lasted more than a day or two, but not by much. She balked at the idea of having another woman join them in bed, a request he made at the very beginning of their marriage. Shortly after their wedding ceremony, he told her he was going to New York—there was some vague talk about kinky sex. He also told her that he'd be flying alone.

About five days later, Lawford called her from New York. He sounded drunk and drugged. As Deborah related to biographer James Spada, her estranged husband sounded frightened. "He told me that there were some weird friends of his with him at a hotel. He also claimed that he was scared because they are into necrophilia." She was flabbergasted and not really comprehending, being completely unfamiliar with the fine points of necrophilic love. "I nearly died when I heard him say that," Deborah told Spada. "I said, 'What?'"

"Yes, I know, it's awful," Deborah quoted her husband as saying. "I can't handle it."

Supposedly this was an accurate statement, and there is no evidence of any kind that the actor himself had any inclination toward necrophilia.

Yet he seemed amazingly informed on the subject, even discussing it with his friend

Looking far happier than they were, **Judy Garland** and **Mickey Deans**--Judy's final husband--are all smiles after their wedding on March 15, 1969 at London's Chelsea Registry Office.

In the picture above, they celebrate their marriage at Quaglino's in the West End, where Judy and Mickey danced as the band played "Over the Rainbow."

Judy's headdress was inspired by her own design. She told reporters that day, "I just want to be happy." On their wedding night, Mickey confessed to her, "I am hopelessly homosexual."

At least in the film *Easter Parade* (1948), **Peter Lawford** was in love with **Judy Garland**. Peter's mother, Lady May Crawford, as a means of punishing her son, had reported to homo-hating Louis B. Mayer, the studio head, that her son was a homosexual. To convince Mayer that that wasn't the case, Lawford inaugurated affairs with both Judy and Lana Turner.

Judy told Lawford that her first marriage (to David Rose) had failed because he was repulsed by the idea of performing cunnilingus on her. Peter replied, "I'm not! It's my preferred form of sex."

and former lover, Noel Coward, in the presence of others.

The most bizarre story he ever told was about another of his former lovers, Judy Garland. He related this tale to actor Sal Mineo, who would later tell it to author James Kirkwood. Mineo was appearing in a play by Kirkwood, *P.S. Your Cat Is Dead* at the time of his murder.

Kirkwood told the story to James Leo Herlihy, author of *Midnight Cowboy*, who reported it to director George Cukor. Soon it was making the rounds of the Hollywood gossip circuit, and the rumor has even appeared in print. When Judy Garland's loyal fans—many of them gay—gather, the story is often repeated. "It's the rumor that will not die," said David Callio, one of Garland's most devoted fans.

Lawford was sophisticated enough to handle a lot of weird friends in both the gay and straight worlds, between which he moved with his usual grace and charm until the drugs took over. He told not only Deborah but some trusted friends that he had met a "pack of necrophilics in New York."

Although he claimed that he was personally disgusted by that sexual practice—and few things sexually disgusted him—he nonetheless continued seeing these "weirdos," as he called them.

As he told friends, he sometimes went out drinking with them and also took drugs with them. But, as he revealed to his actor/lover, Mineo, on the rare occasion they managed to make a deal to actually acquire a dead body—male or female—"I was out of there," Lawford claimed.

But exactly how does Judy Garland fit into this tangled web in the twilight zone?

The journey for Judy Garland had been a long one before she finally arrived at a cemetery

Fired from his job at the chic Arthur's disco in New York, Mickey Deans became Judy's last manager. At this point in her fading career, she had less to offer even than Edith Piaf during her final year.

Looking frail as a bird at her wedding, Judy was eating almost nothing, surviving (if it could be called that) almost exclusively on drugs and liquor. At this point in her career, only the most ghoulish of her diehard fans sought her out, including a spastic who claimed that she learned to walk while listening to Judy's "You'll Never Walk Alone."

The best man at Judy's final wedding was the fading homosexual singer Johnny Ray, who only the night before had gone to bed with her groom.

Bette Davis, John Gielgud, James Mason, and Ginger Rogers (all of whom were in London at the time), each sent their regrets for being otherwise engaged and for not being able to attend this ill-advised wedding.

171

in Westchester County, about an hour's drive north of New York City.

As the world knows, Judy and her gay husband, Mickey Deans, flew from New York to London on June 17, 1969. She had only days to live.

For her final days, Judy settled with Deans into their modest home at 4 Cadogan Lane in the very posh Belgravia section of London. He was 35 years old and her fifth husband. Before marrying her, he ran a famous disco in New York named Arthur. Judy told her friends that "at long last I've found happiness," although Deans often left her alone at night, while he went cruising for young men in the parks of London.

Phil May from the band "The Pretty Things" used to live near Judy. His flatmate was Brian Jones, an early member of *The Rolling Stones*. Phil claimed that Judy used to break into their apartment all the time, stealing their booze and drugs.

On the evening of Saturday, June 21, 1969, both Judy and Deans were watching a TV documentary on the House of Windsor. After the show, they got into an argument over finances.

The fight, like nearly all their fights, was about the lack of money. Judy was in debt for more than $4 million. "Where has all the fucking money gone?" he shouted at her. "You told me you've made ten million dollars in your life. Where in the fuck is it?"

Judy had moved to England to avoid being hounded by her creditors. A string of overspending, back taxes, lawsuits, child custody battles, liens, and other mounting debts had led to her status as a virtual pauper.

She ran screaming into the street, waking the neighbors. Finally, he persuaded her to come back into the house. When he woke up the next morning at 10:40am, she was not in the bed beside him. He tried the bathroom door, finding it locked.

At long last the aftermath of too many pills, too many gay husbands, too many on-

Judy spent her final days with Mickey at this small mews house *(above)* on London's Cadogan Lane, near Sloane Square. Her final hours were spent listening to her hit records. Mickey later claimed that she played "Over the Rainbow" at least 30 times that day.

His career in decline, Johnny Ray visited the house occasionally, informing Judy and her new husband that his only singing gigs derived from gay bars in such cities as Stockholm and Malmö. In response, Judy predicted that in her own declining future, "I'll be able to work the gay circuit for at least another 20 to 30 years. My boys will never desert their Judy. They'll be with me to my grave."

When Judy's director, **George Cukor** *(below, left)* learned about her affair with **Peter Lawford** *(below, right, taken years after their original romantic involvement),* Cukor called her and insisted, "Peter is not a good lover...not at all."

stage collapses, too many illnesses, and too many audiences booing her were over. There were no *boos* on the day of her funeral. The reaction of virtually everyone who heard the news was, "WE LOVE YOU, JUDY!"

If Judy had had her way, her funeral would have been sooner. At the age of 28, she slashed her golden throat, the channel from which emerged some of the greatest musical sounds of the 20th century.

Deans tried the bathroom door, finding it locked. This was not unusual. Judy often went into the bathroom and stayed there for hours.

When she refused to answer his alarmed calls, he exited onto the building's roof from a second-floor window and walked across to the bathroom windowsill. He raised the window, after which he could see her sitting on the toilet, slumped over. When she still didn't answer him, he managed to crawl in through the narrow opening.

As he reported, "I went over and said, 'Hon. . . .' I picked her up. I noticed that her skin was discolored, with both a red and bluish tinge, and that her face was dreadfully distorted. Blood came from her nose and mouth, and the air escaping from her mouth sounded like a low moan. 'Oh, my God, no! Oh, my God, no!'"

To prevent pictures from being taken of Judy's corpse, she was draped over an attendant's arm like a folded coat and covered with a blanket. That was the way she was removed from the house and delivered to Westminster Hospital for an autopsy.

Scotland Yard found her body unmarked, and foul play was ruled out. An autopsy was performed

(Top photo, above) A grief-stricken **Liza Minnelli** *(left)*, **Lorna Luft** *(center)*, and **Mickey Deans** attend Judy's funeral.

On the night of Judy's death, Mickey had been cruising for hustlers in a park near their mews cottage. Judy is known to have passed away sometime between 3 and 4:30 in the early morning of June 22, 1969. She had died without dignity and was found sitting on a toilet with her arms on her lap and her tired head resting on her arms.

Judy's funeral in New York on June 27, 1969, was legendary, drawing 25,00 fans, including hundreds of gay men.

At **Campbell's Funeral Chapel** *(lower photo, above)*, her emaciated body was placed in an open coffin so fans could get a final look at her.

The following day, during the early morning hours of Saturday, June 28, angry, bitter gay men launched the Stonewall Riots. Was Judy responsible? Had she, in fact, been the catalyst that brought on the Gay Revolution?

Sunday afternoon, the day after her death, on Judy's 47-year-old body. It was discovered that massive doses of Seconal had been slowly consumed over a considerable period of time, thereby ruling out suicide. Judy had been addicted to Seconal for years.

The London coroner later ruled that the fading star had died of an accidental overdose of sleeping pills. "There is no evidence at all of a deliberate action by Miss Garland, and I want to make that absolutely clear," said Gavin Thursdon at a brief inquest. "I shall consider the cause of death to be an incautious self overdosage of the sleeping drug Seconal."

Deans announced that he was "taking Miss Garland's body to New York," where it would be placed on public view, with the funeral and burial set for the following Friday.

And so it was. For all the world to see, a heavily made up Judy was displayed in a glass-topped steel coffin lined with blue velvet. "WE LOVE YOU JUDY!" said the inscription on a rainbow-shaped spray of multi-hued carnations.

Under threatening skies, thousands of Judy's most loyal fans, including tribes of gay men, made their way to Campbell's Funeral Home, at Madison Avenue and 81st Street in Manhattan, where Rudolph Valentino had lain in state some 43 years before.

Thousands filed past the bier. Over the sounds of the morning rush hour of Madison Avenue could be heard Judy singing "Over the Rainbow."

Judy was surrounded by yellow chrysanthemums and daisies. Her eyelids were shadowed in blue, and she wore the long silver lamé gown in which she'd married Deans three months ago. Her famous mouth from which had emerged all those songs was painted an orange hue. Wearing a single belt of pearls, Judy had had her hands clasped over a prayer book.

Actor James Mason, with whom Judy had starred in one of her most famous films, *A Star Is Born*, delivered the eulogy. The mourners included Jack Benny, Cary Grant, Katharine Hepburn, Frank Sinatra, and Lana Turner.

Deans had selected a niche for the storage of

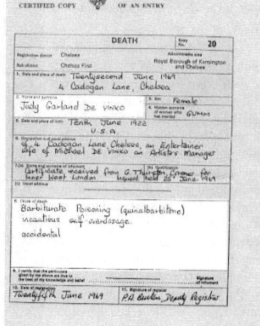

Judy Garland's death in London electrified the world. An ambulance carried her body to Westminster Hospital. On Wednesday, June 25, Dr. Derek Pock, a pathologist, announced the verdict:

Her demise had resulted from "an accidental death by an incautious overdose of barbiturates. In her body lay an equivalent of ten one-and-a-half grain Seconal sleeping tablets--but no food." The report concluded that all her systems, including her liver, had completely shut down, and that at the time of her death, she was completely dehydrated.

Privately, the hospital staff concluded that what was the most surprising was that she'd lived as long as she had in such a deteriorated condition.

Judy's remains at Ferncliff Cemetery in Hartsdale, New York, at a cost of $37,500. But he was nearly broke. Consequently, Judy was placed in temporary storage, actually just a hole in the wall.

Peter Lawford claimed that in the 1960s there existed a "homosexual funeral parlor" on New York's East Side, catering to gay necrophiles.

A prominent New York doctor, so it was rumored, often supplied recently dead bodies to this strange group. Surprisingly, for a time, he was a close buddy of the actor Montgomery Clift, a friend of Judy's. Clift broke off the friendship with the doctor when he discovered his fascination with the dead.

Lawford had met the doctor at a number of parties given by his "weird" friends. The actor later claimed that "fans of Judy's," each a devotee of necrophilia, had bribed a night guardian at Ferncliff and had the body of Judy Garland removed to this homosexual funeral parlor.

According to Lawford, these so-called ghouls "desecrated" the body of Judy. He refused to explain what he meant, but those to whom he told the story later speculated that the men—"as an act of love"—deposited their semen on her body. Lawford did not believe that there had been any sexual penetration of the withered corpse. Such sexual acts, or so it was said, were confined to young bodies who had recently died and been delivered to the funeral parlor.

Lawford went on to say that one of Judy's hands, the one used to sign all those autographs, was severed from her corpse "as a souvenir."

Months later, when rumors reached the office of the *National Enquirer*, a spy from that tabloid, Iain Calder, visited Ferncliff, pretending to be a plot buyer. Once there, he located the resting place of a crypt marked JUDY GARLAND DEANS.

"My heart nearly stopped," Calder claimed. "I touched the marble. It wobbled enough for me to fear it might fall out. It looked like it had been moved and not placed back in its vault with care. Behind this unstable slab of stone, just inches away, lay one of the world's greatest performers, a star who'd electrified audiences and moviegoers all over the world. In life, she wanted to go 'Over the Rainbow,' but, in death, she hadn't even been given the respect of a proper burial." Back at his office, he wrote the headline: JUDY GARLAND IS STILL NOT BURIED. The article caused a scandal.

Liza eventually paid the money and the official burial took place on November 4, 1970, a year or so after Judy's

Judy Garland, 47, Found Dead

Judy Garland during an appearance at the Palace in 1967 Continued on Page 31, Column 1

FERNCLIFF CEMETERY
EST. 1902

← Main Office   Rosewood Mausoleum →
Chapel   Shrine of Memories
Ferncliff Mausoleum   Hillcrest Garden
Crematory   Hickory Terrace

Hours: 9 AM - 4 PM

Judy Garland finally came to rest at Ferncliff Cemetery and Mausoleum in Hartsdale, in New York's Westchester County, 25 miles north of midtown Manhattan.

But did she really find "peace at last" or was her body disturbed?

In death, Judy's "neighbors" at Ferncliff also include Joan Crawford, John Lennon, and Ed Sullivan. It's ironic that Harold Arlen (1905-1986), composer of "Over the Rainbow," is also interred at Ferncliff.

JUDY GARLAND
1922   1969

death. The vault in polished marble reads: JUDY GARLAND 1922-1969. The word DEANS was removed.

Today Liza brings flowers to her mother's grave on Judy's birthday, June 10, 1922.

In the wake of Judy's death, Deans, with Ann Pinchot, wrote a memoir, *Weep No More My Lady*. In the years to come, he eventually drifted to Ohio where he opened a gay bar. He lived until July 11, 2003, when he died of congestive heart failure in Cleveland. His ashes were sent to a private individual in Florida, and he was not interred with Judy at Ferncliff. The great star is the sole occupant of her lonely crypt.

Another rumor that will not go away is that one of Judy's hands is today preserved and kept in the mansion of a wealthy collector and "obsessive fan" in a country estate in Surrey outside London.

The day Judy died, as legend has it, there was a tornado in Kansas.

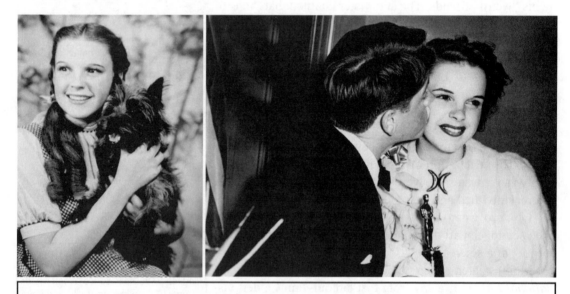

To gay men of a certain age, Judy Garland will always be **Dorothy** who wandered Over the Rainbow, or perhaps the girl they wished they had actually kissed, or at least invited to the prom. In fact, in the days when homosexuality used to be illegal, gay men often referred to themselves as "Friends of Dorothy."

Her career went up and down, as did her personal life, which was filled with emotional turmoil, ill-fated marriages (often to homosexuals) and severe addictions to drugs and alcohol.

"There will never be another Judy Garland," said her tap-dancing friend, Ann Miller. "When she sang, she had the power to make you feel great sadness or great happiness."

"When you've lived the life I've lived, when you've loved and suffered and been madly happy and desperately sad--well, that's when you realize that you'll never be able to write it all down. Maybe you'd rather die first."

Judy Garland

Judy and Her Monster Man

It was called "a marriage from hell" by the press, and during the 1950s, its tumultuous scenes were played out in headlines before the voyeuristic eyes of the world.

That famous coupling breathed its last sigh on September 17, 2005 when the Associated Press moved a small obituary announcing the death in Santa Monica of the gruff-talking, hard-drinking producer, Sid Luft. He was dead at the age of 89.

In 1952 he'd married Judy Garland—her third marriage and his second. Riddled with frequent separations, the stormy relationship would last for 13 years and produce two children, the singer, Lorna Luft, in 1952 and a son, Joey, in 1955.

The most famous of Judy's offspring, Liza Minnelli, had been born in 1946, when Judy was married to director Vincente Minnelli. Of that marriage Judy later said, "He was more in love with Gene Kelly than with me."

At time of her marriage to Luft, Judy was on a "slippery slope to fade-out," having been fired by MGM during her attempt to film *Annie Get Your Gun,* the role eventually going to the equally troubled Betty Hutton.

An amateur boxer, Luft was a barroom brawler and left a trail of broken noses on both coasts. Judy called him "my self-made monster."

Studio boss Jack L. Warner said, "Luft's one of those original guys who promised his parents he'd never work a day in his life—and made good on that promise. He saw Judy Garland as a meal ticket."

That was a cruel, but often accurate appraisal. Nonetheless, Luft did resurrect Judy's fading career. He not only produced one of Judy's all-time great musicals, *A Star Is Born* in 1954, but he launched her into concerts all over the globe, beginning at The Palace in London where she broke attendance records.

An overweight Judy in one of her happier moments with third husband, Sid Luft. One night, around the time she first met him, Luft joined Judy and her then-lover, Fred Finklehoffe, to hear Billy Daniels sing. On the way home, Judy sat between Finklehoffe and Luft in the car's front seat.

Right in front of Luft, Finkelhoffe warned Judy about Luft. "He's the dirtiest, lowdown S.O.B. you'll ever meet. He's bad news, and I'm warning you. He'll call you. I get the vibes. He's on the move. You're a cooked pigeon, baby."

During her divorce proceedings, she testified to having suffered beatings by Luft. But she brought trouble to the marriage as well. On more than one occasion, Luft had to break down a bathroom door to discover Judy bleeding profusely. She'd slit the throat from which emerged one of the great voices of popular music of the 20th century.

Judy herself died at the age of 47 in London. Although her death was ruled as "an accidental overdose of sleeping pills," much of the world defined it as suicide.

Luft survived to take two more brides and faded from the headlines until 1993 when he attempted to auction off the Oscar Judy had won in 1939 for best juvenile actress in *The Wizard of Oz*.

The Academy of Motion Picture Arts and Sciences sued him and won, claiming it had the first option to buy back the Oscar at the price of $10. When he attempted to sell the Oscar again in 2002, the Academy sued him once more, and the court ordered him to pay $60,000 in damages.

Delivering a final comment on his famous spouse, Luft said "She had the most kissable lips of any gal in Hollywood, and I should know, having sampled all the others."

After his death, the most sarcastic appraisal came from a producer in Hollywood who didn't want to be named. "So Sid Luft is what a girl finds over the rainbow?"

In one of the great mistakes of the Academy Awards, the Oscar in 1954 wen to Grace Kelly for her performance in *The Country Girl* instead of to Judy for *A Star is Born*. The icy blonde goddess was born in a Philadelphia mansion, Judy in a vaudeville trunk. Of all the telegrams and letters Judy received, the one from Groucho Marx best summed it all up: *"Dear Judy, This is the biggest robbery since Brinks."*

Shooting of *A Star is Born* took ten months and cost more than $10 million. The completed film came in at a length of three full hours, the longest film at the time since *Gone With the Wind*. After the premiere on Hollywood Boulevard, the *Evening News* wrote, "In this case, a star is re-born because Hollywood had written off Judy. Yet she gives a performance that far outshines anything she did at the height of her triumphs."

(Far left photo) **Frank Sinatra** with **Judy**. Their sexual relationship developed into an enduring friendship. *(Near left photo)* Putting on weight, **Judy** is pictured with **Sid Luft** and their children, Joey and Lorna. He was a witness to her deterioration, and often found himself searching for her hidden caches of Seconal and Benzedrine under carpets, behind books--even in the seams of her dresses. "You missed your calling, Sid," said a drugged and sarcastic Judy. "You're a gumshoe."

Bordello-Hopping With Ava Gardner

Ava Gardner

Ava Gardner: She was The Naked Maja. The Barefoot Contessa. Lady Brett. The rise of a beautiful North Carolina farm girl – barefoot and with a thick Southern accent – to the pinnacle of Hollywood is the stuff of legend. She became Mrs. Mickey Rooney, Mrs. Artie Shaw, Mrs. Frank Sinatra. She loved booze, bullfighters, and bitches of the night. Her close friends ranged from Ernest Hemingway to Adlai Stevenson.

Her own life, however, was more dramatic than any role she portrayed on the screen.

What Are Those Cathouse Pros Saying About Ava?

"Straight women, at least at some point in their lives, fantasize about lesbian sex as much as horny men fantasize about lesbian sex. Include Ava Gardner in the first category."

Paulette Goddard

*"Lesbians! You're a bunch of <u>lesbians</u>! All of you lesbians! **Lesbians**! LESBIANS!!"*

Frank Sinatra in Beverly Hills, 1952, before storming out of a restaurant where he had found Ava Gardner dining with her "best pal" Lana Turner.

"She's not a dyke. But Ava likes to pick up ladies of the night and spend the rest of the evening smoking and drinking with them and listening to their low-life tales of lust in the dust. Life on the hustle, the raw edge."

Marlon Brando

"Howard Hughes pursued Ava Gardner, but all he got from her was a terrific blow-job after that plane crash. Ava told me she never let him screw her. But Mr. Hughes screwed Lana Turner and her boyfriend, Tyrone Power, on a number of occasions. What he really wanted was to go to bed with Lana and Ava, at the same time. Ava said no, but she agreed to make love to Lana and let Mr. Hughes watch one drunken night. He had to settle for that. I think Mr. Hughes told me he masturbated through the entire encounter."

Johnny Meyer, pimp to Howard Hughes

"As much as I would like to believe Ava went for the gals as much as for the cocky bastards like that wop, Frank Sinatra, I just couldn't buy it. In my view, she was too much of a man-eater to like to do it with the girls. At least that was my first impression of her when my son, Peter Lawford, was having an affair with her. But after a thorough interrogation of my son, I now believe Ava was a switch-hitter. Peter supplied names, dates, places, and detailed descriptions of what Ava liked to do with women. I can't stand faggots. Peter was always bringing them around our house in Hollywood. I would retreat upstairs until the perverts were gone. Then I'd order the maid to fumigate the living room. As for lesbians, I'm more like Queen Victoria on that subject. The very thought of woman-on-woman sex makes my blood curdle."

Lady May Lawford

"Ava was so drunk half the time she would have gone to bed with a porcupine."

Mia Farrow

"I always knew Frank would end up with a little boy."
Ava Gardner learning of Frank's marriage to Mia Farrow

"Ann Sheridan and I were fucking Ava Gardner around the same time, but individually—not as a ménage à trois. I think I would have preferred the latter."

Peter Lawford

181

A Temptress Who Drove Sinatra to the Brink of Suicide

Most Ava Gardner biographers make no mention of the star's lesbianism. Lee Server, who wrote the definitive biography of the beautiful star, *Love Is Nothing*, at least was aware of it, as were some of the latest Frank Sinatra biographers like Anthony Summers.

Although unbelievably savvy about what went on when the lights went out in Hollywood, Sinatra became aware of Ava's fondness for the girls only during the course of their marriage, and that was because the even hipper Rat Packer, Peter Lawford, informed him.

Sinatra learned even more about Ava's Sapphic streak when Donna Caldwell, a Hollywood madam of the 50s, told Sinatra that she had once supplied some of her girls to both Ava and him. "You mean, Ava and I have fucked the same pussies?" Sinatra shouted in rage.

Lawford liked lesbians and used to hire them to perform sexual acts together in front of him. Sinatra had almost zero tolerance of lesbians. In his later, more mellow years, he began to at least tolerate gay men, even though he continued to call them "faggots" throughout his life. But he never softened his position on lesbian sex.

Tout Hollywood mainly learned of Ava's lesbianism through the mouth of Yvonne de Carlo. Ava and she often dated some of the same men, notably Howard Hughes. They both shared the lovemaking technique of actor Howard Duff, who later became the third "Mr. Ida Lupino." Clark Gable, Burt Lancaster, and Robert Taylor were other men they shared in common. Ava learned at one point that De Carlo had sampled the charms of two of her former

Ava Gardner was called "the world's greatest beauty." But in the golden age of movie-making, the tabloids, who documented her steamy private life, had a lot more to say than that.

Studio packaged, Ava was one of the last of the great Hollywood sex goddesses. But studio chief Louis B. Mayer went ballistic trying to keep her personal scandals from destroying her career.

"Unless he was a gay blade," said an MGM studio publicist, "every red-blooded male who ever saw an Ava Gardner movie wanted to take her to bed."

Ava's rival, both on screen and in the boudoirs of Hollywood, was **Yvonne De Carlo** (*both photos, above*). "Howard Hughes told me I was the most beautiful woman in the world," claimed Yvonne. "That bitch, Ava Gardner, is a liar telling people that Howard claimed she, not me, was the most beautiful girl in the world."

Yvonne added a footnote, "Prince Aly Khan begged me to marry him. He only got Rita Hayworth when I turned him down. Another thing: both Clark Gable and Robert Taylor told me I was far better in the sack than Ava."

husbands, Artie Shaw (the musician who had originally been married to Lana Turner) and Sinatra himself.

De Carlo claimed that one night Ava invited her to her home, and she accepted. "After all, Ava was a big star at the time." De Carlo said that she feared that she might encounter a drunken Ava who was going to be in a jealous rage and attack her for "sleeping with her boyfriends."

"When I got there, Ava could not have been more charming," De Carlo later told friends. "Not once did she bring up the subject of our shared boyfriends, with one exception. She warned me that Howard Hughes might have given me VD, and that I'd better go and get my vagina checked out by a doctor. When I started to leave around two o'clock in the morning, Ava detained me in the hallway. She invited me to spend the night, fearing I was too drunk to drive. She said she could never stand sleeping alone. I agreed to share her bed. At that point, there was no suggestion of sex."

"In her bedroom, Ava stripped nude—after all, she had a great body—but I modestly retained my lingerie," De Carlo said. We'd been in bed no more than thirty minutes when Ava moved in on me for sex. I was horrified. I have lived and worked with gay people all my life, and I have no problem with their preferences, but anybody who knows me knows I don't go that route. I jumped out of bed and grabbed my clothes, running toward my car. I might have been drunk when I got in bed with Ava but I was sober when I drove away from her place."

The story of De Carlo's night with Ava was just too good to keep to herself. Besides, De Carlo always thought that she—not Ava—deserved the title of "Most Beautiful Women in the World." At parties and dinners, De Carlo widely repeated the story of her private encounter with Ava, telling some of her lovers such as director Billy Wilder, actor Robert Stack, and even Prince Aly Khan, who knew Ava. Soon the word was all over town.

In his biography of Ava, Lee Server accurately wrote: "She had a continuing curiosity about the sexual demi-monde and through the years paid visits to gay bars, red-light zones, and brothels all over the world."

On her most notorious brothel visit, she was accompanied by—of all people—Grace Kelly.

It all began when Grace and Ava signed to co-star in *Mogambo* in 1953, a film to be shot in Africa. The male star was Clark Gable, who, ironically, had appeared in the first version, called *Red Dust*, released in 1932 and co-starring Jean Harlow.

When **Clark Gable** arrived in Africa to film *Mogambo* in 1953, he was accompanied by two of the most beautiful women in the world: **Grace Kelly** and **Ava Gardner.** "I always had trouble deciding whether I liked chocolate or vanilla better," Gable told director John Ford.

He of course was referring to Grace's blonde hair and Ava's dark curls. Mogambo translates from Swahili as "passion," and no other word could better describe the off-screen sex going on during the making of this film. After Frank Sinatra showed up to drag Ava from Gable's tent, the aging actor turned to Grace Kelly instead.

Ava's all-time favorite movie was *Red Dust* in which a young Gable had starred opposite Jean Harlow as "Honey Bear," a slut in the bush. Now Ava was replacing her idol, Harlow, in Gable's arms. "As you know," Ava told Grace, "Clark doesn't have all that much to penetrate with, but Frankie's weapon sure knows how to reach virgin territory."

183

Ava later said that she wanted Grace to sample Gable as a lover, claiming that she'd already been sexually intimate with him in 1947 during the filming of *The Hucksters*. "I felt it was Grace's turn," Ava was quoted as saying.

When she had first met Ava beside the Kagera River in Central Africa, Grace had been shocked by Ava's heavy drinking, her "potty mouth," and her uninhibited behavior. Witnessed by Grace, Ava went around lifting up the breech-cloths of the big, handsome Watusi tribesmen hired as extras. Grace commented to Gable that "Ava is a mess and a half."

But during the long weeks of shooting, Grace gradually warmed to Ava, and in time they became "friends for life."

At the completion of the film, Ava invited Grace to stop over with her for a few days for a Roman holiday, and Grace accepted. According to the testimony of Guido Volta, a chauffeur in Rome in the 1950s who hauled around everyone from Elizabeth Taylor to Frank Sinatra, Ava took the future princess of Monaco on a tour of the city's brothels. At first, Grace declined but Ava could be persuasive.

With Guido as their guide, the two women set off for visits to establishments that included (according to their English translations), "The World of Earthly Pleasures," "One Hundred and One Desires Fulfilled," "No Pleasure Too Great or Too Small," "Memories Are Made of This," and "The Garden of Delights." At the various Roman bordellos, Ava bought drinks for all the hookers, introducing them to Grace and urging them to tell "only their best stories."

According to those who knew her well, her **Most Serene Highness, the Princess of Monaco** in private did not resemble the ice-cold blonde goddess she played on screen. Gary Cooper, who costarred with her in *High Noon* (1952), said, "She looked like a cold dish with a man until you got her pants down. Then she'd explode." A former lover, Don Richardson, claimed, "She screwed everybody she came into contact with who was able to do anything good for her. She screwed agents, producers, directors. And there was really no need for it. She was on her way."

Director Henry Hathaway's wife once said, "Grace wore those white gloves, looking all prissy and proper, but she was no saint. Just ask Bing Crosby, Cary Grant, William Holden, Prince Aly Khan, David Niven, Spencer Tracy, Ray Milland, Jimmy Stewart, and countless others."

At the final bordello, according to Guido, "Miss Kelly became fascinated by a strikingly handsome young man, Antonio Guarnieri, who at the time was about 23 years old, and who worked as a waiter in the joint. Just before dawn, I drove Ava, Miss Kelly, and Antonio back to the women's suites at the Hotel Excelsior on the Via Veneto. Ava sat up front with me, while Miss Kelly and Antonio got acquainted in back. At the hotel, the future princess invited Antonio up for a nightcap. That must have been one long drink. It lasted for three days and nights and ended only when I came back to drive Miss Kelly to the airport. At the airport, Antonio and Miss Kelly engaged in the world's longest goodbye kiss. When I drove Antonio back to Rome, he cried all the way."

Back in Los Angeles, when Ava wasn't with one of her male lovers, she cruised Santa Monica Boulevard at night, often picking up as many as three or four prostitutes and bringing them home with her. Sometimes she didn't want sex with them, but just wanted them to talk to her, smoking, drinking, and sharing their experiences with her.

She did have sex with any number of these hookers. According to reports, she paid them well and treated them kindly. Many of Ava's pickups often preferred women to men anyway, and were only too happy to disappear into the night with what the press called "The World's Most Beautiful Animal."

One night Ava rented herself out as a hooker.

One of Ava's most famous films, *The Barefoot Contessa*, was actually based on the life of another screen sex goddess, Rita Hayworth. When the film's director, **Joseph Mankiewicz** *(with Ava in photo, above)*, still beaming from his success with *All About Eve*, called Ava in Rome, she invited him up to her suite. He was startled to find her lying naked on the sofa, sipping champagne.

"I can play more than barefoot," she said, wiggling her naked toes at him before raising her legs in the air. "Hop on, big guy."

Frank Sinatra was just one of the men that **Lana Turner** and **Ava Gardner** both sampled. "Friends" of both women claimed that Frank barged in on Ava and Lana in bed with each other one night in Palm Springs. He'd already told Peter Lawford that he suspected they would shack up with each other when a man with a big dick wasn't around.

Screaming "LESBIANS! You're both *LESBIANS!*" Frank chased both Lana and Ava – "jaybird naked" – out through his front door in Palm Springs.

The director, Joseph Mankiewicz, wanted to cast Marlon Brando and Ava Gardner in the role of *The Barefoot Contessa*. Brando turned down the role, the part going to Humphrey Bogart. Taking the director into his confidence, Brando revealed that Ava liked to attend bordellos. She became particularly interested in a bordello that specialized in offering "movie stars" to its male clients, and to a few female clients as well.

The madam of the bordello claimed that "if you can't fuck the real thing, we offer you the mock." Clients got a look-alike, and were allowed to spend time with their screen favorite—"Joan Crawford," "Marilyn Monroe," "Elizabeth Taylor," "Jane Russell," "Judy Garland," and even "Margaret O'Brien" for those who liked them really young.

Brando told Mankiewicz that Ava wanted to be taken to the bordello to meet the madam. "That's not all," Brando said. "With the permission of the madam, Ava wanted to exchange places that coming Saturday night with her stand-in."

"That's wild!" Mankiewicz said. "It's incredible. May I be the first customer to hire the real Ava for the night?"

Brando pondered the request for a minute. "If you showed up as Ava's first client, I would just shit my pants. I don't know what Ava would shit."

Brando escorted Ava to the bordello that Saturday night and made the arrangement for Ava with the madam. Ava was in a bedroom awaiting her first customer when Mankiewicz arrived downstairs to be introduced to the madam. She personally escorted him to Ava's bedroom, while Brando wandered off "to do my duty with 'Betty Grable.'"

The story was spread around Hollywood, and many men queried Mankiewicz about his evening in Ava's whorehouse bedroom. "The lady—and she is a lady—deserves her privacy," Mankiewicz said.

The next day Sinatra learned what had happened. Instead of phoning Mankiewicz, an angry Sinatra called Brando. "Listen, creep, and listen good. I know all about you and Ava. Stay away from her! Don't ever come within twenty feet of her even at a party. You got that? First offense, broken legs. Second offense, cracked skull. If you live through all that, cement shoes. One more false step and you've had it."

He slammed down the phone.

185

STEPPING OUT! The love affair and eventual marriage of Frank Sinatra and Ava Gardner were doomed from the start. Initially, Ava wasn't impressed with the bag of bones until he took off his clothes, and then she had nothing but praise for "my Frankie boy." She told Lana Turner, "Only Porfirio Rubirosa is better hung, but then, he's the Ninth Wonder of the World."

She was referring to the diplomat/playboy from the Dominican Republic who went on to marry the world's two richest women--Barbara Hutton and Doris Duke.

In the beginning, Ava was torn between Sinatra and the minor gangster, Johnny Stompanato, a close friend of mob boss Mickey Cohen. One night she received a call from Stompanato, who told her that even though she'd never received an Oscar, she would get one that night if she invited him over.

> "What on earth do you mean, honey chile?" she asked.
> "Oscar and I share the same dimensions," he bluntly told her.
> "Get over here at once, baby, and let's see how much you exaggerated," she said.

When Sinatra learned of their affair, he called Cohen and warned him, "Tell your boy to leave Ava alone or else he might find himself in a ditch somewhere some dark night missing a pair of *cojones."*

> "Oh, Frankie, baby, go back to your wife," Cohen barked at him. "You belong with Nancy--not Ava."

AGING AVA: Years of sexual dissipation and heavy boozing caused Ava to lose her legendary beauty. Her housekeeper reported that she'd often stare at her face in the mirror and say to her image, "Too many bullfighters, baby. Too many dicks. Too many George C. Scotts. Too many Artie Shaws. Too many Roberts." (No doubt, among others, she was referring to Robert Walker, Robert Taylor, and Robert Evans.)

At night, she'd watch reruns of her old movies, many of which she'd never seen before. After seeing such films as *The Snows of Kilimanjaro,* she'd call one of her former co-stars to reminisce. In that instance, it was Gregory Peck:

"Greg, baby, could it have been true? Was I really the most beautiful woman on the face of the earth, and you its most beautiful man?"

Gallantly, Peck answered: "That's true in your case, Ava, my dear, but I had serious competition back then. After all, Jerry Lewis and Broderick Crawford were two good-looking studs."

"We Want Rudi in the Nudi!"

Oft-Repeated Chant of Rudolf Nureyev's Gay Male Fans

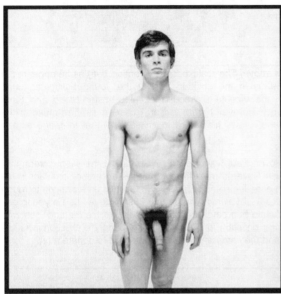

The homosexual actor, **Rudolph Valentino** *(photo below)*, darling of millions of women, died mysteriously in New York City during the hot August of 1926. He was only thirty-one years old.

Almost half a century later, a homosexual dancer, **Rudolf Nureyev** *(two photos, above),* was cast as the lead in *Valentino (1977)* in an attempt to bring the legend of the silent screen back to life.

The movie was a box office failure, yet it remains one of the great camp classics when viewed by 21st-century audiences.

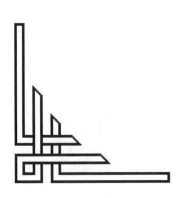

A Star Portrays Another Star and a Legend Is Reborn

The 1977 film, *Valentino*, starred Rudolf Nureyev playing Rudolph Valentino, and was directed by British director Ken Russell. Nureyev said that the director had to develop *des couilles en fer* (iron testicles) to guide him through a difficult role where he either appeared almost naked, or in a bizarre combination of gangster-style pinstripes, flowing Moorish *djellabas,* or Argentinian-style *gaucho* pants. In one of screen history's most exaggerated performances, Leslie Caron appears as Nazimova, a deliberate send-up of the extravagantly theatrical 1920s-era actress known as America's Eleanora Duse.

The movie opened to bad reviews on both sides of the Atlantic. According to film critic Pauline Kael: "There is no artistry left in Ken Russell's work. By now, his sensationalist reputation is based merely on his going further than anybody else. His films have become schoolboy Black Masses, a mixture of offensiveness and crude dumbness. Spitefulness is almost the sole emotion of *Valentino.*"

(Two photos above) The real Rudolph Valentino *(left)* as he appeared in the early 1920s in the coveted role of the young bullfighter, Juan Gallardo, in the Vicente Blasco-Ibañez blockbuster *Blood and Sand (1922).* Rudolf Nureyev *(right),* in Ken Russell's 1977 re-make of the Valentino saga, draws his sword in imitation of that long-ago screen matador.

Valentino's lover, Paul Ivano, once revealed that the silent-screen star wore his Juan Gallardo matador costume as an erotic stimulant in his bedroom, re-enacting some of his bullfight scenes as a prelude to rough sex. On the set of *Valentino* in the mid 70s, Nureyev had a young gay stagehand fellate him before stuffing himself into his matador costume and appearing on set. In one scene, the dancer's erection was too prominent, and the cameraman had to wait for it to deflate a bit.

The other Rudi, almost in the nudi, early 1920s

Valentino (1921) imi-tating Nijinsky

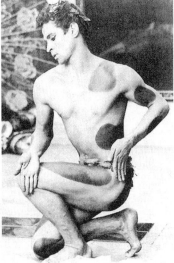

Nureyev (1976) imitating Valentino imitating Nijinsky

In the early 1920s, in a private photo session, Valentino evoked Nijinsky as Nijinsky had appeared about a decade previously in the Stravinsky-Diaghilev ballet *L'apres-midi d'un faune.* Prior to their marriage, Valentino's second wife, a lesbian, Natacha Rambova, asked him to pose for the faun pictures.

And although it was viewed as almost unbelievably pretentious at the time, it was her way of paying homage to Valentino's "Greek god body," and to her Russian compatriot, Nijinsky. When Valentino's first wife, Jean Acker, also a lesbian, filed for divorce, she vengefully introduced these pictures to the press. Headlines immediately blared FAUN PICTURE CAUSES STIR.

In 1977, in a scene from the Ken Russell film, Nureyev played Valentino imitating Nijinsky.

Rudolph Valentino   *Rudolf Nureyev*

Unlike Rudolf Nureyev, who never married, Valentino took two wifes, Jean Acker, and later, Natacha Rambova. There is strong evidence that neither of the two marriages was ever cosummated. In fact, Acker announced her intention of permanently locking Valentino out of her bedroom only minutes after the marriage ceremony ended. Other lovers, however, were far more willing to receive *The Sheik (1921)* into their bedrooms, including "Rae" Bourbon, the female impersonator, and Norman Kerry, once a famous silent screen actor. Even Ramon Novarro, the star of the original film version of *Ben-Hur,* fell madly in love with Valentino. Valentino's greatest role remains *The Sheik,* in which he played a swarthy Arab seducer in a film about desert sex and machismo. In theaters across America, women fainted. *The Sheik* would seal Valentino's legend as the World's Greatest Lover. Baring his chest and popping his eyes, Valentino also attracted thousands of gay male fans who knew "he was one of us."

In director Ken Russell's 1977 *homage* to Valentino, another Rudolf (in this case the Russian-born emigre ballet superstar Rudolf Nureyev) played the desert scenes almost nude. Most critics found him far more seductive than the original.

Before Nureyev, and even before Valentino,

Nijinsky

Defined the Way Men Should Move

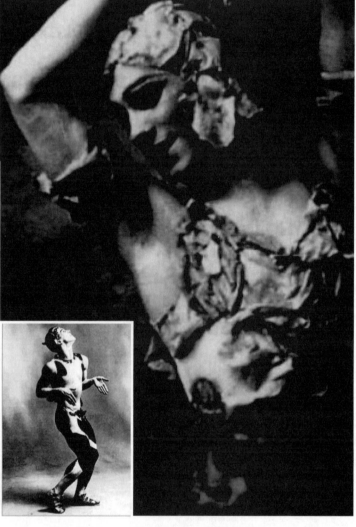

Of Polish descent, but born in The Ukraine in 1880, Vaslav Nijinsky was the most celebrated male dancer in history. At the age of 18, he garnered leading roles in St. Petersburg's Marinsky (aka Kirov) Theater. It was here that he met Sergei Diaghilev, a wealthy impresario and patron of the arts, who soon after became his lover.

Diaghilev wanted his *protégé* to break free of the Marinksy. As a means to this end, Nijinsky appeared at a performance in honor of Russia's royal family without a jockstrap, an accessory that was otherwise obligatory for the troupe's male dancers. The Dowager Empress Marie Feodorovna complained that his appearance was obscene, and that she could see Nijinsky's penis and testicles in complete detail. As a result, he was dismissed from the company, leaving him available to pursue a more radical (and potentially more profitable) style of choreography within Diaghilev's dance troupe, *Les Ballets Russes*.

In Paris, Nijinsky, having developed a "modern" style inspired by Greek antiquity and radically angular movements, helped define a form of choreography "that was an assault" upon traditional classical ballet. In May, 1913, in Paris, a riot broke out among the otherwise black-tie audience at the Théâtre des Champs-Elysées after he mimed masturbation with the scarf of a nymph during the premiere of a joint Stravinsky/Diaghilev production, *Le Sacre du Printemps* (The Rite of Spring).

Despite almost universal charges of obscenity, such luminaries as Rodin and the gay author Marcel Proust aggressively and loudly defended the work, and Nijinsky's dance, as an expression of genius.

Much to the jealous fury of Diaghilev, who had not accompanied his dance troupe on a recital tour of South America because of his morbid superstition of drowning during a sea voyage, Nijinsky eventually married Romola Pulszky, an obsessive Hungarian countess who had been virtually stalking him for months. In 1919, he suffered a nervous breakdown. Diagnosed with acute schizophrenia, he spent the rest of his life in and out of psychiatric hospitals. Before his death in a London clinic in 1950, he recorded a bitter exposé of his relationship with Diaghilev.

Born in Soviet Siberia in 1938, Rudolf Nureyev was the greatest male ballet dancer of the 1960s and 70s, expressing himself in both classical and modern roles. Nureyev cut his ties with the Soviet Union on June 17, 1961, seeking political asylum in France at Le Bourget Airport in Paris, just before his scheduled flight back to the USSR and probable imprisonment for his self-defined status as a gay man.

He never married, although he formed several long-lasting relationships with men over the years, especially Erik Bruhn, the Danish ballet dancer.

Trading on his fame and charisma, he became something of a Kennedy family seducer, enjoying intimacies not only with Lee Radziwill but with Jackie-O herself. And if "Rudi" is to be believed, he and Robert Kennedy, one drunken night in Los Angeles, jointly shared the sexual favors of a handsome American G.I.

(Photos right) Looking macho and particularly virile, Rudolph Valentino created a sensation when he appeared as a gaucho in *Four Horsemen of the Apocalypse,* a 1921 film adaptation of the novel by Vicente Blasco-Ibañez. Valentino kept himself busy tending to the needs of his two male lovers at the time, the young Ramon Novarro, working as a nude model, and Paul Ivano, an adviser to the film's battle scenes.

Novarro later confessed that Valentino became "the great love of my life," even though The Great Lover viewed their sexual liaison as "passionate but loveless, mere ships that pass in the night." As a goodbye gift, Valentino gave Novarro a life-sized replica of his penis, a ten-inch Art Deco dildo.

Valentino in 1921

Nureyev in 1977

Nureyev's re-enactment of Valentino's portrayal followed the original with flair. The script detailed the plot of a playboy wastrel who evolved into a man thanks to wartime suffering. A Muselman Tartar who had been born in a Soviet Trans-Siberian railway car near Irkutsk, near Vladivostok, Nureyev managed to play an Argentinian rather well.

In Ken Russell's film, the willowy blonde singer and songwriter, Michelle Phillips *(three photos, left)* played Natacha Rambova, the notorious second wife of Rudolph Valentino. In the film, a nude Natacha lures Nureyev (playing Valentino) into her tent. Her provocative poses, and their sexual passion, was a mere screen fantasy. In real life, Natacha spent far more time in the arms of Alla Nazimova, the flamboyant actress (and godmother of First Lady Nancy Davis Reagan) than she did eating Valentino's famous spaghetti.

Phillips is best known as one of the founders of the 1960s pop group "The Mamas and the Papas." Phillips and Nureyev clashed often. "I hope you understand that I have no interest in women," he said to her at the time of their first meeting. After working with her for a week, he told her, "Just because you play cunt in film doesn't mean you have to be cunt in life."

Savvy insiders asserted that Natacha aggressively "steered" Valentino's career and public image. Their stormy marriage reflected the legend of Pygmalian and Galatea--in reverse. The impresario, Jacques Hébertot, once claimed that "Natacha was an absolute cow--snotty, rude to Valentino in public. She treated her dogs better than she treated him. He told me that he had slept with her many times, but that she always refused to have sex with him." Hébertot also claimed that whenever he was with Valentino, it was he who took care of the actor's sexual needs.

Nureyev, however, while playing the Sheik, never had trouble finding a bedmate. Just ask Cecil Beaton, Leonard Bernstein, Anthony Perkins, actress Ultra Violet, Mick Jagger, Freddie Mercury, Robert Mapplethorpe, and most definitely the designer, Roy Halston. "All I remember of him," said Marlene Dietrich, "was his constant complaints about his legs--he considered them too short. But he was proud of something else which he talked about as if it was longer than it actually was."

Coco Chanel stood virtually alone in utterly dismissing Nureyev, his allure, and his legend: "If you've known Nijinsky, you don't want to see Nureyev."

They danced divinely: Director Ken Russell discovered during his research that Valentino had actually taught the tango to the great Nijinsky when the young Russian dancer visited New York at the turn of the (20th) century.

"A re-enactment of that scene would be the most sensual introduction to the picture I know," Russell declared.

Originally, Russell had wanted Nureyev to interpret the role of Nijinsky, and in negotiations to that end, offered a goodly sum for the two-day shoot.

But eventually, Russell realized that Nureyev would be even better playing Valentino. Sir Anthony James Dowell *(right-hand figure in photo, left),* who later served as the artistic director of England's Royal Ballet, was cast into the role of Nijinsky instead.

"Nureyev was the living symbol of what Valentino was all about," said Russell. "He was the perfect man for the part. It just *had* to be Nureyev."

As the director of *Valentino,* the very flamboyant **Ken Russell** *(right figure in photo below)* hawkeyes the final touches on Nureyev's slicked-down hair before releasing him to the cameras as Valentino.

Before his career as a director, English-born Russell was also a dancer. His third feature film, the X-rated adaptation of D.H. Lawrence's erotic *Women in Love (1969),* made him internationally famous. He took an enormous gamble in casting Nureyev as Valentino, since the dancer had not at the time been proven or tested as a screen personality.

Another of Russell's cinematic gambles failed in the early 1980s, when he insisted that Liza Minnelli play *Evita* in his abortive attempt to launch a film adaptation of the Argentinian dictator's life. That movie, of course, was eventually made by Alan Parker, who cast Madonna in the role instead.

Russell, during various stages of his life, has been variously dubbed as both "England's Orson Welles," and "The Fellini of the North."

Valentino portrayed a scene from its namesake's life wherein Nureyev (playing Valentino) is arrested because his second marriage license was processed before his divorce was finalized. In this enactment of an L.A. prison, female prostitutes attempt to undress him, and male inmates taunt him and threaten him with rape. A warden mixes a diuretic drug into a mug of coffee, which Valentino unsuspectingly drinks. In the film, he tries not to wet his pants, but his bladder eventually, and very visibly, gives up.

During the shoot, Nureyev fought bitterly with Russell about the size of his penis, since the scene portrayed him pissing his pants. To suggest the long length of his penis, Nureyev kept demanding that the hose (a prop) in his pants be pushed farther and farther down the leg of his pants. Finally, an exasperated Russell told his cameraman: "It looks like Rudy is wrestling with a snake halfway down his pants. No one, not even John C. Holmes, is hung like that!"

(above and left) Ken Russell

Margot Fonteyn *(with Nureyev, right)* became the most famous ballerina of the 2nd half of the 20th century, dominating British ballet for more than four decades. She achieved all that before what has been called her "wonderful Indian summer," a chapter of her late career based almost entirely on her association with Rudolf Nureyev.

After his famous leap to freedom in Paris, he shortly thereafter teamed with Fonteyn, who invited him to London as her dance partner in *Giselle.* Their first performance startled the world, and the most celebrated partnership in the history of ballet was born. They were referred to as "The Dream Duo," and their interpretation of *Giselle* "the success of the century."

Despite the 20-year difference in their ages, Nureyev became her friend and occasional lover, exhibiting enormous tenderness to the *duenna* during her bout with terminal cancer.

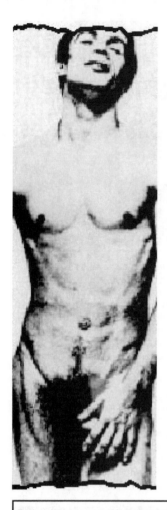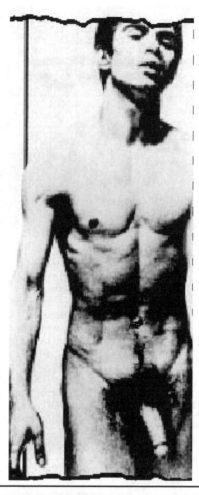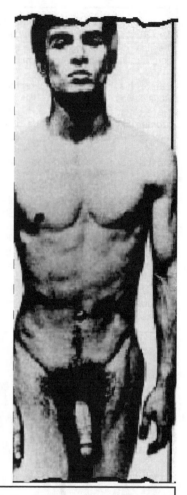

Richard Avedon was the most famous photographer of his day, his subjects including Pablo Picasso, T.S. Eliot, Ezra Pound, Marilyn Monroe, Mae West, Igor Stravinsky, Jean Cocteau, Alfred Hitchcock, Leonard Bernstein, Brigitte Bardot,...and Rudolf Nureyev. Avedon's life and career inspired the screenplay for *Funny Face,* the 1956 film that starred Fred Astaire as a fashion photographer.

Photographed in Paris at a dance studio, Nureyev appeared completely relaxed around Avedon. The photographer's camera captured all of Nureyev's glamour and beauty as exemplified by his rumpled hair and his sexy, languidly sensual eyes. At the end of three hours, Avedon told Nureyev: "I want to photograph you in the nude. Your body at this moment in its history should be recorded at the peak of its glory. Every muscle. Because it's the body of the greatest dancer who ever lived." Nureyev acquiesced.

At first Avedon photographed the now-nude Nureyev in a series of flying leaps. Then, in Avedon's own words, "He slowly raised his arms, and as his arms went up, so did his penis. It was as if he was dancing with every part of himself. His whole body was responding to a kind of wonder at him. I thought this was the most beyond-words moment--too beautiful to be believed. A narcissistic orgy of some kind. An orgy of one."

The next morning, Nureyev confronted Avedon and demanded that Avedon destroy the previous day's final frames. The photographer turned over his negatives to Nureyev, begging him not to destroy them. "When you're an old man, you'll want to look at these pictures to see the miracle that you were." Later that afternoon, Avedon found an unfinished roll left in his camera from the end of the previous day's shoot.

Those remaining nudes were pirated from his studio and sent around the world, in one instance configured into a street poster enticing gay men into a male porno house in the Times Square district of New York during the 1970s. Avedon himself published a full frontal of Nureyev in his book, *The Sixties.* Nureyev later charged that Avedon sold the nudes of himself to the CIA. "The agency used my nudes in an anti-homosexual booklet," Nureyev claimed for years to anyone who would listen.

194

The Love of His Life

There are those in the dance world who claimed that one of Rudi's most compelling motivations for escaping from the Soviet Union involved his fixation on Erik Bruhn, the Danish-born *danseur noble*. Born in 1928, Bruhn danced for the Royal Danish Ballet School from 1938 to 1947, eventually evolving during the 1950s into the world's premier male classical dancer.

All of Rudi's antennae were working. From the moment he met Bruhn in 1961, "It was love at first sight. I had to possess him. More than that, I had to move inside his body and take over his soul. I had to inhabit him. I had to work it so that Erik would become obsessed with me--and he did."

Bruhn, 32, and Rudi, 23, were as different as Apollo and Dionysus, yet they were fiercely attracted to each other. Bruhn later referred to their turbulent relationship as "pure Strindberg."

As expressed by Rudi's biographer, Julie Kavanagh, "A totally reciprocal deep passion existed between the two men. Their emotional intimacy coexisted with an extraordinary artistic interchange. They began each day at the *barre*. Home-movie footage shows them working together in a studio, both dressed in black. Erik raises one arm into an arabesque position. Rudolf, facing him, does the same. They study themselves in the mirror, not with vanity but with the self-critical scrutiny of dancers. Then they change sides. Still facing each other, they move in close, their heads almost touching as they begin an arabesque exercise. A faintly homoerotic undertone now emerges, which also plays on the idea of gender reversal as they partner each other."

Of course, there were arguments and a clash of personalities, Erik being his Hamlet-like veiled, inscrutable self, Rudolf filled with a remarkable candor and a child-man impetuosity. In the words of Glen Tetley, "Erik just responded to that very powerful thing in Rudolf, who could suddenly open everything and let you see his soul."

There were even arguments over Bruhn's ballet tights. Rudi was generously endowed, Bruhn was not. Rudi protested that Bruhn embarrassed him on stage and suggested that he use padding to show off more genitalia. In Rudi's words, "For me, sexually in our bedroom, it doesn't matter, since I am a top. But many young gay men attend the ballet just to see the outline of a dancer's genitalia. You don't want to disappoint them, Erik." Despite those blandishments, the Dane steadfastly refused to pad his crotch.

Rudi was never faithful to Bruhn. It was not in the Russian's makeup to be sexually loyal to anyone. He often flaunted his affairs. One night at Maxim's in Paris, he told Bruhn, "I was just in New York. I fuck Jackie Kennedy. Now I take you back to hotel, and I fuck you--all night."

Bruhn seemed to understand his friend's promiscuity. He once said, "I do not like for love to be something possessive. I find it smothering. For me, loving does not mean owning." Bruhn defined his friendship with his lover like this: "My friendship with Rudi has been intense, stormy, and at times, very very beautiful. I have probably done plenty of things that have hurt or upset him. And he has done the same to me. And still, we are very close."

Bruhn died in Toronto of lung cancer on April 1, 1986, leaving Rudi devastated. He even threatened suicide. As he told his long-time dancing partner, Margot Fonteyn, "The only man I've ever loved lies cold somewhere on a marble slab in a morgue. I will never love again. My life ended today."

Rudolf Nureyev never did love again, and tried to blot out the memory of Bruhn in a series of one-night stands with cheap street hustlers or chance encounters in the steam baths of such cities as London.

He continued to perform classical ballet far beyond his prime, making his last public appearance on October 8, 1992, for the premiere of his staging of the Paris Opera Ballet's *La Bayadère*. He ignored critics who carped that he should abandon ballet and retire. "For me, dance and life are one. I will dance to the last drop of blood."

On January 6, 1993, at the age of 54, Rudi died of cardiac complications brought on by AIDS. On the day he died he said, "I will soon be joining Erik somewhere, someplace. He and I will dance a *pas de deux* into eternity."

Photographed here on the French Riviera, the blond beauty with the bulging basket (**Tab Hunter,** *left*) was enthralled with **Rudolf Nureyev,** whom he described in his autobiography as a "bone white body with blue veins clad only in a sliver lamé swimsuit. Rudi looked like a finely chiseled corpse freshly risen from an ancient crypt, and he walked as if the world was far beneath him."

Eventually, shacked up within Nureyev's exquisitely styled home at 6 Fife Road in the Richmond Park district of London, "Tab & Rudi" abandoned their posturings and got down to some primal intra-male bonding.

Nureyev in those days was known for "fucking like a rabbit." Another of his lovers, Monique Van Vooren, the actress, claimed that Rudolf liked "street boys, toughs, the lowest of the low." Obviously Tab, the ultimate example of a handsome blond beach boy of the 50s, was an exception to the dancer's usual conquests.

(Upper left), Nureyev with Margot Fonteyn in *Paradise Lost*, 1962. *(Right),* Interpreting choreography by George Balanchine, Nureyev evokes *Apollo.*

(Lower left) Russell was fascinated with the historical fact that in 1926, at his memorial service, the 31-year-old body of *The Sheik* lay on a block of ice to preserve it in the stifling heat of a New York August. In a separate room, thousands of fans filed by, and fussed over, a wax replica of Valentino's body, thinking that they were paying their respects to the real Valentino. Nureyev, as the dead Valentino, lies in state, oblivious to the adoring crowds.

Errol Flynn, Vietnam,

and the Torture and Disappearance of His Son

Sean

"Satan's Angel," the right-hand figure in the father-son photo above, smiles. He is depicted with his son, **Sean**.

During his 1930s heyday, **Errol Flynn** was a symbol of masculinity and virility. Young men and boys, including Sean, were inspired to be like him. But as time would painfully reveal, Errol was not a good role model for anybody – most of all, himself. Trying to live up to his father's adventurous image may have led to Sean's ultimate destruction.

Pictured shirtless above on the right, Sean grew tired of his father's fans telling him, "You're not as handsome as your ol' man." Other fans disagreed, and considered Sean more "classically" handsome than his father.

Father & Son Swashbucklers on the Road to Hell

On April 6, 1970, Sean Flynn, handsome son of that dashing swashbuckler, Errol Flynn, disappeared mysteriously in Cambodia and was never seen again, at least in the West.

Along with his friend and fellow journalist, Dana Stone (working for CBS), Sean left Phnom Penh on a red Honda motorbike, hoping to take pictures of frontline fighting between U.S. ground troops and the Vietcong. He was under contract as a freelance photojournalist to *Time* magazine. His disappearance remains a lingering Hollywood mystery, and he wasn't declared legally dead until 1984. Recent investigations and revelations have provided some tantalizing clues as to his fate.

He and Dana are believed to have been captured by the Vietcong, who later turned them over to the murderous Khmer Rouge.

Sean was the only child from the tumultuous

Looking like Peter Fonda in Easy Rider, **Sean** *(above, on the left)* poses for his last photograph (circa 1970) as he and his pal, Dana Stone, set out on a journey into captivity and death.

Cameras ready, the two men attracted gaping onlookers as they prepared to leave on their perilous journey into territory controlled by the Viet Cong. Older men in the village warned the two young Americans of the dangers of such an excursion.

That very morning, Sean had said, "Don't you watch movies? Flynns always emerge victorious."

This studio portrait *(right)* of **Sean** in 1962 reveals him to be as handsome as his father, but a very different physical type.

According to Louella Parsons, "He was so 1950s handsome that he could have been another Troy Donahue or Tab Hunter." Then, in words that stung, the gossip maven continued: "Sadly, in spite of his superb physique and his tallness – more than six feet – he lacked not only Errol's talent but his charisma. Errol Flynn was one of a kind. We may never see the likes of him in our generation."

1930s marriage of Errol Flynn and the French actress, Lili Damita. He was born on May 31, 1941, inheriting the beauty of his two famous parents, who were notorious bisexuals. Errol seduced a roster of people whose combined total he estimated at around 14,000. They included the two richest women on earth: Doris Duke, the tobacco heiress, and Barbara Hutton, the Woolworth heiress. He even seduced America's first billionaire, Howard Hughes. The list would go on and on, taking in South America's most famous dictator, Evita Peron, as well as "the world's most beautiful man" (Tyrone Power) and "the world's most beautiful woman" (Hedy Lamarr). Lili's affairs ranged from Dolly Wilde (Oscar's niece "and the only Wilde who liked sleeping with women") to King Alfonso XIII of Spain.

Errol was hardly a model parent. Before Sean turned 15, his father was escorting him to brothels where he taught his son to share the same prostitute in the same bed at the same time of his own seduction. At one point Lili considered hauling her now-divorced husband into court when Sean broke down and confessed to her that his father was forcing sex upon him, and had once brutally raped him. Errol's lawyers, after a financial settlement, persuaded Lili to drop her case. A charge of

These two scantily clad beauties – French-born **Lila Damita** on the left, **Errol Flynn** on the right – embarked on one of Hollywood's most disastrous marriages of the 1930s. Errol had been attracted to her sensual beauty. But with a marriage license in the safe, he found out that she was a hot-tempered "Tiger Lil" as he called her. "She's too hot to handle," he told his male lover Tyrone Power.

These bisexual newlyweds did not practice fidelity in their marriage. "She essentially disliked men," Errol said, "and I essentially disliked women."

Both **Sean** (*on the left*) and **Errol** were each a photographer's delight. Errol taught his son what to do with one leg during a shoot. "It's sexier that way," Errol told his son. "Women know how to position a leg during a photo shoot. Men can learn from them."

Errol told Sean that he, Errol, was "the perfect specimen," the name of his 1937 movie, and that his son should work hard to develop a body that would "thrill the girls ... and the homosexuals too. Don't overlook them. The boys are among my biggest fans."

homosexual incest would surely have ruined Errol's film career.

Following in his father's footsteps as he grew older, Sean attempted a film career of his own, appearing as *The Son of Captain Blood* in 1962. Although handsome and striking in appearance, he lacked the magnetic screen charm of his father and eventually abandoned movies altogether for a career in photojournalism.

In southeast Asia he took reckless chances. Dana Stone claimed Sean "had a death wish as big as the English Channel." It took a lot of convincing to get Dana to ride on another Honda with him toward a Vietcong roadblock. But that is just what they did on that steamy hot April morning back in 1970.

Like the boomerang he's holding in his hand, **Sean** *(left)* was obsessed with the mythical reputation of his father. "I can never escape his heroic reputation," Sean told Lili Damita. "I can't even escape his infamy. The only way I can get back at him is to be more of a daredevil off the screen than he was on the camera."

Errol *(right)* faces a photographer's camera for the last time on October 12, 1959. After a life of dissipation, the gorgeous male beauty of the 1930s was preserved only on screen. One reporter described his face as if "a thin layer of spongy tissue had been inserted between skin and bone."

Perhaps thinking they were U.S. spies, the Vietcong captured them and held them prisoner, moving them from one jungle cage to another in the wake of U.S. bombings and the advance of American forces. The retreating soldiers eventually handed the two young men over to the Khmer Rouge, who did not believe in keeping prisoners.

Recently unearthed "new" evidence and eyewitness accounts have revealed the sad scenario of these two prisoners. To protest their brutal treatment and starvation diet, Dana refused to recognize the authority of the Khmer Rouge over him. For that rebellion, he was handcuffed and taken into an open field where he was beheaded with a sharp-bladed hoe as a means of saving ammunition.

Sean, who did not protest, was allowed to live because the Khmer Rouge was informed that he was an American movie star. Heng Pheng, a former Khmer Rouge pharmacist, has revealed to British journalists that Sean, after a few months of captivity, developed a severe case of malaria and was taken to a badly run and poorly staffed hospital. His condition worsened day by day.

The doctor in charge, according to Pheng, decided that they could do nothing for him. He injected him with three ampoules of Largactyl solution (an anti-psychotic sedative akin to Thorazine, at the time the drug of choice for the treatment of LSD overdoses) which sent him into severe shock and unconsciousness. While still alive, he was buried in an unmarked grave near the hospital sometime during June of 1971.

Lili herself paid vast sums of money to send search parties into the jungles of Cambodia looking for her son at war's end. Living in Palm Beach, she left a sample of her blood in a blood bank so that if Sean's remains were found after her death, DNA tests could identify him. She wanted his remains buried next to hers. His body was never recovered.

At the time of her death in the spring of 1994 in Palm Beach, she was suffering from Alzheimer's disease and did not remember her son or even her former life when she was a famous movie star—"and the toast of two continents."

"In Hollywood," wrote author Jeffrey Meyers, "Errol could ride into an enemy roadblock and survive; in Vietnam, Sean could not."

(photo, left) In 1958, best pal **Steve Cutter** *(left)* visited Havana during its pre-Castro heyday. Cutter was Sean's best pal in Palm Beach. The two young men engaged in a "rite of passage" in the 1950s – that is, they visited the degenerate bordellos of Havana where the staff advertised "there is no passion we can't satisfy."

The two men gambled away their traveling money at the casinos, then called home for more. Lila Damita sent more funds but refused a third request when Sean appealed yet again. Strapped for cash, Sean went to his favorite whorehouse and made a deal to round up tourists flying down from Florida. He promised to direct them to the *casa de putas* for "the best sex in Havana and the prettiest girls."

Son of Captain Blood

The original movie, **Captain Blood** (1935; *see poster, left*) was one of Errol's greatest hits, and has been shown for decades. While making the film, Errol carried on a torrid affair with actor Ross Alexander, who later committed suicide. "I never loved Lili, but I was truly in love with Ross," Errol told his close confidant Johnny Meyer, pimp for Howard Hughes.

In 1962, hoping to capitalize off Errol's reputation, filmmakers cast Sean in *The Son of Captain Blood. (See poster, right.)* Unlike its predecessor, the swashbuckling sequel was ridiculed as a commercial failure. Sean suffered terrible comparisons with his father's screen image.

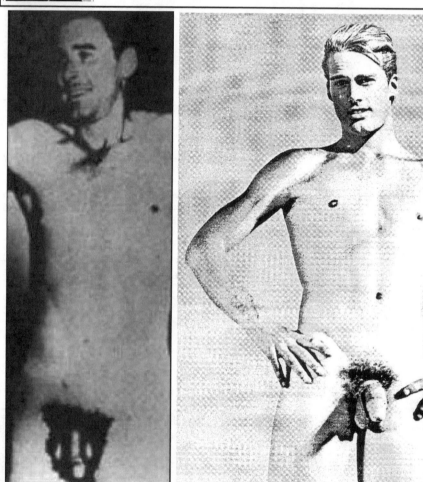

Father and son nudes. Errol *(above, left)* was not inhibited about stripping down – even on film sets. If anyone, regardless of gender, seemed curious about his genitalia he would often whip it out on set – but not before he'd manipulated it to grow an inch or two. He was rather vain about his cock. To anyone interested, he would reveal his biggest sexual secret: a bit of cocaine on the tip of his penis before penetration.

Sean *(above, right)* didn't totally follow the "wicked wicked ways" of his father, but he did strip down in Havana for a gay photographer who offered him a hundred dollars to pose for the nude shots. The offer for a role in a pornographic film, however, was refused. Later he explained the posing by saying, "Nobody wants to be on the streets of Havana without some *dinero."*

202

The Sad Story of *Cary Grant,*
His Troubled *Millionairess,*
and His Beloved *Lancelot*

Cary Grant, Barbara Hutton, and her son from another marriage, **Lancelot Reventlow**, enjoyed the dubious distinction of being the most dysfunctional family of the early 1940s.

Lance had been born on February 24, 1936, the by-product of a marriage for which Miss Hutton had renounced her citizenship to become the wife of a Danish count. It was a bitter marriage, leading to endless custody fights over Lance. But when Hutton divorced the count and later married Cary Grant, Lance at last found the "father" he'd been looking for. However in time, the new relationship with his movie star dad would become a hushed-up Hollywood scandal.

A terrified Lance is seen on the left. In October of 1939, a bodyguard, Bobby Sweeney, shielded his own face – not that of the three-year old - - as reporters stared into the limousine. Lance was later taken out of the car and put aboard the *Conte di Savoia* to sail across the Atlantic.

An Heiress, a Movie Star, & a Million-Dollar Baby

Lance Reventlow was born with a silver spoon in his mouth, in a London townhouse. His parents were Barbara Hutton and a sadistic Danish count, Court Heinrich Eberhard Erdman Georg Haugwitz-Reventlow.

His mother, America's most famous heiress, was receiving as much press as Adolf Hitler or Ernest Hemingway. She was the five-and-dime heiress to the Woolworth fortune, and in a decade she would spend $25 million. That would be the equivalent of $250,000,000 in today's currency.

After divorcing her count, Barbara married Cary Grant at Lake Arrowhead, California, on July 8, 1942, during one of the darkest years of World War II. News of the event immediately redefined them, after Eleanor and Franklin D. Roosevelt, as the most famous couple in America. Almost immediately, the press nick-named the couple "Cash 'n' Cary."

Lance was just six years old at the time his mother took another husband. Instead of resent-ing his stepfather, as many boys do in such cir-cumstances, it was "love at first sight" between Lance and the handsome actor.

Guests at Hutton's mansion were astonished to see Lance running to greet Cary when he returned from a hard day at the studio. The boy would plant a kiss on Cary's lips that "seemed to linger forever—much too long," in the opinion of one of Barbara's guests. He immediately wrote the count about this indiscretion, claiming that "I suspect something is going on here."

That opinion was reinforced when Cary would disappear upstairs with Lance for a long, leisurely bath that often stretched out for an

Fulfilling her pretensions to aristocracy, Woolworth heiress Barbara Hutton married Count Court Haugwitz-Reventlow in May of 1935. He would turn out to be the most sadistic and greedy of her many husbands, as he tried to steal her inherited fortune.

Headlines at the time of her marriage screamed THE PRINCE IS DEAD, LONG LIVE THE COUNT! The ref-erence to the so-called prince was to Barbara Hutton's ill-fated marriage to Prince Alexis Mdivani, an interna-tional hustler intent on marrying her for her money.

Her marriage to her new aristocrat, Count Reventlow, was marked by violence and humiliation. When in Paris at the Ritz Hotel, he raped her on the floor of their suite. In her diary, she later wrote, "When he finished with me he dragged me by the hair into the bathroom. 'You've always had an interest in scatology, Barbara. Now's your big change to experience it.' He forced me to sit in his lap while he excreted into the toilet. Then he locked me in the bathroom overnight."

hour or so. Barbara would be furious when Cary would not even show up for dinner to join her fellow guests.

By his seventh year, Lance was calling Cary "General," and demanding that his mother's seamstress sew the words, "Lance Grant," into all his clothing. Under Cary's protective wing, Lance blossomed, telling the General all his secrets.

In the summer of 1944, Lance was sent to New York to live in an apartment with his father. It was a time of dreadful loneliness for the boy, who claimed his father would beat him so severely that he couldn't walk for a day.

Back in Hollywood, Cary told Elsa Maxwell: "Strange how the little chap has gotten under my skin. When he's away from us, I can never get him out of my mind."

Under threat of brutal beatings, the count forced the boy to reveal the most intimate details going on in the Grant/Hutton household. Breaking down in tears, Lance confessed to his father that Cary had "touched me down there." The count was well aware of Cary's homosexual lifestyle, whose details were especially visible during the 1930s when Cary had openly lived with his gay lover, Randolph Scott. The couple had done little to conceal their romantic involvement with each other, even posing together for revealing pictures.

Infuriated, the count decided to take legal action. He was about to embark on what would become one of the most bitter custody battles in the history of café society.

In his dossier, the count charged that Cary had consistently used "foul language" around his son. Even more damaging, the count charged that Lance had told him that the movie star had "fondled my son in an inappropriate way." Reventlow lawyers talked the count out

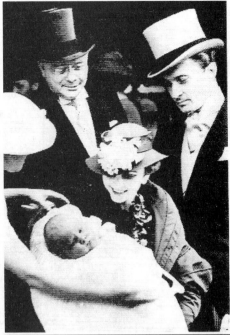

Hutton holds a fifteen-week old Lance in her arms as her top-hatted father *(left)* looks on and her husband, Count Reventlow *(right)*, seems to approve. A photographer caught this troubled family leaving their London townhouse for the boy's baptism in the Chapel of Marlborough. This was one of the more peaceful moments in their tumultuous relationship.

Marriage to the Danish count would not only cost Hutton her U.S. citizenship, but a $4 million bundle. Their divorce was said to have given England "its greatest sensations since King Edward VIII renounced the throne eighteen months ago for the love of Mrs. Wallis Warfield Simpson." Their divorce decree did not come through until March 6, 1941 since King Christian of Denmark had to sign it.

CASH & CARY, the press had called Cary Grant's marriage to Hutton on July 8, 1942. In spite of that label, Grant did not try to hustle money from his wife, the second richest woman in the world after tobacco heiress Doris Duke. In that, he differed substantially from her "prince" and her Danish count. However, in spite of his charming screen presence, Grant too had a history of physically abusing women, as related by his biographers.

Despite his marriage to Barbara Hutton, Grant *(right)* still loved handsome actor Randolph Scott *(left)*. Both Grant and Scott had previously lived together in domestic bliss on and off for almost a decade, yet throughout their co-habitation, each of them got involved sexually with the bisexual billionaire, Howard Hughes.

There were ill-fated involvements with women as well, including Grant's marriage to his first wife Virginia Cherrill. Grant's closeted homosexuality could not be written about openly during his lifetime because of libel laws. However, Grant appeared in Melville Shavelson's *roman à clef*, Lualda, as America's number one screen lover, Bart Howard. In the novel, Howard is a closeted homosexual and feels forced "to make love to women when the whole sex repulses him."

Jimmy Donahue, pictured dancing in the Sahara sand dunes in front of North African tribesman, was the flamboyantly gay cousin of Barbara Hutton. In fact, he became the symbol of the archetypal postwar playboy. The grandson of "Mr. Moneybags," Frank W. Woolworth, Jimmy loved to shock. In 1950, at the age of thirty-five, he courted the Duke and Duchess of Windsor and became the secret lover of both of those world-famed personages. Utterly indiscreet, he later said, "Going to bed with the Duchess was like going to bed with a very old sailor. And going to bed with His Majesty was an almost impossible feat. I had to search and search to even find his penis, much less make love to it."

of pressing that charge of child abuse, which would have made headlines around the world and possibly damaged Cary's stellar career for all time, as similar charges would have that effect upon Michael Jackson in the 90s. But the count demanded nonetheless that his son be prevented from speaking to Cary.

Fearful of a court ruling that could go against him, the count "kidnapped" his son and took him to Canada. Eventually, lawyers persuaded the count to drop his charges and return Lance to Barbara and Cary, providing the heiress parted with $500,000. Back in Hollywood, Cary confessed to Elsa Maxwell, "Lance is the only thing holding this marriage together."

Barbara was reunited with her son right before she launched divorce proceedings against Cary in 1945. Despite their breakup, the couple agreed to be friends, and Barbara asked Cary if he would continue his role as Lance's unofficial guardian. The actor readily agreed.

Lance discovered the world of Grand Prix motor racing at the age of 12, when Barbara, in 1947, married Prince Igor Troubetzkoy, who'd won the Targa Florio (a hysterical, haphazardly organized series of automobile races across the public roads of southern Italy) that year. From that moment on, car racing would dominate Lance's life until one day he suddenly abandoned it.

At the dawn of the 50s, Lance was growing up and becoming an attractive and sought-after young man. He stood six feet, had light brown hair, and an athletic build. Cary would often get angry at him if he chose to spend his weekends away from him.

One night, Jimmy Donahue, Barbara's notoriously gossipy and flamboyantly homosexual cousin, invited the teenage boy to dinner at his apartment. Opening the door to receive Lance,

Jimmy was attired in a long flowing gown, Joan Crawford stilettos, and super large falsies. Ushering the boy into his apartment, Jimmy introduced Lance to Francis Cardinal Spellman, who was irreverently known as "Nellie" Spellman within the Vatican.

Later, Lance would tell Cary that the gay cardinal had tried to seduce him. He also revealed a more serious charge, claiming that after the cardinal left, Jimmy had gotten him drunk and had held him down and raped him. Cary threatened to beat up Jimmy. He immediately confronted Barbara with the charge and was shocked by her reaction. "Oh, that's Jimmy," she said. "Ever since he was a kid, he's always been such a naughty boy."

While James Dean was filming *East of Eden*, a film released in 1955, Barbara asked her driver to take her to the late night bistro, Googie's, in Los Angeles. Here she encountered Dean, who walked right up to her. She was used to men clad in tuxedos, but seemed delighted to see this young man in his blue jeans and

On scooters far too small for them, Bruce Kessler *(left)* goes for a ride with his best friend, Lance Reventlow, who had blossomed into a handsome young man. Although he was later to marry two beautiful young women, Lance went through a sexually confused period during his teenage years and early 20s.

His mother, who had been surrounded by homosexuals all her life – and even ended up marrying some of them – was initially alarmed when she discovered a love letter Lance had written to her former husband, Cary Grant. "If Lance must be with a man," she told friends, "let it be Cary rather than some of those other hoodlums he hangs out with."

Looking serene in her gilded salon, Barbara Hutton had a one-night stand with – of all people – a struggling young actor: James Dean. Dean was a troubled, sexually confused young man, much like her own son. At the time of her brief fling with Dean, Hutton didn't even know who he was, much less the legend he would become.

From the very beginning, she suspected that he was a homosexual because he claimed that "the heightened moment, that intense experience of knowing that you are truly alive" can only be achieved "man to man." She seduced him anyway. He never came back for more, though she would have welcomed it. But he did become involved romantically with her son, Lance (right). Like Grant, Lance developed a severe crush on Dean. "I understand it," Hutton told her friends. "James Dean is easy to love." By then, she knew who James Dean was.

turtleneck sweater.

She shooed her bodyguard away and invited Dean to sit down with her. They talked for two hours until she agreed to be driven home on the back of his motorcycle. Outside the bistro, she dismissed her limousine for the night and went tearing off with Dean, holding onto him tightly.

The next day she reported the experience in her notebook. "It was late and he was drunk and I was drunk, so I asked him to stay. He removed his shirt and pants and climbed into bed, and I snuggled in next to him. We made love and then we made love again. It seemed the right and natural thing to do, although I couldn't help but wonder about his sexuality. He talked so fervently about men and adventure and masculinity. We talked and dozed and made love until long after the sun rose. In the morning he ordered black coffee and scrambled eggs and the waiter served it in the dining room. Then I watched as he climbed on his motorcycle and disappeared around the bend. Forever."

Lance was asleep in one of the bedrooms. Since he slept 11 hours every night, he did not meet Dean until a month later. His future friend had arrived, seduced his mother, and departed before Lance woke up. But James Dean definitely lay in Lance's future.

It is believed that they met at a rally for race car drivers somewhere in the desert between Los Angeles and Palm Springs.

Rogers Brackett, long-time older "patron" of Dean, was informed of the Lance/Dean meeting within ten days. Even though Dean knew that Brackett was madly in love with him, Dean still insisted on relating all the details of his affairs. "It was one of the most passionate man-on-man affairs in the history of Hollywood," Brackett said. "Jimmy himself confided in me that 'sparks flew' when he and Lance got together. He also told me that bedding Lance was the single greatest sexual high of his life. Of course, I, as an older man, felt very jealous. But I always knew I could never have exclusive rights to Jimmy."

Brackett claimed that Lance and Dean harbored none of the "happily ever after" concepts of love. "From the very beginning they were free to pursue other part-

The homosexual TV producer, Rogers Brackett *(pictured above, 1973)*, is often cited as the discoverer of James Dean. If not that, he was an early sponsor and helped launch Dean's career in acting. Dean was not physically attracted to Brackett, but easily submitted to his sexual demands while pursuing more passionate affairs with the likes of Marlon Brando and actor Nick Adams. Dean often delivered what he called "mercy fucks," notably to Tallulah Bankhead and Howard Hughes. Brackett later told biographers that he had a "father-son relationship with Jimmy – but it was incestuous."

More great news from
WOOLWORTHS

In the wake of the kidnapping of the Charles Lindberg baby, Hutton hired security guards and a nanny to protect her son wherever he went. Here he is pictured arriving in Palm Beach at the age of three. Almost monthly she received ominous notes from deranged people threatening to kidnap Lance and hold him for ransom. During her bitter custody battles with Count Reventlow, she faced the greatest kidnapping threat from her former husband.

ners, both male and female. But they saw each other at least three or four times a month."

Dean told Brackett that during one weekend in Palm Springs, Lance had sodomized him nine times.

On September 30, 1955, Lance became the last person to speak to Dean when they met by pre-arrangement on their way to an auto race in Salinas, California, where Lance had booked a hotel room for them. Dean and Lance pulled into Blackwell's Corner, a general store at the junction of Highway 33 and Route 466. They chatted for about fifteen minutes and made plans to have dinner together before Lance retired to their hotel room. It was the last time these two lovers would ever see each other. A few hours later Dean was killed when his Porsche 550 Spyder collided with another vehicle.

In the years that followed Dean's death, Barbara and her son had a violent argument that centered around Dean. Much to Lance's shock, his mother shouted at him: "I had him before you did!"

It was only at this point that Lance became aware that his mother knew about his affair with Dean.

Lance continued to devote most of his time and his $25 million inheritance to his passion for racing. He would often show up at events with Cary in tow, although the actor didn't show much interest in racing. Lance's win of Nassau's 1958 Governor's Cup Race—in a car he both designed and drove—established his credentials in the car-racing world.

Using a special fuel-injection system, Lance developed the Scarab, a low, shovel-nosed racer that could outrun Europe's long dominant Maseratis, Jaguars, and Ferraris. It was the Reventlow Scarab that eventually competed in the 252-mile Nassau Trophy race.

One night at a private dinner at the house of Cary's friend, the homosexual director, George Cukor, Cary seemed particularly troubled and burdened with guilt. Before the evening ended, he broke down and confessed to Cukor what was bothering him. He claimed that when Lance had turned fifteen, their father/stepson relationship

As predicted by virtually every Hollywood columnist, the marriage of "Cash & Cary" would not last. On February 15, 1945, they separated for the final time, although they would remain friends. In her divorce petition, she charged "grievous mental distress, suffering and anguish." She found his making of movies boring, and he detested her friends. But Cary loved his stepson, Lance, and would remain devoted to him until the young man's tragic death in 1972.

The saddest scene in the troubled life of Barbara Hutton was when she was shown this photograph. The single engine Cessna 206 crashed on a bleak mountainside outside Aspen, Colorado on July 24, 1972, taking her son's life. Her only child died far too early, at the age of thirty-six.

She later said, "He gave the greatest gift of all to the gods – an unfulfilled life. I wish I could have been a better mother to him. I will never smile again." She obsessed over his death for the rest of her life, and somehow blamed herself for his accidental death: "I bear more guilt for his death than the pilot of that plane." After that, she "walked a stairway to a dark gulf from which she never came back," claimed her still loyal friend, Cary Grant.

had become sexual.

The actor claimed that it was Lance who had come on to him. "I didn't want it to happen," Cary allegedly told Cukor. "But things got started and followed to their natural conclusion."

Cary admitted to Cukor that he had continued with the affair and "could not bring myself to end it." Apparently, the affair—on again, off again—continued until the day of Lance's death. "I've never been so completely satisfied sexually—except for Randy, of course," Cary told Cukor. Cary was referring to his long-time love, actor and heartthrob Randolph Scott.

Perhaps in an attempt to establish heterosexual credentials, Lance asked the beautiful Jill St. John to marry him. When she accepted, he planted a spectacular ring—set with 100 diamonds—on her finger.

The marriage took place in 1960 and lasted for three troubled years. Lance spent part of that time with Cary. Future partners lay in both of their futures. Today, St. John, who is said to have a genius I.Q., is married to Robert Wagner who wed her when he'd recovered from the mysterious death, off the coast of Catalina Island, of his wife Natalie Wood.

In 1962, Lance visited his mother at her mansion in Cuernavaca, Mexico. Jimmy Donahue was there. Lance was in a belligerent mood, wanting to confront Barbara with all her failures as a mother. He also found it offensive that she was shacked up with Lloyd Franklin, a man younger than Lance. Looking for his mother, Lance asked Donahue: "where's that drunken cunt of a mother of mine?"

Gossipy Donahue went directly to Barbara and told her what her son had said. That afternoon Barbara instructed her lawyers to cut off Lance "without a cent." That meant his trust fund as well. With almost no money, he sold his California home and bought a small place in Benedict Canyon. At that point, he was living apart from St. John; Cary told him that his wife was having an affair with Frank Sinatra. During this trouble time, Cary spent many a night just holding Lance in his arms to comfort him. As Cary later told Cukor, "It wasn't about sex—it was about love."

Lance recovered from his mother's belligerence and his break-up with St. John. He told friends, "Regardless of what happens to me, Cary is always there for me."

In 1964 Lance married Cheryl Holdridge, a member of TV's original Mickey Mouse Club in 1955. That marriage was also troubled, and Lance and Cheryl were estranged at the end of his life. Nevertheless, he left her his fortune.

In the last hour of his life, on July 24, 1972, Lance, who maintained a home in Aspen, set out with real estate brokers to

The wives of Lance: Hollywood insiders were shocked that Lance had married at all, because his home (dubbed "Camp Climax") became notorious for its orgies and daisy chains, both gay and straight. "Lance Reventlow invented the swinging jet set," claimed Louella Parsons. Jill St. John *(top)* was the first, followed by a final ill-fated marriage to Cheryl Holdridge *(center and lower photo)*.

Lance met the buxom Jill St. John – and her high IQ – shortly after he turned 21. The relationship ended in divorce. His second marriage was to Holdridge, a former Mouseketeer on the hit Walt Disney TV series. Lance, then twenty-eight, showered this ingénue with mink coats and diamonds, but told Grant that he suspected the young actress was "still in love with Elvis Presley."

CHERYL

examine a region of Colorado that seemed ripe for the construction of a ski resort. He was a passenger, not the pilot, of a Cessna 206. The actual pilot was an inexperienced 27-year-old student who flew into a blind canyon and stalled the aircraft. While trying to turn it around, the small plane plunged to the ground, killing Lance and other men aboard.

Cary later told friends, "It was the single darkest day of my life." He experienced something akin to a nervous breakdown, but pulled himself together to fly to Aspen for the memorial service which had been organized by his widow, Cheryl. The next few months were very hard on Cary who entered a deep, dark depression that he tried—rather successfully—to conceal. Close friends said he was almost suicidal.

"He was my son," Cary told friends. "Don't even use the word 'step' in my presence. I will love that boy until the day I die. If I've known any joy in my life, it is the hours, days, and weeks I have spent with Lance. Just the two of us. If there is a God, he got jealous of such a bond—and had to take Lance from me."

Hutton, shortly after divorcing Cary Grant

Barbara Hutton (left) was a doomed, tragic figure whom the press labeled, "Poor Little Rich Girl." Truman Capote called her, "The most incredible phenomenon of the century."

Her gold-plated life fueled the tabloids. In today's terms, she spend $250,000,000 in a decade on parties, clothing, furs, jewelry and hustling men – most of them homosexual. Descended from the "robber barons" of the 1890s, she was a weak, vulnerable woman who was haunted all her life by loneliness. Lance (center), like his lover James Dean, was a racecar driver. Hutton once predicted that her son would meet his death racing cars, but he fell from the skies instead.

Grant (right), like Hutton, also led a lonely life in spite of the fact that he was surrounded by the rich and famous and adored by millions. His glamorous facade was a mere front to hide the tortured, closeted homosexual who lived behind that shield. The most revelatory statement about him was made by the actor himself. "There was no such thing as a Cary Grant until I invented him."

Lance (far right) looks on mournfully as his mother gets a peck on the cheek from her new husband. Her wedding to the Dominican playboy, Porfirio Rubirosa (nicknamed "Rubi"), took place at three o'clock in the afternoon on December 30, 1953. Hutton looked regal with her upswept hairdo and diamond brooch, wearing a black taffeta dress with a school neckline – the design of Balenciaga.

She told the press that her son was "all in favor of the marriage," but he wasn't. Earlier that day, upon learning that Lance had homosexual tendencies, Rubi whispered to his stepson-to-be, "Go ahead, feel it." Forget about that small dick of Cary Grant. I've got one that stretches to the moon." In horror, Lance declined the offer.

At the time of Rubi's marriage to Hutton, he'd been involved in a torrid affair with Zsa Zsa Gabor. Wearing a black patch to cover a black eye she'd been given by Rubi before his upcoming marriage, Zsa Zsa held up a wedding picture of her estranged lover and the Woolworth heiress. She then publicly mocked the marriage.

At the time of her wedding, reporters asked Hutton what she thought of Zsa Zsa. "I'm terribly sorry," she said. "I don't know the lady. I read the remarks she made, but I have no comment." Rubi quickly responded, accusing Zsa Zsa of staging a publicity stunt. "Everything she says is fabricated." Actually, Zsa Zsa was telling the truth.

In her palace in Tangier, Hutton became known for her notorious parties. Dressed as Peter Pan in green velvet tights, Hutton is seen dancing with David Herbert, the second son of the Earl of Pembroke. Hutton had recovered for this party, after downing a bottle of vinegar the week before. Apparently she had discovered that her servants had stolen all her alcohol and sold it to tourists in the local bazaar.

She confided to Herbert that during her marriage to Grant, "neither of us wanted sex, but I liked having him around the house. He's a charming fellow." At the time this picture was taken, Hutton was taking gerovital shots, telling friends it was "the elixir of perpetual youth." She was also taking many painkillers and would soon become an addict, ingesting massive amounts of drugs to overcome her increasing tolerance.

The twilight of a tabloid goddess is bitterly evident in this shocking photograph of an aging heiress on her last legs.

Here she is seen in 1972 with the handsome Spanish matador, twenty-four year old Angel Teruel. Draped in a mink stole, Hutton was sixty years old when the photo was taken but her so-called friends cattily remarked that she looked eighty-five.

Hailed in Madrid as the greatest bullfighter since Dominguin, Teruel was known in Spain for killing bulls in the arena, and for being a bull at night with the ladies. Hutton fell for him and, although she hated the brutality of bullfighting, had a bodyguard carry her to a front row so she could watch her beloved. As she aged, she wore more and more diamonds to the corrida. Teruel would present her with the blood-soaked ear of the bull at the end of the fight. In return, she showered him with gifts such as a gold-and-diamond ring and a new Rolls-Royce.

Hutton was bitterly attacked in the Spanish press for "tempting our national hero of the ring by waving her ill-gotten Woolworth millions in his bedazzled eyes." She got the point and bid her lover *adios* before fleeing back to the horrors of Tangier. In Tangier, party guests and her own staff were systematically looting her treasures, and her bank accounts dropped precariously.

One of the world's richest women died bankrupt on May 11, 1979, at the age of sixty-six. There were only ten mourners at her funeral, which took place at the Woodlawn Memorial Cemetery in the Bronx. One obit claimed, "America's Gilded Age officially ended today with the death of its last standard-bearer, Miss Barbara Hutton. Peace at last for the troubled heiress."

Either thinly veiled or directly attributed, the notorious life of Barbara Hutton has been the subject of many novels, films, and biographies. The most controversial, and the one which catalyzed the greatest number of threatened lawsuits, was *Poor Little Rich Girl, The Life and Legend of Barbara Hutton* by C. David Heymann.

One of Heymann's more recent biographies discusses Caroline and John F. Kennedy Jr., and alleges that young John was bisexual.

The saga of Barbara Hutton reached its largest audience when Farrah Fawcett brought it to the screen in 1987. Called *Poor Little Rich Girl--The Barbara Hutton Story,* the film was a soapy and somewhat romanticized version of the life of one of the richest women in the history of America. It took great liberties with the facts of Ms. Hutton's life, defining her as a woman who had "vast wealth and seven husbands, but who never found lasting love."

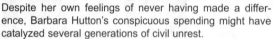

Despite her own feelings of never having made a difference, Barbara Hutton's conspicuous spending might have catalyzed several generations of civil unrest.

Above, waitresses at Woolworths staged an eight-day sit-down strike in 1937, singing, dancing, exercising, doing each other's hair and nails until finally management recognized their union and gave them a five-cent per hour pay hike.

The richest man in America, Howard Hughes, and one of its wealthiest women, Barbara Hutton, had a brief fling together in London in 1939 before she married Hughes's longtime lover, Cary Grant.

Hughes and Hutton weren't sexually compatible. "He could not bring me to orgasm," she wrote in her diary. "He sees that I have difficulty reaching orgasm, tries desperately to make me do so the first time, thereafter pleases himself and tells me I won't have one anyway. If I touch myself, he brushes my hand away with an angry snort. He can't take it when a woman loses herself in pleasure. Howard feels he has to be able to control a situation. When he doesn't, panic sets in."

A world very different from Barbara's: Staff portrait at Woolworths in Miami, Oklahoma, April 1957

Bette Davis
Off-Screen Murderess

As the conniving "witch, not a bitch," playing Regina Giddens in Lillian Hellman's *The Little Foxes* (1941), **Bette Davis** looks like she could murder anyone.

Tallulah Bankhead played Regina on Broadway, but lost the movie role to Bette. Later, confronting her at a party, Tallulah said, "So you're the woman who gets to play all my parts in the movies. And I play them so much better."

Whatever Happened to Bette's Mysterious 2nd Husband?

Bette Davis faced a murder investigation during the darkest days of World War II. Surely we're talking about on-screen Bette Davis, not the star in private life. Perhaps we're rehashing one of her famous movie plots, such as W. Somerset Maugham's *The Letter* from 1940. But in real (not reel) life, Bette came very close to being charged with the murder of her second husband, Arthur Farnsworth Jr. in 1943. Instead, under murky circumstances, she was never charged.

Some tantalizing background on this strange case came about during a series of interviews conducted with Jim Dougherty in the 1970s. Ostensibly, we were meeting with him to discuss his former wife, Norma Jean Baker, who went on to become Marilyn Monroe. But as a longtime officer of the Los Angeles Police Department, he had a lot of other tales to tell about Hollywood and its stars, including Miss Bette Davis. She had appeared with his former wife, Marilyn, in the memorable 1950 film, *All About Eve*.

Dougherty reported that on one slow afternoon as he was going through police files, he came upon a thick document labeled BETTE DAVIS. He said he read the complete file "for voyeuristic pleasure." The screen's greatest tragedienne at the time had been investigated on a charge of murder in the mysterious death of her second husband, Arthur Farnsworth Jr., whom she called "Farney." She'd met this handsome New Englander when she was on vacation at Peckett's Inn in Franconia, New Hampshire, where he was assistant manager.

She immediately became infatuated with him and invited Farney to come back with her to Hollywood, which he did. At the time, Bette was at the pinnacle of her career, making her most successful movies for Warner Brothers. Love bloomed and eventually, Miss Bette Davis, 31, married Farney, 33.

Cutting the wedding cake: **Bette Davis** and her new husband, New Englander **Arnold Farnsworth Jr.** (she called him "Farney"), were a vision of domestic bliss. But not for long.

The marriage started to unravel during their honeymoon. She married him on December 31, 1940, when he was a perfect male specimen, in robust good health. He died on August 25, 1943 under suspicious circumstances.

Like all of Bette's marriages, this one started to fail almost from the beginning. Farney had a lot of male charm which he turned on other ladies as he indulged in a number of secret affairs. Bette wasn't exactly the faithful wife either. She was also having affairs with actor John Garfield, her "chum" at the Hollywood Canteen, and with the director Vincent Sherman, who was to guide her through two of her most critically acclaimed films, *Old Acquaintance* in 1943 and *Mr. Skeffington* in 1944.

On the afternoon of August 23, 1943, Farney lunched with Bette's lawyer, Dudley Furse. After lunch, which ended at 2:30pm, he strolled down Hollywood Boulevard toward his car. In front of a cigar store, he suddenly screamed—"a blood curdler," reported an eyewitness. He fell backward onto the sidewalk with a dull thud, hitting his head. David Freedman, the owner of the cigar store, rushed to his aid, discovering Farney "bleeding profusely from both ears and nostrils." An ambulance was summoned.

In the hospital, Farney lived in a coma for two days until his heart gave out. The news of his death flashed around the world. From the very beginning, it had an unsettling air of mystery about it. How could a young man in apparent good health die so quickly? Of course, the public interest in Farney existed only because of his marriage to the woman who at the time was the world's most famous movie star.

A few days after his death, an inquest was called in front of a six-man grand jury. The autopsy surgeon, Dr. Homer Keyes, claimed that the fall on the sidewalk was not the cause of death. He charged that

Walter Winchell dubbed **Ann Sheridan** *(two photos, above))* as "The Oomph Girl," but **Ronald Reagan**, her co-star *(immediately above)*, later said that she had the "body of a skinny young man." In contrast, she found him "very, very cute" when they filmed *Juke Girl*--a truck farmer's version of *The Grapes of Wrath*. She provided him comfort during those long, cold nights shooting in the tomato fields of inland California.

Fortunately, Reagan's wife, Jane Wyman, never found out. She probably would have felt doubly betrayed, since she considered Ann her best friend.

At a Hollywood nightclub in 1941, **Bette and Farney** *(left)* seemed like a happy couple. But later that night, he accused her of having an affair with Errol Flynn, and she denounced him as a lush. Months later, she would discover that he was spending the money she earned at Warner Brothers on other, even more glamorous, women.

Farney had suffered an earlier blow on the head from "some unknown party."

Called to the witness stand, Bette appeared properly dressed in black mourning clothes, playing the grieving and heart broken widow, "a performance worthy of an Oscar" as she would later tell Sherman. She was questioned about a possible blow on Farney's head. In her testimony, she recalled that in June, about two months before, her husband descended the stairs in his stocking feet at her summer home, Butternut, in New Hampshire. She claimed that he fell, falling the full length of the stairs, landing on his head. "Although he complained of severe headaches for a day or two, he seemed to recover quickly and never consulted a doctor," she testified.

Dr. Keyes disputed Bette's story, charging that the blow to Farney's head with "some blunt instrument" had not occurred in June, but had been sustained "no more than two weeks" before his untimely death.

Dr. Keyes' report stated, "The blood in the fracture was black and coagulated, not merely purple and partially congealed as it would have been if the blow had been received only last Monday [i.e., from Farney's fall on Hollywood Boulevard]." The report went on to say, "After receiving some blow to his head [i.e., prior to his death], Farnsworth had been walking around ever since with the condition fructifying until it eventually caused his death."

A Dr. Moore, a personal friend of Bette's who also happened to be physician to both Farney and Bette, took the stand, confirming Bette's description of the fall on the stairwell. Ironically, he had no direct, firsthand knowledge of that alleged

Farney (*above*) was not as lonely as this photo suggests. He accused Ann Sheridan of betraying him with Ronald Reagan and charged his wife with having an affair with John Garfield at the Hollywood Canteen.

To get even with both of them, he launched a (not-so-secret) affair with that Southern belle, Miriam Hopkins, Bette's co-star in *Old Acquaintance* (1943) and her off-screen arch enemy.

fall and had not examined Farney since early January of that year. Nevertheless, the jury sided with Dr. Moore and Bette, rejecting the report of the autopsy surgeon. It was later revealed that the star-struck jury consisted of men who were ardent fans of the star.

Bette walked. Months later, perhaps over pillow talk, she told a startled Sherman that she made up the entire story. "It never happened." Sherman was not a man to keep secrets. He later reported that Bette told him a completely different story. She claimed that Farney had accompanied her to the train station where she was traveling alone to Mexico. It was later learned she was meeting Sherman there to continue their adulterous affair.

On board the train, Bette and Farney got into an argument over the exact purpose of the trip. She said the train started to move, and she couldn't get Farney to disembark. At that point she told Sherman that she pushed her husband off the platform. As the train left the station, she reported seeing him fall to the ground, but get up as he rubbed his head.

There was one major flaw in Bette's second story, according to detective Dougherty. Farney was in another part of Los Angeles that day consulting with a private attorney about bringing divorce action against Bette. Ignoring his own clandestine affairs, he had discovered her romance with Sherman.

In 1961, in a suite in a Chicago hotel, Bette came up with another version of what really happened to Farney. She was in Chicago appearing as the stage star of Tennessee Williams's

The Night of the Iguana. The playwright urged Bette, after she'd had a few drinks, to tell him the story of how Farney died. Also present at this late night social gathering were Frank Merlo (Tennessee's longtime companion) and Darwin Porter.

In her new version, Bette said that she came home early from the studio one day, having had to take off from shooting at Warner Brothers because of a "splitting headache." When she came into her living room, she heard sounds coming from her bedroom. Going to investigate, she opened the door, only to discover Farney deep into intercourse with some woman.

The object of Farney's affection turned out to be the original "Oomph girl," who, along with Bette, was also a top star at Warner Brothers and one of the most famous women in the world in the 1940s.

It was the actress, Ann Sheridan, in person.

Grabbing a sheet, Ann fled from the bedroom and raced toward her car parked near the garden. That left the temperamental Bette alone in the bedroom to confront Farney. She confessed that she picked up a wrought-iron lamp on a nearby nightstand and crashed it into "Farney's two-timing skull."

Death came to him ten days later, in front of the above-noted cigar store on Hollywood Boulevard. The third version of her story coincided with the findings of the autopsy general.

Tennessee asked Bette if she had any lingering guilt for delivering such a damaging blow to her husband's head. She denied having any remorse, primarily because she discovered after his death that Farney had been spending her money on expensive gifts for other women.

According to her, her only anxiety came when Farney's relatives obtained a legal order to exhume his body where she'd buried it in New Hampshire. "I thought they were going to demand another autopsy and reopen the case. As it turned out, they wanted Farney's body shipped back to their family vault in Rutland, Vermont."

Dougherty felt that the red stamp imbedded on Bette's secret police file said it all:

CASE CLOSED

Bette referred to the New England residence *(above, left)* which she shared with Farney as "The Barn" or "Butternut." It was here that she falsely stated that Farney's untimely death was based on an accident involving a fall on the house's stairs.

Locals, proud of Farney's New England origins, dedicated a plaque *(lower left)* to Farney. Cast in bronze, it referred to him as "the keeper of stray ladies," a title originally bestowed upon him by Bette.

In old age, a reporter asked Bette for some specific details about Farney's death. Her answer? **"No comment."**

Jim Dougherty *(above left)* as he looked on the day he married Norma Jean Baker, and **Dougherty** *(above right)* as he appeared after his retirement from the Los Angeles Police Department. It was during his employment as a police officer, and on a slow day, that he examined the file which the L.A. police department kept on Bette Davis.

Miss Bette Davis, the fading queen of Hollywood, confronts **Marilyn Monroe**, who was about to assume the throne in the months that followed her brief appearance in Bette's greatest film, *All About Eve,* released in 1950.

Bette interpreted the role of actress Margo Channing, modeling her performance on the real-life Tallulah Bankhead.

Marilyn, long since divorced from Dougherty (she had married him when she was only 16), played Miss Caswell, "a graduate of the Copacabana School of Dramatic Art."

Bette wasn't (immediately) jealous of Monroe. She later said, "Not Gary [Merrill], not Hugh Marlowe, not any one of the men in the cast thought she was attractive at all. And I told everybody, 'Wait. She's gonna make it.'"

Rolling His Stones
Getting Naked with Mick Jagger

Hip, hot, and irresistible, **Mick Jagger** may never have gotten "satisfaction," but not from lack of trying.

Jagger and his Rolling Stones have inspired both outrage and devotion, and they seem to continue forever, even if they do look like gnarled trees. A study in contradictions and contrasts, Jagger burst into the Sexy 60s like a firecracker going off. He was a sizzler both onstage and off, both in bed and out. From Rudolf Nureyev to Linda Ronstadt, from Keith Richards to Carly Simon, from Princess Margaret to Madonna, his friendships, feuds, affairs, rocky marriages and lovers titillated his fans. Jagger strutted and swaggered through the many chapters of an explosive life.

Mick Jagger Leaves No Stone Unturned

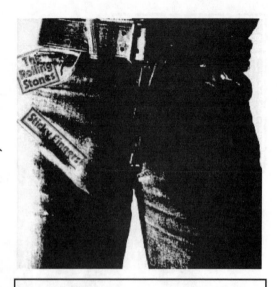

"There's really no reason to have women on tour unless they've got a job to do. The only other reason is to fuck."

Mick Jagger

"The fact is that Mick doesn't like women. He never has."

Christine Shrimpton, model

"Believe me, he's about as sexy as a pissing toad."

Truman Capote

"The Rolling Stones outlined an era and is still the best damn rock and roll band in the world!"

George Tremlett

"His cock's on the end of his nose. And a very small one at that. Huge balls. Small cock. Ask Marianne Faithfull."

Keith Richards,
referring to Mick Jagger

Mick Jagger was never shy about showing his basket. The singer, Etta James, once claimed she knew the reason for the bulge in the star's tight pants.

"It's padding," she claimed, after discovering him backstage. Allegedly his "wad" had slipped out of its position and was hanging down to his knees. He was feverishly trying to readjust his so-called "love bulge" before strutting on stage again.

Cecil Beaton, the British photographer and designer, claimed that **Jagger**'s mouth was "almost too large; he is beautiful and ugly, feminine and masculine – a rare phenomenon."

In a self-appraisal, Jagger himself said, "What really upsets people is that I'm a man – not a woman. I don't do anything more than a lot of girl dancers do, but they're accepted because it's a man's world."

High Testosterone

Abandoning the greasy "soul food" of his childhood, **Michael Jackson** *(above, right)* once became a vegetarian, claiming he wanted a body as lithe as **Mick Jagger**'s *(left)*.

But when he worked with Jagger later, he wasn't impressed. The two did a duet, "State of Shock," for Jackson's "Victory" album. "Froth on the beer," Jagger later complained to his friends about Jacko. "The kid's a lightweight, as limp as his handshake and as boring as a pussy that's already been worked over ten times." When he heard the recording, Jacko shot back with: "He can't sing. I don't get it. How could someone with absolutely no talent become a star?"

Rivaled only by Michael Jackson as the most controversial rock star of the 20th century, Mick Jagger is said to have led three lives—on stage, off stage, and in bed. His phenomenal fame derives mostly from the first and the last of those three categories. Swaggering and strutting, with occasionally sinister streaks of cynicism, he's one of the most recognizable figures in pop culture, even today, some 35 years since he took the world press by storm.

Is he a world-class seducer of women? Definitely yes to that one. A bisexual? Probably, though some of the evidence is inconclusive. Perhaps we'll have to dig up Rudolf Nureyev for a definite answer. Carly Simon and Linda Ronstadt surely could supply more details about his life as a womanizer.

The rocker's high-testosterone appeal to young men and women has always been strong. In the musical *Hair,* one of the attractive male actors asserted that he'd turn gay for Mick Jagger. His life has been permeated with scandal, high drama, and pure, unadulterated musical genius.

Jagger's naughtiness, particularly his involvement with Anita Pallenberg, has been back in the news again because of the March, 2007, re-release (on DVD) of *Performance,* in which Jagger's acting skills are notoriously featured. Shot in 1968, it was concealed within a bank vault until 1970, thanks to it having being judged as too pornographic for viewers at the time. Some of the 16mm footage of sex scenes were so explicit that the film-processing

At the height of his male beauty and with those "child-bearing lips" (in the words of Joan Rivers), **Jagger** mesmerized fans around the world. Eventually, he came to personify sex, drugs and rock 'n' roll.

When reports leaked out about his secret life, Jagger brushed aside anyone who might be shocked. "Obviously I'm no paragon of virtue."

Often seen under a hairnet in his dressing room, Jagger said he was "the son of an Avon lady who taught me all I know about fashion, hair care, and cosmetics. I could hire out as a beautician."

lab processing it at the time refused to develop it. Citing obscenitiy laws then in effect, a team of film developers destroyed key parts of the film with a hammer and chisel.

Eventually, accompanied by violent opposition, a test screening before a live California audience was scheduled for March, 1970. Many members of the audience walked out of the first preview screening and demanded their money back. In one well-publicized incident associated with the preview, the shocked wife of a Warner Brothers executive vomited after seeing the film.

Its featured actors included Jagger, Pallenberg, and James Fox.

By today's standards, the film seems a bit tame and relatively harmless. Its plotline involves Chas, a violently psychotic thug from East London, who needs a place to lie low after he commits a murder hit that should never have been executed. The thug's role was interpreted by Fox, who was actually the second choice of the film's director, who would have preferred the (then unavailable) Marlon Brando instead. Before rejecting the offer, Brando privately told friends, "If called upon, and only in the interest of art, I'll perform a 69 with Jagger any day. He can even climax in my mouth if he wants to, and I'll return the favor." Was Brando joking? He did like to put people on, but then again, we may never really know.

In the film, the character of Chas gets emotionally involved with Turner, portrayed by Jagger as a decadent, sexually ambiguous, over-the-hill rock star. In their reviews, critics questioned whether Jagger's performance, and the film itself, was intended to be biographical, or at least self-satirical.

The film contains many full-frontal nude portrayals of Jagger (see photos) putting to rest forever the long-standing question about whether or not he padded his crotch onstage. And before its ending, the onscreen character of Chas seems to eerily swap personalities with Turner after the lead characters share a hallucinogenic dose of magic mushrooms.

Although she's a virtually forgotten figure today, Anita Pallenberg is still remembered by

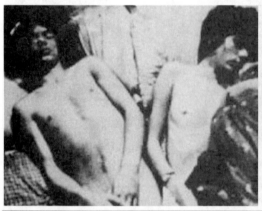 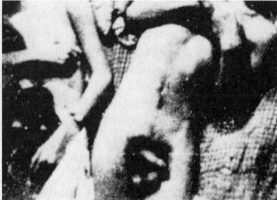 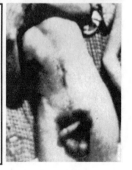

Stills from the notorious film, *Performance*, shot in 1968, starring **Mick Jagger** and **Anita Pallenberg**. It was the story of a hit man on the run who encounters a washed-up rock star (as played by Jagger himself). The hoodlum makes Jagger's character doubt his own heterosexuality.

Marlon Brando turned down the role of the hoodlum, which was subsequently awarded to James Fox. According to Donald Cammell, the movie's producer, Fox and Jagger had a "sort of romance, but they were such closet queens."

Jagger (upper left and on the left) was cast opposite Anita Pallenberg, who was the lover of Keith Richards and pregnant at the time with his child. After a day off for an abortion, she returned to the set.

The once notorious **Anita Pallenberg** (*above, far left*). The actress, model, and fashion designer admitted that she was stoned during the entire shoot of *Performance*.

In the world of rock 'n' roll, Pallenberg is a legend. Her romantic involvement with the Rolling Stones began with **Brian Jones** (*pictured with her in the center*) in 1965. She dumped him in 1967 and took up with **Keith Richards** (*she's pictured with Richards and his children on the far right*). She was Richards' common-law wife from 1967 to 1980.

During the filming of *Performance* she was alleged to have had an affair with Jagger himself, which seriously pissed off Richards. In her 70s heyday, Pallenberg was said to have been obsessed with black magic, and she carried a string of garlic with her everywhere to ward off vampires.

Rolling Stones fans as a pivotal associate and artistic collaborator during the sex-crazed 70s. Today, both Pallenberg and Jagger have become symbols of the era's decadence. With the recent release of *Performance* on DVD, new generations of viewers can see firsthand what all the fuss was about.

Pallenberg's off-screen interest in the Rolling Stones has always been the source of controversy. She had a torrid affair with Brian Jones in 1965. In 1967 she left Jones for Keith Richards, and is rumored to have had a brief affair with Jagger during the filming of *Performance* in 1968. Years later, in 2007, she strongly denied this final liaison during the release of film's DVD version.

Incidentally, she not only co-starred in *Performance*, but co-wrote the script. She may have based the character of Turner on Brian Jones. The scalding sex scenes between Jagger and Pallenberg were said to have infuriated Richards.

Pallenberg was the common law wife of Richards from 1967 until their parting in 1980. She is believed to have had an enormous influence over the Rolling Stones and their music during the late 60s and throughout the 70s.

Throughout her life Pallenberg seemed to develop a knack for generating scandalous headlines, some of which involved an arrest on a charge of heroin possession in Toronto in 1977. The charge was later dropped. In 1979, a 17-year-old boy, Scott Cantrell, from a location within Pallenberg's bed, shot himself in the head, with a gun owned by Richards, in the home she shared with Richards in South Salem, New York.

Pallenberg was rumored to have been involved romantically with the boy. Although she was arrested, in 1980, the death was ruled a suicide. Rumors still persist that Pallenberg and Cantrell were playing Russian roulette with the gun at the time of the teen's suicide. However, police later asserted that Pallenberg was not on the same floor of the house when Cantrell fired his fatal bullet.

Such Rolling Stones' songs as "Angie" and "You Got the Silver" were written for

Pallenberg. Today she has her own line of clothing, having evolved into a fashion designer in the 1990s.

She remains an icon in the history of rock 'n' roll, a beautiful woman with a mysterious past. The press called her a "dangerous, powerful personality." Some music critics still consider her "the sixth member of the Stones."

Movie fans remember her playing the Black Queen in *Barbarella* starring Jane Fonda (1968).

In the movie, Fonda is baffled by the Black Queen's advances. Pallenberg calls Fonda "my pretty pretty." The world was more innocent then about lesbianism in films. Duran Duran, whose name was taken from the mad scientist character in *Barbarella*, used the movie clip of Pallenberg as the Black Queen in their video for their 1985 hit, "Wild Boys."

During the early 70s, Jagger seemed to encourage rumors of bisexuality, and subtly played his role in *Performance* as a switch-hitter. Headlines at the time linked him, sexually, to both men and women. Most notable among the journalists who "Outed" him was respected author Christopher Andersen in *Jagger Unauthorized.*

Jagger, in fact, actually laid the groundwork for gender-bending, incarnating a style known as "Glitter Rock." David Bowie and Elton John cashed in on it, too. Suddenly, as if from out of nowhere, Jagger in a white Elvis-like jumpsuit slashed from its collar to his pubic hair appeared onstage in purple eye shadow with gold sparkles—and always with bulging genitalia inspired by Jagger's oft-expressed wish to look as if he had a perpetual erection.

In his biography of Jagger, Andersen leaves the suggestion that the rock star had affairs with each of his fellow Stones (including Brian Jones and Keith Richards), as well as with icons who included Andy Warhol, Rudolf Nureyev, Eric Clapton, and Allen Ginsberg. And also with virtually countless numbers of both male and female groupies.

According to Andersen, in the late 1960s, Jagger also had a fling with David Bowie. Bowie's girlfriend, Mary-Angela Barnett, caught the two men in bed together. Bowie, who would, in 1970, marry Angela, later claimed, "We were both laying the same bloke."

Jagger reportedly was also discovered naked and in bed with Eric Clapton by Marianne Faithful,

Film director Julien Temple revealed that **Jagger** *(above)* attempted to use an ancient Amazonian marriage ritual while filming scenes for *Fitzcarraldo* (1982).

"It involved putting bamboo over his male member and filling it with stinger bees so that the penis attained the size of the bamboo. Mick spent months in the jungle of Peru. He was going mad out there, I think."

A former U.S. supermodel, Janice Dickinson, had humiliated Jagger when she told TV chat hose Jonathan Ross: "Mick has a very small penis."

Tom Driberg, the British left-wing politician and MP, was the author of a notorious autobiography, *Ruling Passion*, which gave a racy account of his sexual behavior.

His sexual preferences often got him into trouble. The Kremlin was able to blackmail him into becoming a KGB agent – codenamed *Lepage* – after one blowjob too many in Moscow.

But, as one writer put it, "Few people really care whether or not he's a Russian spy. What we want to know is: Did he really seduce Mick Jagger?"

Jagger's girlfriend at the time. Reportedly, she claimed that she'd rather have found him in bed with a man than with another woman.

In further revelations, Andersen reported that Tom Driberg, a notorious member of the British parliament, had a three-way with Jagger and Allen Ginsberg. Apparently, the affair began one night when the trio was drinking together. Ginsberg admitted that "I had eyes for Jagger myself."

But it was Driberg who broke the ice by sitting down next to the rock star and placing his hand on the star's thigh, close to the strategic area. "Oh, my Mick," Driberg is alleged to have said, "what a big basket you have." If reports are to be believed, all three men ended up in bed together, a sexual romp later to be repeated on other occasions.

Jagger's seduction of women, including famous women, is far more impressive than seductions of their male counterparts. The list is long, highlights including Brigitte Bardot, Patti LaBelle, Madonna, Linda Ronstadt, Carly Simon, Uma Thurman, and Margaret Trudeau, wife of Canada's former prime minister.

His most surprising seduction was of Princess Margaret. The Princess, whose attraction to younger men was widely known, reportedly found Jagger a "magnetic animal."

Still in her 30s and still attractive when she met the rock star, she became intimate with him. They were seen dancing together. Even in public, she possessively put her hand on his knee. In spite of Queen Elizabeth's disapproval, the affair of Princess Margaret and Jagger further developed on the island of Mustique, one of the Grenadines in the Caribbean. Both of them had vacation homes there and were frequently seen together.

Jagger was born in 1943, in the middle of World War II. That he is still performing today makes him the Grandfather of rock 'n' roll.

Reportedly, he is still finding "Satisfaction."

This is not a police lineup, but three legends in a row: **Eric Clapton** *(above left)*, **David Bowie** *(center)* and **Allen Ginsberg** *(above right)*.

Jagger met the up-and-coming guitarist, Eric Clapton, before he formed the Yardbirds. It was a relationship that would grow even after both of them became superstars. There has been much speculation about how intimate they really were. Jagger may have created the gender-bending "Glitter Rock," but friend and rival Bowie cashed in on it. Both stars helped make bisexual chic outrageously popular.

After the American beat poet, Ginsberg, met Jagger at a party in Greenwich Village, he told friends, "I'm instantly smitten," an odd choice of words for Ginsberg.

  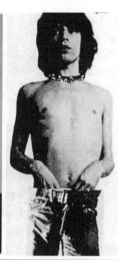

Keith Richards *(left-hand figure in left-hand photo, above)* was famously associated with the provocative T-shirt, WHO THE FUCK IS MICK JAGGER? during their 1975 "Tour of the Americas." Mick's stylist, **Piere Larocce**, wore the T-shirt on the same tour. The shirt is now something of a legend, and vintage ones are collector's items. Although **Jagger** *(upper right)* tried to maintain an androgynous appeal, the basket on display, real or fake, suggested only one thing—masculinity.

Princess Margaret *(center photo, above)* was "far too intelligent for her station in life," wrote Gore Vidal in his memoirs, *Point to Point Navigation*. He recalled a conversation with her in which she discussed her public notoriety. "It was inevitable," she said. "When there are two sisters and one is the Queen, who must be a source of honor and all that is good, while the other must be the focus of the most creative malice, the evil sister."

Margaret, although married, was attracted to younger men, including Jagger and, for a time, Marlon Brando. Both the princess and Jagger owned homes on the Grenadine island of Mustique in the Caribbean. According to locals, "there was a lot of traffic at night" between the two homes.

Billy the Kid
Howard Hughes's Toyboy

Forget Roy Rogers and Gene Autry, and let William S. Hart of the Silent Era continue decaying in his grave. "The Aviator" (also known as the billionaire playboy and movie producer, Howard Hughes) brought a new type of Billy the Kid to the screen with his notorious release of *The Outlaw* in 1943.

Hughes' kept the Dallas-born young stud **Jack Buetel** *(photo above)* under an iron-bound contract for much of the actor's working life. He also kept Buetel under virtual sexual bondage. "With that trim waist and those broad shoulders, Jack was what you wanted Santa Claus to bring you for Christmas," said the gay casting couch agent Henry Willson.

The Aviator
As Sexual Outlaw

Billionaire **Howard Hughes** *(above)* led a life of almost unprecedented debauchery – at least, for his era. In that pursuit, he had the collaboration of many dozens of A-list legends, men and women, including both Katharine Hepburn and Cary Grant.

The Aviator was the greatest Lothario of the 20th century, seducing an all-star roster of movie stars that was greater even than the one Marlene Dietrich compiled during her entertainment of U.S. troops in the field during World War II.

"Bossman was an equal opportunity seducer. The gender of the victim didn't matter. He had just one requirement. Beauty."

Howard Hughes's pimp, **Johnny Meyer**

Having hired publicist Russell Birdwell, Howard Hughes summoned him to his spooky mansion, Muirfield, at two o'clock one morning. The former publicist for *Gone With the Wind* had understood he was working for an eccentric billionaire, but the pay was good. His new boss had no regard for the time of day.

At Muirfield, Hughes instructed him to begin the search for an unknown to play the title role in his upcoming film, *Billy the Kid* (later retitled *The Outlaw*). Hughes informed him that he was going to make the first sex western.

"But Mr. Hughes, in westerns, men ride off into the sunset with their horses—not the girl."

"Not in this western. Billy the Kid will actually fuck Rio—that's the name of the gal."

"What kind of guy are you looking for? A Tyrone Power type? Errol Flynn? Certainly not Ronald Reagan?"

"I have one requirement. I want him to look like he's carrying a ten-inch cock between his legs when he walks," Hughes said. "And we're talking soft."

Three weeks later, Howard called Birdwell. "Call off the search for Billy the Kid. I found him last night in a bar. I'm signing him to a contract. He's from New England. Good fam-

Despite *The Outlaw's* weak plot and many shortcomings, big-busted **Jane Russell** was the "shill" that, it was hoped, would draw the American movie-going public into theaters. As studio publicists described it, *The Outlaw* was "Too Startling to Describe."

If only the public had known what was going on behind the scenes!

ily. A perfect physical specimen. Name of David Bacon. We'll keep the name. David to suggest Michelangelo's statue. And Bacon means pork—get it? A dude feeding a gal the pork as we say in Texas."

"I get it," Birdwell said. "Let me meet this stud. I'll go to work to create a bio for him."

"I want you to bill him as 'the handsomest man in Hollywood.' He may not be, but it'll set off a debate as to who's the prettiest boy in show business."

David was married at the time to Greta Keller, the Austrian chanteuse who in the 1930s was Hitler's favorite singer. It was rumored that they'd had an affair. When Joseph Goebbels found out that she was part Jewish, Greta fled to New York where she launched an affair with Greta Garbo. In lesbian circles they were known at the time as "the two Gretas."

Going to Hollywood, Greta launched another affair with screen vamp Pola Negri, eventually giving her up when she met David. "He aroused a latent motherly instinct in me," Greta later said.

After marriage, Greta had an understanding with David that he could carry on affairs with men, while she indulged her passion "for the girls," as she put it. At one time, one of those "girls" included Joan Crawford, who got Greta cast in a small part in *Reunion in France* (1942).

Hughes rented a bungalow in the Hollywood Hills where he and David spent days at a time. Greta estimated that the affair lasted three months before Hughes dumped David for Jack Buetel,

Howard Hughes (above) is pictured in his favorite post, in the proximity of an aircraft, one of which nearly took his life.

Some of the facts of that life are known to the general public – the filming of *Hell's Angels* with blonde goddess Jean Harlow, his transglobal flight, the bra he designed for Jane Russell, and the Senate investigation associated with his notoriously grandiose "Spruce Goose." But during his lifetime, most Americans knew little, if anything, of Hughes' phobically secretive private life.

New England blueblood **David Bacon** *(above, left),* once called the "handsomest man in Hollywood," became known to World War II audiences for his starring role in the Republic Pictures serial, *The Masked Marvel.* He became even more celebrated for his murder which occurred on September 12, 1943 in Venice, California. Was Hughes responsible for the death of his lover? Speculation continues to this day about one of the most notorious unsolved murders of the 20th century.

Bacon formed a famously lavender marriage to the Austria chanteuse, **Greta Keller** *(above, center, and above, right)* whose hit record, "Lili Marleen," became the most popular song of WWII, especially when sung by her rival, Marlene Dietrich. The song itself became misspelled as "Lili Marlene," not Marleen. Bacon and Ms. Keller had an arrangement: he was allowed to pursue his love affair with Howard Hughes, and she could continue her affairs with Joan Crawford and Pola Negri.

signing him for the part of Billy the Kid.

David's exclusive contract with Hughes, however, was still binding, and called for payment of a monthly stipend with the understanding that he was forbidden to look for work with another studio without the approval of Hughes. In effect, David had been locked into a binding exclusive contract and hung out on a clothesline to dry.

Furious, David came up with a blackmail scheme. He began to record, in writing, the details of his affair with Hughes.

"I urged David not to do it," Greta claimed. "But he sat at a typewriter and pounded out almost ten pages a day. I saw some of it. It was very pornographic. There was one very explicit scene where David described in graphic detail just how far Howard would go with him orally."

"My husband never actually planned to offer his manuscript to a publisher," Greta said. "Instead he wanted to show a typewritten copy to Howard Hughes. He said that he was going to demand that his former lover part with forty thousand dollars, which would give Hughes the rights to the manuscript. Of course, the belief was that Hughes would then burn it."

Through Noah Dietrich, whom David knew, he arranged for what was tantamount to a blackmail threat delivered directly to Howard. Subsequently, a meeting was arranged between Howard and David.

"I warned David that he was playing with dynamite, making threats to a man as powerful as Howard Hughes," Greta claimed. "But my husband was very stubborn and wouldn't listen. Three days later, he walked out of our house in a white bathing suit and claimed that he was going swimming at Santa Monica beach. I often knew he met his boyfriends there, but nothing was said about it between us. I knew that he was getting something outside the home that I couldn't give him. He didn't say for certain, but I believe he was meeting Hughes."

Four hours later, a maroon-colored British-made sports car—a gift to David from Howard—was seen moving along Washington Boulevard in Venice. It was a Sunday. The driver was manning the wheel like he'd had two bottles of whisky. Fortunately, there were no other cars on the road or else the car would surely have crashed in a head-on collision.

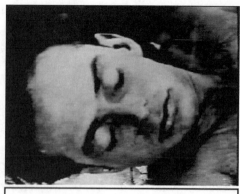

In this rare photograph, **David Bacon** is captured in death after a stiletto pierced his lung and he bled to death. Only an hour before his death, his possible assailant had taken a nude picture of him on the beach, indicating he must have known who killed him.

At the time of his death, Bacon had been writing a tell-all memoir about his affair with Hughes, which, according to Greta Keller, Bacon planned to use as a weapon of blackmail in the hopes that Hughes would make a big financial settlement on him.

Police Hunt Killer of 'Masked Marvel'

MRS. GRETA KELLER BACON, former Austrian singer and wife of David Bacon, is shown at home near collapse at news of her husband's slaying. Mrs. Bacon is an expectant mother.
—Los Angeles Examiner photo.

232

Suddenly, the driver slammed on the brakes of the small car and rolled to a stop, jumping the curb. Sheila Belkstein was walking her German shepherd that day and later reported what she'd seen to the police. "I was walking my dog near a field of cabbage. At the sound of brakes, I spun around. My dog barked hysterically. From the car emerged a man wearing only a pair of white bathing trunks which showed blood stains. Across the street was a gas station. The attendant there must have seen the man. He called the police, I learned later. I was a little afraid at first, and I was having a hard time restraining my dog. I moved toward the man. I'll always remember the sunken look of despair on his face. 'Help me!' he said in a very plaintive voice. 'Oh, God, please help me. Please help me!' That was all he managed to say. His eyes rolled back in his head, which seemed to loll to the side like it was separating from his body. Then he fell to the ground. A stiletto was lodged in his back."

A coroner later confirmed that the stiletto had pierced his lung, and that David had bled to death. A thorough examination of his body revealed no bruises, no signs of struggle. Police surmised that David had known his assailant, and that he had driven the car while hunched over the steering wheel.

For weeks to come, David Bacon's death was the talk of Hollywood. Several years later, the youngest-ever editor of *The Saturday Evening Post*, Cleveland Amory, listed the David Bacon murder among the Top Ten Unsolved Murders of the 20th Century.

Police discovered a leather wallet, soaked with blood, in the pocket of David's bathing trunks. The wallet contained one hundred and fifty dollars, which was remarkable for the time, as few men carried around so much money, especially as part of a visit to the beach. In the sports car, the police discovered a camera containing a roll of film. The roll was developed by the police. Only one picture had been taken. It depicted David standing happily on a beach completely nude, his white bathing trunks not shown anywhere within the frame. From this, police concluded that David knew the mystery man who stabbed him, and that he had actually posed

Agent Henry Willson met **Jack Buetel** (*right*) in a bar on Hollywood Boulevard where he picked him up.

After he'd paid the out-of-work budding actor for a night of sex, Willson promised this "physically perfect young man" that he'd help him break into films and introduce him to Howard Hughes. "You'd be ideal for the role of Billy the Kid," Willson told the handsome hunk.

Later, Buetel confided this to his roommate about Willson, "That fat queer is insatiable. Like a hog slurping at the trough."

A nighttime scene of **Hughes** (*pictured standing in the photo, left*) directing *The Outlaw* during the early days of World War II.

The hottest scenes were not with the film's star, **Jane Russell** (*right*), but were private semi-pornographic footage of Hughes shot with a partially naked Billy the Kid and a "hot Mexican enchilada from a whorehouse in Phoenix."

THE PICTURE THAT COULDN'T BE STOPPED!

Howard Hughes' GREAT NEW PICTURE

THE OUTLAW

In Person!

JANE RUSSELL

1943'S MOST *exciting* NEW SCREEN STAR

for his murderer. (The police reports used the word "man" when referring to the unknown murderer. Of course, his murderer could have been a woman, but no one at the time seemed to have raised that as a possibility.)

After the investigation, the nude photograph and the blood-stained wallet were returned to Greta Keller, although the case was never officially closed. Today, the wallet and the photograph are the property of author Darwin Porter, a gift to him from Greta Keller.

After David's death, Greta evolved into an internationally celebrated cabaret singer with a sophisticated coterie of devoted fans on both sides of the Atlantic. Movie audiences last heard her singing the song "Married" (*Heirat*) in the 1972 movie, *Cabaret*, which won eight Oscars that year but not for best picture.

Greta Keller died in Vienna in 1977, symbolizing a nostalgic, esoteric, and glamorous figure from a faded golden age. Until the end of her life, she maintained to anyone interested that she knew who stabbed her husband. "I can't prove it, but Howard Hughes murdered my David."

In the late autumn of 1940, insider Hollywood knew that David Bacon had been removed from the list of candidates hoping to play Billy the Kid, having lost the role to Jack Buetel, a devilishly handsome, lean but muscular, "walking streak of sex" with a slight leer and a cocky gait.

"He was a homosexual's wet dream," said his agent, Henry Willson, when this darkly good-looking stud was dressed in tight-fitting jeans and buckskins revealing his ample assets. "With that trim waist and those broad shoulders, he was what you wanted Santa Claus to bring you for Christmas. Regrettably, Jack was hopelessly straight. But not so straight he wouldn't drop his jeans for the right producer or agent. That was the limit of it, though. No fucking. And no reciprocation."

Henry Willson, Hughes's pimp, had picked Jack up one night at a bar on Hollywood

Austria-born **Greta Keller** *(left photo, above)* became legendary in Europe during the 1930s when she became Hitler's favorite chanteuse – that is, until Goebbels learned she was partially Jewish and sent out warrants for her arrest.

Marlene Dietrich copied her style and her famous voice. "I'm going to sing in my next picture," Marlene told Greta back in the early 1930s. "I have all your records."

After her death, Ms. Keller was honored in her hometown of Vienna with a plaque marking the building where she had lived. In 2007, a street was named after her.

Boulevard. Willson promised that he'd help "this physically perfect young man" break into films.

"If getting a blow-job from a guy, something I find a little bit repulsive, is the way to break into movies, then why not play the game?" the already street-smart Jack told Willson. "A guy who looks like me and bums around Hollywood Boulevard for several months either learns the ropes or is a fool."

Willson told Buetel that if Howard Hughes found him suitable in bed, and that if Buetel would submit to Hughes's sexual demands, the role of Billy the Kid would be his.

Within a week, Jack had become Hughes's new protégé, the equivalent of Faith Domergue on the female side. He signed Jack to an eight-year contract at $75 a week, $25 more per week than he'd later pay Jane Russell, who had been cast as Rio. "He kept a lid on Jack's salary all during the years he had him under contract," Willson later said. "It was a form of holding that dear boy under sexual bondage."

"When Jack put his name on that contract with Howard, it was like selling himself as a sexual slave to some Caliph of Baghdad centuries ago," Willson said. "Of course, Jack could have broken with Howard, especially when Howard did nothing for his career after *The Outlaw*, but he remained in bondage and did Howard's bidding until the very end of their relationship."

In a bizarre twist, Howard confessed to Jack one night that he believed by drinking his semen it was rejuvenating him. In an even more bizarre twist, Hughes began to prescribe a carefully controlled diet so that Jack's semen would "rejuvenate my dying cells." For some reason not known, Hughes focused on the pomegranate as his source of rejuvenation. Instead of eating pomegranates himself, he forced Jack to consume six a day, feeling that this fruit would make the young man's semen more enriched and ultimately more beneficial to him. He even selected the exact pomegranates that Jack would eat. "Here he was," Jack told Willson, "the busiest man on the planet spending time selecting just the ripest and juiciest of pomegranates for me. I hate pomegranates! I would have preferred an apple a day."

Throughout the rest of his life, until he died on June 27, 1989, he remained friends with Jane Russell, having drifted north to Portland, Oregon. Apparently, he never confided in her what was going on behind the scenes.

Jane Russell (*upper right photo above*) survived this notorious assemblage of stars associated with the filming of *The Outlaw* and went on to become a gospel singer.

Hughes never seduced her but fell passionately in love with **David Bacon** (*lower right*). That is, until he met that "walking streak of sex," **Jack Buetel** (*upper left*). Then it was lights out for Bacon and "hello, you big Texas stud."

Hughes himself (*lower left*) was also a big Texan stud.

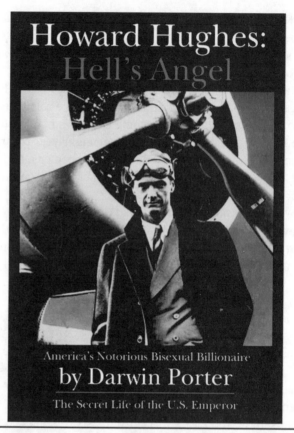

Schwarzenegger
The Last Action Hero

No American immigrant's tale is quite as extraordinary as that of **Arnold Schwarzenegger**, pictured on the left as a mighty warrior in one of his most famous roles as *Conan the Barbarian (1982)*. Had the laws of the U.S. Constitution been different, this young bodybuilder might have risen from the gyms of Germany and Austria to become President of the United States. As it is, he's had to settle for being the governor of the great state of California, even though he can't pronounce it.

On the long road to Sacramento, "*Ah-Nold*" became the greatest bodybuilder in history, and the number one movie star in the world. And despite his status as a Republican, he eventually married one of the princesses of the Kennedy clan.

Do These Photographs Represent the Next President of the United States?

America's "cockmania" reached its zenith with the publication of a spring issue of *Spy* Magazine in which there appeared a nude photograph of **Arnold Schwarzenegger**. As *The Bay Area Reporter* proclaimed: "Celebrity penis! What an immense and delectable scandal! More significant than the public frenzy over Arnold's penis is the reason the photo was run--as punishment." The suggestion was that Arnold had been manipulating the media too much, and the nude was a sort of pay-back."

"Arnold has been re-creating his biography and buying respectability by building a power-wielding publicity machine," the paper said. "He's been hiding his history and personal habits to promote an all-American image—he's denied, despite contrary evidence, both steroid use and homosexual hustling during his bodybuilding years and, tried to suppress photographs taken by gay millionaire playboy Paco Arce which showed Arnold in tight undies and ones in which he's smoking big phallic cigars. How does Spy humble him? By exposing the greatest shame of any red-blooded American: his penis."

In the late 1970s, when Arnold Schwarzenegger posed for this nude photograph (*with towel, left*) for *After Dark*, a gay-oriented New York City arts magazine, it set off a debate among crotch watchers. Was Arnold cut or uncut? The answer is, he's uncircumcized, but he had pulled his foreskin back for this controversial photograph, which later made the pages of *The National Enquirer* as part of an exposé.

"When Arnold posed for this photograph, he wasn't thinking of his future, but his present," said Warren Beatty, once rumored to be considering a bid against the bodybuilder for governor of California. "But all of us have done things in our past that we'd like to rewrite."

Reaction was swift when Governor Schwarzenegger referred to California Democrats as "girly men." Stating the case for the opposition was Matthrew Fraguela in *The New York Daily News.*

"Does Schwarzenegger realize that it is most emasculating to dye one's hair for fear of looking one's age? Why not go to grey, tough guy? Anyone who wears skivvies, oils his body and flexes his muscles in a room full of other men, while ogling himself in the mirror, is not too masculine either. Schwarzenegger is the epitome of vanity, of the metrosexual, and despite his bulging appearance, he has a puny bicep within his skull."

In another reaction, California State Senator Sheila Kuehl, a Democrat from Santa Monica, said, "It's really painful to hear the governor resort to such blatant homophobia. It's an old-fashioned way of talking about gay men as to indicate they're not as strong. It's like he can't get his way so he resorts to name-calling."

Eve Ensler, author of *The Vagina Monologues,* responded quickly when California governor Arnold Schwarzenegger attacked opposition members of the legislature in Sacramento, calling them "girly men."

Ensler, whose group hawks "Vagina Warrior" T-shirts, came up with an idea for a new souvenir to distribute. "I am all for girly men. I think we should get buttons that say, 'I'm a girly man and proud.' Because what is a girly man? A person who listens, a person who negotiates, a person who doesn't escalate violence."

Following in the footsteps of Burt Reynolds, Schwarzenegger also posed for a nude centerfold in a 1977 edition of *Cosmopolitan.* News vendors claimed that more gay men than women bought the mag.

When Arnold posed in his BVDs, gay collectors around the world elected him "male pinup of the year."

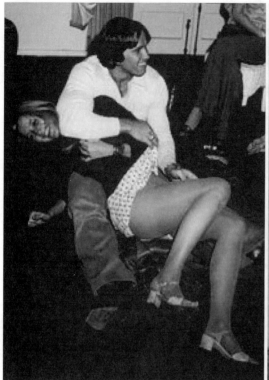

In the 1970s, Arnold was a barely articulate, pumped-up bodybuilder with a closet full of skeletons. He was also a wild man about town as pictured here at a party in 1977. At the time, he said "I am treated like a god by my sponsors but, then I am a god! They provide me with everything but, everything I desire—five hours of solid training, good food, sound sleep and, all the women I can handle—and that's a whole lot of women!"

Columnist Bob Herbert in *The New York Times* stated the case for the opposition: "He may once have admired Hitler for whatever reasons but, I'm sure if you asked Arnold Schwarzenegger whom he admires most, the honest answer would be *'Ah-nold!'* Welcome to the world of undiluted narcissism. The man has spent a lifetime pirouetting in front of cameras and mirrors, contemplating his navel and every other part of his once-buff bod. Adoration is the thing. In the mad, mad world of Hollywood stardom, the undiluted narcissist doesn't have to worry about what to say. Image is everything."

Heil, Ah-Nold!

As a young bodybuilder, Arnold didn't always keep his penis well concealed—even when posing with his genitals covered.

His past came back to haunt Arnold when he ran for governor of California. For most politicians, an exposé of past infidelities, marijuana use and, even an unknowing cameo in a gay porno would derail their run for office. But not in the case of *The Terminator*.

Before becoming governor, Arnold promised to be a "champion of women" if elected. "Yes, I have behaved badly sometimes," he admitted. "Wherever there is smoke, there is fire." Women came forward to testify that the action hero had made crude comments and advances; not to mention having run his big hands under their shirts or skirts to grab their privates.

"I have done some things that were not right, which I thought then was playing but now I recognize that I have offended people," he said. "Those people that I have offended, I want to say to them, I am deeply sorry about that –and I apologize."

Since becoming governor, Arnold isn't so touchy, feely anymore and, in fact, he has promised to keep his groping hands to himself. "I learned my lessons," he told members of the Hollywood Foreign Press Association. He admitted to no wrong-doing in his past but, claimed that "The world has changed so much that any kind of comment you make to a woman now, about her clothes or about this and that could be misinterpreted and open the door to a lawsuit."

ATTENTION
CROTCH WATCHERS

****

****

ARNOLD SCHWARZENEGGER

WHAT---NO JOCKSTRAP?

"THOSE OF YOU WHO INSIST THAT
THE NUDE PHOTO OF ARNOLD
IN *AFTER DARK* SHOWED HIM CUT
WILL WELCOME THIS PHOTO.
WITH OR WITHOUT
A FORESKIN, ARNOLD'S GLANS
IS CERTAINLY PROMINENT"

Photo and caption courtesy of author Chuck Thompson

THEN

"I'll be back!"

NOW

"Oh, my back!"

In 2004, Gov. Arnold Schwarzenegger of California said he would be interested in running for president if the U.S. Constitution were amended to allow foreign-born citizens to seek the nation's highest office.

"Yes, I'd run if possible. Why not? I mean, with my way of thinking, you always shoot for the top. But, first, I have to straighten out this mess in California."

"I still look back today on my incredible life's journey," said Arnold, "and I say to myself, 'How did all this happen? How did that become reality?' Only in America, or only in my beloved California. My life as a movie script would not be believed. Some director would reject it as improbable."

Daniel Radcliffe's Equus
Most of Harry Potter's Fans Denounced It as "Teenage Porn"

When **Daniel Radcliffe**, who rose to worldwide fame as the hero of the Harry Potter film series, appeared nude on the London stage in *Equus,* it set off a worldwide scandal, at least on the web. Some horny young girls found Radcliffe sexy; others attacked him for destroying the wholesome image of Harry Potter. Perhaps that's what Radcliffe wanted. As a young actor, he still has decades of work ahead of him, and perhaps he didn't want to be forever typecast as the pubescent teen, Harry Potter. Debate on the size of his penis raged around the world. The poor boy's dick was trivialized by some, but praised by others, especially gay male pedophiles.

Was there ever a fear on Radcliffe's part about getting a hard-on on stage? "It's the least arousing process," he claimed. "My girlfriend in the play is beautiful, but after you've gone through it a hundred times with an audience there...to be honest, when you get naked in front of 900 people, quite the opposite happens. I feel OK about my body," he said. "Not totally, of course, but no one my age does. But I've been going to the gym to make sure. And many of the actors I admire, like Gary Oldman, have gone naked--in his case, a lot."

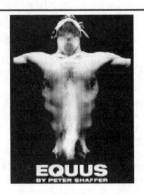

"Daniel, you're really, really, really hot! And I hate people who don't think you're hot!"

--Danya, young blogger

The producers of the newest version of *Equus,* which opened in February of 2007 at the Gielgud Theater in London, sure knew how to sell tickets. *Equus* is an abstract and difficult sell about a troubled young man who blinds horses. The novelty that sold tickets to this reprise of a play which was originally introduced in 1973 was the appeal of stripping the world famous star from those Harry Potter movies, Daniel Radcliffe, and sending him buck naked onto the stage. Tickets sold like hotcakes as theater audiences flocked to see how the then-17 year old was hung.

Radcliffe worked hard in the weeks before opening to tone his body, and defended his decision to appear nude. He insisted that his role in the revival of Peter Shaffer's thought-provoking play would be "rubbish," if he didn't appear *au naturel.* "I'm fine about appearing nude," Radcliffe said. "The nude scene is part of the play. I can't do it with my pants on. I had no particular qualms. There's nothing that would stop me getting my kit off if

Born in London on July 23, 1989, **Daniel Radcliffe** is now one of the world's most recognizable people. After his appearance on the London stage in *Equus*, he also has one of the world's most recognizable dicks.

Radcliffe says he tried to read the first Harry Potter adventure when he was eight, but was unable to finish it. It's ironic that he has now earned six million British pounds for portraying the main character of that novel, making him the second richest teenager in Britain. In terms of wealth, he's second only to Prince Harry, who reportedly controls 14 million pounds.

On making a Harry Potter film, Radcliffe said, *"I like them, but it's hard to concentrate when the bats fly about – they pee when they fly."*

On considering himself a heartthrob, he said, *"Personally, I can't see it, but if other people can, fine. Cool!"*

How did he deal with the paparazzi swarming outside the John Gielgud Theatre after *Equus*? *"I came up with a cunning ruse. I would wear the same outfit – a different t-shirt underneath, but I'd wear the same jacket and zip it up so they couldn't see what I was wearing underneath, and the same hat. So they could take pictures for six months, but it would look like [they'd all been taken on] the same day, so their photos became unpublishable. Which was hilarious, because there's nothing better than seeing paparazzi getting really frustrated."*

that's what the work demands. The key to serious acting involves losing your inhibitions, to become free and fearless." Posing for the explicit promos had giddy repercussions for Daniel. "When we did those pictures, I was tensing my muscles for about two hours – I almost fainted."

Radcliffe had starred in the first of the Harry Potter movies when he was eleven years old. As he passed puberty, he pleaded with his fans to accept that he was grown-up and had become a teenager with sexual desires. "I think people are shocked that I've had girlfriends, which I have. They think I'm a 'Peter Pan' figure, but I'm not – I promise you." The young actor's decision to go nude disappointed many of his fans. Blogger Kara asserted on her website, "I am disgusted at Radcliffe degrading himself. I thought he was going to be Britain's most inspiring young actor – not an underage porn star. Posing in the nude is not OK at his age. He isn't even good looking and doesn't even reach 5'7". Inflated ego?"

In his review of the play, Charles Spencer wrote, "I never thought I would find the diminutive (but perfectly formed) Radcliffe a sinister figure, but as Alan Strang, the play's teenaged antihero who undergoes psychotherapy after viciously blinding six horses, there are moments when he seems generally scary in his face and confusion. There are fleeting instants when you even detect a hint of Voldemort-like evil in his hooded eyes."

J.K. Rowling, the author of the Potter books, was said to have been angered with Radcliffe's decision "to defame the Harry Potter character by appearing nude. Complaining about his wilfulness, she said, "He knows my tactics and has apparently acquired some sort of protective amulet to block my spells."

Daniel Radcliffe *(left)* and his sidekicks from the Harry Potter series, Rupert Grint *(center)* and Emma Watson *(right)*. Die-hard fans of the series have watched all three of these actors advance relentlessly from pre-puberty to their late teens.

Rupert played the young wizard Ron Weasley, Potter's redheaded friend at Hogwarts School of Wizardry. He answered an open casting call to get the part, and his bank account reflects his success today.

Born in Paris, the daughter of two English lawyers, Emma began her involvement as an actress in the Harry Potter series when she was nine. Since then, her interpretation of the always-sensible Hermione has won her several awards and more than ten million pounds.

The nude sex scene in *Equus* between **Radcliffe and Joanna Christie** *(photos, above)* had all the media in a tizzy. Radcliffe and Christie beautifully captured the awkward tenderness of young love before the action moved into altogether darker territory. Radcliffe plays a young psychotic with a sexual and religious fixation on horses. Even worse, at the beginning of the play, he can't articulate anything except advertising jingles.

Theater critic Benedict Nightingale in *The Times* (of London) wrote: *OK, it was exactly what all that prurient hype promised. For his theatrical debut last night, 17-year-old Daniel Radcliffe was brave enough to perform the denouement of* EQUUS *without wearing so much as the specs that are his Potter insignia…. Radcliffe proves an assured actor and makes a perfectly able equimaniac."*

It was Daniel Radcliffe's penis – not necessarily the play – that captured the attention of bloggers around the world. The West End Whingers wrote: "And that scene! You have to wait until the last 15 minutes of the play for it – no leaving at the interval here. Our hearts went out to poor Danny boy as 900 pairs of eyes concentrated on one small area of the stage. As he dropped his drawers, the focus of the play became very different indeed. However sophisticated and mature the audience believed themselves to be, this was the big (or perhaps not) moment. All coughing stopped as one special cast member took the spotlight."

How Sirius Black (a.k.a. Gary Oldman) Taught Harry Potter to Get Naked

When he learned that he'd be showing the full monty onstage in London, Daniel Radcliffe admitted that he felt "extremely nervous baring it all onstage." He turned to a more experienced actor for advice.

"I was nervous and a little bit worried. I talked to Gary Oldman about it, because we got on very well and I know he's been naked onstage. I said to him, 'What's it like?' He said, 'On the first night you'll be terrified and on the second night you'll be terrified, and after that you won't care.' And that's absolutely true. When you've done it twice, it doesn't matter anymore."

Photos, right, show Oldman as Sirius Black in *The Prisoner of Azkaban,* as well as in a playful, more candid moment that would probably never have been included in any Harry Potter serial.

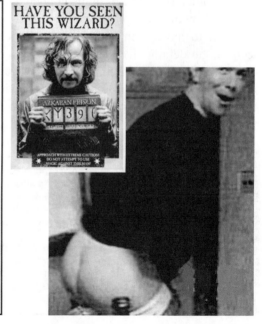

246

Tony Randall

Life in the Closet Isn't Funny

It seems that everyone **Tony Randall** worked with, from blonde bombshells Jayne Mansfield to Marilyn Monroe, from Jack Klugman to Rock Hudson, knew that Randall was gay. But in spite of his closeted private life, he could never admit that he was a homosexual.

Nonetheless, when he appeared in the situation comedy, *Mr. Peepers*, he had an affair with its star, Wally Cox. Cox took time out from servicing Marlon Brando to devote some time to Randall.

Cox was a foot fetishist. Years later, Randall confided to Hudson, "During the time I knew Wally, I had the cleanest feet in town – no toe jam when you're in bed with Wally."

Merv Griffin (of all people) also seduced Tony when they made the campy *Hello Down There* (1969), but it was a one-night stand. The two entertainers decided it was "better to remain sisters than lovers."

Secretly Gay Offscreen and Secretly Gay Onscreen, Too.

"*That Jack Parr was right. On nationwide TV he said 'What's ruining television are those big productions—the fairies who come in and sing with the big balloons. It's the fairies who are going to ruin television.' I myself always felt there are too many pansies on TV. Let's face it. The gay boys—I call them camera-swishes—are dictating what you see on TV. It's appalling. TV is going to pervert America's teenage boys to their perverse world. It's odd when you turn on the TV and don't see a limp wrist.*"

Tony Randall

Maybe reading more into the TV series than they should have, gay men felt that fussbudget Felix Unger in *The Odd Couple* was one of them. **Randall** (left) played the role like a prissy wife to **Jack Klugman's** more macho performance as a lovable slob.

"*The limpest wrist on television belongs to Tony himself. If they were the same size, he and J. Edgar Hoover could exchange gowns.*"

Rock Hudson

The only thing missing from the plot was that Felix and Oscar never actually maneuvered their way together into the sack..

A talented specialist in light comedy, the late Tony Randall was born on February 26, 1920, in Tulsa, Oklahoma, the same state from which emerged the homophobic orange juice queen, Anita Bryant.

He became a brilliant character actor, usually playing an articulate, obsessive, and well-meaning *schlub*. Postmortem (he died in 2004), he's best remembered for his interpretation of fussbudget Felix Unger in *The Odd Couple*, the small-screen adaptation of Neil Simon's play.

His greatest screen success came in 1959, when he played Doris Day's "unsuitable suitor" in that smash hit *Pillow Talk*. As seen today by more sophisticated audiences, Randall appears to be more interested in Rock Hudson, the film's co-star, than in the bouncy, chirpy, strong-willed blonde, as played by Doris.

Indeed, he was. Rock Hudson told his buddy George Nader and others that "Tony came on to me real strong. I think he fell in love with me one day when I was dressed in a bathing suit. The elastic of the athletic supporter inside the suit was loose. One of my balls fell out. Tony was entranced. Knowing how much he wanted it, I let him give me a blow-job. In fact, he gave me quite a few."

Hudson also revealed that Randall told him that he'd had an active gay past, particularly in the 40s and early 50s. He also said that "like Marilyn Monroe and her calendar shot, I've posed nude. But I never showed it erect. Only tasteful nudes. You know, the Greek ideal. Classical."

Universal was so delighted with the Day-Hudson-Randall *ménage à trois* that they re-teamed them in *Lover Come Back* (1961) and again in *Send Me No Flowers* (1964). That meant a lot more blow-jobs for Hudson.

In 1981-83, Randall did another series for TV called *Love, Sidney*. It was spun off from a telefilm in which his character is clearly gay. But TV suits "cleaned it up" for its weekly run into America's households.

One TV critic claimed that Randall always played it gay, most definitely as Felix Unger in *The Odd Couple*. "If Felix isn't a gay man, I don't know who is. Those prissy characters he played were a 1950s and 60s version of Edward Everett Horton or Franklin Pangborn, most definitely Clifton Webb. In fact, Randall was following in Webb's footsteps. Webb lusted after that beautiful Robert Wagner, and Randall went for that handsome hunk with the super-sized dick, Rock Hudson."

Perhaps as a means of concealing his own homosexuality, Randall gave a number of interviews on the subject of homosexuals, many of them decidedly homophobic. One such interview, bizarrely entitled "Evening Out the Odd Couple," was delivered to journalist David Johnson, who printed it in the September, 1972 issue of *After Dark*.

In the article, Randall described the time when he took a group of friends to what he described as "an all-male house in Los Angeles."

RANDALL: *"Oh, that was really bad, really bad. Just terrible. Just disgusting. But also not good. Oh, guys sucking each other's cocks. There's nothing to watch in that. It confirms something I've always suspected about homosexuality—they don't like it. These guys never got aroused. Whereas in today's modern straight porn, these kids really go at it. Yeah. Oh, it's awful to see great big guys . . . definitely not my bag. There's no such thing as homosexuality—it's just something invented by a bunch of fags."*

At this point in the interview, Randall broke into hysterical laughter, as if at his own wit. *"I believe that!"*

Pillow Talk in 1959 launched a surprising comedy team: **Rock Hudson, Doris Day**, and **Tony Randall**.

Randall, playing a thrice-married millionaire, pretended to want Doris to become wife number four, but gay men in the audience knew he was secretly in love with hunky Rock. The film and others like it inspired a new term in the Hollywood lexicon: **DFMs** ("Delayed Fuck Movies") where the sexually frustrated protagonists were strictly forbidden, usually by their own volition, from sleeping together until after their (inevitable upcoming) marriage.

Doris Day and **Rock Hudson** *(inset, left)* were pretend lovers on screen, and good friends off screen. She did much to secure his macho image in their screen comedies. Meanwhile, his notorious agent, Henry Willson, fought off homosexual exposés threatening to reveal that his primary bread winner was gay. No one played the standoffish perennial virgin with the daft hats better than Doris.

Author Armistead Maupin noted the irony of *Pillow Talk*: "Here was a gay man, Rock himself, impersonating a straight man impersonating a gay man."

249

In the same interview, Randall went on to claim that he had been bitterly attacked by homosexuals for an interview he gave in *Opera News*, which had expressed *"my attitude toward faggotry."* In the article, he complained about *"hordes"* of homosexuals who went to the opera to *"scream and squeal and support broken-down sopranos. They're a self-appointed claque. This is absolutely true. Same guys that follow Bette Davis movies and all that."*

When Rock Hudson was shown a copy of this rambling and disjointed interview, he remarked, "Tony is a very funny man, but this is about the most ridiculous piece of shit I've ever read. Homosexuals don't like getting it on? Tell that to millions of gay men around the world. I no longer think Tony is smart. From that throat does not emerge the wisdom of the ages. But he certainly opened up that throat to me. I'd rank him as one of the best cocksuckers of all time, even better than Liberace—and that's a high compliment indeed."

Rock went on to say, "Tony once told me that he was caught sucking off a teenage boy in a New York T-room—that's a toilet—but the cop let him off because he thought Tony 'was a riot' in *Pillow Talk*."

WAS TONY RANDALL ALL THAT FUNNY?

Here is what Tony Randall
considered his all-time favorite joke.

Q: How do you wash a genital?
A: The same way you wash a Jew.

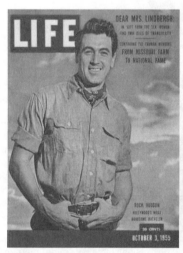

Magazine covers such as *Life (above, left)* did much to enforce **Rock Hudson**'s macho image--he was called "The Second Coming John Wayne."

During a beach scene in *Pillow Talk* with **Doris**, Rock was lying on the sand in his bathing trunks when one of the crew yelled, "Your balls are hanging out!" The scene called for Doris and Rock to kiss, but they laughed so hard that director Delbert Mann had to shoot twelve takes before Rock, his balls safely secured, got it right.

Gay Extortion

How Rock Hudson Coped With Blackmail from the Unscrupulous Lesbian He Married

"**A marriage made in hell**." That's what **Rock Hudson** told George Nader on the second day of his so-called "honeymoon," following his arranged marriage to **Phyllis Gates** on November 9, 1955.

The problems began with the wedding dress – while Rock insisted on "cocoa brown," Phyllis demanded white. Rock won out.

To dispel stories that Rock was a homosexual, Henry Willson, the mega-agent with whom the hunk was sleeping, forced him into this disastrous "shotgun wedding."

Getting a Piece of The Rock:

How Hudson Was Pushed Off the Casting Couch & Into a Lavender Marriage

In the 1950s fan magazines such as *Screen*, with **Ava Gardner** and **Rock** on the cover *(see above)*, were getting suspicious and asking, "Why Rock Hudson hasn't married." Of course, these articles were just for a gullible public; most screen writers knew that "The Rock" was gay. He gave out fake quotes, "If I think of Lana Turner, I can't go to sleep."

John Wayne saw it differently: "What a waste of a face on a queer. You know what I could have done with that face?"

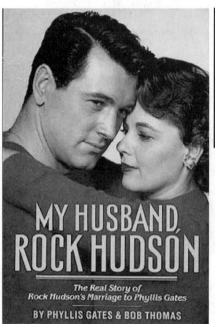

MY HUSBAND, ROCK HUDSON

The Real Story of Rock Hudson's Marriage to Phyllis Gates

BY PHYLLIS GATES & BOB THOMAS

"There is nothing true in this book," said friends of Rock's former wife, **Phyllis Gates**. She pretended to be shocked to find out that Rock was gay, when in fact she knew that and more all along. Exposed intimately to his secret, she eventually used it to blackmail him. Incidentally, she was also a lesbian.

"The Man Who Invented Rock Hudson," gay agent **Henry Willson** *(right)* got rid of the Roy Fitzgerald name and turned the hunk from an ungainly young man into an international star. For this reward, Rock became a virtual male prostitute, regularly satisfying most of Willson's sexual demands.

James Frey's so-called memoir, *A Million Little Pieces*, about drug addiction and alcoholism, became a national scandal and bestseller in spite of its infamy. Oprah Winfrey first promoted the book to millions of her fans, then turned on Frey, exposing him on TV as a fraud and a liar.

But fake memoirs are old hat to insider Hollywood. Bennett Cerf, publisher at Random House, once told Marlene Dietrich that in her memoirs she must have confused her own infamous life with the saintly days of Mother Teresa. Joan Crawford privately admitted that her self-serving 1962 *Portrait of Joan* "was only fodder for fans."

The world took little note in 2006 of the death of another fake memoirist, Phyllis Gates, who died of cancer at the age of 80 in Marina del Rey. On November 9, 1955, this beautiful "farm girl from Minnesota" married Rock Hudson, who at the time was the most popular movie star in the world. In 1985, he died of AIDS at the age of 59. Two years later, Gates wrote *My Husband, Rock Hudson*, portraying herself as an innocent victim who didn't know her husband was gay at the time of their marriage.

Ironically, in ways that were even more shocking than the AIDS-related death of Hudson himself, the innocent-faced Gates was a blackmailer and an extortionist, the memoir a lie. Her boss was Henry Willson, a notorious homosexual agent who ruled the male flesh market of 1950s Hollywood. Almost single-handedly, he created "Rock Hudson" (actually Roy Fitzgerald) as well as Guy Madison, Rory Calhoun, Tab Hunter, and various other good-looking heart-throb male stars. Willson paid Gates $50,000 of Hudson's money to enter into this sham of a marriage before scandal-mongering *Confidential* magazine exposed the handsome macho star as a homosexual.

Before working as a secretary for Willson, Gates was known in lesbian circles of the 1950s. She'd been the "girl toy" of the cross-dressing heiress, Joe Carstairs, whose grandfather had left her mega-millions in petroleum dollars he'd amassed alongside John D. Rockefeller.

After her divorce from Hudson in 1958, Gates became infuriated at the meager terms she'd agreed to, and eventually demanded more money—millions, in fact. She threatened to blackmail her former mate, demanding 75 percent of his future earnings. She warned him that "25 percent of something is better than nothing." She could have destroyed Hudson's burgeoning career.

Willson to the rescue. He presented Hudson's lawyers with a five-inch file on the nefarious blackmailing schemes Gates had attempted with some of her more famous lesbian friends, an activity that brought her to the attention of the FBI. "It was a Mexican standoff," one of Hudson's lawyers once told reporter Darwin Porter. "She had us, and we had her." Gates called off her blackmail threats, returning to a quiet life with her lesbian girlfriends—she referred to them as "my sewing circle."

As many a Hollywood star painfully knows, not all blackmailers look like a white-suited Sidney Greenstreet in an old Bogie film. Some of them, as in the case of Phyllis Gates, looked like she could have reigned as queen of a 1950s senior prom.

HENRY WILLSON'S "BOYS" ALL LINED UP IN A ROW. From left to right: **Guy Madison, Tab Hunter, Rory Calhoun**, and **Robert Wagner**.

With a sharp eye for male beauty, casting couch WIllson was a "sucker" for an attractive man. It is said that he, more than any other figure in Hollywood, defined the concept of the post-war male sex symbol, just as methodically as Hugh Hefner created the Playboy bunny. For Henry's boys, columnist Sidney Skolsky coined a new word – "Beefcake." Willson pretended he was straight, actually dating the president's daughter, Margaret Truman.

Pillow Talk

In a scene from *Pillow Talk* (1959), **Doris Day** and **Rock Hudson** played footsies with each other in their respective bathtubs, separated from one another with either a wall or with a split screen, depending on how you interpreted screen techologies at the time.

That was reel life. In real life, between marriages, Doris pursued other men. Notably, one of them was a failing young actor, Ronald Reagan. Romantic gossip at the time linked her to black men.

Hudson was sleeping around too, screwing the likes of stars who included Errol Flynn and Tyrone Power. "Just because it wiggles, you don't have to fuck it," cautioned Rock's close friend, Mark Miller.

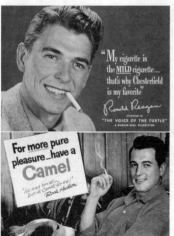

Rock *(left, top photo)*, chose **Mae West**, then 66, for the duet, "Baby It's Cold Outside," which they performed together at the 1958 Academy Awards ceremony. They never actually completed their rendition, since onstage she gave him the giggles. Backstage she told him that she thought all the sex queens in movie history, from Jean Harlow to Monroe, were "bullshit."

Left, center, and bottom, two cute guys, **Ronald Reagan** and **Rock Hudson**, try to give cancer to the American public. A very macho-looking Rock, smoking a Camel, had been drinking heavily and lost his six-pack abs.

Reagan eventually gave up smoking and Hollywood altogether, and went on, with his actress wife, to preside over the Free World.

Right photo: **The Rock**, Superstar

WAS THERE LIFE AFTER ROCK? For **Phyllis Gates** *(above left, and above right, with **Rock** "at home")*, there certainly was, in her case in the form of **Marlon (Joe) Carstairs** *(photo left below from the 1920s, photo right below from the 1960s)*, the ultra-eccentric Texas-born heiress who inherited part of the Standard Oil fortune.

Butch and brilliant, she ruled with a bemused but iron grip over her own private Bahamian island, Whale Cay, which she had converted from a wilderness into a flourishing, mostly self-reliant private fiefdom. Years after Marlene Dietrich had terminated an emotional involvement with her--it was noted by biographers as one of the most flamboyant lesbian affairs in the history of same-sex love--Joe invited Phyllis into her life as a companion and "kept woman," a relationship that endured for years.

More macho than most sailors, Carstairs documented scores of affairs with other women, including Dolly Wilde --the niece of Oscar--and a string of actresses, among them Tallulah Bankhead. "I was never a little girl," Carstairs declared. "I came out of the womb queer."

But despite Phyllis' prom queen good looks, Joe's true love, or at least obsession, was "Lord Tod Wadley," a 12" tall doll that's visible, despite the 40-year span in the chronology, in each of the photos below. At the time of her death at the age of 93, she was virtually never seen without it, having attached very personal fetishistic powers to it. As a friend observed, "Wadley was her religion." "I was never entirely honest to anyone," she confessed later in her life, "except to Wadley."

According to Kate Summerscale, Joe's biographer, when Wallis Warfield Simpson, the Duchess of Windsor first saw Wadley, she asked "Who is that?". Carstairs introduced her: "That's my boy, that's Wadley."

"My God!" said the Duchess, for whom her husband had abandoned the British throne: "He's just like my husband."

255

In Memory of Rock Hudson

At a reception at the White House, it was First Lady Nancy Reagan who first spotted an open sore on Rock Hudson's neck. He dismissed it as a minor infection. But it wasn't. In time, the world would learn that the big, strapping, sexy hunk of male flesh known as Rock Hudson, a former sailor and truck driver, had AIDS.

He was the first major celebrity known to have come down with the disease, which was thought at the time to attack "only limp-wristed fairies, junkies, and Haitians." The public was much more naïve in the 1980s. Many did not realize that macho he-men could also be gay.

Hudson was the first friend of the Reagans to contract the disease, and as such, it made the President painfully aware that it could strike anywhere. Up until then, in the words of Brigadier General John Hutton, the White House physician, Reagan believed that AIDS "was like measles and would go away." In an ill-conceived move, Hudson agreed to join his longtime friend, Doris Day, for the launch of her cable show, *Doris Day's Best Friends*. Because of her invitation, the world saw a shockingly diminished version of the Rock Hudson they thought they knew. No longer the macho beauty they knew from *Pillow Talk,* his image was broadcast virtually everywhere. It was *Variety* that first broke the news that Rock Hudson had Kaposi's sarcoma. Doris, regretting the invitation she'd extended, but with compassion and grief, said, "Rock shouldn't have come."

Flown to Paris for experimental treatment at the American Hospital there, Hudson finally issued a formal statement admitting that he was not only gay, but that he had full-blown AIDS. At the time, he hadn't yet informed his lover, Marc Christian. When authorities realized he didn't have long to live, Hudson was flown back to Los Angeles on a private chartered jet, where he died on October 2, 1985. One of his last public statements was, "I can at least know that my own misfortune has had a positive worth." Perhaps he meant that his association with the disease would give AIDS a face. However, it took two additional years before President Reagan would even acknowledge the existence of AIDS, much less provide funding for research. By then, AIDS was claiming the lives of both men and women, gay and straight, and children as well. In time, millions would die, and continue to do so.

After Hudson's death, since he had continued to have unprotected sex with his lover for a year after he knew he had contracted AIDS, Marc Christian sued his estate for $5 million. The jury awarded Christian $14.5 million--almost three times more than he had asked for. Soon thereafter, the Prudential Life Insurance company abandoned forever its long-standing advertising slogan, **GET A PIECE OF THE ROCK.**

Live Fast, Die Young

The Unexpected Links Among
Elvis, James Dean, & Johnny Reb

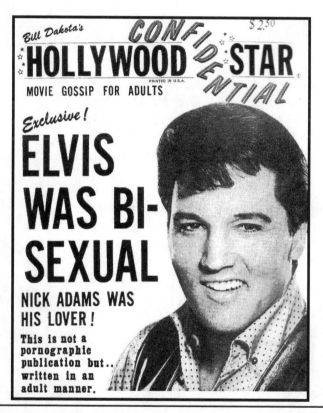

Elvis Presley was fascinated with James Dean and would endlessly watch *Rebel Without a Cause*. So when he got to Hollywood, he sought out and befriended a young actor, Nick Adams, who had been Dean's best friend.

After only a few weeks, Nick became best friend to Elvis, launching a troubled relationship that witnesses claimed turned sexual. Nick himself loudly proclaimed that he'd had affairs both with Dean and later with Elvis.

Their romance began when Elvis accepted an offer to be Nick's "date" for a preview of the film *The Last Wagon* (1956).

The Unexplained Death of Show-Biz Rebel, Nick Adams

"All of Hollywood knows Nick Adams was knocked off. It's hushed up—one of those things you dare not talk about because Hollywood likes to keep as many scandals from the public as possible. It's bad for business."

Forrest Tucker

"Movies were my life. You had to have an escape when you were living in a basement. I saw all the Cagney, Bogart, and Garfield pictures, the ones where a guy finally got a break. Odds against the world—that was my meat."

Nick Adams

Nick Adams *(three photos this page)* was known as a "star-fucker." His closest friends said he'd go to bed with any star – male or female – who might advance his career. Rock Hudson. John Ford. Natalie Wood. James Dean. Elvis Presley. It didn't matter to Nick as long as the fuckee was a star or possibly a director.

In the words of Albert Goldman, Nick was "forever selling himself: a property which, to hear him tell it, was nothing less than sensational – 'the greatest little actor to hit this town in years.' In fact, he had very little going for him in terms of looks or talent or professional experience. He was just another poor kid from the sticks who had grown up dreaming of the silver screen."

The handsome, blond-haired actor, Nick Adams, became the fourth member of the doomed young crew of *Rebel Without a Cause* who would die young and violently.

In death, he joined the actual stars: James Dean (died September 30, 1955), Sal Mineo (died February 12, 1976), and Natalie Wood (died November 29, 1981).

Born on July 10, 1931, in the gritty coal-mining town of Nanticoke Pennsylvania, actor Nick Adams (whose name at the time of his birth was Nicholas Aloysius Adamshock) was the son of Ukrainian immigrants. As a young man, he inherited his mother's anxiety that the breadwinner of the house would face doom one day in the mines.

But it was Nick's uncle, not his father, who was eventually trapped beneath a cascade of fallen rock. Rescued and hauled back to his house, there wasn't much the company doctor could do for him but let him die in peace. His uncle, on his death bed, patted Nick's head. "You're a fine lad and one day you'll be a good miner." Nick pulled away as his uncle drew his last breath. "No, I won't!" he protested. "I want to be a movie star like Bogart and Cagney."

Abandoning the mines after his brother's death, Nick's father moved to Jersey City, a suburb of New York City, where the family scraped by on $30 a month, the money earned by his work as a janitor in Audubon Park. Mired in poverty, Nick never forgot his dream of stardom.

Stealing money for his fare to New York, a teenage Nick escaped to the city one weekend. His parents didn't know where he had gone and feared the worst. He had some vague idea about wanting to be an actor. That dream came about when he'd read in the *New York Daily News* that heartthrob Guy Madison had hitchhiked to Hollywood and soonafter had been discovered by the movies.

Madison was currently making $2,000 a week. Nick

Nicholas Ray directed **James Dean** *(right-hand figure in photos above and below)* in *Rebel Without a Cause* (1955). Also appearing in the film were **Natalie Wood** *(left-hand figure in photo above)* and **Sal Mineo** *(left-hand figure in photo below)*. All three stars were destined to end their lives tragically and prematurely. Many reports claim that the concept "Live fast, die young, and leave a good-looking corpse" came from that film.

Actually, the phrase was uttered within the context of another Nicholas Ray film, *Knock on Any Door* (1949). It was said by Nick Romano, the character played by John Derek.

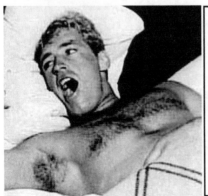

The well-established heartthrob **Guy Madison** *(left)* became one of Nick Adams' early Hollywood lovers. Guy's birth name was Robert Moseley.

His Hollywood career began when he took a train to Los Angeles for a 48-hour leave granted in San Diego by the U.S. Navy. He wandered into a movie theater where the gay agent, Henry Willson, spotted him and was immediately enthralled with the sailor's sunbleached hair and the way he fitted into his navy whites. "I'm a scout for David O. Selznick. You should be in the movies."

Years later, Willson proclaimed to his pre-eminent star, Rock Hudson: "Guy was a *Tom of Finland* fantasy drawing come to life."

decided that when the time came he, too, was going to hitch-hike his way to California. Little did he know that in just a few years he would become the lover of movie star Madison.

In New York, he sought out a bookstore where he hoped to find a used textbook on acting. As he was reading a Sean O'Casey play, an actor approached him and told him of an audition being held that day at Carnegie Hall. With no acting experience at all, Nick showed up at the audition, thick New Jersey street kid accent and all.

Sitting next to him was a rugged looking actor named Jack Palance, who was understudying for Marlon Brando in *A Streetcar Named Desire*. As they talked, the two men discovered that they both came from the Nanticoke region of Pennsylvania.

Palance introduced Nick to the director, but Nick was turned down for the part. Palance didn't give up so easily. He took Nick upstairs to a junior theater, The Interplayers, and convinced the director to cast him as Muff Potter in *Tom Sawyer*.

Nick had no money, but Palance invited the handsome young actor wannabee to dinner. Nick was already street smart at this point and knew what was going to happen later that night when Palance asked him back to his apartment.

Nick had never had sex with a man before, although he'd seduced at least three virgins back in New Jersey. He found the experience "strangely satisfying," as he later told his new *confidants* in Hollywood. "I still like girls, but I would soon learn that gay men are very attracted to what is hanging low between my legs." Palance was no exception, and the older actor fell in love with Nick and moved him into his apartment.

After a few weeks, Nick felt nothing was happening to advance his career in New York. Packing his clothes without telling Palance good-bye, he set out hitchhiking, with $80 in his pocket, on the long road to Hollywood. He survived by getting picked up by gay men who seduced him at night in cheap motels after buying his dinner. On his lone suitcase, he'd pasted the letters, HOLLYWOOD HERE I COME.

In time, Palance came to Hollywood to film *Panic in the Streets* (1950), but Nick was unable to get in touch with him. He was inspired, though, when he saw his former lover two years later score it big in *Sudden Fear* starring opposite an aging Joan Crawford.

Nick finally landed a two-day job in Griffith Park in a Coca-Cola commercial where he had to dance the jitterbug around a jukebox. He was given lunch and ten dollars for the job.

Few of his movie fans knew that veteran movie actor **Jack Palance** *(above)*, a product of the Lattimer Mines, in Pennsylvania, was a professional heavyweight boxer in the early 1940s. Fighting under the name of Jack Brazzo, the tough kid, who stood 6'4", won his first 15 fights.

During World War II he was wounded in combat, for which he received the Purple Heart. Even fewer of his fans knew that this tough guy was a closeted gay. Nick Adams soon found out. So did **Joan Crawford**, his costar in *Sudden Fear*. She said, "I never met a homosexual I didn't like until Palance came along."

Before Hollywood, Palance understudied Marlon Brando in the Broadway version of *A Streetcar Named Desire*. Palance agreed to teach the star how to box. He deliberately missed the punching bag, and his fist landed square on Brando's nose, a hit so vicious it put him in the hospital and altered his face for all time. Palance went on as Brando's understudy that night. He'd already alerted Hollywood agents that he'd be playing Stanley Kowalski that night. That appearance led to a contract with 20th Century Fox.

The "star" of the commercial was a young actor named James Dean. Meeting Dean for the first time, Nick bonded with him, even when Dean told him that for future jobs he had to go with him into the office of an assistant director, who wanted to give both boys a blow-job.

Somewhat reluctant, he trailed Dean into the office, where the two young actors chatted amicably while the much older man performed fellatio on each of them, going from one to the other and back again until they'd both climaxed. Zipping up, Dean and Nick headed out into the night. After a few drinks, Dean invited Nick back to his apartment where "he made love to me all night. When I woke up the next morning, Dean asked me to move in with him. I gladly accepted."

Dean urged Nick to join him "in hustling the queers along Santa Monica Boulevard." Again reluctant, Nick finally agreed. "A hungry boy has to do what a hungry boy has to do," he later said. Partly because of his large endowment, Nick became one of the most successful hustlers along the street, especially with size queens. Other men found Dean more appealing because of his devilish bad boy look.

Dean was much kinkier than Nick, who would not take some of the gigs offered. Dean volunteered for almost any job. At an all-male party, he performed an exhibition with "a Mandingo type" before 30 spectators. Dean also went with sadistic clients, some of whom turned him into a human ashtray. When he returned to join Nick in the apartment, his friend often had to treat his burns. Nick kept urging Dean "to give up all this weirdo shit," but Dean continued.

Although friends and occasional lovers when they had any energy still left, the two actors were very competitive. Nick read that the director of *See the Jaguar* was auditioning actors. He slipped out of the house to attend the audition, but when he arrived at the studio, he found that Dean had beaten him there, even though he'd left him sleeping in bed. Dean got the role, and Nick was rejected.

After endless struggles trying to break into the business, Nick was drafted into the Coast Guard in 1952. Some of his fellow servicemen were gay and were impressed with what they saw of Nick in the shower. Throughout his stint in the Coast Guard, "I didn't have to go hungry again," Nick later told friends. "Those guys took care of me, and I had all the sex and

Two famous directors, **John Ford** (*left*) and **Mervyn LeRoy** *(right),* were instrumental in the career of Nick Adams. Nick soon learned that the macho Ford was a closeted homosexual, something such actresses as Katharine Hepburn and Maureen O'Hara had discovered long before.

Nick learned that Ford had seduced John Wayne back in the late 1920s. Wayne still called him "Pappy" decades later. Nick later admitted "I virtually dangled my cock in front of LeRoy, but he just wasn't interested – a true ladies' man."

LeRoy's claim to fame today: He introduced Ronald Reagan to starlet Nancy Davis, privately telling the future president that Nancy, in spite of her prissy demeanor, "gives the best blow-jobs in Hollywood."

money I wanted."

When his ship docked in Long Beach for a 90-day leave in June of 1954, Nick headed for Hollywood, city of his broken dreams (at least so far). He'd read that John Ford was casting the film version of the hit Broadway play, *Mister Roberts*. Henry Fonda and James Cagney had already been cast in the leads.

In tight-fitting sailor whites that emphasized his endowment, he took the bus to Warner Brothers in Burbank. Casting director Solly Baiano met Nick and took him over to see John Ford. "The great director looked me up and down so closely I felt he was stripping my sailor pants right off of me," Nick later told Dean and others. Finally, Ford took off his eye patch and addressed producer Leland Hayward. "Spunky, little bastard, isn't he?" Ford asked.

Nick later claimed that Ford took him back into his office where "he French kissed me and felt my meat. He asked me if he could give me a blow-job. I said, 'Why not?'"

At that time, Ford was known as the most straight shooter among the directors of Hollywood. But since then, he has been outed by actress Maureen O'Hara and other biographers.

Ford cast Nick in the film but shortly thereafter, Ford abandoned the project after a fight with Henry Fonda. Ford was replaced by Mervyn LeRoy. "Although I gave him plenty of chances, LeRoy never made a pass at me," Nick said. "I think he was more into the Lana Turner type. Contrary to popular belief, not all directors in Hollywood are gay."

One day when Nick was doing his best impression of Cagney, the actor himself walked up behind Nick. When he realized who was behind him, Nick felt embarrassed and apologized profusely. Cagney seemed amused. "So, that's how I sound, kid?"

Far from being offended, Cagney was impressed with Nick and invited him to lunch where they bonded. Lunch evolved into dinner and drinks that night, which was so successful that Cagney offered Nick a weekend vacation in Palm Springs. Awed at being in the presence of one of his all-time favorite movie stars, Nick eagerly accepted, knowing what would be expected of him.

After seeing the picture of **Audie Murphy** (left), America's most lavishly decorated soldier of World War II, on the cover of *Life* Magazine, **James Cagney** (right) got in touch with the hero and invited him to come and live with him in Hollywood.

Cagney pretended to the press that it was just an act of patriotism on his part, but secretly he had seduction on his mind. The movie tough guy managed, after some initial protests, to seduce Murphy and promised him a movie contract. More seduction and more promises followed in the year to come.

Eventually Murphy moved out and slept in a gym at night, fed up with having to prostitute himself. He would later be discovered by Alan Ladd who gave him a small role in *Beyond Glory*. But as Murphy soon discovered, "I had to sing for my supper once again!"

"I figured something was up," Nick said. "The first night in Palm Springs, Cagney asked me to remove my underwear before getting into bed. At that point, I knew what was going to happen. My God, James Cagney gay? When he was giving me some of the best head of my life, I became convinced."

Over the years Nick liked to brag to his male friends about his sexual conquests with movie stars. "It was more than Cagney could handle," he later claimed. "Jimmy boy told me I was two or even three inches bigger than Audie Murphy."

The most decorated hero of World War II—and a movie star himself—Audie Murphy used to live at Cagney's house.

Back in Hollywood, Nick still couldn't believe what had happened to him. "John Ford and James Cagney gay?" he kept saying to himself. "If they are gay, then that means almost any director or star I meet might possibly be gay."

Because of his involvement with Palance, Cagney, and Ford, Nick decided that as soon as he got out of the Coast Guard, he'd abandon ten-buck tricks forever.

"No more showing off my meat on Santa Monica Boulevard," he vowed. "I still want to be a movie star, but I plan to support myself in another way. Before I become a big-time movie star, I'll become known as the biggest star-fucker in Hollywood. Man or woman, it doesn't matter to me. If they are a star, they can put their shoes under my bed any time."

True to his intentions, when his military service was over, Nick returned to Hollywood and Dean, who got him a small part in *Rebel Without a Cause* (1955). Nick seduced Dean as well as the other stars of the picture, Sal Mineo ("an easy conquest") and Natalie Wood.

Nick had been the man to whom Natalie had surrendered her virginity when she turned fourteen. He always told his friends that it was Natalie's mother who'd asked him to "deflower my daughter—she needs to be taught the ways of the world. I trust you to do it more than some of the men hovering around Natalie like bees around a flower."

In the watershed year of 1955, **Elizabeth Taylor** befriended **James Dean** on the set of *Giant*. She was already a friend of Rock Hudson, the star of the film. Rock, Dean and another of her friends, Montgomery Clift, were each closeted homosexuals.

For years, she refused to discuss the sexuality of these actors. Finally, however, in 1977, she revealed, "The men that I knew – Monty and Jimmy and Rock – if anything, I helped them get out of the closet." Dame Elizabeth gave herself too much credit. With the exception of Rock, when he was dying of AIDS, these men never really came out of the closet.

After completing his role in *Giant* (1956) with Rock Hudson and Elizabeth Taylor, Dean died tragically in a car accident. Director George Stevens had Nick dub Dean's voice in one drunken scene where the actor's words were inaudible.

After doing that, Nick plunged into a dark, moody period, driving too fast, as if trying to kill himself as his friend had done. In one year alone, the police of Los Angeles arrested him nine times on traffic violations.

A close bond between **Elvis** and **Nick Adams** was established on the first night they met. Nick told Natalie Wood, "Elvis is going to replace Jimmy in my life."

Right from the beginning, Nick offered his services to Elvis: Friendship, a guide to "Inside Hollywood," a bosom companion, a homosexual lover. "Whatever it is you want, I've got it ... and plenty of it," Nick told Elvis. "If you want to meet movie stars, I know them. Want to fuck Natalie Wood? I can set that up." And so he did.

When Elvis, a closeted bisexual, arrived in Hollywood in 1956 to make *Love Me Tender*, the mega-star fell in love with his co-star Debra Paget. She gave him his blue suede shoes and told him to keep on walking. Lonely and depressed in California, and having been told that James Dean had been Nick's best friend, Elvis contacted Nick, telling him that James Dean had been his all-time favorite actor. He'd seen *Rebel Without a Cause* an astonishing 44 times. Elvis had also memorized all of Dean's lines in the film.

Elvis wanted to "hang" with Nick, and asked him to show him Hollywood. Partly because he hadn't really found anyone to replace Dean in his life, Nick readily agreed. When Elvis and Nick met, "the chemistry exploded" between them and an instant friendship developed.

Within a week, as Nick later told another lover, Sal Mineo, Nick and Elvis were sleeping together. Elvis preferred oral sex and mutual masturbation. Penetration, apparently, was never an option between them.

In those days Elvis could drive his white Cadillac all over Los Angeles with Nick beside him. There was never any fear of molestation from fans. Fan magazines of that era were quick to pick up on this new friendship. However, they misinterpreted its real purpose and accused Nick of riding on Elvis' coat-tails to promote his own career. (Previously, the same accusations had been leveled about Nick when he developed his friendship with Dean.)

Nick took Elvis to the same places he'd frequented with Dean, including the old Villa Capri when it was on McCadden Place. They were seen dining frequently at Googie's Restaurant on Sunset Boulevard. Elvis wanted to know what foods Dean had liked, and he asked for the same dishes.

When Elvis had to return to Graceland, he left Nick an airplane ticket. To avoid suspicion, Nick flew to Tennessee two days later, telling friends that he was going to New York to seek work on the stage.

Sometimes at Graceland, Elvis would have a lover's quarrel with Nick, and Nick would be forced to sleep with Vester Presley, Elvis's uncle.

A tabloid ran a story that Nick and Elvis shared the same bed at Graceland. When that news broke, Elvis—ever sensitive to charges of homosexuality—

When Elvis moved into **Graceland** *(above)*, it was a relatively isolated spot that occupied a country-comfortable spread of 14 acres. But as Elvis's fame, and Memphis' population, grew, Graceland's perimeter was eventually surrounded by shopping malls, supermarkets, souvenir shops, and record stores.

Before his death, Elvis said that living in the building was "almost like living in New York's Times Square. I'm real proud of my Graceland. I'll never leave. I got a lot of decorating ideas, including a wonderful idea to make the ceiling of my bedroom all velvet. I like bright colors like orange, red and yellow – they look real nice. I only feel at home in Graceland."

Nick Adams *(right)* "deflowered" **Natalie Wood** *(center)* at the request of her mother, after which the actor invited **Elvis** *(left)* to "sample the wares."

Elvis' involvement with Wood was brief – mainly because of his mother, Gladys. When Elvis brought Wood to Graceland, Gladys "hated the bitch on sight." One night, a drunken Gladys confronted Wood in her bedroom, claiming, "You're latching onto my son because you're after his money. You're nothing but a goddamn gold-digger, and if it's the last thing I do I'm gonna see that you don't get into my boy's pants."

264

ordered that a cot be put in his bedroom. He told friends that Nick slept on the cot and not in the same bed with him, which—according to the hired help—was not true. A maid later told the press that the covers on that cot were never turned down the mornings after Nick slept over with Elvis.

Late at night, Elvis and Nick could be seen on the streets of Memphis, riding their twin Harley Davidson motorcycles.

Elvis's girlfriend, June Juanico, claimed that when she dated Elvis all he ever did was talk about Nick Adams.

To legitimatize their relationship, Elvis hired Nick to accompany him on cross-country tours. Nick came out first to warm up the audience by doing his impressions of the famous actors he'd learned to mimic as a kid, notably Cagney and Bogart. Elvis warned Nick not to allow them to get trapped alone together by a photographer. Elvis always insisted that he be photographed with some pretty young girl in the picture, most often a fan. On several occasions that pretty little girl was Natalie Wood herself.

In the hotel suites they co-inhabited during their tours, Elvis also insisted that Nick walk around in a pair of tight-fitting white jockey shorts, arranged so that his pubic hairs would peep out. He confessed to Nick that this was his ultimate turn-on.

"Elvis was into oral sex and enjoyed getting a blow-job more than intercourse," Dennis Miller, a former friend and companion, confirmed. Nick later claimed that when Elvis was watching astronauts land on the moon, he was "getting head" from Nick. Nick would later boast to such lovers as Rock Hudson or Guy Madison that "Elvis claims I give the best head in Hollywood. What Elvis doesn't know is that some women claim I do too, especially Natalie."

Whenever he flew to Graceland, Nick brought a stash of pornography given to him by Hudson. On a daily basis, handsome, well-endowed young men across America mailed nudes or pornographic pictures of themselves to Hudson, hoping to entice the star to call them for a date. Nick later claimed that he and Elvis would often masturbate while looking at the most enticing pictures.

Pictures of **Elvis** *(second from left)* in his jockey shorts – taken when he was being inducted into the Army – made the underground rounds of his fans (especially his homosexual ones) in the 1950s. They were coveted collectors' items, in spite of Elvis' avowed "hatred" of gay men.

In the Army, Elvis was mercilessly kidded and called a stripper. His coworkers begged him to do "bumps and grinds" for them. These soldiers had a point, as Elvis had borrowed some of the moves from burlesque dancers, including his former lover, Tempest Storm.

"He would shoot out his legs in a series of hot shots that were the pimp-walkin' daddy's equivalent of a bump," wrote biographer Albert Goldman. "But his erotic pantomime suggested not so much the coitus of the burlesque dancer or the masturbation of the go-go girl so much as the aggressive and brutal motions of rape."

Although he was straight, actor **Robert Conrad** *(left)* thrilled the gay heart of Nick Adams. Adams befriended Conrad and offered to help him break into the movies. Today Conrad is best remembered by an older public for his starring role as James West in *The Wild Wild West* (1964).

As regards his friendship with Elvis, Conrad never publicly commented on it. However, in 1961 he told *Photoplay,* "I think there are men who need many women in order to bolster their egos – half the time, they don't remember the girl's name afterward. But I've got a good ego to start with, and I'm too sensitive for a quick relationship with a dame – and sex alone would never be enough for me."

Dutch-born "Colonel" **Tom Parker** *(upper left)* had worked both as a carnival hustler and dogcatcher before talking a naïve **Elvis** into signing a management deal that gave him as much as fifty percent of Elvis' earnings. On hearing of his star's death, the colonel placed a quick call to an Elvis merchandiser.

Stripper **Tempest Storm** *(above)* was a good friend of Marilyn Monroe's and lover to both John F. Kennedy and Elvis. She met Elvis in 1957 before he went into the Army. He climbed a fence into her backyard, tearing his pants. Her French poodle, Stormy, kept barking all night as she and Elvis locked the bedroom door and went at it.

THREE LOOK-ALIKE BLONDES lined up in a row for Elvis. They were all bombshells: **Mamie Van Doren** *(above, left)*, the British actress **Diana Dors** *(center)*, and heavy-hanging **Jayne Mansfield** *(right)*.

Actually Elvis considered all blondes prostitutes, demanding that his wife, Priscilla, keep her hair dyed jet black at all times. Married during the period that Elvis pursued her, Mamie later said that she could have "kicked myself for not succumbing to Elvis' magnetic personality."

Diana Dors, "the English Marilyn Monroe," later claimed that she amused Elvis by showing him a press clipping that claimed she was "the only sex symbol Britain had produced since Lady Godiva." Diana also showed Elvis a picture of herself when she won a local beauty contest. Although she had claimed to be much older, she was only thirteen at the time she won the contest. He told her, "I wish I had known you then."

Jayne Mansfield, describing her affair with Elvis, said, "I felt something wiggling around down there, teasing me, but to achieve orgasm I require a deep, thick penetration from a man like Mickey Hargitay."

Nick later revealed some of Elvis's sexual secrets, claiming that the star was uncircumcised. He told Nick that when having sexual intercourse with a woman, or even masturbating, his tight foreskin would often tear, causing him to bleed.

Elvis constantly bragged to Nick about his conquests with women. But he claimed that he could not have sex with a woman who had borne a child. "Fucking a woman who's given birth is like plowing your dick into a tub of fat," Elvis said. "She's too loose to provide any enjoyment for a man."

In the months following Dean's death, Nick learned that Robert Altman was going to film *The James Dean Story*. Elvis became excited and lobbied to play his hero on film. "This would be my greatest achievement," Elvis told Nick.

Elvis was bitterly disappointed when he learned that Altman had decided to make the film using still photographs, film clips, and narration by everyone from Natalie Wood to Clark Gable (of all people).

Elvis still persisted, however, insisting that he wanted to be the narrator, for which he agreed to appear free. Altman wanted Marlon Brando for the job, but Marlon turned down the job, which eventually went to Martin Gabel instead. The most sardonic moments in the film are when Dean appears in a TV commercial advocating safe driving.

Warner Brothers hired Nick to travel to Marion, Indiana (James Dean's birthplace) for the premier of the Altman film. On site, Nick visited Dean's aunt and uncle, Marcus and Ortense Winslow, who introduced him to a handsome young actor/singer, Robert Conrad.

In spite of his short arms, Conrad was an exceptionally good-looking man with a most photographic "beefcake body." Nick persuaded him to go to Hollywood to become an actor and

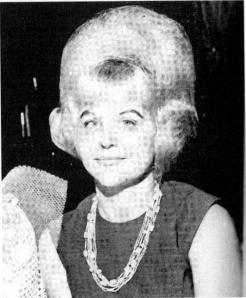

Young Elvis *(left-hand photo, above)* is pictured with his parents, **Vernon** and **Gladys Presley**. The Memphis Mafia claimed that a devoted Elvis never recovered from Gladys' death. After she died, Elvis shut himself up in his room, allowing entrance only to Nick Adams. He ordered Nick to call the funeral parlor and have his mother's tomb inscribed with the words: SHE WAS THE SUNSHINE OF OUR HOME. Her death resulted from acute hepatitis and water retention, a deteriorating condition brought after years of compulsive overeating, an addiction to diet pills, and acute alcoholism. She was 46.

Vernon's second wife (Elvis' stepmother, **Dee Stanley;** *right-hand photo, above)*, claimed in her published autobiography that her stepson had maintained a sexual relationship with his mother. She also alleged that it was guilt over this incestuous involvement that caused Gladys to drink herself to death.

promised "to open doors for you," which was a bit strange since Nick could not open that many doors for himself.

Soon Conrad and Nick were seen riding along Hollywood Boulevard in Nick's '57 Thunderbird or dining in the same restaurants where Nick had eaten previously with either Dean or Elvis.

Word of this burgeoning new relationship soon reached Elvis in Memphis. He threw a jealous fit and threatened to cut off his relationship with Nick.

Using his facile charm, Nick convinced Elvis that he was "still true to you." Elvis was particularly impressed that Nick flew to Tennessee to hold his hand when he got news from the Memphis Draft Board that he'd been drafted into the army on March 24, 1958. Nick waited outside the draft board building in a pink Cadillac belonging to Elvis.

Eventually, when Elvis returned to Hollywood from Memphis, Nick persuaded him to meet Conrad. Elvis was impressed with the actor's looks and charms, and soon Elvis, Nick and Conrad were playing tennis every Sunday afternoon.

For some reason, Elvis became obsessed that "I look like a faggot on film." Night after night he sat with Nick watching his own movies. He asked Nick to warn him if he were "making any limp-wrist moves like one of those goddamn effeminate swishes." To his male friends, Elvis, in spite of his own nocturnal adventures, often attacked "swishes" or "faggots," never wanting to be identified with

Gay agent **Henry Willson** (*left photo above*) seduced both **Rory Calhoun** (*left-hand figure in right-hand photo, above*) and **Guy Madison** (*right*) from his "stable of stars" that included Rock Hudson.

Willson told his gay pals, "I definitely believe in the casting couch. I tell my boys, including Rock, that it's the only way to get ahead in Hollywood." Rory was a far greater stud than Guy. One night Willson stumbled upon Rory and Guy making love in a parked car during a thunderstorm. "Rory was fucking Guy!" Willson later claimed. "And they always told me they didn't like to do it with men – except me, of course."

His wife in a troubled marriage, **Carol Nugent** (*center*) visits **Nick Adams** on the set of *The Rebel*. Nick enjoyed his greatest success playing a Confederate soldier in the TV series. Such acclaim would never come again. Unfortunately, despite its popularity and success, the series was pulled after two seasons because of studio politics. As an actor, Nick had a brief reprieve when he was nominated for Best Supporting Actor in *Twilight of Honor* (1963), losing to Melvyn Douglas, who played opposite Paul Newman in *Hud*.

When Nugent and Nick divorced, he won custody of their two children, Allyson and Jeb.

Nick Adams
THE REBEL

them in any way. When Nick pointed out some scenes where Elvis raised his wrist limply, Elvis would go into a rage and denounce Nick. At one time Elvis got so angry that he ordered Nick from Graceland and tore up his return ticket home. But the next day he forgave his friend and welcomed him back.

Elvis's manager, Colonel Tom Parker, handled the Elvis/Nick affair calmly. "At least he's not impregnating another gal and leaving me to abort another brat."

Col. Parker appreciated Nick's support of Elvis in the wake of the death of his mother, Gladys Presley, on August 14, 1958. "Nicky Admas [sic] came out to be with Elvis last Week wich [sic] was so very kind of him to be there with his friend."

For three days Elvis locked himself in his darkened bedroom with Nick, refusing to eat or to see anyone else. Nick later claimed that Elvis talked for days about Gladys, and Nick recorded all he'd learned in journals which he'd been keeping ever since he arrived in Hollywood.

At one point he revealed Elvis's darkest secret to both Natalie Wood and Rock Hudson, suggesting that he feared "Elvis's relationship with Gladys was incestuous."

Afraid that news of Elvis's homosexuality would leak out, the colonel spread stories of what a stud Elvis was, even linking him to the stripper Tempest Storm, whom previously Elvis had seduced.

Elvis told his stepmother, Dee Presley, that he'd slept with more than 1,000 women before marrying Priscilla. Over the years he claimed to have had sex with everyone from the British sexpot Diana Dors to the American sexpot, Jayne Mansfield, even Cybill Shepherd, Nancy Sinatra, Connie Stevens, Tuesday Weld, Mary Ann Mobley, Natalie Wood, and Ann-Margaret, among countless others.

With all his commissions, ancillary deals, and trinket sales, Col. Parker was actually making more money—an outrageous 50% split—than Elvis himself.

In the words of biographer David Bret, Col. Parker had a "Svengali-like grip over Elvis because he continually threatened to reveal that Elvis had romanced Nick Adams."

Every time Elvis would get fed up with the colonel's larceny and try to fire him, Parker would threaten to blackmail him. Only after Elvis's death did revelations about his bisexuality appear in print, notably in Dee Presley's memoir, *The Intimate Life and Death of Elvis Presley*.

Sadly, the worst scene is missing from *Frankenstein Conquers the World*, a monster movie shot in Japan (1965) during the twilight of **Nick Adams'** career. What's missing is the scene within the office of Nick's agent when he persuaded Nick to sign the contract to appear within this horrible movie, which turned out to be one of the worst films ever made.

(Photo below) When Nick was cast in the highly popular *Pillow Talk* with **Doris Day** and Rock Hudson, he settled for fifth billing. "Unlike the reel version where Doris got Rock, I got Rock in real life," Nick later said.

269

When he wasn't hanging with Elvis, Nick had become part of Henry Willson's "boys." The casting couch agent had helped launch the career of not only Rock Hudson, but Guy Madison, Rory Calhoun, and even Robert Wagner. Nick had an on-again, off-again affair with Hudson before falling for Madison, who at the time was the lover of Rory Calhoun. Eventually, Nick stole Calhoun from Madison. Hudson was responsible for getting Nick cast in a small part in his famous box office hit, *Pillow Talk* (1959), with Doris Day.

Nick's biggest hit had come the year before *Pillow Talk* when he was cast in *No Time for Sergeants*, where he was united with Mervyn LeRoy again. Roddy McDowall had turned down the role of Andy Griffith's sidekick.

Nick's luck turned when a producer, Andrew J. Fenady, created a character for Nick to play in a TV series. It was Johnny Yuma, a young ex-Confederate soldier who helps restore law and order as he roamed the West after the Civil War. The series became known as *The Rebel*, and premiered on October 4, 1959. It didn't occur overnight, but eventually, Nick Adams became a household word throughout America. No more did columnists refer to him as "The Leech," and even today, many viewers from the Age of Sputnik can remember the catchy jingle that opened each episode of the series. But in spite of its success, ABC canceled the series after two seasons. Nick was bitterly disappointed.

Amazingly, through no help from Nick, Conrad also hit it big that same year, becoming a sensation in the popular TV series, *Hawaiian Eye*. That show lasted four seasons on ABC.

Somewhere along the way, Nick's straight side asserted itself. On May 10, 1959 he married Carol Nugent, a former child actress. They would have two children— Allyson Lee, born February 23, 1960, and a son, Jeb Stuart, born April 10, 1961.

William Kern, a journalist who edited the infamous *Hollywood Star*, writing under the name of "Bill Dakota" in the 60s, claimed that "Carol turned out to be a real bitch. She would call Nick on the set and say, 'Guess what I'm doing?' And then she'd tell Nick who she was fucking." For a while, Kern worked as Nick's private secretary and learned all his secrets, including details about his ongoing affair with Elvis.

"At first Nick tried his best to please Carol, but she never seemed to get enough of anything," Kern claimed. "Nick would eventually commit suicide—or was murdered— and Carol's second husband fatally shot himself in the head. Nick loved her too much."

When he learned that she was unfaithful, Nick resumed dating men. His affair with Elvis had never really ended.

Nick Adams wanted a piece of "The Rock," and managed to get him on occasion. But **Rock Hudson** was America's biggest male star, and the line of young men waiting to go to bed with him "stretched around the block," according to best friend George Nader.

When Hudson finally achieved box office clout, he told Nick, "Now I'm so big I don't have to give mercy fucks to the likes of Joan Crawford, Errol Flynn, Liberace or Tyrone Power. I can fuck who I want to for a change."

Nick later countered, "Rock might have said that, but he didn't always live up to his word. One night we were at a party, and he sent word to old-time star Mickey Rooney that he wanted him to come home with him. Mickey declined, sending word to Rock, 'I thought you knew that I liked girls.'"

Ultimately Nick had a devastating effect on Elvis. He was the man who introduced Elvis to drugs, supplying him with his first bennies.

Nick didn't sit at home pining away for either Carol or Elvis. He'd roam the Hollywood Hills or visit the homes of one of Henry Willson's boys. In later life he spent several nights a month with Rory Calhoun, who spoke of his affair with Marilyn Monroe when he co-starred with her in *River of No Return* (1954).

Sometimes Nick arrived at his "love nest" with Carol at three or even four o'clock in the morning. Reportedly one night when he came in late, he tossed his Johnny Reb hat on the sofa. "Guess who just fucked me?" he reportedly announced. "Rock Hudson. His dick is as big as mine. I'm practically bleeding."

Nick wanted to win an Oscar and thought he might have the coveted prize sewed up when he appeared in *Twilight of Honor* (1963), opposite gay actor Richard Chamberlain (there were rumors). Nick got a nomination and campaigned for the Academy Award, only to see it go to Melvyn Douglas for his brilliant performance as Paul Newman's dying rancher father in *Hud*.

After that, Nick's career sunk lower and lower. The low point occurred in 1967 when he starred in *Frankenstein Meets the Giant Devil Fish*. He ended up playing in low-budget Japanese sci-fi films.

His on-again, off-again marriage had actually come undone before that when Carol filed for divorce in September of 1965. The gossip columnist, Rona Barrett, once wrote that during his final years Nick had "become the companion to a group of salacious homosexuals." According to Barrett, these gays told Nick he was a superstar "and poisoned his mind against Carol, convincing him that she was the real reason he was a failure."

In spite of struggling efforts to revive it, Nick's career was on a downslide. His finances were in disarray as legal bills piled up, mainly from his extended custody battles with Carol over his children.

On January 20, 1967, his former wife's new boyfriend filed a $110,000 defamation suit against Nick for remarks he'd made during the procurement of a restraining order prohibiting Carol's new love from coming into the family home and appearing in the presence of Nick's

2126 El Roble Lane was one of the most idyllic cottages in Beverly Hills. But despite the fact that it was at the time relatively inexpensive for such an elite neighborhood, Nick couldn't afford to buy it, so he rented it. Neighbors reported strange comings and goings at all hours of the day or night.

(Above, right), Gossip columnist Rona Barrett.

Known to baby boomers as Sergeant O'Rourke in the classic TV sitcom *F Troop* (1965), **Forrest Tucker** *(above, left)* was a close friend of Nick Adams. After Nick's mysterious death, Tucker went to the police and presented his theories about who killed Nick – and why. He later said, "The police listened politely before dismissing me and my theories."

Another close friend of Nick's, veteran actor **Broderick Crawford** *(above, right)*, said, "Nick Adams was murdered. It was not a suicide. He knew too much about too many stars, especially Elvis Presley and John Wayne. He was flirting with death. Of course, the whole thing was staged to make it look like a suicide."

children.

Nick hired an attorney, Ervin ("Tip") Roeder, a "very, very tough guy" who'd worked for the L.A. Police Department. His hope was that Roeder would find some way to help Nick out of his legal and financial problems.

On the verge of bankruptcy, Nick flew to Graceland for a meeting with Elvis. Their passion for each other had long ago cooled.

Nick arrived drunk for his showdown with Elvis. Alone in Elvis's bedroom, Nick demanded that the star give him a check for $100,000 for all the services rendered over the years.

Elvis was drugged. He accused Nick of being "The Leech," applying the exact same words used by tabloid columnists during the late 50s and 60s. Elvis refused to give him any money, even his return fare to Los Angeles.

At that point, Nick made a fatal mistake. He threatened Elvis, claiming that he was going to write a tell-all memoir. Throughout the course of his star-fucking career, he'd kept extensive journals, even describing the pornographic details of sexual bouts with both male and female stars. Nick used to tell friends, "I take the advice of Mae West. Keep a diary while you're young, because it will keep you when you get old."

The exact details of Nick's final confrontation with Elvis aren't known, but when Elvis steadfastly refused to "give you one buck, you bastard," Nick delivered his final, perhaps fatal, threat. He warned Elvis that he was not only going to write about their affair, but tell all the secrets he'd learned about Elvis and Gladys during the three days and nights he'd spent with Elvis in the wake of his mother's death.

Col. Parker "threw a fit" when he heard that Nick was writing about his affair with Elvis.

Nick Adams found peace at last on February 6, 1968, after his dead body was discovered by his lawyer, Ervin Roeder at his house in Coldwater Canyon. His body was propped up against the bedroom wall. An autopsy revealed that he had overdosed on a cocktail of the anti-anxiety medications Paraldehyde and Promazine. A coroner's report determined that the death was "accidental, suicidal and undetermined." But persistent reports of foul play continue to this day. No drugs or needles were found in the bedroom. There was no suicide note.

"He's joining those tabloid vultures," the colonel told his *confidants*.

As part of "another brushfire to put out," the old showman mistakenly heard that another reporter was ready to expose the Nick Adams/Elvis Presley affair. The colonel went to him, offering him $20,000 in cash. The reporter was only too glad to accept this manna from heaven. Ironically, he had been researching an exposé of the Nick Adams/Rory Calhoun affair and had had no previous knowledge of Nick's romance with Elvis.

Over the years that he managed Elvis, Col. Parker shelled out many thousands of dollars to buy off the many tabloid magazines that arose after the demise of *Confidential*. "I spend half my day shelling out dough to faggots," he once said. "Hollywood is full of cocksuckers to buy off."

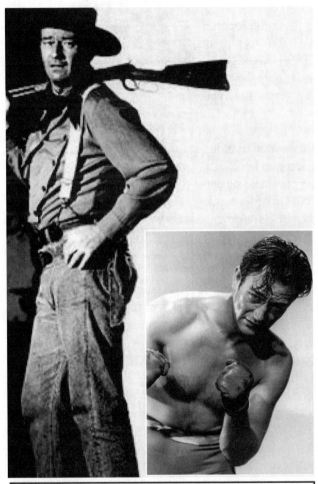

The exact details of **John Wayne's** *(two photos, above)* mysterious, and often quite intimate, relationship with Nick Adams may never be known. Nick died before he ever recorded the full extent of his relationship with either Elvis or Wayne.

What is known is that Wayne used Nick as a sounding board for almost anything. Wayne confided in Nick that, "Women make me feel inadequate." He claimed that he had not known that women were capable of having an orgasm until Paulette Goddard, his costar in *Reap the Wild Wind* (1942), rather crudely informed him.

Nick carried through his threat and began to write his memoirs, confiding in his friends, Broderick Crawford and Forrest Tucker, what he planned to do.

Nick set up a dinner date for Wednesday evening, February 7, 1968, with Roeder to discuss his mounting problems. Mainly Nick wanted Roeder's advice about how to approach Col. Parker with an offer to sell the memoir "for top dollar. I'm sure the colonel wouldn't want any bad news out there about his cash cow. I'm certain that Parker will acquire the manuscript—not for publication—but for his private library."

Roeder arrived at their pre-designated restaurant, even though he hadn't heard from Nick in 48 hours. On a normal day, Nick called him anywhere from five to seven times. After waiting at table for nearly an hour, Roeder called Nick but got no answer. Fearing Nick's car had broken down. Roeder left the restaurant and followed the most logical route Nick would have taken to the restaurant, thinking he might find him along the road in a stalled car waiting for a tow truck.

Finally, the attorney pulled up at Nick's rented house at 2126 El Roble Drive in Beverly Hills. At the front door, he rang the doorbell three times. No answer.

He went around to the back of the house, finding the door locked. Impulsively he forced open a window and slipped inside. Finding no one downstairs, he climbed up to the second landing and headed for Nick's bedroom. Here he came upon Nick sitting in a chair, his open eyes staring accusingly. He was dressed in a plaid shirt, blue jeans, and red boots. He was 36 years old at the time.

Roeder called the police at once. When they arrived fifteen minutes later, Nick's body was removed on a stretcher and placed in an ambulance. As this was being done, the house was searched. There were no signs of a robbery, and the police even noted some loose cash and two valuable rings on a nearby nightstand.

When Roeder searched through Nick's desk, he reported that the exposé manuscript which Nick had been working on was nowhere to be found. Even more significant were Nick's journals which were also missing. He'd kept them for years. Nick's tape recordings were also missing, even his typewriter, a cherished gift from James Dean.

An autopsy performed that night by the L.A. County Coroner revealed that Nick's body contained a massive dose of the sedative paraldehyde. The drug had acted in lethal concert with the tranquilizer Promazine. But no paraldehyde container was found in the house. A chemical cousin of formaldehyde, paraldehyde had been prescribed by Nick's brother, a doctor, Andrew Adams.

Dr. Thomas Noguchi, "coroner to the stars," finally concluded on March 3, 1968, that, "The mode of death is certified as accidental suicide and undetermined." What was not said was that at first Nick's death had been ruled a homicide.

Although blasted by the critics, *Charro!* (1969) cast **Elvis Presley** in a different type of role. Colonel Parker decided that he wanted his chief money-maker to follow in the footsteps of Clint Eastwood and get on the Spaghetti Western bandwagon.

In spite of his mumbled dialogue and misplaced direction, Elvis still managed to shine. He played a bearded, unglamorous role as the reformed outlaw, Jesse Wade. Initially, Elvis wanted Nick to appear in the film with him but Nick's death came too soon for that wish to ever be fulfilled

The case would become fodder for a legend. The tabloids went wild, speculating that Nick's so-called suicide was actually murder.

One of his closest friends was the Oscar-winning actor Broderick Crawford. "Nick was very outspoken to me in the weeks before his death," Crawford said. "He told me about the memoir he was writing about Elvis. I warned him that if Col. Parker found out about it, 'you're dead meat, kid.' But no one could tell Nick anything. Until my dying grave, I'll believe that Parker ordered Nick killed."

A fellow actor, Forrest Tucker, agreed with him. "In the weeks before his death, Nick told me that he feared bodily harm from Parker. He also told me that he kept two guns in the house just in case of a break-in. When the police searched the house, no weapons of any kind were found. Whoever broke in to steal the incriminating journals and manuscript even took his Johnny Reb cap. Nick always told me he wanted to be buried in that cap one day. I just hope that hip gyrator, Elvis, had nothing to do with this."

"Absolutely, it wasn't suicide," Robert Conrad was quoted as saying. "We were so close that if he'd intended that, I'd have known about it. Murder? I don't know. It could be foul play."

Jeb Adams, Nick's son, claimed in 1992 that he was "99.99% sure" that his dad had been murdered.

The autopsy had revealed that Nick was not strangled nor had he been injected with a dangerous fluid.

The police found no pills, bottles, syringes, or needles. Nothing indicated that Nick had met foul play. The police privately speculated to Roeder that Nick had been force-fed a lethal dose of paraldehyde mixed with sedatives.

A policeman, who did not want his name used, said, "We know that Nick had been in the habit of taking paraldehyde for a severe nervous condition brought on, we think, by his divorce and the long custody fight for the kids he adored. But he had been warned by his doctor how dangerous it was and to be careful of his dose. He knew exactly how dangerous it was, and I'm sure he would not take an overdose, or mix it with booze."

The same policeman concluded that, "Word had gotten out that Nick was writing a tell-all book. He should not have announced it, but just published it quietly. It was sure to be a best-seller. But if a lot of stars learned of such a book—and apparently they did—I know several of them who would want Nick to go bye-bye."

The items taken from Nick's home, including those controversial journals, have never turned up. It is not known who owns them today. Perhaps they were destroyed.

Who or what killed Johnny Yuma? The mystery remains unsolved, along with the murders or suicides of William Desmond Taylor, Marilyn Monroe, Thelma Todd, Bob Crane, and George (Superman) Reeves.

A final baffling but tantalizing clue came from Roeder himself in a talk with his close friend, Kenneth Bullis. "Tip [Roeder's nickname] told me that Nick was also going to 'expose' John Wayne in his memoir. John Ford had introduced Nick to Wayne during the *Mister Roberts* shoot. Years ago Nick went to Wayne to seek acting tips on playing Johnny Yuma. Tip said Wayne and Nick were very close, but Wayne always insisted on meeting his friend in out-of-the-way places or late at night. There was a very mysterious aura surrounding their relationship, a vibe which led Tip to bouts of bizarre speculation. 'Surely not,' I said to myself. I wondered, though. I'd heard all those casting couch stories about John Ford and Wayne during the late 1920s. One of Nick's neighbors, according to Tip, claimed that she saw John Wayne leaving Nick's house about 5:30pm on the day of the actor's death. She later reported that she was watering her back lawn about an hour later when she saw two delivery men appear at the back door. One of the men had a key. She saw both men go inside the house."

"The woman was called to the house, but Tip later speculated that the men had been sent by someone to remove incriminating evidence," Bullis said. "Tip also felt that one or both of the men had killed Nick, if he wasn't already dead. Tip took this information to the police, and the woman was willing to testify about what she'd seen. But the police told Tip that the case was officially closed. Tip never knew why the police didn't question Wayne since he was the last known person to see Nick."

"To his dying day, Tip felt there was a cover-up that may have stretched to some very high level," Bullis claimed. "Tip even felt that he knew too much about the case himself and that his own life might be in danger. Exactly what Nick had on Wayne, or the exact nature of their clandestine relationship, may never be known. But Nick hinted to Tip that John Wayne, not just Col. Parker, might also want to purchase (and subsequently suppress) Nick's memoir."

Tip Roeder continued to speak out about Nick's death in the years to come, and even gave some interviews. Disturbingly, in June of 1981, almost 13 years after Nick's death, both Roeder and his wife, Jenny Maxwell Roeder, were shot and killed by an assailant as they entered their Beverly Hills apartment house. Ironically, Jenny, playing a bratty nymphet, had appeared with Elvis years previously in *Blue Hawaii.*

Forrest Tucker, an actor known for being outspoken and candid, was once asked about Nick's relationship with John Wayne. "I know the Duke. He's a friend of mine. Nick told me the whole story, and I'll go to my grave not telling. What the fuck. No one would believe it. Not about Duke Wayne!"

CAVEAT EMPTOR: Only a few graying fans, mostly homosexual men, still visit the **grave site of Nick Adams**. Born Nicholas Aloysius Adamshockor on July 10, 1931, he was buried near his birthplace in Berwick, Pennsylvania. The restless son of immigrant parents from the Ukraine, Nick always maintained a burning ambition to become a movie star.

After a brief success, his career began to slip into oblivion. Faced with mounting bills, he played a dangerous card. That move may have cost him his life.

Rebel Without a Cause

The doomed lovers of *Rebel Without a Cause*, **Natalie Wood** and **James Dean**, "lived fast and died young." Both stars not only seduced the director, Nicholas Ray, but slept with each other as well.

After their initial meeting in the autumn of '54, Ray was startled by a late night knock on the door of his bungalow at the Chateau Marmont. It was James Dean, in tight jeans and an unbuttoned shirt.

Wood was just sixteen years old when Ray took her back to the same bungalow, where he told her, "I want to make love with you." She later confided to Dean, "Ray took me to a tiny, candlelit restaurant where the tablecloths were pink. We drank pink champagne. After that, I was head over heels in love with him. After all, pink is my favorite color."

The "Chemistry" Between James Dean & Sal Mineo

Who of us alive in 1955 didn't flock to see James Dean in *Rebel Without a Cause*? Arguably it gave birth to the "Atomic Age" teenager. The film's bisexual director, Nicholas Ray, cast several young actors still tormented by their burgeoning sexuality—not only Dean, but sixteen-year-old-Natalie Wood, as well as baby-faced Sal Mineo and Nick Adams (later to become famous for "The Rebel" series on TV). Talk about a casting couch. Ray seduced Dean, Wood, Mineo, and Adams in quick succession. He could have been arrested for having sex with Wood and Mineo, as both of them were minors.

Every generation since its initial release has rediscovered *Rebel Without a Cause*. Celebrating its 50th anniversary in 2005,

James Dean told **Natalie Wood** that the two of them had "lived our roles" in *Rebel Without a Cause*. Later, she claimed that his words acted upon her like an aphrodisiac. After accompanying him to the Egyptian Theater in Hollywood for a screening of *East of Eden*, she told friends, "I'm gonna marry him."

Dean found her crush on him "intolerable." Once, in an attempt to break her infatuation with him, he invited her to his place. He told her he'd leave the door open and she could just walk in. "I've got a big surprise for you," he promised.

When she arrived promptly at eight, she found the "love of her life" sodomizing Mineo on the living room sofa.

The performance of **James Dean** in *Rebel Without a Cause* – coupled with his early, tragic, and violent death – made the actor a legend. Today, he's an icon, in critic Geoffrey O'Brien's words, of "the cult of the dead teenager."

Dean's other two films, *East of Eden* and *Giant,* did not fuel the engine of posthumous fame the way *Rebel* did. Years after his death, fans continued to deluge Warner Brothers with letters refusing to believe that Dean was really dead.

The film was an immediate box office success and is watched by each new generation. "It created ripples that would continue to open out for decades," said author Lawrence Frascella. "Ray and company offered up a romantic, charismatic, sexually charged archetype – a heroic ideal of what being a teen might mean. The film took teenagers as seriously as they took themselves."

Rebel is still showing in some movie theaters around the world. It made recent headlines when a circa 1947 screen test of Marlon Brando trying out for the role was re-discovered after having been lost for many years. The film was shelved for eight years until 1955, when James Dean was eventually cast as its "anti-hero."

Authors Lawrence Frascella and Al Weisel recently released a book, *Live Fast, Die Young*, devoted to the making of this film. The title derives from the fact that each of its stars—Dean, Adams, Mineo, and Wood—met violent, unusual, and sometimes suspicious deaths during their prime.

As audiences in the 1950s watched a father-son conflict between Dean and Jim Backus rage on-screen, they didn't know that it was inspired by real father-son conflicts in the director's personal life. In 1948 Nicholas Ray had married sultry Gloria Grahame, the quintessential *film noir* blonde. One afternoon he came home early from work and caught Gloria in bed with his 13-year-old son, Tony, from his first marriage to journalist Jean Evans. He immediately kicked Tony out of the house and soon thereafter divorced Gloria.

In 1960, to the shock of *le tout Hollywood*, Gloria married her former stepson, making him the new stepfather of Timothy, a child who Gloria had produced during her marriage to Nicholas Ray. All of this sounds like material for a Jerry Springer show.

More scandals were later revealed. For months, Bronx-born Sal Mineo had pursued Ray, even seducing him, hoping as a result to win the role of Plato, the closeted gay teenager smitten with Dean's character in *Rebel*. Ray kept rejecting Mineo for the role, claiming, "I don't see any chemistry between you and Jimmy."

In *Rebel Without a Cause*, teenage **Sal Mineo** fell hopelessly in love with James Dean, both on and off the screen. The first rushes of Dean and Mineo horrified the censor, Geoffrey Shurlock. In a memo to producer Jack Warner, he warned: "It is of course vital that there be no inference of a questionable or homosexual relationship between Jim and Plato."

Meeting Dean was one of the highlights of Mineo's life. "I realize that from the moment I met Jimmy, my whole life took on a completely different meaning. It was only years later that I understood I was incredibly in love with him."

In addition to Nicholas Ray, Mineo had many other male lovers, including Rock Hudson and Peter Lawford. He even spent a "nude weekend" with (of all people) Mickey Cohen, the Mafia mobster.

All that Cohen ever said about that notorious weekend was, "Sal Mineo is a fine young man." But to his gangster pal, Johnny Stompanato, he said, "That kid's got a great ass on him!"

279

Finally, Ray gave in, inviting both Dean and Mineo to his bungalow in the gardens of Hollywood's Château Marmont one Sunday afternoon.

In a meeting in 1972 in an apartment in New York's Chelsea district, Mineo told Darwin Porter what happened that long ago afternoon. "I came face to face with Jimmy in Ray's apartment. We were awkwardly reading the script to each other. Perhaps Ray was right about no chemistry. But I was determined to get that part. Trying to get us to relax with each other, Ray told us to improvise. Suddenly, as we talked about very personal things, we relaxed—and how! We even wrestled. At one point Jimmy kissed me. That's all I needed. I came on to him like gangbusters and seduced him right in front of Ray. We must have gone at it for an hour. When we finally got up, Ray relented, saying, 'I have never seen such chemistry between two actors before.' I got the role of Plato. And from that Sunday on, I knew I was incredibly in love with Jimmy."

On the night of February 12, 1976, returning from his rehearsal of a new play, *P.S. Your Cat is Dead*, Mineo was stabbed to death in front of his West Hollywood apartment. Three years later, a "career criminal," Lionel Ray Williams, was convicted and sentenced to life in prison for the murder. Eventually, in 1990, he was released on parole, but many questions still remain unanswered about Mineo's sudden and tragic death.

Blonde bombshell **Gloria Grahame** became famous in *film noir* for her pouting upper lip and an arched eyebrow that spoke volumes. She was one of the sexiest stars ever to emerge from 1940s cinema, and Nicholas Ray was so taken with her he made her his second wife.

Big mistake. Their troubled marriage lasted from 1948 until 1952, but she later admitted that during the course of the marriage, she infinitely preferred having sex with his 13-year-old son, Tony. She continued to have sexual relations with him after divorcing Nicholas Ray, and finally in 1960, Tony Ray and Gloria Grahame were married.

Gloria later articulated some *über*-sophisticated remarks about love and sex: "A woman should enjoy a young boy when he's at his peak – say, between 17 and 19 – and not wait for him when he can no longer get it up – say, age 31."

Had the original casting vision of director Nicholas Ray prevailed, Marlon Brando would be driving that car instead of James Dean. Wishing him luck would be Debbie Reynolds instead of Natalie Wood.

Even though Dean knew that Wood was madly in love with him, he perversely taunted her throughout the filming. When she was intently studying her script one afternoon, he walked up to her, whipped out his penis, and pissed on her pages.

She always forgave him, claiming that Dean as a Method actor, was always just staying in the character of Jim Stark, the alienated outsider. Dean taunted Wood for "being too Hollywood," claiming he loved the innocence of actress Pier Angeli. By the end of the film, Dean bluntly told Wood, "Stop your dreaming. I'll never marry you. You don't even know how to crush out a cigarette butt on my ass and make me enjoy it."

Was James Dean
A Child Molester?

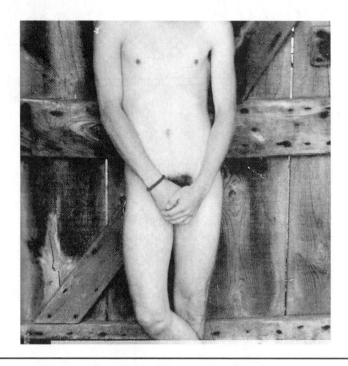

"There's only one true form of greatness for a man," James Dean once said. "If he can bridge the gap between life and death, if he can live on after he's dead, then maybe he was a great man. Whatever's the truth, you've got to live fast." And so he did, dying tragically at the age of twenty-four, just before he evolved into one of the biggest superstars in Hollywood history.

His enigmatic image of youthful rebellion included faded blue jeans, a slouching stance, and an angelic face. That image, now an icon in its own right, seems more famous today than ever. Dean is a man of myth, and one of the most enduring legends associated with that myth has involved his widely touted but heretofore unexplained sexual involvements with an underaged boy.

Dean had utter contempt for authority. When his patron/lover, Rogers Brackett, learned about Dean's romance with this young boy, he demanded to know why. In response, Dean told him, "I refuse to let society's rules dictate my life. If I have certain feelings, and certain things I need to explore within myself, I'm not going to supress them. To hell with that!"

Boulevard of Broken Dreams

"You know, I've had my cock sucked by some of the big names in Hollywood."

James Dean

"I don't mean to speak ill of the dead, but he was a prick."

Rock Hudson, on James Dean

"I've known many actors who have been twisted up in their sex lives, but never anybody as, I guess, unhealthy is the word, as sick and unhealthy as Dean was."

Elia Kazan, on James Dean

"He was small, ugly, hunchbacked with a potbelly, and bow-legged. If he'd had lived, he'd have a larger potbelly, wear a wig, and have died of AIDS."

Marlene Dietrich, on James Dean

For at least two decades after the death of James Dean on September 30, 1955, one of the most talked about aspects of his admittedly secret life was the legendary star's clandestine involvement with a twelve-year-old boy.

Even before the release of *East of Eden* in 1955, the studio feared news of the scandal would break. *Confidential* magazine had some of the facts, and was about to run with the story, but one month before publication—for reasons not known—the exposé was suddenly canceled.

Nonetheless, studio head Jack Warner of Warner Brothers hired a private investigator to check out the rumors. Subsequently, the private eye trailed Dean and his underaged companion to the site of one of their rendezvous, eventually delivering a detailed report. Warner planned to use this explosive information as a means of keeping his rebellious new star in line. In the event that he became as big a star as Montgomery Clift or Marlon Brando, Warner would use the information as a means of blackmailing Dean into signing a long-term contract, presumably at fees well below what his true market value might be worth.

In 2006, through a chance introduction in Hollywood, Blood Moon's reporters finally tracked down this pre-teen boy of the 50s, the one said to have had an affair with Dean. After a lot of maneuvering, wavering, and reluctance, the former partner of Dean agreed to be interviewed in depth, providing his identity was kept undercover.

In his 60s today, John Smith (not his real name) is a successful businessman living in the Greater Los Angeles area. Occasionally, some Dean fanatic will track him down, somehow learning of his identity, and will stalk him. One fifteen-year-old boy appeared almost nightly on John's block, waiting for the man to return home from work. The boy never approached him and never caused him any harm.

"But he spooked me out," John said. "He always wore the same James Dean T-shirt and dressed as Dean did back in the days when he rode his motorcycle along Santa Monica Boulevard."

John claimed that he met Dean at the time he was rehearsing his lines for *East of Eden*, wherein he played the tormented teen, Cal Trask, in the Elia Kazan adaptation.

"My father had parked to go into a hardware store and told me he'd be a while," John said. "I was told to sit in the car and wait for him. He'd been gone for only a few minutes when I saw this good-looking guy get out of a car and walk toward the store too. At the last minute, he looked back at me before going on his way. Then he stopped. I never figured out what made him stop. But he walked toward the car and came over to me. All he said was, 'Hi.' I wasn't afraid of him. He had such an honest face—such openness. He might have been cast as a tormented teen in the movie, but I was a tormented pre-teen

When the aspirant actor James Dean met Marlon Brando in New York, he fell hopelessly in love with him, and would virtually stalk him throughout the rest of his life. Brando ultimately gave Dean sex--not love. Brando always remembered how Dean first attracted his attention.

In front of Brando, Dean claimed, "I have this uncanny ability to predict deaths." To demonstrate his skill, he predicted that his own death would occur in 1967, and that Brando would die on December 24, 2010.

Dean was a talented and charismatic actor, but not a prophet. As it happened, Dean died in 1955, Brando in 2004.

in real life. I was very confused about my sexuality at that point. I feared that I was attracted to men. I found Jimmy the handsomest man I've ever met."

"You must have been an extraordinary beautiful boy at the time, a regular Tadzio," Blood Moon asked John.

"I wasn't at all," he said. "I was a very ordinary kid, and I also had some really wicked pimples at the time. I was skinny, had mousey looking hair; I was very bad at sports and not doing too well at school. No other kid wanted to be my friend. This stranger and I talked for about fifteen minutes. I was afraid my father would come out and catch us talking. I was worried that he'd think it wrong somehow that this older man was talking to his kid. Before he left to go into the store, he told me he'd meet me after school tomorrow. But we needed a place to meet. He didn't want to be seen driving up to my school playground where I would get off at three. So we agreed to meet about three blocks away. I'd be standing on a street corner. My mother worked and my father worked, and they never got home until around seven. So I knew I had some time to spend with this exciting new friend. At the last minute before he left me, he turned and said, 'by the way, I never told you who I was. I'm James Dean. Some people call me an actor but I'm not so sure about that. Time will tell.'"

To this day, John doesn't know what there was about him that made Dean walk over to his father's car. "Maybe he felt my radar. I was staring at him when he parked his car and headed for the store. I didn't know men came in packages like that. I wanted him but I didn't know what that meant. What did wanting an older man mean? What did I have to do? Or, even more frightening, what would he make me do to him? Whatever it was, I wanted to find out. I knew enough from the boys at school to know that some men fucked young boys—and not always a woman. We were warned to be on the lookout for men like that and not get into a car with a stranger offering us a ride home. I wasn't really sure what fucking really meant—or how it'd feel. They didn't show things like that on TV in those days. I knew enough to fear it might hurt me, yet, somehow, I trusted my new friend. His eyes were kind. During our talk, he told me that my own eyes were the most beautiful he'd ever seen. 'I'm an eye man,' he said. 'You can tell a lot about someone by looking deep into their eyes,' he told me."

"The next day in school I didn't pay one bit of attention to what the teacher was saying. All I knew was that at three o'clock I was going to have a secret meeting with my new friend. I couldn't wait. I thought three o'clock would never come."

"He was waiting for me even before I got to that corner," John said. "Without saying a word to him, I got into his car. He told me he was going to take me to a secret place he'd discovered. 'No one will bother us there,' he said. 'I've checked it out many times. I go there just to think about my life sometimes. It's a beautiful place.' I didn't care where he was taking me."

"I would have followed him anywhere. He had a wonderful, mischievous look about him—and that special smile could melt the coldest heart. I think I was in love for the first time."

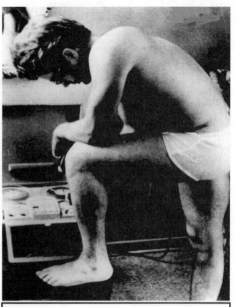

Privately, James Dean admitted to his gay friends that he'd had brief affairs with some of the biggest producers, directors, and stars in Hollywood, but he never specifically named them. For the most part, the names of most of these bigwigs have eluded James Dean biographers. One of the pursuers, however, was Howard Hughes, who stalked Dean, had him trailed by private dectectives, and eventually flew him to a villa in Acapulco. Their host, Ted Stauffer, later said: "I think their affair consisted almost entirely of a series of blow jobs--and rather frequent ones at that."

Simultaneous with Hughes' pursuit of Dean was Hughes' involvement with actress Terry Moore, who later claimed to have married the reclusive billionaire at sea.

"The drive was long, but I didn't even look at the road," John said. "I kept staring at his jeans which were pulled up tight around his waist. He noticed where my eyes kept glancing. 'You want it real bad?' he finally asked. 'You can't wait until we get there, can you?' I was so embarrassed I couldn't say anything. He unfastened his jeans and pulled out his cock which was already hard. I had never seen a man erect before. It was so much bigger than mine."

"He told me to 'lay your head in my lap so no one will see us.' I did what he said. 'Go on,' he urged. 'Take it in your mouth.' I followed his instruction and took the head in my mouth. The taste was strange to me. He told me to 'lick it' and I did. He then issued orders for me to start to suck but quickly jerked back. 'Watch those teeth!' he cautioned. I did and tried to use my tongue more. I didn't want to piss him off. Finally, I seem to get it right. 'You're doing fine,' he said. 'We're going to make a cocksucker out of you yet.'"

"When he exploded in my mouth, I was taken by surprise. I tried to spit it out, but he ordered me to swallow it. 'Lovers always swallow each other's cum,' he told me. I did what he said. I swallowed. It was a strange taste. In some ways it had almost no taste at all, but then it did. I didn't particularly like the taste of it, but I loved the man who made me swallow. I was hooked. From then on, I'd do anything he wanted."

"He turned the car down a dirt road and drove us to a little glen where there was a bubbling creek. He ordered me out of the car. He called me 'little buddy' and 'little sucker.' He got out of the car with me. 'I'm still hot. I'm gonna show you what a girl feels like when I slip them the rod.' He ordered me to take off all my clothes. I was afraid but I pulled off everything but my underwear. He yanked my shorts down for me. He had me lay down in the back seat facing him. Then he slapped one of my ass cheeks real hard, then the other one, and it really stung. He grabbed my legs and pulled me over to the edge of the seat. Instinctively I must have put my legs up in the air."

"He fingered me and warned me that the first time really hurts, but I was mesmerized by him and wanted to please him. He slowly guided himself to my entrance. All of a sudden he lunged forward. I screamed. I felt my insides were splitting. He didn't allow me to get used to it. I was crying and begging him to take it out, but he was too far gone to stop. I didn't think I could take it. 'Oh, oh, you're tight,' was all he said, as he kept ramming me real hard. I begged and begged. He answered me by saying, 'Take it. Learn to take it!'"

"At last he exploded again and pulled out real quick. I was left gasping for breath at the sudden withdrawal. I closed my eyes and tried to stop crying. I felt like some dumb little kid."

"'C'mon,' he said. 'Wipe yourself clean. Get your clothes on. I'll take you for a ride.'"

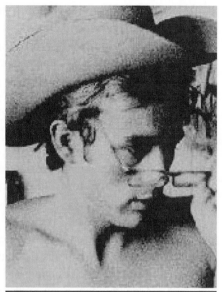

Despite the fact that Marlon Brando always claimed that he hated parties, he attended quite a few of them while making *On the Waterfront* in 1953 and 54. One night in Brooklyn, he showed up with his "date," James Dean. "All of us along Broadway knew that Dean and Brando were carrying on," said actor Jimmy Schauffer, who attended the party. "It was the worst-kept secret. From what I observed that night, Brando was definitely in charge of the relationship. Dean was tagging along like a puppydog after its master. We'd also heard rumors that there was more than a little S&M being expressed within that relationship. Guess who the 'S' was?"

"My ass still hurt, and I bled a bit but not much. I got dressed and went for a ride with him. He bought me two hot dogs and a cone of chocolate ice cream, my favorite. I didn't care what he did to me. I didn't want to leave his side. If having him hurt me for pleasure was what was needed and wanted, I was willing to go for it."

"Jimmy let me out of his car about two hours later two blocks from my house. He told me to walk the rest of the way home. He warned me if I knew what was good for me, I'd be on that same street corner at three o'clock tomorrow. 'You're my new boy friend,' he told me. Ass still aching like hell, I actually skipped all the way home. I'd never been so happy in my life."

John claimed that for the few months that remained in Dean's life, the actor continued to see him and that his parents never really found out. "They mostly neglected me and would divorce in 1957. Jimmy kept hurting me, and I kept taking it. Then, after about a dozen times, it started to feel real good. It got so that I wanted it more and more. Usually he obliged. I knew he was dating adults, probably both men and women. He only talked about the women he was fucking. Never the men. I was as jealous as hell but I tried not to show it."

"Sometimes we'd park and he'd kiss me for an hour or so. He didn't seem to mind my pimples. He even squeezed a few for me. He didn't find such things disgusting. He was real natural about functions of the human body. He'd even stop by the road and take a shit in front of passing cars. Sometimes people would yell at him but he didn't seem to mind."

"He was afraid to give me presents, because that would make my parents suspicious. But he gave me money to spend on special treats and things. I loved him for that. He always seemed to have money on him. When the film came out, all of Hollywood, even the guys at school, were talking about James Dean. He went on to make *Rebel Without A Cause*, and he talked about Sal Mineo. I suspected they were having an affair, but I was afraid to ask. He still saw me, but not as often."

"When he went to Texas to make *Giant* with Elizabeth Taylor, I feared she'd take him away from me. I sat by the phone, and he often called me in the afternoon from Texas, knowing that my parents would be out of the house. When he came back, I was the happiest boy in the world. I think my pimples had cleared up a bit. I tried to make myself as attractive to him as I possibly could."

"I wanted him to live with me one day when I got old enough to leave home, and he said he would. I was listening to the radio when the news flashed of his death. At first I couldn't believe it. I must have cried for weeks. My mother even took me to a doctor, and he said nothing was wrong with me. There was talk of sending me to a psychiatrist. But that never happened. When I was eighteen and left home, my first trip was to visit his grave in Indiana. He was from a town called Fairmount. I met other kids my age there. They were weeping at his gravesite."

John claimed that he eventually went to college and into the workplace. After college, he built up a successful business and, at the age of twenty-four, settled down with one of his salesmen, with whom he still lives today.

"There's not a day that goes by, even after all these years, that I don't think of Jimmy. He got under my skin and has stayed there forever. They say that time heals all wounds. That's crap! I love my lover, and I love him dearly, but Jimmy Dean will live in my heart forever. There was never an electrifying presence like him. He was tenderhearted but could be tough on me when I didn't do what he said."

This nude picture of James Dean with an erection has sold around the world: Many of the most avid Dean fans, male and female, own a copy of it.

The gay newspaper, *The Advocate*, once wrote: "The alleged [nude] photo of Dean has sold in New York like hotcakes. It is purported to be a scene from a gay porno movie that Dean made before he became a star. It is difficult to say who is attached to that mammoth, erect cock, but to millions of men and women, it sure looks like Dean, a *Giant* in more ways than one."

"All in all, except for my sadness and loss, I think I turned out okay. Jimmy Dean made a man out of me. He taught me how to experience true joy in life, and that only comes when you love and are completely dedicated to another human being. All other experiences are like eating cardboard."

James Dean, who had seduced everybody from Tallulah Bankhead to Rock Hudson, from Marlon Brando to Howard Hughes, was only twenty-four and still single at the time of his brutal death.

Ever the iconoclast and an exhibitionist as well, Dean wrote to his friend, William Fox, in the autumn of 1952 that he'd posed for a nude picture. This is probably it.

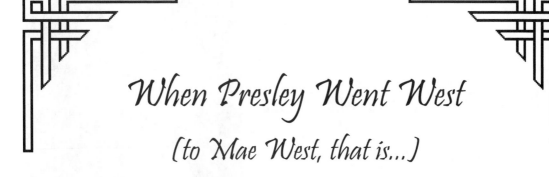

When Presley Went West

(to Mae West, that is...)

The love affair of the century was NOT launched on the night Elvis Presley came to call upon Mae West. Mae would have been willing if Elvis hadn't bolted. He might even have gone along with it had he not suspected that Mae was a female impersonator. After all, he didn't always go for 14-year-old girls, and he'd been known to seduce older women before, including Doris Duke.

"Let's face it," Mae declared to Elvis. "There are only two great sex symbols left in the world today-- yours truly and the man I'm looking at right now in those tight pants. I wish I'd been born in a different era, when men wore tight pants and not those bagggy trousers they used to wear. After all, a gal should know what she's getting. Don't you agree?"

Elvis didn't think the question required an answer.

When Elvis Came Up to See Her... Sometime

The film, if it had ever been made, would have become *the* jawdropping camp classic of the 20th century.

Elvis harbored a dream of appearing opposite, not Marilyn Monroe or even Jayne Mansfield, but Mae West, who at the time was 72 years old.

He didn't care that her last film, *The Heat's On*, had bombed shortly after its release in 1943. Watching the Oscar ceremonies in 1958, Elvis had been fascinated when West, with Rock Hudson, generated wild applause with a hilarious duet, "Baby It's Cold Outside."

In 1964 when Elvis was evaluating the script for *Roustabout*, he decided that the role of the fairground owner, Maggie Morgan, would be ideal for the ageless sex goddess. He demanded that his producer, Hal Wallis, offer her a contract, and announced that he intended to sing three separate duets onscreen her.

The next day Wallis told Elvis that West would agree to the role only after a private audition with him "to check on our mutual chemistries." Elvis called West, and she invited him to "come up and see me sometime like tonight at eight."

Aware of her reputation for seducing young men, he invited his sidekick, Nick Adams, to join him.

West greeted "the boys," as she called them, in a long, white, rhinestone-studded gown that evoked her 1934 film, *Belle of the Nineties*.

West and Elvis were sympathetic souls, and gen-

Mae West was impressed that Elvis was called **"Elvis the Pelvis."** In her one and only meeting with The King, she claimed that the hip action of the pelvis was almost as important as the sex act itself. She also revealed that a "sexercise" of her pelvis was a work-out she performed every morning to prepare herself for the action to follow that evening. "You've got to keep the pelvis muscles really firm," she told Elvis, "Completely toned. Pelvis exercise also tones the leg muscles and thigh muscles as well. Even the stomach muscles. In sexual activity, you've got to use not just your pelvis, but your thighs and your stomach."

At the age of 72, she demonstrated her technique. Lying on her stomach upon the thickly carpeted floor of her living room, she extended her arms into what she called a "T Position." She proceeded to demonstrate her pelvis exercise, the rules of which she later defined within her infamous book, *Mae West on Sex, Health & ESP*. She had three rules: "Take a deep breath and lift your legs as high as you can but keep them straight. Hold that position for the count of five. Maybe even ten on a good day. Now exhale slowly and bring your legs to the floor. Now take it easy for a minute or so to get your breath. Repeat that same exercise five times. You'd be surprised how good the sex act will feel later if all your muscles, including the pelvis, are in tiptop shape."

She admitted that Elvis shaking his pelvis onstage would achieve the same effect as her sexercise. "With all that pelvis action, I bet you're a treat for the gals."

uinely seemed to like each other. She regaled the men with indiscreet stories of her decades in show business. When she excused herself to "powder my nose," Elvis whispered to Adams that he'd heard rumors that West was a drag queen. "Now that I've met her in person, I'm sure of it."

Had he wanted to, Elvis that night could have learned first hand if West were a man or a woman. After three hours of additional dialogue, he excused himself, claiming he had another appointment. Actually, he had a late-night date with Ann-Margaret.

In urging him to stay, West claimed that she liked to "audition" her leading men before signing a contract. "I want to know if they swing my way." Seeing doubt on Elvis's face, she assured him, "I have the body of a 26-year-old gal."

In spite of the offer, he politely excused himself and headed for the door with Adams trailing. The next morning Wallis told Elvis that West had liked him and would sign the contract. But before the deal could be finalized, Elvis's manager, Col. Tom Parker, intervened. He threatened to shut down production on the picture if West were signed. The savvy old showman knew that she'd rewrite the script, zapping it with her famous *double-entendre* one-liners. "*Roustabout* would be a Mae West picture with Elvis as her stooge," Col. Parker shouted at Wallis.

Elvis was bitterly disappointed when he learned that West was out, the role going to Barbara Stanwyck instead. The former speakeasy dancer from Brooklyn was the biggest female star Elvis had ever appeared with. She was available only because she, along with Joan Crawford, had been fired from the latest Bette Davis movie, *Hush...Hush, Sweet Charlotte.*

Elvis and Stanwyck hated each other on sight. On the second day of the shoot, Stanwyck overheard Elvis telling some of his Memphis Mafia boys that she was "the most closeted dyke in Hollywood."

She never spoke to him again except when delivering her lines in front of the camera. When the picture wrapped, Stanwyck told Wallis, "As an actor, Mr. Presley is pathetic. *He has no star quality.*" Then she stormed off the sound stage.

Nick Adams, at the time, Elvis' best pal, attended the historic meeting between the King of Rock 'n' Roll and the aging Queen of Sex, Miss Mae West. Unlike Elvis, who did not succumb to Mae's vintage charms, Adams was the eternal star fucker.

"Age or sex didn't matter to Nick," said one of his best pals, Forrest Tucker. "All he demanded of the fuckee was that he/she/it be a star. And there was no doubt that Mae West stood for stardom." During his meeting with Mae, Elvis got up and requested to "go to the little boy's room." It was then that Nick moved in on Mae. "Little boys like Elvis are fine, but, as you know, sometimes a lady such as yourself needs a big boy," Nick said. "Accent on big."

Size-queen Mae got the point and accepted the phone number offered. She made Nick wait three weeks before calling him. She phoned and he visited, and he hadn't exaggerated his male charms. But when Mae called again for a repeat performance, Nick was unavailable. He later told Rock Hudson, "I woke up to reality. At this point in her career, Mae West couldn't do anything for her own career – much less mine. Now John Wayne, that's a guy who can get parts for me. In the future, you're gonna see me hanging out with the Duke." And so it came to be.

Miss West

Mae West became the all-time gay icon among movie divas and was for decades the single most impersonated actress by drag queens. One of her first plays, *The Drag*, became notorious for dealing with the then-taboo subject of homosexuality. When the show opened in New York, there were fears it would cause a riot.

For a woman born in 1892, she was rather tolerant of the gays she encountered in vaudeville, and later the movies. Yet even at their best, many of her views on homosexuality were Victorian. She referred to gays as "The Third Sex" and claimed that "the homosexual act" was really a form of masturbation, "bringing temporary relief but no real satisfaction." She also felt that a "bitchy homosexual can be worse than a bitchy woman." (EDITOR'S NOTE: PERHAPS SHE WAS RIGHT.)

In contrast to her tolerance for gay men, Mae had a disdain for lesbians. She once recalled her meeting with Marlene Dietrich, whom she claimed had "made a bigger name through her publicity than her talent."

"I've always washed my own hair when I was shooting a picture," Mae wrote. "I'd get to the studio very early to do it the way I liked. One day I was standing at the sink rinsing my hair when the door opened. I turned off the water and felt a towel being placed on my head, then hands moving it around as they dried my hair. I still didn't know who the hands belonged to, and when I turned around, I was surprised to see Marlene Dietrich staring at me, wearing nothing but a flimsy robe."

"'You are very beautiful,' I told her. 'I've always been an admirer of yours.'"

"At that point, Dietrich's robe opened, and she stared at me waiting for me to catch the pass she was throwing. Never at a loss for words, I found the right ones. 'You'd better button up dearie. You're gonna catch cold.'"

According to Miss West, Miss Dietrich left and never returned,

Things Are Getting Campier All the Time

Sofa *(right)* designed by the world's premier surrealist **Salvador Dalí** "in Honor of Mae West's Lips."

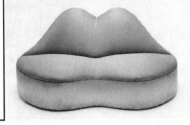

Miss Dietrich

Barbara Stanwyck was a great actress, as these pictures with Elvis in the 1964 film, *Roustabout*, indicate. Although personally, she detested Elvis, her on-screen chemistry and sense of professionalism made it appear that she adored him.

Elvis made a mistake on the first day of the shoot by suggesting to Stanwyck that he was going to learn a lot from her and be as devoted to her as he was to his own mother, Gladys. "I know I can learn a lot about acting from you. I'm sure you'll be like a mother to me and get me through this damn picture."

"I'm nobody's mother," Stanwyck shot back. "And certainly no mother to Elvis Presley."

Actually, Stanwyck did have an adopted son, Dion, an arrangement finalized during her marriage to her first husband Frank Fay. But throughout his life, she virtually ignored Dion, sending him away to boarding schools or to live with relatives.

Perhaps as a means of getting back at her, Dion exposed details about her marriage to Robert Taylor in the pages of *Confidential*. The headline blared, DOES MY MOTHER, BARBARA STANWYCK, HATE ME? The article was published in 1959, around the time Dion was arrested for selling pornographic materials.

Colonel Tom Parker, Elvis' control freak, money-grubbing manager, nixed the deal to star Elvis with Mae West in *Roustabout*, preferring Barbara Stanwyck instead. Stanwyck later admitted that she was shocked when Hal Wallis called and asked her to appear with Elvis. "The idea of working with Mr. Presley intrigued me, because that would bring me into a younger audience than I'm accustomed to. And I thought it would be rather fun."

How wrong she was. To the press she said, "Elvis was a wonderful person to work with. His manners are impeccable, he is on time, he knows his lines, he asks for nothing outside of what any other actor or actress wants."

Privately she denounced him to Joan Crawford as, "A shithead, a selfish, uneducated oaf, surrounded by Southern redneck retards, and no doubt a closeted homosexual like my dear cock-sucking former husband, Bob Taylor."

Stanwyck had first seen Elvis on *The Ed Sullivan Show,* which she watched faithfully every week. In the picture to the immediate left, **Col. Tom Parker** *(left figure)*, **Elvis** *(center)*, and **Sullivan** *(right)* face a tense moment behind the scenes.

Sullivan had just told the colonel and Elvis that the rock 'n' roll star was to be photographed or filmed only from the waist up. His gyrations, according to Sullivan, were deemed obscene for young TV audiences. Elvis voiced strong objections to this, but Parker calmed him down. After Sullivan had left, Parker told Elvis, "We'll just take the fucker's money and run to the bank with it."

"Nobody Gyrates Like Elvis"

Elvis

and the

Richest Woman in the World

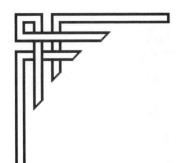

Elvis Presley was an unlikely conquest for **Doris Duke**, the steel-gloved tobacco-industry heiress. Although she had an affair with the less well-endowed, more homosexually inclined Cary Grant, she preferred men like her second husband, the heavy-hung Porfirio Rubirosa, the Dominican playboy-diplomat.

Her lovers included actor Brian Aherne, who claimed "Doris had the most beautiful legs in the world." She often wrapped those legs around his neck. Others of her lovers included Errol Flynn, David Niven, Aristotle Onassis, Gilbert Roland, George Sanders, General George C. Patton, and lots of Hawaiian beach boys. She told Truman Capote that she had a sexual preference for "dark meat."

When Doris Duke Met Her Idol

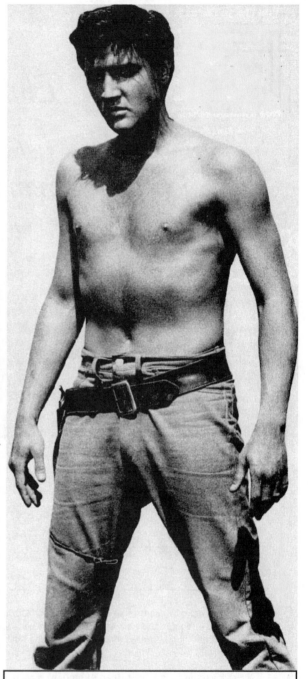

An Odd Couple is a concept that refers to more, much more, than merely a hit TV comedy series with fussbudget Tony Randall and lovable slob Jack Klugman. The phrase more often refers to bizarre couplings in unexpected combinations.

Everybody's heard of the affair between President Kennedy and Marilyn Monroe. Less well-known is the brief sexual encounter between tobacco heiress, Doris Duke, the world's richest woman, and Elvis Presley.

In 1967, having just healed from "history's finest plastic surgery," Duke flew to Las Vegas to see Elvis "in the flesh," so to speak.

Still slender and attractive, she was a ripe 55, Elvis only 32.

He'd been born into poverty, she with a silver spoon in her mouth—or a least a cigarette.

Yet they shared some common ground, as both of them belonged to the Self-Realization Fellowship in Los Angeles. Each of them had the same fashionable guru, and both of them adored black soul music.

At one time, Duke had even taken dancing lessons from "Bojangles" Robinson and singing lessons from Aretha

Doris Duke developed a fixation on **Elvis Presley** after seeing him go shirtless in the movie, *Flaming Star* (1960). She was said to have seen all of his movies, some films more than once. Jokingly, she summarized all the plots of the Elvis films to Truman Capote. "A Southern boy beats up a guy and then sings to him." Duke even sat through such mindless crap as the ditsy *Tickle Me*, and claimed that her favorite song of Elvis' was from *Paradise – Hawaiian Style*.

She even predicted that "Queenie Waheenee's Papayan Surprise" would become "immortal Elvis."

Franklin's father. Her favorite singer, however, was Elvis, upon whom she'd developed a lingering crush, almost a fixation.

For dinner in her Vegas hotel suite, Duke invited not just The King, but the gossipy and rather effeminate Truman Capote. At dinner, she served Capote lobster and caviar, but for Elvis, she offered fried bacon and melted cheese sandwiches with thick chocolate milkshakes.

Years later, Capote revealed the subject of this strange trio's conversation. "Toilet paper." She urged Elvis to install paperless toilets at Graceland, as she had recently done at her estates. "Otherwise, the servants will use so much toilet paper that you'll go to a pauper's grave," she warned Elvis.

Capote claimed that at some point, way after midnight, Elvis disappeared with Duke into her bedroom, leaving the author alone to finish off the vintage champagne.

A year later, at a dinner party at Duke's palatial estate in New Jersey, Capote asked her how it had gone with Elvis. She frowned before admitting that she'd proposed marriage to him. "I found him very, very sexy. But he turned me down." Then she sighed. "American men have no talent for marrying rich women."

Doris Duke was not alone in sampling the wares of Porfirio Rubirosa (1909-1963), who had once been married to the sluttish Flor de Oro Trujillo, daughter of The Dominican Republic's dictator, Rafael Trujillo, an autocrat who was nicknamed "The Goat" because of his sexual excesses.

Duke took Rubirosa as her second husband, but had to share his sexual favors with, among others, Joan Crawford, Evita Peron, Ava Gardner, Veronica Lake, Jayne Mansfield, and Marilyn Monroe. He even seduced Patricia Kennedy Lawford, the U.S. president's sister. When John F. Kennedy heard about that, he bluntly asked her, 'Is it as big as they say?" His sister refused to answer, but her husband, Peter Lawford, claimed he had the exact measurements: "Eleven inches long and thick as a beer can. That guy can balance a chair with a telephone book on it on the tip of his erection."

Duke *(left)* is photographed on her wedding day in 1947. Having been coerced a few moments before the ceremony into signing a prenuptial agreement, Rubirosa smoked a cigarette during the delivery of his wedding vows and later fainted in her arms.

Rubi, Doris' husband, a man with a talent for marrying rich women, appears in the photo *(right)* with Doris' rival, the almost-as-rich-as-Doris **Barbara Hutton**. After his divorce from Duke, the Latino fortune hunter would marry Hutton, the Woolworth heiress, in 1953.

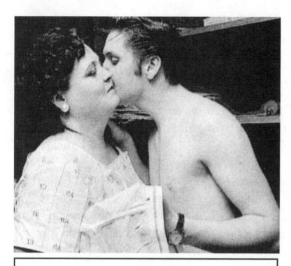

The relationship between **Gladys Presley** and her son, **Elvis**, was defined as "incestuous, if not physically, then spiritually" by Elvis' stepmother.

Gladys was horrified when she heard Elvis was sleeping with the tobacco heiress. She warned her son to "never see that evil woman ever again."

"Don't worry, mama," Elvis said. "It didn't work out. The bitch wants her toes licked, then sucked for hours. I told her, 'white boys don't do that.'"

For some reason, Doris Duke kept extending invitations to both Elvis and **Truman Capote** at the same time. Privately, Elvis told Duke that Capote was a "faggot," but Capote's satirical wit and razor sharp parodies of the rich and famous soon had Elvis in stitches. Capote, known for stretching the truth, told Elvis that, "Jacqueline Kennedy – my closest friend – has a secret crush on you. I can arrange for you to have a rendezvous with her to fuck her."

Elvis said he'd be eager to accomplish that mission, but Capote, of course, never followed through with his promise. After some time at Duke's palatial and aptly named Shangri-la in Hawaii, Elvis left while Capote stayed behind for a dinner Duke had planned with Greta Garbo.

Duke later said of that evening, "Garbo is the most boring woman in the world."

When Elvis and Truman Capote dined together at Duke's estate in Hawaii, Capote later reported on the only serious conversation they ever had. Capote complimented Elvis for having the courage to be an "ass-kicking rocker willing to take on all the bullies at school who mocked you for your Tony Curtis hair-do and punk look, even your blue suede shoes. In many ways – as a straight, of course – you behaved like a young gay male who dresses in drag walking down the meanest street in town, knowing that your very appearance will get the shit beat out of you."

Elvis was quick to respond. "I'm not a guy to be pushed around. I was in pursuit of a dream and I was never willing to let anybody come between me and my dream."

"So how do you respond to critics who say your act is a male burlesque show?" Capote asked.

"I move my pelvis with the same gyrations I use in the fuck," Elvis claimed.

Another Year, Another President

MM's Fling With Ronald Reagan

During World War II, **Captain Ronald Reagan** was stationed in California, handling PR for the Army. In that capacity, Captain Reagan ordered his staff photographer, Private David Conover, to go to a local factory to take pictures of women on the homefront who were turning out aircraft, munitions, and parachutes. These morale-boosting photos of pretty girls contributing to the war effort were for publication in *Yank* magazine. .

One of the girls he photographed that day was named **Norma Jeane**. She could hardly know at the time that she'd eventually have an affair with Private Conover's commanding officer – or that the officer would become, long after her own death, the President of the United States. Conover later claimed that the eyes of Norma Jeane "held something that touched and intrigued me. She should be a movie star."

After lunch, he requested that she change into a red sweater, and he took more pictures of her in which her breasts were more prominent. When Conover came into the office of his boss (Reagan) a week later, he noticed that he'd pinned up that picture of Norma Jeane. Reagan said, "This young lady, not Lana Turner, should be called **The Sweater Girl**."

Reagan's Tough Choice
for a First Lady:
Doris? Nancy? Patricia?

But NOT MARILYN!

Ronald Reagan, of course, was the only Hollywood actor and the only divorced man to ever become President. But the road to the White House had a few romantic potholes.

As early as 1950, he was dreaming the impossible dream of one day becoming President of the United States, even though he'd recently divorced actress Jane Wyman. He dated a lot of starlets, mostly one-night stands, but had settled on two women he particularly liked, Doris Day and Nancy Davis.

He was the president of the Screen Actors Guild but had loftier ambitions in politics because his screen career had stalled. Actor/dancer George Murphy, who'd been Guild president from 1944 to '46, was his role model. Murphy also wanted to go into politics and would indeed become a U.S. Senator from California (1965-71).

Reagan turned to Murphy not only for political advice but for affairs of the heart. "If you want to be president one day, you've got to have a suitable First Lady," Murphy told him. "Nancy is too mousy with no personality. Doris is nothing but personality. She can sing, too. Even if you bore your audience with one of your long-winded speeches, they'll stick around to hear Doris sing 'Sentimental Journey.'"

At this same time yet another starlet was about to enter Reagan's life. In 1948 Marilyn Monroe had met Fred Karger, a musician, who was also working as a

Had Ronald Reagan pursued his first "first choice" for a second marriage after his divorce from Jane Wyman, **Doris Day** *(above)* might conceivably have become First Lady of the United States. Both Day and Reagan had been cast in the film, *Storm Warming* (1951) about the KKK. It also starred Ginger Rogers. Although Rogers was famous for her dancing and Day for her singing, neither star was called upon to do either. Both instead were cast in dramatic parts.

Reagan dated Day, who said that "two things about Ronnie impressed me. How much he liked to dance and how much he liked to talk. There was a little place on La Cienega where he used to take me. It had a tiny dance floor. When he didn't dance with me, he talked to me. Not talk, really. Not real conversation. It was rather talking at you, sort of long discourses on subjects that interested him. I remember telling him he should be touring the country making speeches. I turned out to be a prophet. He was very good at it. He believed everything he said, or at least he made you think he believed."

Unknown to Day, Reagan was also dating Patricia Neal who was still in love with Gary Cooper. "From what I heard, Gary's a tough act to follow, " Reagan said.

Could he have been referring to Coop's legendary endowment? At this time, starlet Nancy Davis was dating Reagan, but not going steady with him.

vocal coach at Columbia. Almost within days she'd fallen in love with him, even though he was bitter about women. "No female is capable of genuine love," he told her. At the time, he'd just been dumped by Rita Hayworth. In spite of what he said, Marilyn wanted to marry him. But he did not think she would make a proper stepmother for his young daughter from an earlier marriage. Marilyn was bitterly disappointed.

Unknown to Marilyn at the time, another woman had also fallen for Karger. At the peak of her star power in Hollywood, Jane Wyman, the ex-Mrs. Ronald Reagan, also wanted to marry Karger. He ended up proposing to Jane. Marilyn was furious and wanted to get even.

In one of those coincidences that often occur in life, a drunken Marilyn encountered Jane in the women's room of Chasen's Restaurant in Los Angeles. In an altercation, Marilyn lunged for Jane, accidentally ripping her wig off. Jane was wearing a wig that night to conceal a scalp irritation. When novelist Jacqueline Susann heard of that catfight, it inspired the most dramatic scene in her *Valley of the Dolls*, one of the best-selling novels of all time.

Marilyn couldn't have Karger, but she went after Jane's "discard," hoping that would make her rival jealous even though she'd divorced him. Marilyn called Reagan, ostensibly to discuss problems with her membership in the Guild. This led to a dinner date and a subsequent affair.

Later when Reagan had business in Miami Beach, he invited Marilyn to fly down to join him. He bought her a ticket on a separate plane. He

When **Nancy Davis** *(above)* latched onto **Ronald Reagan**, she held tightly and was determined not to let go. Unlike Jane Wyman, Nancy pretended to be "vitally interested" in Reagan's political views, listening to him talk for hours. She used every feminine wile to attract his attention, and later told her old friend, Spencer Tracy, "I am wholeheartedly in love." But Reagan wasn't ready to commit. At first, he saw other women while dating Nancy on and off.

At the time, Nancy's career was in serious jeopardy. Her starring roles in *The Next Voice You Hear* (1950) with James Whitmore bombed at the box office, as did *Night into Morning* (1951), a maudlin melodrama she made with Ray Milland (who, by the way, was still in mourning after having been dumped by Grace Kelly).

On September 7, 1951, Nancy received bad news from MGM. After her series of box office failures, her three-year contract would not be renewed.

Ronnie and Nancy *(right)* at their wedding in 1952. She'd finally won her long sought-after prize. They are flanked by **Ardis Marshall** *(left of Reagan)* and **William Holden** *(right of Nancy)*.

At the time, Mr. and Mrs. Holden were Reagan's best friends. Known on the screen as Brenda Marshall, Holden's wife had appeared opposite Errol Flynn in *Sea Hawk*, opposite Alan Ladd in *Whispering Smith*, and opposite Joel McCrea in *Espionage Agent*. Holden became a role model for Reagan, who copied his style on screen all the way down to the way he lit a cigarette. He began dressing like Holden and even adopted the actor's cynical raised eyebrow.

even insisted on booking her a suite in a different hotel from his own on Miami Beach, stashing her secretly at the Helen Mar.

Why the secrecy? Reagan was between marriages and could date whomever he chose. But he did not want Doris or Nancy to know he was seeing yet another starlet. The only time Reagan and Marilyn were seen together in public was during their secret "date" in a dimly lit Miami Beach night club that starred Sophie Tucker. As a fading star, Reagan attracted no attention, and Marilyn was yet to become a household word.

Flying back to the West Coast again on a different plane from Marilyn, Reagan had a final dinner date with the star, telling her "it's over between us." She burst into tears. He also broke up with Doris, who married Marty Melcher in 1951. During the course of that marriage, his profligate spending nearly drove Doris into bankruptcy.

Ignoring Murphy's advice, Reagan went on to marry Nancy on March 4, 1952. He was 41; she was 30. "We had a kid in the oven," he told Murphy. Their daughter, Patti, was born that October 21.

Wyman married Karger in 1952, but divorced him in 1954. She remarried him in 1961 but walked out on him in 1965, divorcing him again. She never remarried.

After reigning as "the queen of TV" on the soap opera, *Falcon Crest*, while Reagan presided over the Free World in the 80s, she went into seclusion, suffering from arthritis and diabetes.

Her last public appearance was in 2004 at Reagan's funeral. Concealed behind sunglasses, she was hidden in the background, and most of the much-younger paparazzi and journalists didn't recognize her. Jane had wanted to attend

Nancy never achieved her goal, which was to become as famous as another actress named Davis – Bette, that is. After appearing in some duds, Nancy was cast in *Talk About a Stranger* (1952), with song-and-dance man and Reagan's friend, George Murphy. Neither Murphy nor the movie-going audiences were impressed with Davis' acting. Nonetheless, determined to make a career, she signed on for yet another project. *Donovani's Brain*, starring Lew Ayres, was possibly her best film. The irony of Davis starring with Lew Ayres was certainly amusing: Ayres had been the lover of Jane Wyman during Wyman's marriage to Reagan.

In 1957, the producers of *Hellcats of the Navy* came up with what they believed to be an inspired idea – casting the husband-and-wife team of **Ronnie and Nancy** in the same picture. Ironically, it sent Nancy's Hollywood career into a tailspin. The only other film that followed was the aptly titled *Crash Landing* in 1958.

Ronald Reagan's film career was also winding down. When Nancy announced her retirement from the screen in '58, people paid little attention. F. Scott Fitzgerald once wrote that there are no second acts in American lives. Both Reagans proved him wrong.

With her husband facing an uncertain film future, Nancy Reagan decided she couldn't afford a maid and did her own cooking and housekeeping. As a means of maintaining an aura of glamour, she sometimes wore high heels while doing the daily chores. This *(below, right)* is how Reagan found **Nancy** when he returned from shooting his last film for Warner Brothers in 1952.

In that film, entitled *The Winning Team*, Reagan portrayed Grover Cleveland Alexander, one of baseball's immortals. Doris Day was cast as his wife, but received top billing. At that point, her romance with Reagan had already cooled. Reagan departed from the Warner Brothers lot on January 28, 1952, after fifteen years of involvement. There was no fanfare. "Not even a gold watch from Jack Warner," he told Nancy when he got home. "I thought an *adios* from Jack might be possible. I only got silence. I asked for my final paycheck. They told me, 'It's in the mail.'"

As he pulled his car out of the studio lot that day, he noticed an attendant removing his "permanent" nameplate. Although facing an uncertain future, Nancy and Ronald were married on March 4, 1952.

to pay her respects but privately told friends, "This is Nancy's time to shine—not mine."

She died at the age of 90 on September 10, 2007, at her home near Palm Springs. Her adopted son, Michael Reagan, issued a statement in which he said, "Hollywood has lost the classiest lady to ever grace the silver screen."

SAILOR, CAN YOU SPARE A DIME? Fans of **Jane Wyman** *(four photos above)*, who knew her only from her TV role in *Falcon Crest*, may never have known that a younger, brassier, sexier Wyman ever existed. She trained as a dancer in her younger days, but ended up as a radio singer. Taking the last name of her first husband, whom she'd divorced in her teens, "Jane Wyman" went through the Warner Brothers casting mill and came out a B-rated chorus girl, a dumb blonde backup in a "Torchy Blane" mystery (she played a hat check girl). In *Brother Rat* (1938), she played a blonde chasing cadet Reagan. She caught him in real life and married him in 1940.

"Jane was a fly-away girl," said Glenda Farrell. "Very blonde – too blonde, in fact. She was a party girl. Word at Warners was that she was available, if you know what I mean."

"I just had to go dancing and dining at the Troc or the Grove or some nightspot every night to be happy," Wyman said. She was seen in a booth kissing John Payne one night, and flirting with attorney Greg Bautzer another. (Bautzer's sole aim seemed to be to screw every major female star in Hollywood; he was most visibly successful with Lana Turner and Joan Crawford.) Wyman even fell for Bing Crosby when they costarred in *Here Comes the Groom* (1951).

Jane **Wyman** (the ex Mrs. Ronald Reagan) and **Rock Hudson** made two successful movies together, both of which were soapy: *Magnificent Obsession* in 1954 and *All That Heaven Allows* in 1955. During the filming of both pictures, Wyman had a fling with the handsome actor, eventually learning that he was a homosexual. Wyman wasn't as savvy as Hudson, and found it "a bit incomprehensible that Rock can make love to a woman so successfully even though he's gay." Despite her eight-year real-life role as Mrs. Ronald Reagan, "the talker" had never explained the finer points of homosexuality to his first wife. Previously, Hudson had even made love to an aging Joan Crawford, who'd praised the size of his equipment.

Magnificent Obsession was the granddaddy of all tearjerkers: A handsome, reckless playboy accidentally blinds a woman and then falls in love with her. Searching for spiritual meaning in his life, he returns to medical school, becomes a doctor, and cures her blindness. Director Douglas Sirk later said, "Rock rode into stardom on the skirttails of Jane Wyman."

Because of the success of *Magnificent Obsession,* the studio cast Wyman and Hudson together in *All That Heaven Allows,* with filming beginning in January of 1955. It was another older woman/younger man-themed film, and was almost guaranteed to thrill middle-aged women across the country, most of whom were completely unaware that Hudson was a closeted gay.

By the middle of the shoot, Wyman had lost all interest in Hudson, having learned too much about his private life from well-meaning friends. Even so, the public drew parallels between *All That Heaven Allows* and the star's personal life. She caused a scandal when the public learned that at the age of 38, she'd become engaged to a dashingly handsome 26-year-old, Travis Kleefeld. Public opinion turned against the marriage, and Wyman dropped Kleefeld, not wanting to further alienate her fans.

Evelyn Keyes convinced **Fred Karger** *(with Wyman in photo, left)* a musician at Columbia, to put together a band to play at a party hosted by the John Hustons. Escorted by Reagan, to whom she was married at the time, Wyman was introduced to Karger that night. Little knowing that she would eventually marry him--not once, but twice--she eloped with him in November of 1952 after the termination of her marriage to Reagan. By doing so, she seriously pissed off gossip maven Louella Parsons, who had wanted the scoop.

The public was eager for details about Wyman's "mystery man." Reading the papers, Marilyn Monroe said, "I could tell them plenty about Fred Karger, more than they'd be able to print. And I'll get even with that bitch Wyman if it's the last thing I ever do.

Upon hearing of his marriage to Wyman, Rita Hayworth told friends, "Jane is welcome to him! Frankly, I don't know why Marilyn is so crazy about the guy." Previously, Karger had been involved in Hayworth films which included *The Loves of Carmen* and *Affair in Trinidad.*

Even though Wyman's second marriage to Karger lasted longer than the first, it wasn't successful. This was despite the fact that her career was winding down and she had more time to devote to him.

In March of 1965 he charged her with "desertion." She counter-charged, citing "grievous mental cruelty," and that he had "an uncontrollable temper."

Marilyn Monroe *(three photos, above)* had two objectives when she pursued Ronald Reagan: She told best pal, Shelley Winters, that she thought Reagan was cute, but more important than his good looks was her personal vendetta against Jane Wyman. A few months earlier, Wyman had taken Fred Karger, a musician, away from Marilyn. In Marilyn's view, sleeping with Jane's former husband was a suitable revenge.

Marilyn later recalled details of her affair with Reagan to Winters. "He was the only man I know who took a shower and brushed his teeth before and after sex. He was very clean. Not terribly passionate, though. It was sort of automatic, and he went directly to the spot. No preliminaries. He did feel my breasts but didn't go in for all that armpit licking and toe sucking that some guys like. No wonder Arrow shirts used him as a model. Reagan is straight as an arrow. He told me that he was shopping around for a wife, but she'd have to be suitable as a president's wife. I was disqualified because he said I was a showgirl and had posed for nude pictures. For some reason, my background disqualifies me for everything except to play a dumb blonde on the screen."

Anyone who visits the Ronald Reagan Presidential Library, in the Simi Valley of California, might never know that Jane Wyman even existed, since it contains few, if any, references to her role in his life. Yet during the 1940s, she was married to Reagan for eight years. She was a far bigger star than her husband ever was, having won an Oscar for her portrayal of a deaf mute in *Johnny Belinda* (1948). As George Murphy put it, "When Ronnie lost Jane, a really big star, he married down. Nancy Davis never made it. She couldn't even be called a Grade B star. How about going down the alphabet a bit? She never had any charisma on the screen … or off, as far as I'm concerned."

By 1941, the differences between **Reagan and Wyman** *(photo left)* had become painfully apparent. As he became more political (she hated politics), she became more and more withdrawn, devoting nearly all her time to the advancement of her film career. The tension brewing between them exploded one night at a Hollywood party given by William Holden. "So you don't think I'm spending enough time at home?" she shouted. "One day I'm going to win an Oscar. That's something that will never happen to you."

After **Rita Hayworth** *(right)* dumped musician Fred Karger, he fell into the arms of Marilyn Monroe. Hayworth later said, "Fred got off on the legends about me – not me. He particularly liked the fact that GIs pasted a pinup photo of me on the first atomic bomb dropped on Hiroshima. *Talk about incendiary.*"

During her affair with the musician, Hayworth maintained no particular loyalty or fidelity to him. She enjoyed on-again, off-again affairs with Kirk Douglas, Glenn Ford, Howard Hughes, Peter Lawford, Victor Mature, Tony Martin, David Niven, Tyrone Power, and James Stewart.

"She liked to go to bed with movie stars," said her second husband, Orson Welles. "But then, so did I."

As his marriage to Wyman deteriorated, Reagan spent more and more time socializing with MGM star, **George Murphy**, pictured above left *(headshot)* and above right with **Judy Garland** and **Gene Kelly** in *For Me and My Gal* (1942).

Dick Powell *(above, right)* also became part of that circle. Both he and Murphy were ardent Republicans who greatly influenced Reagan's political direction. Although firmly entrenched as the (Democratic) President of the Screen Actors Guild, Reagan would eventually switch his allegiance from the Democrats to the Republicans.

Preoccupied with her own career, Wyman resented Reagan's attempt to expound on everything. One evening while Reagan was debating with Dick Powell about politics, Wyman leaned over to Powell's wife, June Allyson, and said, "Don't ask Ronnie what time it is because he will tell you how a watch is made."

Murphy entered politics before Reagan, running successfully for the seat of a California senator. He urged Reagan to enter politics by running for the governor of California. "From that position, you can parlay your fame into the presidency, but only if you run on the Republican ticket."

Nearly broke, and with bills accumulating, **Ronald Reagan**, centerpiece of the two photos immediately above, accepted a two-week vaudeville gig in Las Vegas which began on February 15, 1954. Best pal George Murphy had once told him that Las Vegas was a land of "has-beens, almost-rans, and never quites." Even so, Murphy agreed to help Reagan privately with his dance routines.

The future president was booked to appear with **The Contintentals** *(above, left)*, a dimestore version of the zany Marx Brothers. Other than horsing around, using a guttural German accent, and acting drunk, Reagan played straight man to the slapstick comics and told bad Irish jokes that got him booed.

At one point he appeared in an apron advertising Pabst Blue Ribbon Beer with the German phrase – *Vos vils du haben?* – incorrectly written. As part of the same act, Reagan also appeared with **The Adorabelles** *(above, right)*, gorgeous showgirls clad in Carmen Miranda-inspired Brazilian costumes and plumed headdresses that towered more than two and a half feet high.

With Nancy sitting out front every night cheering him on, Reagan attracted only modest business. After his opening night, a local critic asked the question, "Is Las Vegas going to become a retreat for fading Hollywood stars?" At the wheel driving back to Los Angeles, Reagan told Nancy, "I'll never sink that low again." Fortunately, an offer was pending at General Electric which eventually designated Reagan as host of the syndicated TV series, *The General Electric Theater*, launching him on what would eventually become the road to the White House.

In the 1940s, before Ronnie,

and long before she realized that it would be discussed around the world,
aspiring ingenue and Hollywood starlet <u>Nancy Davis</u>
dallied in some romantic experiments en route to the White House

Marlon Brando
(pictured here with Grace Kelly)

Milton Berle

(clockwise from left)
Spencer Tracy, Alfred Drake, Yul Brynner

JFK's brother-in-law,
Peter Lawford

Frank Sinatra (photo courtesy
of Bergen County, NJ)

Robert Walker

Clark Gable (pictured here
with Vivien Leigh)

As Angela Channing, empress of *Falcon Crest*, **Jane Wyman** became the highest-paid actress on television in the 1980s. The hit series made its debut one year after Ronald Reagan was inaugurated as U.S. president, with Nancy, not Jane, as his First Lady. Industry insiders pointed out that "there were dozens of aging actresses in the Hollywood Hills who would be ideal for the part." (Bette Davis? Anne Baxter? Eleanor Parker?) But the studio wanted to take advantage of Wyman's unique status as the president's ex-wife. At the White House, Reagan was said to have been a faithful fan of the series, even though Nancy left the room whenever it was aired.

Wyman was in the California wine country filming an episode when she received word that Reagan had been shot by a would-be assassin, after he'd been president for only two months and nine days. She retreated to her dressing room and didn't emerge until the following morning, when she announced abruptly, "It's back to business, fellows! The nation goes on, and so does *Falcon Crest!*"

Portrayed *(left)* on a cover of *TV Guide* with some key cast members of *Falcon Crest*, Wyman received massive publicity because of the series, but consistently refused to talk to reporters about the nation's new president.

WHATEVER DID JANE WYMAN HAVE TO DO WITH VALLEY OF THE DOLLS, AND WHY WAS SHE SO ANGRY WITH ITS AUTHOR, JACQUELINE SUSANN?

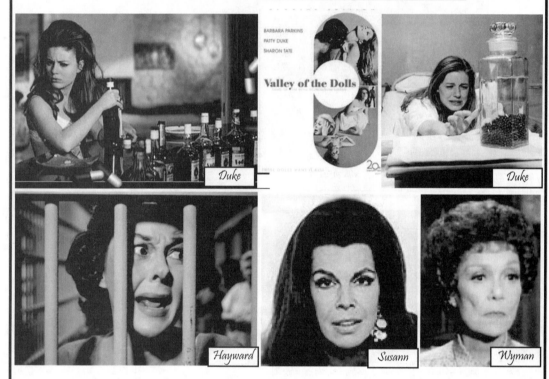

Duke *Duke* *Hayward* *Susann* *Wyman*

Judy Garland knew a thing or two about pill addiction, but when she was fired from the original cast of *Valley of the Dolls,* the role of the aging star, Helen Lawson, went to **Susan Hayward**. In one of the most dramatic confrontations within that film, **Patty Duke** (seen above caving in to her character's substance abuse issues) grabbed Hayward's wig, ripped it off her head and then flushed it down a toilet. By the end of the scene, Lawson, as played by Hayward, was revealed as a grotesque, wrinkled, has-been, way beyond her prime.

The hair-pulling battle between Duke and Hayward has entered camp movie history as one of its grander episodes. Jane Wyman saw *Valley of the Dolls* and was furious, knowing that its author, **Jacqueline Susann**, had ripped off an episode from her own life--i.e., her confrontation many years previously with Marilyn Monroe over Fred Karger in a Los Angeles restaurant. Several decades after that episode, at a party, when Susann came up to Wyman to greet her, Wyman tossed her drink in Susann's face and stormed out of the room.

Susann, incidentally, lived a life that paralleled many of her best-selling novels, a life filled with tragedy and triumph. Her most successful novel, and one of the most successful novels of all time, was *Valley of the Dolls,* whose theme involved pill addiction and sexual betrayal in Hollywood. Naturally, bidding for its movie rights was intense. Some critics suggested that the role of Helen Lawson was based on the life of Judy Garland, who was a personal friend of Susann's. Actually, however, it was based on the life of another faded musical star, Ethel Merman, with whom Susann had once suffered through an abortive lesbian love affair. Susann, who died in 1974, never forgave Merman, and "got her revenge" by depicting the star as a dumpy, semi-psychotic, over-the-hill monster.

Among other ironies, the film also starred the ill-fated Sharon Tate, who met a grisly death two years after the 1967 release of the film at the hands of the lunatic Charles Manson clan.

Dream Couple
MM and Elvis

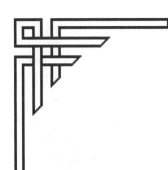

Take dozens of **Marilyn Monroe** and **Elvis Presley** biographies, and in most cases, you'll never find any cross-references indicating that either of them ever even met, much less got intimate. Yet because of recent media revelations, news of the Elvis/Marilyn affair has become public knowledge.

What isn't known, except to some longtime Hollywood insiders, is that the affair lasted longer and was more intense than had originally been known. Spilling the beans were Nick Adams, Elvis' closest pal, and Shelley Winters, former roommate of MM's and a life-long, rather gossippy *confidante*.

Although Shelley kept most of Marilyn's secrets during MM's lifetime, after the star's tragic death in 1962, Shelley became a virtual "talking head" about Marilyn's secret life and passions.

"It's true," Shelley said. "Marilyn and I fucked some of the same guys, but I never got around to Elvis. From what I hear, I didn't miss all that much. Give me Burt Lancaster or John Ireland any day."

Love Me Tender

Elvis and Marilyn forever regretted that Col. Tom Parker, Elvis' manager, nixed the deal for them to co-star together in *Bus Stop* (1956). Even so, Marilyn's 24th film, made shortly after *The Seven Year Itch*, offered a vehicle for her greatest performance to date.

As Bosley Crowther noted in *The New York Times*, director Josh Logan got Marilyn to "do a great deal more than wiggle and pout and pop her big eyes and play the synthetic vamp in this film. He got her to be the beat-up B-girl of Mr. William Inge's play, even down to the Ozark accent and the look of pellagra about her skin. He got her to be the tinseled floozy, the semi-moronic-doll who is found in a Phoenix clip-joint by a cowboy of equally limited brains."

When The Colonel turned down the part for his money maker, the role intended for Elvis went instead to actor Don Murray, who was credible, but not brilliant, as the young and innocent cowboy, Bo Decker.

"Try as he could, Don Murray was no Elvis," said a disappointed Logan. "Marilyn and Elvis together would at least have had the power of the atomic bomb dropped on Hiroshima, maybe a nuclear blast that would have made them the screen team of the century."

A poll taken in the summer of 2007 of presumably straight adults (ages 21 to 35) revealed the names of the two sex icons of the 20th century that these Americans would most like to bed. By overwhelming majorities, women went for Elvis Presley, the men predictably going for Marilyn Monroe.

There was always talk in Hollywood of pairing this dream couple in a film, especially the picture, *Bus Stop* (1956), one of Marilyn's most successful hits. But Col. Tom Parker, Elvis's greedy manager, always blocked such deals, insisting that Elvis keep turning out such quickie junk as *Blue Hawaii* (1961).

Nearly all biographers agree that Elvis and Marilyn met, but only briefly, in the mid-50s. Those books will have to be rewritten in the wake of revelations in October of 2006 by Byron Raphael, a retired William Morris agent who worked for Elvis. He spilled the beans on a salacious secret he'd been harboring for nearly half a century, revealing a "one-night stand" between Elvis and the blonde goddess in 1956.

"**Elvis** could deliver, I guess," Marilyn confessed to Shelley. "But he sure wanted to postpone penetration as long as possible. In my opinion, I think his ideal form of sex would be mutual masturbation. He sure likes to play with you down there. But he likes to use his fingers more than he likes to use the rod. One night, I was a bit drunk and jokingly kidded him, 'Spare the rod, spoil the fuck, Elvis.' He didn't like that at all. In fact, he got up and put on his pants and told me to go home. But he called the next day and apologized."

Raphael claimed that he received a call one night from Elvis, requesting that Marilyn be brought to him at the Beverly Wilshire Hotel. The agent called Marilyn, doubting if she'd accept such a request. Even though she'd been recently married to playwright Arthur Miller, Marilyn took the bait and agreed to the secret rendezvous. At the time, she was also secretly dating a handsome young senator from Massachusetts, who would one day become the President of the United States. Actor Peter Lawford had set up that liaison.

Raphael reported that when Marilyn came into Elvis's suite, the famous pair started kissing even before saying a word to each other. Finally, Marilyn broke the silence, telling Elvis, "You're not bad for a guitar player." After only a few minutes on the living room sofa, according to Raphael, they got up and disappeared into the bedroom. He waited in the living room to take Marilyn home, but fell asleep, awakening hours later to find Marilyn and Elvis, both nude, emerging from the bedroom.

Not knowing when their sexual gymnastics would end, Raphael said he "bolted" from Elvis's suite. Five days later when he encountered Elvis, Raphael asked how it had gone with Marilyn. "She's a nice gal, but a little tall for me," Elvis said. She was also nearly a decade older than Elvis, but he was too much of a Southern gentleman to bring that up.

Raphael got the "historic" coming together of Elvis and Marilyn right. But there was much more to the story than what he knew.

One night in 1966, at an actor's hangout off Times Square in New York, Shelley Winters, Marilyn's roommate when she first hit Hollywood, revealed to actor John Ireland (star of the 1949 version of *All the King's Men*) and Darwin Porter a lot more about Marilyn and the King. She claimed that their one-night stand blossomed into an on-again, off-again affair that lasted for the rest of the 50s, interrupted only by Elvis singing the *G.I. Blues* when he was stationed in Germany with the U.S. Army.

A lifelong friend and confidant of Marilyn, Shelley said that Marilyn also told her that Elvis the lover didn't match the allure of baseball legend Joe DiMaggio (Marilyn's former husband). She also claimed that Elvis "didn't have Joe's bat to hit home runs with."

When Shelley asked Marilyn why she continued to see Elvis over the years, MM said, "Other than me, he's the most famous person there is. How could I refuse? I don't think Albert Einstein would be a great lover either, but if he called me to his bed, I'd come running. After all, I think he invented the atomic bomb or something."

Porter also knew a young actor, Nick Adams, who arguably was Elvis's best all time male friend. Nick had appeared with James Dean in *Rebel Without a Cause* (1955), but is remembered today chiefly for his 1962 TV series, *The Rebel*. Nick died, allegedly from a drug overdose, in 1968. Many Hollywood insiders, including actor Forrest Tucker, insisted that he was murdered.

In 1964 when he was making *Hell Is for Heroes*, Nick Adams confirmed to Porter details about the Elvis/Marilyn tryst, telling much the same story that Shelley did.

"Elvis was never really *that* attracted to Marilyn," Nick claimed. "Not only was she an older woman, she wasn't really his type. He much preferred Ann-Margaret."

"Then why did he keep seeing her?" Porter asked.

Elvis read less than one percent of the fan mail he received, and **Marilyn** read even less. But the two of them liked to share some of their more outrageous letters with each other. Men throughout America sent Marilyn nudes of themselves, telling her in graphic detail just what they'd like to do with her in bed. And dozens of lesbians wrote, with similar requests.

Most of Elvis' mail – some ten thousand letters a week – came from young girls. Many of them wanted Elvis "to take my virginity," and most enclosed photos of themselves ready, willing, and eager to be deflowered. Some of them threatened suicide if Elvis didn't agree to meet them. The strangest letters came from distraught parents, who threatened to kill themselves if Elvis didn't "cool down his act."

"You're turning my girl evil!" was a typical comment among these parental letters. "I don't see how I could be a threat to any parents' daughters. I'm just up there on that stage doing what comes naturally," Elvis said.

"Forget it," Marilyn told him. "You're doing fine. Just keep doing what you're doing. Speaking of doing what comes naturally, why don't you come over here and join me in bed and we'll let Mother Nature take her course?"

Marilyn's most memorable evening with **Elvis** – at least according to Shelley Winters – was when he danced "Jailhouse Rock" for her in the nude. "I giggled as I watched him flipping up and down. It was very funny and strangely erotic," Marilyn later confessed.

Sometimes Elvis didn't want sex at all with Marilyn, and told her, "I just want to cuddle." During some of these evenings, he would talk about his beloved mother, Gladys. Marilyn confessed to Elvis that mental illness ran in her family and that her maternal great-grandfather, Tilford Hogan, hanged himself at the age of 82. Her maternal grandmother, Della, died in a mental asylum at the age of 51 – one year after Marilyn's birth. She also told Elvis that her grandmother tried to smother her before being shipped off to the mental ward. But it is unlikely that Marilyn could remember such an incident, since she would have been barely 13 months old. Elvis later confided to Nick Adams that "Marilyn fantasizes a lot about her past. Shit, man, she even told me that Clark Gable was her father."

"It was an ego trip for him," Nick said. "At the time, she was the world's most beautiful and sexiest woman. And she probably found it thrilling to fuck with the man every other woman wanted. Hanging out together was a thrill for both of them. The sex was mere icing on the cake--not the cake itself."

After Elvis and Marilyn stopped dating, around 1960, and as a token of his gratitude, he bought her a moon-shaped bed whose headboard was upholstered in "shocking pink" leather with scarlet-red sheets and accessories.

When a truck pulled up with the bed at Marilyn's bungalow, she refused to accept delivery. "Tell Mr. Elvis that I don't rock and I don't roll in a Valentine box," she told the deliverymen. "I would never sleep in a bed that would attract more attention than me. After all, I'm the star!"

Marilyn died on August 5, 1962, and **Elvis** was depressed about it for weeks. "I'm next," he told his cronies. "First Marilyn, then me. Me and her always talked a lot about it. We both knew we were going to die young. I don't know when my time is coming, but I know it's coming soon. I got a lot of people out there wanting to get me. My death will probably be faked to look like a suicide. But I bet they'll get me the way they got Marilyn."

Until the day he died, Elvis refused to believe that Marilyn's death was a suicide. "It was Robert Kennedy," he said. "That son of a bitch had Marilyn murdered. She knew too much. She was threatening to destroy the Kennedys, and she could have if she'd wanted to."

So incensed was he at Marilyn's death that Elvis hired two private detectives to prove that Robert Kennedy had flown to Los Angeles for "a final meeting" between Marilyn and himself. Allegedly, Marilyn had angrily told Peter Lawford, "I refuse to be treated like a piece of meat by either Bobby or Jack. I'm gonna make them pay for that." It was when Lawford informed Robert Kennedy of that threat that he allegedly flew to LA to deal with Marilyn.

Kennedy later claimed that at the time, he was at Gilroy, a ranch 300 miles northwest of Los Angeles. But Elvis said that his detectives discovered that the attorney general had secretly flown to Los Angeles only hours before Marilyn's untimely death.

According to Elvis, "By making that threat to that cocksucker Lawford, Marilyn sealed her doom."

Elvis told Marilyn that the one thing he hated about working in films was that he was always pursued by homosexuals. "I can't stand fags," he once told her. "And Hollywood's full of them. I'd run a hundred miles to get away from a fag."

"Now, now, Elvis," Marilyn cautioned, "We're both in show-business. A little tolerance is called for. Homosexuals are people too. God loves all his children." Marilyn was well aware of Elvis' own involvement with Nick Adams. She knew Nick personally, and they shared many a conversation about Elvis.

In 1962, at the time of Marilyn's death, Elvis was filming *Fun in Acapulco*. In one scene, Elvis had to emerge from the sea being carried aloft by six men, in a sort of victory march. Elvis kept blowing the scene because he couldn't stop wiggling around. Finally he went to his Memphis Mafia and said, "Boys, there's a fag in that bunch. Every time they pick me up, one of them six guys grabs me by the balls."

During the next take, the assistant director, Mickey Moore, spotted the guy and fired him on the spot. "He just told this fag quietly that there were too many people in the scene," said Red West, one of Elvis' pals. "We, of course, near died laughing. Elvis wasn't as amused. He was very upset at being handled in a most intimate way by a fag."

When Elvis confessed to **Marilyn** that he was always being pursued by homosexual gay men, she also claimed that she was often the object of desire from lesbian or bisexual women. She said that she had met the bisexual actress, **Marlene Dietrich** (center), in New York on January 7, 1955.

She'd called a press conference to announce the formation of Marilyn Monroe Productions, Inc., with theatrical agent **Milton Green** *(right)*. "I'm tired of sex roles," she told the press. "I want to do dramatic parts like *The Brothers Karamazov*."

"Do you want to play one of the brothers?" one of the reporters asked jokingly. Marilyn almost lost her temper. "No, I want to play Grushenka, the girl part."

After meeting Dietrich, Marilyn was invited to visit her apartment. "I stayed over," Marilyn confessed. "But lesbian sex is not really my thing. Although like most actresses in Hollywood, I have indulged. Marlene is very oral. She did her own thing down there, but I didn't reciprocate. In the morning, she made her famous scrambled eggs for me."

Elvis told her that he never objected to two lesbians getting it on. "In fact, I rather enjoy watching bitches going at each other."

Marilyn sometimes confessed amusing tidbits about her life to Elvis. She claimed that at the Empire Theatre in London at a Royal Command Film Performance, she was introduced to the Queen.

"Let's face it, we're both Queens. She's the Queen of England and I'm the Queen of Hollywood. Before Her Majesty extended her hand to me, I caught her running her eyes up and down my figure and looking right at my breasts. Do you think she's a lesbian like Princess Margaret? Marlon Brando told me all about that one."

In the receiving line, Marilyn stood next to **Victor Mature** *(left of Marilyn)*. "He screwed the hell out of me," Marilyn claimed. "His dick's too big. He made me bleed. He wanted repeats. No way!"

The Rape of Marilyn Monroe

According to Shelley Winters, MM's former roommate and longtime friend, "Marilyn Monroe was the biggest liar who ever set foot in Hollywood. Don't get me wrong. I loved the gal dearly. But the biographers of Marilyn's early life each bought into her fantasy."

Shelley continued: "Marilyn confused her real life as Norma Jeane with the movie script of Norma Jeane that she kept rewriting in her head. I remember a story she told me about childhood rape. Over the years she told me three different versions of the same story, forgetting what she'd said previously. In time, I think Marilyn could no longer distinguish between what was real and what wasn't. To her, the movie script of Norma Jeane became more real than the actual events. Marilyn became the star of a Greek tragedy that was her life. The only thing that Marilyn was ever completely honest about was the inevitability of the casting couch. In her early days, she spent far more time on that couch than she did in front of a camera. But as for the rest of it, it's too late now--no one will ever know the complete truth."

Marilyn's former lover, Ted Jordan, understood her contradictions better than most. He wrote that she was "the extremely vulnerable child-woman incapable of hurting a fly, who was also a hardheaded bitch consumed by ambition; the innocent *ingenue* moving through life in a kind of daze was also petty, vindictive, and cruel, a woman consumed by a need to be loved who was also manipulative and uncaring."

When Marilyn posed for the photo, above, she was only 13 years old, but made herself up to look like a seductive 19-year-old woman.

Goodbye Norma Jeane, Hello Marilyn Monroe

The world took little note in 2005 of the passing of a man known throughout his life as "Mr. Marilyn Monroe."

A retired Los Angeles detective, James E. Dougherty, lived for decades in the shadow of sixteen-year old Norma Jeane Baker, whom he married on June 19, 1942, before going off to sea as a merchant marine. Death came to him at the age of 84 in San Rafael, California, where he'd be suffering from leukemia.

Throughout most of his life, Dougherty refused to talk about his life with Marilyn. Gordon Howard, the California tycoon, arranged for reporter Darwin Porter to meet Dougherty several times over a period of three weeks in Los Angeles in 1968.

In Porter's words: "I felt that Gordon, a generous person, had paid Dougherty for granting me that privilege, but I don't know that for a fact. The soft-spoken, unassuming, and rather kind detective, who still maintained a slight trace of his former good looks, had nothing in common with Marilyn's later two husbands: Baseball great Joe DiMaggio and playwright Arthur Miller. At first, Dougherty wanted to talk only about his hobby (special weapons), but I eventually steered him onto the subject of

One of **Norma Jeane's** few family-friendly poses was shot with her breasts carefully concealed and with this fluffy white lamb in 1946. Usually her photographs were much sexier, but this photographer decided he wanted her looking "farm girl wholesome."

When he saw the photograph, her modeling agent told her, "There's no way, gal, with a face like that, that you're going to look wholesome. From now on, we're sending you out on different jobs."

After making a voyage around the world, Dougherty arrived home and waited three hours for his wife to return. She claimed she had run overtime on a modeling assignment. Actually, she was detained giving the photographer a blow-job.

James Dougherty *(with Marilyn, right)*, in an interview later in life, revealed, "I should have known who Norma Jeane was when I married her. It's funny how I kidded myself into thinking her innocent like I wanted her to be.

The clue came the first night I took her dancing. With her eyes shut extra tight, she pressed her body as tight as she could against me. Naturally, I got a hard-on. The third night when I took her dancing, she pressed so hard against me that I almost came. I was shocked when she took that delicate paw of hers and felt my hard-on. "Oh, my God, I almost ruined my pants on the spot. When the music stopped, I had to stand on the dance floor until my erection came down."

314

Marilyn. Dougherty insisted that I refer to her as Norma Jeane, saying, 'I don't know any Marilyn Monroe.' Dougherty admitted that he'd married 'a very damaged woman, unloved for most of her life.' But he was quick to dispel some rumors about Marilyn's early life. The one I found most intriguing was the claim he made about Marilyn's virginity—or lack thereof," Porter said.

"Norma Jeane came to our marriage bed a virgin," Dougherty claimed. "She and I had never had sex before. Her delicate threshold had never been crossed before. She cried out in pain, and I was aware and sensitive to her." *Those were his exact words*. After losing her virginity to her new husband on her wedding night, Norma Jeane "just fell crazily in love with sex," Dougherty claimed. "I was one lucky man!"

But what of all those other stories, as detailed in countless biographies, about Marilyn's abuse and rape in foster homes?

"Pure fantasy on Norma Jeane's part," Dougherty insisted. "She made up those stories to win the public's sympathy when she was revealed as the model who'd posed for that nude calendar hanging in every men's toilet in every garage in America. She got the sympathy vote. Her ploy worked. Her career was saved."

Once he was launched into the subject, Dougherty had a lot to say about Marilyn, enough to fill a book.

The marriage of **Norma Jeane Baker** and **James Dougherty** on June 19, 1942 was doomed from the start. She was just three weeks past her sixteenth birthday. He wanted a faithful and dutiful housewife who would be waiting for him when he returned home from work. He also wanted a woman to cook his dinner, wash his underwear, and succumb to his sexual demands. Finally, he'd wanted a virgin, thinking he was getting one when he married her.

He had no way of knowing that the sixteen year old he'd wed would one day become the sex goddess of the century -- a *femme fatale* whose sexual conquests would include two American presidents, Joan Crawford, and Barbara Stanwyck.

The debut of **Norma Jeane's** modeling career marked the beginning of the end of her marriage to James Dougherty. To be fair, the relationship had been rocky from the beginning.

The photographer who shot her photo for the cover *(right)* of *Diary Secrets* later said, "she had a 35-inch bust at the age of nineteen – and knew how to project those tits to the last centimeter." Marilyn disagreed with this appraisal, and in 1954 said her epitaph should read: **HERE LIES MARILYN MONROE – 38-23-36.**

After her appearance on the cover of *Diary Secrets,* modeling jobs began to pour in, especially after word spread that Norma Jeane had a surprise waiting at the end of every shoot. She truly lived up to the promise on the cover of *Diary Secrets*: **I PLAYED KISS AND RUN.**

In her late teens, Norma Jeane still kept her hair color dirty blonde. But she noticed it became lighter in the summer sun of California. She liked that look and decided to go blonde all the way and all year round. She later told Shelley Winters that "all the way" meant dying "down there," too.

"I'm a skeptical reporter," Porter said, but 'the first husband' talked so convincingly and provided so many clinical details about his wedding night with Norma Jeane that I believed his account. He did provide one unsettling detail about his honeymoon. 'Unknown to me at the time, Dougherty claimed, 'Norma Jeane had trench mouth.'"

If the detective's story rings true, and there is no reason to believe otherwise, only one man as far as it's known—ever raped Marilyn Monroe.

His name was Jumpin' Joe DiMaggio, and it happened one night in Los Angeles.

Marilyn Monroe and James Dougherty had very different impressions about Monroe's teenage sexuality. When Marilyn married Dougherty in 1952, she claimed, "There were no thoughts of sex in my head." Dougherty concurred, stating "She began our married life knowing nothing, absolutely zero, about sex. My mother had cautioned me to go easy on Norma Jeane, knowing I was to be the first to pierce her hymen. I went gentle with her, crossing a delicate threshold that had never been crossed before. Not ever! It didn't hurt her at all. She took to it like a pig to shit and couldn't get enough of me. She wanted it all the time. God, I was one tired man."

Nearly a decade later, Marilyn had a different story: "Marriage just added to my lack of interest in sex. Jim enjoyed himself. I did not. He didn't even seem to know that he wasn't satisfying me."

Over the next several years, Norma Jeane would come to know men with far greater endowments than Jim's.

During the first weeks of their marriage, **James Dougherty** was shocked to discover that his new wife wanted to have sex in public places – especially movie theaters. "I would keep telling her, 'Wait, Norma Jeane, until we get home.'"

"Sometimes in the theater, she'd get down on her knees on the dirty floor and unbutton my pants and blow me. She also liked to get fucked in dangerous places where a policeman was likely to discover us. She preferred side streets or even back roads in San Fernando Valley."

"One night some hunters found us and shined a flashlight into our car. I quickly concealed myself but Norma Jeane let the four guys get a free look. When I drove her home, I told her I didn't want to have sex in public places anymore."

"Why not?" she said. "We're married, aren't we? It's not like we're doing anything illegal."

"Marriage Without Kisses!" The headline on this edition of *Personal Romances* might have described Norma Jeane's deteriorating relationship with her first husband, James Dougherty. When he came home on leave, she was no longer passionate. She seemed distant and removed from him, and only submitted to sex. He later told friends, "It was like fucking a zombie."

Norma Jeane had moved out of her home with Dougherty's parents—"I needed more freedom." What she actually needed was privacy in order to bring home tricks to help launch her modeling career. James was furious when he found out she'd quit her job for modeling – he feared that she couldn't count on getting modeling jobs all the time.

Placing her hand on her hip, Norma Jeane challenged Dougherty, "Do I look like a factory girl?" With that, she stormed out of the house and didn't return until three o'clock the following morning. She refused to tell him where she'd been. When he threatened physical violence, she claimed, "I was out with the girls."

True Experiences

The Magazine About Real People

25 Complete Features For Only 25¢

May

Do I look happy?

I should —
For I was a little
nobody wanted
A lonely girl with a
dream — who awakened to find
that dream come true —

I am Marilyn Monroe...
read my Cinderella story on page 22 →

After posing for this cover, **Norma Jeane** sent a letter to Dougherty informing him that she was no longer "your Norma Jeane – **from this day on, I am Marilyn Monroe!!!**" (The three exclamation points were her own.) "One photographer told me today that I should go to Hollywood and replace Betty Grable who's getting a little long in the tooth." That photographer turned out to be a prophet.

Although the magazine was called *True Experiences*, the story it ran about Marilyn's Cinderella-like childhood was completely false. The only true confession it contained was that she was, "A lonely girl with a dream – *who awakened to that dream come true.*"

The full actualization of that dream, however, would be a long time coming, if, in fact, it ever came at all. Even at the time of her death, Marilyn still remained that "lonely girl" looking for a love she would never find, except for perhaps "a few good days" with Joe DiMaggio.

In need of money to pay the rent, **Marilyn** posed nude for photographer Tom Kelly in 1949 when she was 21 years old. He eventually sold the pictures for $200 to Western Lithograph Company, who subsequently reproduced a calendar series three years later. The tantalizing nudes of Marilyn were hanging in garage and barbershop walls throughout America until some hawkeyed fan did some research – the face on the calendar belonged to Marilyn Monroe, the new blonde goddess at 20th Century Fox.

In the early 1950s, such a display of nudity could have easily destroyed the career of a young actress. Exposure in the press, however, had the opposite effect for Marilyn. If anybody in America had not heard of her already, the massive media coverage it generated soon remedied that. Marilyn truly became a household word. A legend was born.

But at first the executives at Fox considered not releasing *Clash By Night*. Marilyn had starred in the movie with bisexual actress, Barbara Stanwyck, with whom she'd had a brief affair.

Marilyn, far ahead of the Fox executives, sensed that the country and its mores had changed – no doubt due to the upheaval brought about by World War II. The nude calendar, bestseller of all time, is still a hot seller today. Over the decades it has generated revenues in the millions. Marilyn received fifty dollars. One of the nude calendar shots was purchased for $500 by Hugh Hefner, and it was featured in the first edition of his startling new magazine, *Playboy*. On its cover, Marilyn appeared fully clothed.

An original of this first edition is now a valued collectors' item. In 2007, Playboy printed 20,000 replica copies and sold them for $25 each. Many collectors who purchased these copies have been fooled into thinking they own an original.

This tantalizing picture of "Marilyn Monroe" on the cover of a 1979 edition of *Playboy* is not the real thing. Chicago model Cheryle Larsen replicated the blonde bombshell of the fifties. Playboy's executive art director, Tom Staebler, gave Larsen the hairstyle, beauty mark, and glossy red lips. Larsen did the rest, parting those succulent lips in her best come-hither style.

The magazine itself contained an exposé of "The Private Life of Marilyn Monroe," a memoir as revealed by Lene Pepitone, her personal maid and seamstress. In 1957, Pepitone rang the bell of Marilyn's New York apartment where Marilyn was waiting, nude, to interview her as a job applicant.

"She was anything but what I had expected. Her blonde hair, which appeared unwashed, was a mess. Without makeup, she was pale and tired-looking. Her celebrated figure seemed more overweight than voluptuous. I was astonished by the way she smelled. She needed a bath. Badly. Still, she was pretty."

Hired for the job, Pepitone noted that Marilyn spent an unusually long time in the bathroom. "One day, thinking Marilyn was out, I went into the bathroom to straighten up, and I found her perched on the toilet, legs up, performing an elaborate ceremony with a bottle of some chemical and two toothbrushes. She was bleaching her pubic hair blonde. She shrieked with embarrassment. Both Marilyn and I were beet red with embarrassment. Then she started laughing uncontrollably. 'Now you know my secret!' she told me. 'You know, it has to match my hair.' I had always assumed Marilyn was a natural blonde all over. Now I knew better. 'With all my white dresses and all, it just wouldn't look nice to be dark down there. You could see through, you know,' she said."

The marriage of "The Last Hero," **Joe DiMaggio,** with **Marilyn Monroe** became a glamorous tabloid fiesta and ended in heartbreak and grief. The last hero, as we now know, wasn't a hero at all, and Marilyn was hardly a romantic heroine. When a blind date was arranged between Marilyn and DiMaggio, she claimed, "I've heard that name. He's that Italian actor, isn't he? Don't tell him, but I've seen none of his pictures."

"Marilyn, he's the greatest baseball star in America," said business agent David March.

"Okay, big guy," she said, "If you know so much about sports, tell me the difference between baseball and football."

Almost before their honeymoon began, the tension in the marriage began to surface. Always zealously guarding his privacy, DiMaggio was horrified at how she immediately went into her "Marilyn Monroe act" every time she saw a photographer. "She's a total exhibitionist," DiMaggio told his pal, Frank Sinatra. "Publicity is to Marilyn what fresh meat is to a tyrannosaur."

Even though she claimed to enjoy sex with DiMaggio, she admitted to Shelley Winters, "I can't have a climax with him. That's something no man can seem to give me. Maybe one day I'll meet the man who can – Porfirio Rubirosa with that rubber hose of his went at me all night, and he was mighty determined – but even he didn't succeed. The only climax I get is the one I give myself."

Despite of her ongoing lack of fulfillment, the sexual attraction between Marilyn and DiMaggio was a powerful link. Within two weeks, she'd nicknamed him "Slugger."

Despite their public displays of affection, the clashing egos of **DiMaggio** and **Marilyn** – called "Mr. and Mrs. America" – appeared as a match made in heaven. In reality, it was nine months of hell. Marilyn wasn't the first movie star DiMaggio had fucked. His pal, Frank Sinatra, had arranged liaisons with lots of other stars, including Marlene Dietrich. After their brief fling, DiMaggio complained to Sinatra about Dietrich's bad breath.

During his marriage to Marilyn, DiMaggio was insanely jealous, as his wife continued her affairs with other men. One night he arrived home and found Sinatra leaving Marilyn's room in only his underwear.

Sinatra and DiMaggio were both first generation Americans, the two most famous Italians in the world. Although they'd been pals for years, their friendship was severely strained that night, as Sinatra quickly dressed and left the apartment. DiMaggio later told his cronies, "I gave Marilyn the beating of her life that night. I even threatened to ruin her face for life, and I was so mad I almost did it. As for Frankie boy, I'm not going to banish him from my life forever. We've been too close for that. I'm still going to speak to him, maybe even hang out with him from time to time. But it will never be the same between us. I'll get even. The first thing I'm going to do is call up Ava Gardner and go over and fuck her. She's nothing but a whore anyway. Just like that blonde I married."

In spite of his secret fury with Sinatra, DiMaggio continued to see his old friend from time to time. His deep-seated resentment became obvious when he refused to invite Sinatra to Marilyn's funeral, despite Sinatra's pointed requests to pay his final respects.

In what could be viewed as a fortuitous prediction of her young death, Marilyn had always stated that she wanted Sinatra's music to be played at her funeral. Instead, DiMaggio ordered that Judy Garland's "Over the Rainbow" be played. Days after the funeral, DiMaggio told friends, "Sinatra, and the others, including those God damn low-life bastards, the Kennedys, killed Marilyn. That faggot, Peter Lawford, also had a hand in it. If one of those Kennedys had showed up for Marilyn's funeral, I would have taken a baseball bat and bashed in their faces. All of those sons of bitches killed Marilyn."

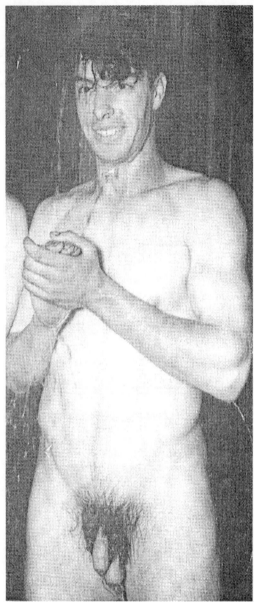

"He's a grower, not a show-er," Marilyn told Shelley Winters when describing her lover/husband **Joe DiMaggio**. His uncut penis didn't initially impress some of the showgirls he seduced, but from most reports it usually rose to the occasion and was quite impressive when fully extended.

After his divorce from Marilyn, DiMaggio's reputation as The Great Lover spread. "There was something to that reputation," said author Richard Ben Cramer, "because in those years, more than ever, women just fell all over him. That was partly about Marilyn, too. Every female of a certain age in America had wondered what it would be like to be Marilyn Monroe. (A lot of 'em were willing to try it for a night.) But it was something about Joe, too – because he was so publicly, famously hurt … it gave him a softer edge, a vulnerability, that drew women in, like bears to honey – a lot of volunteers to fix his broken heart."

Behind Joe's back, Marilyn hired the famous lawyer, Jerry Giesler, to begin the divorce proceedings. The usual charge of mental cruelty was cited, along with a "conflict of careers." Considering the latent hostility DiMaggio felt for Sinatra, it was ironic that he chose to spend the night his divorce was finalized, along with Marilyn, in the singer's apartment in LA.

The divorce became final on October 17, 1954. DiMaggio and Marilyn had been married for 286 days. No longer married to her "Slugger," the divorce having gone through only hours before, Marilyn, also in a surprise move, chose to spend the first night of her newly found freedom with her (suddenly former) husband. Joe was no longer in a position to demand conjugal rights, as he had so many times in the past. She later said she just wanted to "be alone with Joe and cuddle with him." He had other plans.

Humiliated by the divorce, he wanted to re-establish his dominance over her. When she refused to have sex with him, he ripped her dress from her body. As was her habit, she wore no underwear. He knocked her down on the carpeted floor of Sinatra's living room and held her firmly. He proceeded to rape her as violently as he'd ever seduced any woman. At one point, she later confessed, she no longer resisted him but began to sob uncontrollably. That seemed to excite him all the more. He became even more brutal. He continued trying to kiss her but she turned her head away. Nevertheless, he forced her lips to meet his. Instead of kissing her, he bit her lip until it bled.

After raping her, he stormed out of the apartment but later reconciled with her. They continued to have sex until her death. She forgave him for his brutal actions. "Only that night, only when he was raping me," she told Peter Lawford, "did I truly understand just how much he loved me."

320

Marilyn, Joe & Me

A Distant, Dubious Relative of the DiMaggios "Tells It Like It Wasn't"

The December 2005 issue of *Playboy* carried the promise of "new evidence" into the mysterious death of Marilyn Monroe. Hugh Hefner's magazine assured readers they would get to read "Her Last Words Uncensored." The so-called revelations were excerpted from one of the most controversial books every written about the star. Entitled **Marilyn, Joe & Me**, it was penned by June DiMaggio who asserted that she was the daughter of Louise and Tom DiMaggio, brother of the baseball icon.

Even her blood link to the DiMaggio family came into question as bloggers cited that June's mother was merely a second wife to Joe's brother, Tom. Although the book is reported to be the first from the usually silent DiMaggio family, researcher Lebh Shomea claimed that "June is not a DiMaggio and she was born June M. Elpine on June 11, 1923 to Rosetta Louise Rovegno and Albert U. Elpine. The assertion is made that her mother married Tom DiMaggio sometime in the 1940s when June was an adult and not living at home. June is not Joe DiMaggio's niece," Shomea claimed.

A minor actress, June states that she was a confidante of Marilyn for eleven years, as have so many other "close friends." Bloggers charged that the book was "another sad, pathetic attempt to make money off a dead legend."

The obvious errors were there, and they were big. Gloria Swanson played an actress named Norma Desmond in *Sunset Blvd.,* not "Desdemona," a character from Shakespeare's *Othello*. Marlon Brando did not star in *The Rose Tattoo*, Burt Lancaster did. The 1952 MM film with Richard Widmark was *Don't Bother to Knock*, not *Don't Bother Knocking*. The book even contains such embarrassing assertions as "Cabina (sic) Wright was a syndicated Hollywood gossip columnist, the Luella (sic) Parsons of her time." Of course, it was Cobina Wright and Louella Parsons.

Jill A. Adams, an MM historian for more than 30 years, called June's book "a complete hoax." Adams cited a Long Beach *Queen Mary* exhibit to which June was connected. The "artifacts" on display were said to have been in the possession of Marilyn herself, although the exhibit was not authenticated. For example, one questionable display was a Clairol hair curling set complete with blonde hair still attached. Since Clairol manufactured that set in 1972 and Marilyn died in 1962, the chances seem slim that she actually used it to curl her hair.

Assertions are made that June cooked a homemade pizza which Marilyn ate shortly before her death. Coroners, however, found Marilyn's stomach empty of food. Even though the (alleged murder) house was tightly sealed by the police, June also claimed that in the early hours of the morning after Marilyn's death, she drove over to the dead star's house and used a pass key she'd been given to open the back door. Her claim is that there was no one in the house at the time. She alleges that from the house she retrieved a teddy bear – Marilyn called it "Barbie Bear" – that she'd given Marilyn, along with her pizza pan. How June managed not to be seen by all the reporters and photographers, along with the idle curious assembled outside Marilyn's house, is not explained.

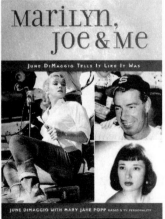

In the most controversial claim within June's memoir, she writes, "Marilyn had been talking with her on the phone, Mother told me, when intruders entered Marilyn's room. In her terror, Marilyn dropped the phone, but the killers never hung it up. Mother told me that she had heard it all – the voices in the room, the struggle, the silence. All accounts that I know of state that when Marilyn was found, her phone was still off the hook."

June alleges that her mother "knew who killed Marilyn but that knowledge absolutely terrified her, and to protect us, she said that she would never reveal the details of what she knew."

When Titans Clash
The Night Jackie Confronted Marilyn

Jackie Kennedy and **Truman Capote** *(above)* had long, drawn-out discussions about the affairs of the Kennedy men, including the founding papa, Joseph Kennedy, and his relationships with actresses such as Gloria Swanson. "I don't think Jackie realized what she was walking into when she married Jack," Capote said. "He was in constant competition with his old man to see who could nail the most women. Jackie wasn't prepared for quite such blatant womanizing. She hadn't expected to find herself stranded at parties while her husband went off with somebody new."

In her anger one night, Jackie told Capote, "Jack has a miniscule body and a huge head." Capote was far more direct. "All those Kennedy men are the same. They're like dogs, having to stop and pee on every fire hydrant."

In another startling conversation, Capote listened to a drugged and slightly demented Marilyn Monroe who shared her dream with him. "Jack told me only last week that he plans to divorce Jackie and marry me. No later than 1964, I will be by his side when he seeks re-election. Imagine me, *First Lady of the land*. I had ambitions when I was struggling in the early days. With Jack, I will preside over America from 1964 to 1968 as his First Lady. I'll be a very different First Lady from Jackie. I'll be more human, more down to earth. I was the most dreamy starlet to ever arrive in Hollywood. I dreamed of becoming the biggest movie star of all time, bigger than Betty Grable, Lana Turner, and Ava Gardner. That dream came true for me. But in my wildest imagination, I never dreamed I'd become First Lady of the United States."

The World Knew Them by their Nicknames:
Jackie Oh! and MM

In the great tradition of Southern storytellers, author Truman Capote was clearly the master. Regrettably, he dined out on more stories than he recorded on paper. There is no doubt that he was privy to many of the secrets of the rich and famous, some of whom he betrayed by writing thinly disguised portraits of them when he published excerpts from his unfinished novel, *Answered Prayers*.

One night in Key West in 1969, Truman told an astonishing story that he claimed was going to appear as an entire chapter in his upcoming novel. Listening with eager ears were Truman's hosts, Tennessee Williams and his longtime companion, Frank Merlo, along with James Leo Herlihy (author of *Midnight Cowboy*) and the co-author of this book, Darwin Porter.

All biographers assume that Marilyn Monroe and Jacqueline Kennedy never met face to face, although they occasionally shared the bed of the same man—namely President John F. Kennedy.

Each woman had met the rising young Massachusetts politician in 1951: Marilyn on May 15, Jackie at a different party 12 days earlier.

By the time the Kennedys moved into the White House, the new First Lady was aware of her husband's affairs with other women, including Marilyn. Jackie called it, "the curse of being married to a Kennedy man."

According to Truman, Jackie tried to ignore the

Truman Capote wanted **Marilyn Monroe** to play Holly Golightly in the film version of *Breakfast at Tiffany's*. But the studio had other plans, and cast Audrey Hepburn instead. Capote later said, "Marilyn would have been absolutely marvelous in the role. She wanted to play Holly and even worked up two whole scenes all by herself and did them for me. She was terrifically good, but Paramount double-crossed me in every conceivable way and cast Audrey. Audrey is an old friend and one of my favorite people, but she was just wrong for the part."

A Question of Size. "What I don't understand is why everybody said the Kennedys were so sexy," said Capote. "I know a lot about cocks – I've seen an awful lot of them – and if you put all the Kennedys together, you wouldn't have a good one. I used to see Jack when I was staying with Loel and Gloria Guinness in Palm Beach. I had a little guest cottage with its own private beach, and he would come down so he could swim in the nude. He had absolutely nuthin'! Bobby was the same way; I don't know how he had all those children. As for Teddy – forget it! I liked Jack, and I liked many things about Bobby. But I wouldn't have wanted him to be President. He was too vindictive. Teddy is crazy. He's a menace. He's a wild Irish drunk who goes into terrible rages. I'd want anybody to be president before Teddy!"

affair but plotted revenge. That would come on the night of May 19, 1962. On learning that Peter Lawford had asked Marilyn to fly in from the West Coast and sing "Happy Birthday, Mr. President" to JFK in Washington, Jackie placed a secret call to Marilyn one week before the event. She advised Marilyn to make the song "as sexy as possible because Jack will adore it." Marilyn told her that she thought that was a "great idea," and that designer Jean-Louis was putting the finishing touches on a dress that Marilyn was describing as "just flesh and diamonds."

Appearing late at the televised event, Marilyn walked onto the stage to sing her song. As columnist Dorothy Kilgallen later so aptly put it: "It was like Marilyn Monroe was making love to the President in direct view of 40 million Americans." Jackie wisely had skipped the event to go horseback riding in Virginia.

Although officially, the President had thanked Marilyn for singing "in such a sweet and wholesome way," backstage he was furious, blaming Peter Lawford for the disaster. Meeting privately with Marilyn, JFK whispered to her that their affair was over, even though he invited her back to his suite at the Hotel Carlyle for "a farewell fuck." He warned her never to call the White House again. Belatedly, Marilyn realized that Jackie had tricked her.

Back on the West Coast, Marilyn was fuming and "full of fury," in Peter's words. She phoned him one night to

Truman Capote not only saw **John Kennedy** *sans* bathing suit *(right)*, but also attended dinner parties with "Jackie and Jack" in the 1950s during the first years of their marriage. At one such party on Park Avenue, Capote showed up with Babe Paley, the wife of William Paley, then chairman of the board of CBS.

After dinner, Jackie and Babe left for a brandy in one part of the apartment while the men retired for brandy and cigars in the library. "Some high roller from Texas was recounting his experiences with a $1,500-a-night call girl in Las Vegas," Capote claimed. "He knew their telephone numbers and their specialty – sucking cock, rim jobs, around the world. He knew how well they did it, how long, how deep, how big a cock they could take, and what they could do with it that nobody else had ever done. That's how he talked. It was nauseating, a real stomach-turner. Jack was lapping it up, practically taking notes. He did write some names and numbers on a scrap of paper for future use. Later when he and Jackie were leaving, she asked him what the men had talked about. 'Plain old politics,' he lied to her. But Jackie knew the score. She knew everything!"

Two months before her death in 1962, Capote dined with **Marilyn**. "In spite of all the pain she was suffering from both Jack and Bobby Kennedy, she had lost a lot of weight for the film *Something's Got to Give,*" Capote said. "George Cukor had been set to direct her. There was a new maturity about her. She wasn't so giggly anymore. I told her, 'Marilyn, why cry over Jack or Bobby? Between the two of them, they can't raise a decent hard-on.' 'Truman,' she chastised me, 'You've always been such a size queen.' If she'd lived and held onto her figure, I think she would have looked gorgeous and glamorous for years. Bobby and Jack didn't really kill her, at least in the literal sense. She committed suicide."

"But they did pay one of her best friends to keep quiet about their affairs with her," Capote claimed. "The friend knew where all the skeletons were. After Marilyn died, Peter Lawford gave this friend a year-long cruise around the world. For that entire year, no one, not even the police, knew where she was. A cover-up, for sure."

inform him that she was going to call a press conference next week and reveal her long-running affair with the President. She also said that after her press conference, "Mr. President can kiss a second term good-bye."

Peter beseeched her not to, but fully believed she'd do it. He placed an urgent call to Bobby Kennedy, urging him to warn the President. Peter also claimed that Marilyn was growing more and more dependent on drugs and sounded "unhinged."

It is not known how Jackie learned about Marilyn's threat, but apparently she did. Through Peter's help, she placed another call to Marilyn and asked to meet secretly with her at the apartment of Truman Capote, in Manhattan, the following week. The author had agreed to play host at this secret rendezvous.

Marilyn flew in from the West Coast to New York, where she checked into The Hotel Carlyle, earlier site of several secret trysts with the President.

Years later, in Key West in 1969, Truman either was being deliberately vague or did not want his audience to know the exact date of this rendezvous. Obviously it had to have occurred some weekend during June or July of 1962. He did reveal the time of the meeting in his apartment, plac-

Capote learned that **Jacqueline Kennedy** *(above)* was so upset over her husband's affair with Marilyn Monroe that she went to Valleyhead, a private psychiatric clinic in Carlisle, Massachusetts, for electro-shock therapy.

Capote had met Jackie when she was a college student working for *Vogue* magazine in New York. He'd been in on her early days of romance with the senator from Massachusetts. "From the beginning, Jackie knew that her husband was dating other women. She even knew that he had begun his affair when Marilyn was the most famous movie star in the world and Jack a relatively unknown senator. At times when I saw her she was coming unglued. I never knew what was wrong with her. She's way out in orbit somewhere most of the time. I don't think she can stand the pressure of being a politician's wife. I think she'll snap."

Her friend, Paul Mathias, said, "Jackie was hurt very young in connection with both her father and mother. She never came out of the shock of growing up. I don't think she was born happy. She fills her days as best as she can, but she suffers a lot. I have great compassion for her. It sinks into me more and more just how irreversibly unhappy she is."

In the 1950s when **Capote** *(right)* met Jacqueline Kennedy, she was married to a handsome young senator from Massachusetts.

"I used to have dinner with her and Jack when they had this awful old apartment on Park Avenue around 86th Street. But mostly Jack was out of town, and she and I would have dinner or go to the theater by ourselves. We used to sit around talking until four or five o'clock in the morning. She was sweet, eager, intelligent, not quite sure of herself and hurt – because she knew that he was banging all these other broads. She never said that, but I knew about it rather vaguely."

ing it at around ten o'clock in the evening. He claimed that Marilyn arrived first, looking "camera ready" in a white satin gown with a white sable, even though it was summer. Jackie, according to Truman, arrived twenty minutes later and wore a plain black and severely tailored business suit.

Marilyn sat on a sofa opposite Jackie, who preferred Truman's favorite armchair. "Marilyn oozed charm, but Jackie was distant," Truman recalled.

After social pleasantries were exchanged, Jackie asked Truman to excuse himself while they conducted private business. He said that he retreated to his bedroom with a drink, and before the evening ended he had a few more. Eventually he drifted off to sleep.

A loud pounding on his door woke him up around one-thirty a.m. Opening it, he encountered a hysterical Marilyn, her makeup smeared. She too, or so it appeared, had been drinking heavily. The First Lady had left the apartment.

"It's all over!" Marilyn sobbed to Truman. As best as he could ascertain, Marilyn had agreed to call off the press conference. She also said that Jackie had forgiven her for her affair with her husband, saying that "only a cadaver can resist Jack when he turns on the charm." Jackie's icy facade had "melted" at some point in the night as she

On December 10, 1967, in the wake of the death of her husband, John F. Kennedy, **Jackie** let years pass before she attended her first public event, a $500-a-plate dinner for the New York Democratic Party. Accompanying her was brother-in-law, **Robert Kennedy** (above).

Behind Jackie's back, Capote betrayed her friendship. Unknown to Jackie – at least at the time – Capote spread the rumor that, "Jackie is having an affair with Bobby."

"Even though those rumors appear to have been true, it was a dastardly thing to do," said Tennessee Williams. He severely chastised Capote for gossiping about Jackie. "The poor woman has suffered enough. Give her a rest. If she is finding some comfort, even some love with her brother-in-law, she should be left alone to do so. The human heart, and its needs, sometimes follows unorthodox patterns. Of all people on this earth, you and I, as artists, should know and respect that."

Biographers such as Mart Martin compile lists of what celebrities have seduced what other celebrities. There are a lot of surprises on most lists. Take John F. Kennedy, for example. On the list of his former lovers, you expect to encounter Lana Turner, June Allyson, Judith (gun moll) Campbell, even Joan Crawford and Marlene Dietrich, or his lifelong best pal, LeMoyne Billings. Billings was a homosexual who had been in love with Kennedy ever since 1933. Robert Kennedy referred to "Lem" as "Jack's second wife."

But what is the playwright **Tennessee Williams** (right) doing on a list of JFK's lovers? Gore Vidal, former friend of Williams, provided a tantalizing clue. When he introduced Tennessee to JFK in Palm Beach and when JFK went away for a moment to get a drink, the playwright told Vidal, "He's got a nice ass on him." Vidal chastised Tennessee, claiming, "You're talking about the President of the United States, Tenn."

In Key West years later, Williams said. "About as far as I got with the President was his allowing me to give him a tantalizing blow-job in the beach house that afternoon. That was the extent of our grand affair."

begged Marilyn "not to publicly humiliate me in front of the world." She also pleaded with Marilyn not to make her children victims of a divorce. According to Marilyn, Jackie even spoke of how John-John's face "lights up when his daddy walks into the room."

True to her word, Marilyn, who had only weeks to live, never held that press conference. But through the rest of June and July, Peter reported to Jackie that Marilyn was continuing to make threats against the Kennedys. When Jackie learned that Bobby Kennedy was flying to Los Angeles, she asked him to call on Marilyn to see what kind of trouble she might make for the Kennedys.

Long after Marilyn's death, and long after the assassination of her husband, Jackie told Truman: "Sending Bobby to comfort Marilyn was like sending the most succulent lamb into the wolf's lair. Bobby didn't have a chance. He'd already had an affair, and was still in love with Marilyn. If Marilyn had lived, she would probably have gotten around to Teddy too."

Marilyn Monroe was found dead in her bed early on the morning of August 5, 1962. Murder? Suicide? The debate will go on as long as the public still remembers the star's brief and incandescent, but tragic life.

One of Capote's biographers (who doesn't want his name revealed) tried to track down this story by hiring a private detective. He later refused to answer questions about the date of the alleged meeting between Marilyn and Jackie, even though he was not going to write about it in his biography. He had a policy of not running stories unless he was able to confirm them with some other source, but wanted to keep the detective's report secret in case he wished to write about it in the future.

All that he would confirm was that Marilyn, on a summer night unspecified, left the Hotel Carlyle around 9:30 and was helped into a private limousine, not the hotel's usual car service. Jackie was also in New York that night to attend some charity event, but called and cancelled at the last minute, citing flu-like symptoms.

There were no paparazzi to record where the two most famous female icons of the 20th century went on that historic night, which adds veracity to Truman's account, although the Secret Service had to be aware of Jackie's whereabouts. The detective, according to the biographer, concluded that "in all possibility" Truman was telling the truth.

After Truman left that 1969 social gathering in Key West, Tennessee Williams virtually echoed the detective's report. He told his remaining guests that, "I think we have to entertain the possibility that Truman indeed is spilling the beans. But even if he's lying to us, it still makes a hell of a good yarn."

Marilyn was studying acting with the brilliant "theatrical dragon," British-born **Constance Collier (1878-1955;** *right, top photo).* Noel Coward once branded Collier as "The Great Dyke of the Western World." Never a great beauty, Collier personified theatrical glamour to Katharine Hepburn, who was rumored to have been her lover. Collier had intuitive good taste, a wicked sense of humor, and "more talent than any actress deserves," Hepburn once said.

As regards Marilyn, the legendary British actress told Capote: "Oh yes, there is something there – a beautiful child, really – I don't think she's an actress at all – certainly not in a traditional sense. What she has is this presence, a certain luminosity, a flickering intelligence. These marvelous traits could not be captured on stage because they are too subtle, too fragile. Her wonder can only be caused by the camera. It's like a hummingbird in flight. Only a camera can freeze the poetry of it. But anyone who thinks this girl is simply another Harlow or harlot or whatever, is mad. I hope, I really pray, that she survives long enough to free the strange lovely talent that's wandering through her like a jailed spirit."

The Saga of Tom Cruise, et. al.

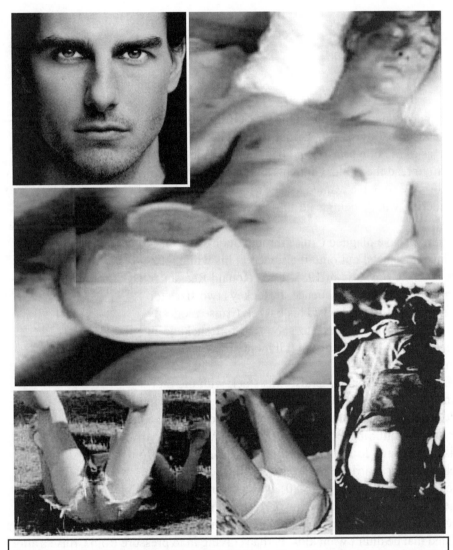

"Break out the butterfly net, New York, and unfurl the straitjacket," are words written by newspaper columnist Andrea Peyser. That's how the press these days greets the arrival in town of fading heartthrob Tom Cruise, who appears in hyperactive midlife crisis--and desperate for a comeback. Cruise in the pictures above makes an ass of himself. Turn the pages if you want to see what secret he's hiding beneath that salad bowl.

Tomfoolery
Mission Improbable

Before becoming the Number One Box Office Star in the world, a handsome, boyish Tom Cruise toyed with the idea of signing on as a Catholic priest. But his dyslexia made it difficult for him to read the Bible. Quite possibly, the very heterosexual actor may not have wanted to face accusations of being gay, considering what's being said these days about Catholic priests.

Gay rumors have plagued Cruise throughout his career, or at least since he danced out onto the screen in his white jockey shorts in *Risky Business* in 1983. Even Ronald Reagan Jr. on TV spoofed the famous sequence. In Jockeys two sizes too small, the president's son showed his basket: Cruise modestly did not. Yet he wasn't adverse to show his full package in *Magnolia* (1999) and he'd gone the full monty in *All the Right Moves* in 1983.

From the very beginning, Cruise was stuck with the pretty boy image, which was one of the reasons those gay rumors started to circulate. One unproven rumor linked him to a handsome pilot from Singapore who worked for American Airlines while based in Chicago.

"It's that big!" I swear it!" Bloggers put those words into the mouth of Tom Cruise when this crazed-look photo was published. Some of Cruise's critics suggested he needed help from the American Psychiatric Association.

There is no love lost between Cruise and America's leading psychiatrists. After his televised attack on psychiatry, shrinks sharply criticized the actor for his remarks in which he denounced their profession as a "pseudoscience."

"It is irresponsible for Mr. Cruise to use his movie publicity tour to promote his own ideological views and deter people with mental illness from getting the care they need," said Dr. Steven Sharfstein, APA president in June of 2005.

Cruise's marriage to Florida-born Mimi Rogers lasted from 1987 to 1990 and was beset with problems. Her marriage to Cruise was the second for this world-class poker player. Her first husband, James Rogers (1976-80), was a Church of Scientology counselor. Does this mean that Rogers is to blame for converting Cruise to this wacko cult?

Rogers didn't help matters at her divorce when she claimed that she and Cruise "had a poor sex life" and that he didn't want kids. Perhaps giving in to pressure from Cruise's attorneys, she later retracted her statement about Cruise in bed.

As his marriage was coming apart, Cruise met Nicole Kidman, who was only 22 years old at the time, on the set of *Days of Thunder*. The picture they made together was a bomb, but they set off personal fireworks, not only on the screen but off-screen as well. By Christmas Eve of 1990 they were married. One of those mysterious sources whose identity was never revealed reported that Kidman and Cruise tried to conceive "but it just didn't happen." Obviously not.

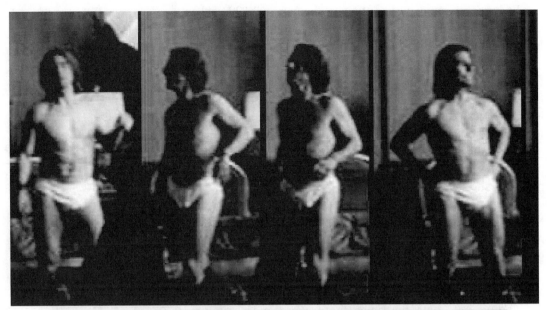

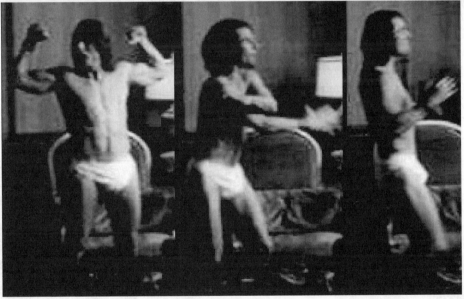

DOES LENGTH MATTER? asked the Hollywood trade papers about Tom Cruise's movie, *Magnolia* (1999). No, they weren't talking about the size of his penis, so richly on display in this movie, where he danced about in his white underpants more provocatively than he'd done in *Risky Business.* Critics were questioning the length of *Magnolia*, since it has a running time of about three hours and ten minutes.

Cruise's "basket" even became the focus of TV news as the 20th century came to its inglorious end. One critic on the air confronted Cruise about the "ample size" of his basket, a question the superstar quickly deflected. The bloggers then went to work with comments as widely varied as the wind. One blogger suggested that Cruise padded his underwear, another "size queen" expressing his disappointment, claiming he had expected "a much larger package" from the Hollywood stud, who, as it turns out, may not be a stud at all.

The movie was an epic mosaic of several interrelated characters from the San Fernando Valley, each searching for happiness, forgiveness, and meaning. Although disappointing at the box office, it did earn Cruise a nomination for an Oscar as best supporting actor.

He lost.

Fatherhood came by adoption in January of 1993 when they took into their home a child they named Isabella Jane Kidman Cruise.

Two months later Cruise picked up the March issue of *Playboy* to see his former wife, Rogers, posed in the nude. The interview she gave to Hugh Hefner's boys was also sensational. She revealed that Cruise talked of becoming a monk. "It looked as though marriage wouldn't fit into his overall spiritual need," she said, "and he thought he had to be celibate in preparation for entering the priesthood." Later, again bowing to pressure, she said "I was only joking."

Kidman was more supportive of Cruise's sexual prowess. She told *Movieline,* "He's the best lover I ever had," without revealing who she was comparing him to. "Is your husband gay?" she was asked.

"Gay? Really. Well, ummm, he's not gay in my knowledge. You'll have to ask him that question."

Throughout their marriage there were more rumors, *McCall's* magazine charging that there existed a contract between Kidman and Cruise. It was alleged from sources worldwide that the marriage was finalized only as a means of beefing up his romantic image. After Cruise formally protested to *McCall's,* that magazine publicly apologized.

Even though Kidman said she wanted a natural child, she and Cruise did not conceive. So in February of 1995 they adopted a second child, Connor Antony Kidman Cruise, an African-American.

During the filming of *Eyes Wide Shut,* Cruise's lawyers brought successful legal action against the British newspaper *The Independent.* The publication ran quotes from Susan Batson, a drama coach. She claimed that she assisted both Cruise and Kidman "to give a convincing sexual performance" in the movie. Cruise's attorneys promptly demanded a retraction, claiming that it was Kidman—not Cruise—who worked with Batson.

Throughout the filming of this movie, the press was filled with speculation that the marriage was on the rocks.

Kidman admitted that she was pregnant early in 2001. But she and Cruise announced shortly thereafter, in February of the same year, that they were splitting. The Australian beauty learned that her ten-year marriage to Cruise was coming to an end through his representatives. She was reportedly both "amazed" and "infuriated" that he chose not to confront her directly with the news.

A few weeks later, on March 13, she claimed that a miscarriage had occurred. She stated that Cruise was the father of the still-born child. Apparently, if true, this was the first child the

Before he became a national joke, Tom Cruise represented good, "clean" sex, not the dirty kinky kind that you might associate with an actor like Colin Farrell on a sex video.

Cruise managed to remain an all-American boy for nearly two decades. "Tom Cruise is to hunks what Velveeta is to cheese," said director Emile Ardolina.

In the infamous dance scene in *Risky Business,* the code language was that dance equaled sex. As one critic said, "Cruise's ecstatic solo gyrations are the best covert wank-off in movie history. And, of course, he's damn cute. Even when he became more overt, it was about 'natural sex,' not the sordid, icky stuff."

star had been able to beget. During her ordeal, he did not visit her in the hospital at UCLA.

There was no prenuptial agreement, which seems to suggest that the story that she was paid a large sum of money to marry him "to clarify his sexual ambivalence," may have been just that...a story. Miscarriage or not, the divorce proceeded.

As part of their private divorce agreement, Cruise agreed to provide Kidman with one half of their community property. That would surely consist of tens of millions of dollars.

Perez Hilton writes what is called "Hollywood's Most Hated Web Site," and Tom Cruise is a favorite target of his.

In one of the most provocative items he ever posted, he wrote:

"For years, Hollywood insiders have whispered (loudly) that Cruise cannot have his

Cruise's first attempt at marriage was with Florida-born Mimi Rogers.

The actress married Cruise in 1987, divorcing him in 1990. Rogers, who posed nude for *Playboy* in 1993, hasn't been too friendly with her ex. She once claimed that they split up because Cruise "wanted to maintain the purity of his instrument."

Cruise proposed to Katie Holmes romantically from one of the platforms of the Eiffel Tower. But Rogers claimed that "with me, he didn't do anything dashing, like going down on one knee. It just, well, it just sort of happened."

Incidentally Mimi Rogers is the greatest poker player in Hollywood.

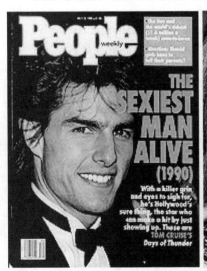

At one time, second wife Nicole Kidman may have agreed that Tom Cruise was "The Sexiest Man Alive." She claimed that she soon overcame any reservation about his lack of height after their first date. "We went to the movies and he was wearing a T-shirt," she said. "I took one look at his biceps and I could not watch the movie. I was a goner after that."

He said, "My first reaction to meeting Nicole was pure lust. It was totally physical. I thought she was amazingly sexy and stunning."

own biological children because his sperm count is too low. That would explain why he and Nicole Kidman adopted their two children. Additionally, though this obviously was never confirmed, the leading theory in LA as to the Kidman/Cruise divorce is that Nicole became pregnant with Scotsman Ewan McGregor's child, which ended up in a miscarriage, during the filming of Moulin Rouge. According to that theory, Tom was furious that Nicole broke their pact. They could each fool around with other men, but she could never get pregnant. Why? Because it'd become obvious when the child grew up that it wasn't his."

Although practically everyone in Hollywood reads Perez Hilton, his allegations about Cruise and Kidman are mere speculation. There was no evidence presented about Cruise's sperm count, Kidman's miscarriage, or any "secret pact" between them.

Set adrift after his divorce, Cruise developed a so-called romance with Penelope Cruz, whom he'd met when they were co-starring in *Vanilla Sky*. Mimi Rogers predicted that "Tom and Penelope will tie the knot before long. Knowing Tom, it will be sooner than later." How wrong a first wife can be. Cruise and the Madrid-born beauty went their separate ways. She ended up with a shirtless but certifiably straight man, Matthew McConaughey, who was named "Sexiest Man Alive" by *People* magazine in 2005. From his arms, Cruz developed the hots for another certifiably straight actor, Josh Hartnett, who seems to be every woman's fantasy boyfriend. From Hartnett, she sailed into the piratical seas of the Caribbean with Orlando Bloom.

During his time with Cruz, Cruise may have developed a taste for Hispanic women. He was next seen with Colombian model/actress Sofia Vergara, who is a much bigger name in South America than in the United States. A former lover of Enrique Iglesias, "La Toti" (her nickname) often makes those lists of the 100 sexiest women in the world, usually ranking somewhere in the 50s. The sexy star downplayed stories that she and Cruise "had been intimate."

During the post-millennium, rumors of Cruise's homosexuality grew more rampant than at any point in his career. "They just wouldn't go away," said one Paramount executive off the record. "The public was taking the position of 'where there's smoke there's fire.'"

To preserve his romantic image and maintain his box office clout, Cruise, as some of his advisers maintained, needed to launch a full-scale romance instead of a series of routine flirtations. The pressure was high to present an uncompromisingly hetero image to his public.

There were totally unconfirmed reports that Cruise went not only shopping for a new girlfriend but a potential wife, perhaps a future mother of his children.

Unsubstantiated reports appearing in the press said that his first choice was Jessica Alba,

After Nicole Kidman divorced Tom Cruise for reasons yet unexplained (there are rumors), she told the press. "At long last I can wear heels." Often, it's Cruise himself in heels, but not the Joan Crawford "fuck-me shoes" of the 1940s. Call Cruise's footwear "lifts." He stands five feet, 7 inches, although some claim he's 5 feet, 5 inches. Shoe experts say that lifts today can be deceptively inserted inside the heel of a standard dress shoe, thereby adding inches to a man's height. Some paparazzi shots show Kidman towering above her husband. Others show their heights as equally matched. You figure.

a California-born beauty. Nicknamed Sky Angel, she's the daughter of a Mexican father. She also has a gift for appearing on those lists of "100 Hot Babes." She threatened to sue *Playboy* when it ran her picture on its March 2005 cover, suggesting there might be nude pictures of her inside. There weren't.

She has claimed she's a modest girl "and would never do a nude scene or pose topless in a magazine," pointedly unlike Cruise's first wife.

Alba was voted "Worst Actress" for her appearance in *Fantastic Four* in 2005. The Cruise/Alba spaceship never got airborne. Alba later attacked the Cruise/Katie Holmes romance, claiming they were using their high-profile romance to boost both of their respective careers. She said, "I don't date actors, and I don't date people to get ahead in my career." In fact, she swore off actors after her failed relationship with Mark Wahlberg (Marky Mark). Perhaps—and this is not known—she hung out with him long enough to find what those Calvin Klein briefs concealed.

Actress Kate Bosworth, between alleged bouts of anorexia, was said to be prospect number two on the Cruise list of potential girlfriends. Ben Widdicome, in his popular Gatecrasher column in *The New York Daily News*, reported on this as a grapevine rumor. The leading Cruise rep (his sister at the time) denied it. Bosworth seemed to have had the hots for the more studly and more handsome Orlando Bloom.

The rumors on the Hollywood cocktail circuit continued in spite of loud and frequent denials. Allegedly, the bimbo mess, Lindsay Lohan, was considered as a candidate but was almost immediately rejected because of her chaotic personal life.

Reportedly fifth on the list, Katie Holmes, baptized a Catholic, began dating Cruise following her breakup with *American Pie* actor Chris Klein. The couple had been together since 2001. She had become famous for her role as Joey Potter on the WB teen TV drama, *Dawson's Creek*, which ran from 1998 to 2003. By June of 2005, she was said to have become engaged to Cruise and had expressed an interest in Scientology. Some fans suggested that she had been coerced or "brainwashed" into this religious cult.

Many young fans posted their opinions on the web, claiming that if they were Katie, they would have preferred a

Tom Cruise and **Nicole Kidman** differed over their sex scenes in *Eyes Wide Shut* (1999), the last film directed by Stanley Kubrick. "Some of the scenes are almost pornographic," Kidman charged. "We shot a lot I wouldn't do for any other director."

Cruise, appearing in an interview with Diane Sawyer, claimed, "It's not pornography. It's me kissing and touching my wife. There's nothing wrong with that."

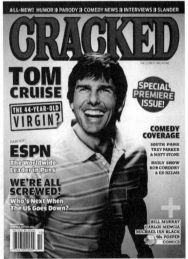

Cruise's devotion to Holmes got icky when he allegedly told *GQ* magazine that he wanted to eat the placenta of their upcoming baby, later named Suri. Surely he was joking. Remarks such as that got **Cruise** onto the cover of *Cracked*.

hottie like Chris Klein instead of Cruise. The Illinois-born, apple-cheeked, translucent-skinned, all-American boy made him a natural for pretty boy jock roles. Holmes may have left Klein because he has one false tooth. He lost the original in a football accident in high school.

Despite Cruise's romance with Holmes, those old rumors persist, and apparently, for a while, they were driving Cruise beserk. He believed, it appears, that he had to fight back but he did it in such a bizarre way that he seemed to be in the midst of an emotional breakdown in May of 2005 during an appearance on Oprah Winfrey's TV show. He admitted that he was smitten with Holmes and in front of millions of witnesses, like a lunatic, he started jumping up and down on Winfrey's sofa, proclaiming "I can't be cool . . . I can't be laid back." Cruise at the time was a middle-age man, 16 years her senior.

Unfortunately for him, Cruise's statements were being evaluated by audiences whose references were far more sophisticated than those which evaluated the private lives of stars during Hollywood's so-called Golden Age. Back in the 40s, practicing bisexuals could escape public scrutiny more easily.

Almost overnight, on late-night TV and on talk radio stations throughout the nation, Cruise went from a pop culture phenomenon to a pop culture punchline.

When Nicole Kidman made *Moulin Rouge* with Scotsman Ewan McGregor, there was the inevitable speculation that they were carrying on a torrid romance. This appears to be untrue, but it fueled the tabloids nonetheless.

Although McGregor (*above*) looks crazed atop his bike, he's taken seriously as an actor. He has a wicked sense of humor, delivering comments such as, "I really want to play Princess Leia. Stick some big pastries on my head." McGregor denied having the hots for Kidman. "I am a married man. I haven't been personally involved with all my leading ladies. It would be somewhat glamorous if I had been, but I have not!"

The *Moulin Rouge* roles, incidentally, were originally intended for Catherine Zeta-Jones and the late Heath Ledger.

"CRUISE CRUISED CRUZ" when they came together (no pun intended) to make the controversial *Vanilla Sky* in 2001. Although he has been accused of homosexuality, and although **Penelope Cruz** has sparked lesbian rumors, they confused their suspects when they teamed up together for some hot nights.

The glamorous pair met on the set when Cruise's marriage to Nicole Kidman was falling apart. The sexy Spanish star fiercely denied that she was the cause of Cruise's split from Kidman. Cruise, in reference to Cruz, annouced to the press, "she is a beautiful human being, but in terms of marriage, there are no particular plans."

He later dumped her. Cruz broke down in a restaurant in Berlin and begged Cruise to "tell me why?" In response, all Cruise could offer was "Tea & Sympathy."

After Cruise's now-notorious appearance on her TV show, Winfrey allegedly told friends that "I don't believe the romance is real." She confessed that she was stunned by Cruise's exhibitionistic behavior, jumping up on her couch like a crazed man. "It was wilder than it was appearing to me. I was just trying to maintain the truth for myself because I couldn't figure out what was going on. I was not buying—not buying and not buying. That's why I kept saying 'you're gone, you're really gone.'"

In polls of their readership, magazines such as *People* or *Us Weekly* found that a majority of their readers were highly skeptical of this Cruise/Holmes romance. Cruise, however, refused to cool it, grabbing Holmes every time he saw a camera and tonguing her in front of the paparazzi. No star had ever gone this public before in trying to prove his heterosexuality before an unconvinced public, certainly not Cary Grant or Rock Hudson.

As a reward for the pains he took to grandstand how hot he was for Holmes, Cruise was voted "most irritating actor in movies" by a poll of readers of *Empire*, the British "film Bible."

Why, everyone asked, was Cruise rushing to identify and define "the love of my life," whatever her name might be? In lieu of hard evidence, bloggers went to work and immediately came up with some theories.

A rumor that started in Los Angeles in 2005 made its way around the world. A "Deep Throat tipster" claimed that model Marisol Maldonado, the wife of Matchbox singer Rob Thomas, had walked into her bedroom to catch her husband, Rob Thomas, *in flagrante delicto*

Candidates for Wife no. 3? Each of these beauties--**Kate Bosworth** (*left*), **Jessica Alba** (*center*), and **Sofía Vergara** (*right*)--were rumored to have been considered as appropriate wife material--or at least "arm candy," as his critics would have it--for Tom Cruise. Of the three, Bosworth seemed the least likely choice. In 2006, *FMH Magazine* ranked her as #69 on their "100 Sexiest Women in the World" contest.

No one ever accused that California beauty, Jessica Alba, of being ugly. The bra she wore in *Sin City* (2005) was later auctioned to the highest bidder for hundreds of dollars. Her movie, *Never Been Kissed* (1999), was absolutely not based on her own life. A *Hollywood.com* poll rated her the fifth Sexiest Female Star, and *Playboy* named her its "Sex Star of the Year" in its March, 2006 issue. Did Tom Cruise get to know her intimately enough to discover a tattoo of a daisy with a ladybug on it on the back of her neck? In 2005, Alba slammed the very public romance of Cruise and Holmes. "I think celebrity couples prostitute their relationships when they reveal intimate secrets. They do so only to sell movies and win roles." Her no-actor rule followed in the wake of her failed relationship with Mark Wahlberg.

The sexy Columbian beauty, Sofía Vergara, may have been too much woman for Cruise to handle. Naturally blonde and consistently rated as one of the sexiest women in the world, she downplayed the idea of a hot romance with the controversial Cruise. "But according to the media," Vergara asserted, "Tom is in a full-fledged sexual relationship with the most irresistible woman in the world--ME!"

with Cruise. According to this completely unverified Internet grapevine, she threatened to go public with her sighting until she was paid off to keep her mouth shut. There is not a shred of evidence to support this allegation, but that doesn't mean it wasn't talked about on the party circuit from the Hollywood Hills to the New York Islands.

"If I were gay," Thomas said, "Tom wouldn't be on the top of my list. It would be Brad Pitt. I'm more offended by the rumors saying I'm a Scientologist."

Of course, bloggers weighed in with their respective opinions. A typical response came from "Rahuli" posted June 30, 2005, at 4:33am, "This is the funniest thing I've ever read, and Tom Cruise gets on my nerves so bad. I hope this whole thing ends with a bang so loud that I never hear about him again."

"X" on July 2, 2005 at 2:04am posted this reaction, "This reminds me of the rumor that TC's first marriage ended because Mimi Rogers found Tom in bed with her brother."

Sometimes a blogger will actually stop speculating about Cruise's sex life and become a

"Hello, my name is Lindsay, and I'm an alchoholic and a drug addict." Or so spoke the messy bimbo, Lindsay Lohan, who is definitely "sobriety challenged."

She accepted a plea deal in her back-to-back DUI cases in August of 2007 that sent her to jail for a day.

Yes, she was stripped naked and searched "for hidden weapons."

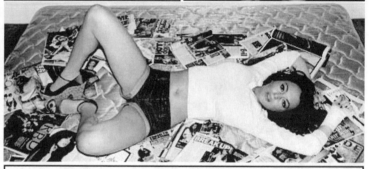

Lindsay Lohan, allegedly rejected from Cruise's list of "acceptable women for dating," raised eyebrows in June of 2005 when she performed a Cruise-inspired couch dance. She appeared on the Jay Leno show shortly after her split with Wilmer Valderrama. The 18-year-old told Leno that she wasn't in love. "But I was watching the show the other day and I saw Tom Cruise and I know he's in love. So in honor of him, and for everyone who's not in love, I'm gonna pull a Tom."

She then jumped up and down on Leno's couch, mocking the megastar. The audience cheered her on. Finally, after sitting down, she said, "I just had to do that."

movie reviewer, as in the case of "Anonymous" on July 2, 2005. *War of the Worlds*, what a piece of junk! Tell Tom it's over for him as an actor. I'm surprised and disappointed in Steven Spielberg in his poor direction and in this stupid movie. Fuck, no wonder people have stopped going and paying ridiculous money for such unbelievable crap!"

What does Bogie's baby, the sometimes scathing octogenarian Lauren Bacall, have to say about Cruise's behavior? "When you talk about a great actor, you're not talking about Tom Cruise," she said. "His whole behavior is so shocking. It's inappropriate and vulgar and absolutely unacceptable to use your private life to sell anything commercially, but I think it's a kind of sickness."

If Bogie could rise from his grave, we bet he'd agree with his former love.

Reporter James P. Pinkerton tried to explain Cruise's space cadet antics. "First, as 'everybody' knows by now, Cruise is out to prove two points. First, that he is an ardent heterosexual: hence his publicly passionate romance with actress Katie Holmes. And, second, that Scientology, the religion, is beneficial to all."

But Cruise went about achieving both goals in such a ridiculous way that he screwed up bigtime. Or, as Marc Babej, a New York communications expert so colorfully put it: "Celebrity PR is like getting Elvis into a corset. Something will come popping out."

That astute observer of the Hollywood scene, Dominick Dunne, wrote that once Cruise made appearances only when he had to. Not so any more, not when he's trying to prove something to the public. "Cruise has thrown all sense of decorum and become more clamorous for attention than Paris Hilton in his public displays of love for Katie Holmes. Surrounded by a mob of paparazzi at a premiere, they stopped and kissed and hugged and smiled and stared deeply into each other's eyes. I felt that he was playing a part, like the one he played in *Magnolia*, but I never felt that he was real or genuinely romantic. To me he seemed less like a man in love than a nutcase." These comments were published in *Vanity Fair*. Dunne's ultimate conclusion about watching Cruise's many TV appearances: "I found him *bitchy*—not a good adjective for a mega-star."

If Cruise thought rumors about his being gay would die with his "mad love" for Holmes, he was dead wrong. The speculation continued at a feverish pitch, even when Holmes announced she was pregnant.

When Lee Anne DeVette, Tom Cruise's sister, took over her brother's PR media campaign, "she completely fucked it up," according to the *Jossip.com* website. Cruise's sister/publicist, for example, failed to rehearse Katie Holmes *(two photos above)* before she went on the David Letterman Show. When the talk show host asked Holmes how she had met Cruise, she stumbled and never answered the question, but instead started talking about her "misadventures" swimming with dolphins.

Cruise has, in the past, threatened law suits when a magazine such as *Life & Style* suggested that his high-profile relationship with Holmes was only a tool for the generation of mainstream heterosexual publicity, or that he and Holmes were about to split. Cruise later referred to the allegations within the magazine report as "malicious fantasies."

Katie Holmes and actor Chris Klein *(above, alone and with Katie)* were an item up until early 2004. The *Phone Book* actress and the *American Pie* funnyman had dated for four years, and their upcoming marriage seemed virtually assured until the arrival of Tom Cruise.

Was Cruise himself the reason for the split? "We grew up," Klein said. "The fantasy was over, and reality set in. We weren't lighting each other's fires any more."

A lot of unflattering pictures of Holmes appeared in the newspaper, her belly protruding. Such obvious evidence didn't stop the bloggers, the tabloids, the gossip columnists, or the general public. The press dubbed the Holmes/Cruise duo "TomKat."

Another rumor spread: that Holmes was impregnated with frozen sperm left behind by L. Ron Hubbard before his death in 1986. It was also suggested that Holmes had been impregnated by the handsome Chris Klein, her former fiancé.

The main question on every gossip's lips: "Was Tom Cruise really the father?" Naturally, Cruise's reps claimed that he was indeed the father and that every other opinion was "trashy, vulgar speculation."

In October of 2005, both Holmes and Cruise had to angrily deny that their baby was conceived in a test tube. The superstar was plagued with rumors that he sought *in vitro* fertilization treatment (IVF) to become a biological papa for the first time.

After some arm twisting by Cruise, Holmes embraced Scientology. After doing so, he placed a $200,000 diamond engagement ring on her finger atop the Eiffel Tower in Paris on June 17, 2005.

At long last, on April 18, 2006, this mysterious baby entered the world. It was a girl. Cruise named her "Suri." That's the name of a breed of alpaca. And when Cruise, Holmes and their tiny baby daughter, Suri, posed for a family portrait that appeared on the cover of *Vanity Fair*, one mocking headline asked: *Who's the Father? Surely Not Daddy Weirdest?*

The famous author, Dotson Rader, went to Cruise's home around this time for an interview for *Parade* magazine. A revealing incident occurred. At the end of the interview, Holmes

Cruise morphed from a public icon to a pop culture joke when he theatrically posed for tongue-kissing photos, the most notorious of which is immediately above. "He became a circus freak and and we lost our biggest star," said a Paramount exec.

Cruise's gushing and ranting about his Romeo-like love for gal pal (later wife) Holmes didn't go over with the public. A survey later showed that 61% "liked him less." In the closing hours of 2005, *Empire* magazine readers voted Cruise as Hollywood's "most irritating actor."

During their wedding in Bracciano, Italy, Cruise finally made Holmes an honest woman in what was called "The Wedding of the Century."

entered the room, towering three inches over her boyfriend. "She seemed dazed, passive, and vacant," Rader wrote. "The minute she appeared, Cruise's now familiar public mode of behavior returned. He began hooting how beautiful she was, touching and kissing her like a teenage boy on his first backseat date, aware that he was being watched."

The executives at Paramount almost went ballistic when Cruise refused to promote *Mission: Impossible III* if Comedy Central aired a cablecast of a controversial South Park episode about Scientology. In the spoof, "Trapped in the Closet," the show poked fun at both John Travolta and Cruise, urging them to come out of the closet.

Viacom owns both Paramount and Comedy Central, and feared that *Mission* would lose millions if Cruise did not promote it. So the executives ordered that the plug be pulled on the "Trapped in the Closet" episode. The staff at South Park were furious at this censorship from Cruise.

Cruise has a history of ball clanking and brinksmanship in Hollywood. He demanded that a sex scene with Holmes, filmed before they started dating, be axed. Jason Reitman had directed Holmes in 2005 in the satirical comedy, *Thank You for Smoking*. Pictures of Holmes showing her tits, but with her vagina concealed behind a flimsy bikini, are available for those who know how to search out celebrity nudes on the web.

In August of 2006, Viacom's aging and very realistic chairman, Sumner M. Redstone, had had enough of Mr. Megastar. He announced that Paramount Pictures was ending its 14-year relationship with the actor's production company. Of course, the link might have fatally deteriorated in the aftermath of the episode on Oprah's sofa, but Cruise's obsequiously declaring his love for Katie Holmes, and grabbing and kissing her every time he saw a camera probably didn't help. And no one at Paramount was charmed or amused when Cruise assailed Brooke Shields for taking prescription drugs to treat postpartum depression. Or for publicly denouncing psychiatry during an interview with Matt Lauer on the widely syndicated *Today* Show, and for repeatedly touting his controversial and sometimes frightening religion, Scientology, despite extremely negative publicity often associated with that sect?

Sci-fi writer L. Ron Hubbard was the founder of the controversial cult of scientology, and today, Tom Cruise is one of his chief propagandists. Hubbard claimed that Xenu, the intergalactic ruler, banished hundreds, maybe thousands, of people on Teegeeack (his name for Earth back then) as a means of alleviating overpopulation.

According to Scientology's dogma, the god dumped these captive aliens into a volcano and blew them up into bits and pieces by nuking them. Their souls were scattered across the earth to "infect humans with misery."

Appearing on the **Oprah Winfrey** show *(left photo)* in 2005, Tom Cruise was just plain batty over his relationship with Katie Holmes. jumping up and down on her couch like an excerpt from a Robin Williams comedy act. Claiming that his love for Holmes is "beyond cool--I can't be laid-back," an exuberent Cruise told a skeptical Oprah, "Something happened and I want to celebrate it." The jack-in-the-box TV appearance made Cruise the butt of jokes across the country.

Later, Cruise appeared on Jay Leno's couch *(right),* pumping his arms and mocking his own ridiculous previous appearance on Oprah.

Had the public already turned against Cruise and Paramount was merely reacting? Or was Paramount seizing the opportunity to sever ties with Cruise before he got worse? Accusations about Cruise's status as a "nut job" grew even louder when Cruise's beliefs in space aliens, ships circling the earth, and the mystic powers of L. Ron Hubbard were more fully known.

Actually, Redstone's ultimate decision to fire Cruise may have been financial. Ironically, during the week it opened, *Mission Impossible 3* earned millions worldwide. But Cruise's huge chunk of the profits may have left the studio just breaking even. Redstone told *The Wall Street Journal* that "Cruise's recent conduct has not been acceptable to Paramount." An executive, speaking off the record, said "*Top Gun* is more like *Rain Man* today. Gay rumors aside, he's destroyed his image as a romantic hero. Instead of a handsome hunk, he comes off more like a space alien."

Ignoring criticism, the evangelizing Cruise continues as the "Jimmy Swaggart of Scientology," with all the negative implications that go with it. But headlines revealed that at one point the "stress of believing" caused him to back away from his full endorsement. The rational part of his brain balked at the idea that the god, Xenu, stacked his alien enemies in volcanoes and then blew them up with H-bombs. But after his Scientology professors gave Cruise some breathing room, he came around again and became a true believer. Let the H-bombs blast.

In his defense of Scientology and his attack on psychiatry, Cruise is not above libeling people himself. He

John Travolta, the second most-famous Scientologist after Tom Cruise, prepares to give a sloppy wet kiss to his handsome and butch, but unknown pilot. Like Cruise himself, the star of *Grease* and *Hairspray* has also been subjected to unwanted speculation about his sexual preference.

Travolta was outed by journalist Paul Barresi in a May 8, 1990 issue of the *National Enquirer*. The tabloid shouted in a headline, "I WAS JOHN TRAVOLTA'S GAY LOVER." The former nude model for *Playgirl*, and the star of some 50 sex videos, asserted that he and Travolta had carried on an affair that had lasted for two years.

Boyish *Matchbox 20* frontman Rob Thomas has slammed rumors that he had sex with superstar Cruise. "L.A. is full of nothing but filthy, filthy liars who would like nothing better than to destroy the man," notes gossip clearinghouse Defamer.com, whose editors concluded that the rumor was baseless. "We live here, we should know."

Most bloggers treated the so-called "romance" as a joke. Wrote blogger "Scholar" on June 30, 2005, "I'll only be interested in Rob and Tom having an affair if one of them gets pregnant. Their lovechild might actually be kinda cute."

attacked psychiatry as "a Nazi science." Cruise then asserted that Carl Jung, the father of modern psychiatry, was an editor for Nazi papers during World War II. The New York Center for Jungian Studies denounced such a libelous accusation. Unfortunately, Dr. Jung is dead and cannot defend himself against such ridiculous charges. Cruise also attacked the drug methadone, claiming that it was originally called "Adolophine," named after Adolf Hitler. This is a widely popular but discounted myth with no basis in fact.

On the www.buzzle.com website, a blogger filed this opinion: "Is Tom Cruise gay? Who knows, maybe he isn't even sure. Whatever the case, these rumors have surrounded him since the beginning of his career, and they probably won't go away anytime soon. People are going to believe what they want and with Cruise's penchant for suing anyone who makes an untoward peep about his sexual proclivity, it makes people wonder all the more. Cruise claims he just doesn't want his children or eventually his grandchildren to read about things he never did. Whatever makes you happy, Tom, sue away."

Even "with baby making three," not to mention the other children, more and more rumors are flying about Tom Cruise, Katie Holmes, and their newfound friends, David Beckham and Posh Spice (a.k.a. Victoria Caroline Adams). But these rumors are too libelous to print. However, gossip columnists have ways of skirting libel, printing such tidbits as the "Fabulous Four," meaning the Cruises and Beckhams, are set to remake that saucy Natalie Wood hit from 1969, *Bob & Carol & Ted & Alice*.

After all of this, we faithfully promise: There will be no more rumors about the very overexposed Tom Cruise till at least another few minutes.

In June of 2005, Matt Lauer and Tom Cruise practically came to blows on *The Today Show*. The TV talk show host asked Cruise about his criticism of Brooke Shields, who had acknowledged the joint role of medication and psychotherapy during her battle with postpartum depression. "You don't know the history of psychiatry," Cruise ranted. "I do. There's no such thing as chemical imbalance. You don't even--you're glib, Matt. You don't even know what Ritalin is. You should be a bit more responsible in knowing what it is because you communicate to people."

Viacom chief Sumner Redstone *(left)* not only fired Tom Cruise but denounced him. "He was embarrassing the studio. And he was costing us a lot of money." Urged on by his wife, Paula, who had long ago soured on Cruise, Redstone gave Cruise the boot, refusing to renew Paramount's megabucks deal with Cruise's production company. "Paula, like women everywhere, has come to hate Cruise." Redstone claimed.

After hearing his attack upon her, Brooke Shields *(right)* dismissed Cruise's antics on TV as "a ridiculous rant," referring to his ill-informed comments as "a disservice to mothers everywhere." In a not-quite-final dig, she claimed, "And I don't take advice from someone who believes in aliens."

TV talk show host, Matt Lauer, disguised as Paris Hilton, pulls off the act better than the hotel heiress herself. If only **he** would make a sex tape video with his critic, Tom Cruise.

As for money, Lauer can effectively compete with Paris herself thanks to his having signed a contract in 2006 calling for a payment of $13 million annually for the subsequent five years. Does Lauer, like the staff at *People,* think that he is all that beautiful? "I get letters from women, and they say, 'I love your Roman nose.' If I weren't on TV and I walked past that same woman, she'd go, 'Did you see the beak on that guy?'"

Chosen in 1997 by *People Magazine* as one of the "50 most beautiful people in the world," TV anchorman **Matt Lauer** *(two photos above)* plants a kiss on one of the succulent lips of Miss Piggy. On the right, TV's "Mr Beefcake" stands ready to challenge Tom Cruise in the battle of the bulge. The press asserted that Cruise's on-air confrontation with Lauer was "the biggest career misstep since fellow Scientologist John Travolta made *Battlefield Earth.*"

Below right, in "Second Coming" headlines, the tabloid press continues to cast a very skeptical eye upon the marriage of Tom Cruise and Katie Holmes in spite of their giving birth to a very furry little girl.

Kate Bosworth *(above, right)* extends a friendly smooch with **Liv Tyler** *(above, left)*, a New York City actress chosen by *People* Magazine as one of the "50 Most Beautiful People in the World" in 1997. She wears a size 10 shoe, hates piercings and tattoos, and gave up smoking at the age of 14. She was born in 1977, but didn't meet her father until 1988. "I have these slumber parties with my father and when we can't sleep, we stay up at night trading beauty tips. He knows all about the good creams and masks."

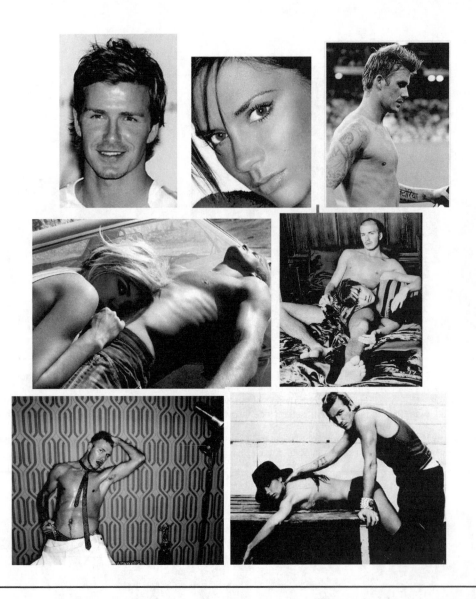

If the celebrity team of the moment, "Posh and Bucks," know nothing else, they know how to pose for provocative, often lurid photos. For as long as it lasts, they are best friends of TomKat.

As *W Magazine* headlined it, "When the soccer star married the pop singer, it was a match made in British tabloid heaven. Now David and Victoria Beckham are determined to become the new American idols." As these steamy photos show, they are not shy about stripping down.

The couple earn more than most corporations, and spend more than some countries. A $250 million deal brought Beckham to Los Angeles to play soccer...and maybe even to become a movie star. As for his relationship with Cruise, Beckham refers to the controversial movie star as "my best buddy."

After Tom Cruise, Penelope Cruz went to the arms of another hottie, **Josh Harnett** *(right and two photos, left)* a San Francisco boy who was voted *Bliss Magazine's* "Third Sexiest Male." And by many indications, he might actually be a nice guy. "I've had my heart broken, and it's not fun. But I'd rather have my heart broken than break someone else's heart."

Harnett tried to give up sex during the shooting of his movie, *40 Days and 40 Nights* (2002), but later admitted that "it made me crazy."

The film is about a man who gave up sex for Lent. "I wasn't gonna go for 40 Days and 40 Nights. You're depriving yourself of this one thing, and it becomes all you can think about."

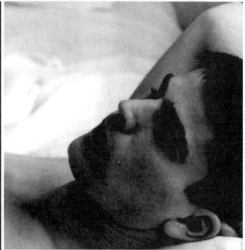

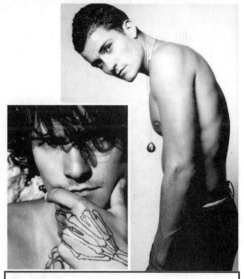

Were **Enrique Iglesias** *(two photos immediately above)* and Tom Cruise once competing for the same beauty, Sofia Vergara of Colombia? It appears so. The Madrid-born singer, son of another famous singer, Enrique has sold more Spanish-language albums than any other directly competing artist of his day. Before the millennium, he made a crossover into the mainstream English-language market. "I don't consider myself a sex symbol," he once said, but much of the world, including sexy actress Jennifer Love Hewitt, might disagree.

In an interview, reporter Ross von Metzke asked Enrique about a rumor. "Did you ever think it would turn into such a huge deal when you said in an interview that you were going to endorse extra-small condoms?"

Enrique shot back, "Yeah, that was so stupid. But I say a lot of stupid things in my interviews. I didn't literally say my penis was small, but I actually didn't care that people said I had a small penis. Maybe it doesn't bother me, because I don't. But even if I did, I wouldn't care. Give me a break."

English actor Orlando Bloom *(photos immediately above)* took up with Penelope Cruz when Josh Harnett wandered elsewhere. Some of his diverse titles includes *People Magazine's* "50 Most Beautiful People," or "The Sexiest Actor in Britain."

As a superstar, he sometimes finds himself pitted against the piratical Johnny Depp, as well as Brad Pitt, Matt Damon, Jake Gyllenhaal, Colin Farrell, and Usher Raymond. One of VH1's "100 Hottest Hotties," Bloom dated Kate Bosworth before they split in 2006. As Orlando drifts on the Caribbean Sea of Love, he admits, "I'm in love with love--it's a heavenly affair." Based on his fan mail, he admits, "The girls have got a bit excited."

Disney sued when Sinful Comics produced a raunchy script depicting Keira Knightley being simultaneously seduced by co-stars Johnny Depp and Orlando Bloom. The studio later referred to it as "pirate porn."

Cruise Control

Putting the Moves on His Girlfriend in the Early 80s

In a high school football movie, *All the Right Moves*, made in 1983, Tom Cruise starred with Lea Thompson, who interpreted the role of his girlfriend, Lisa. There is a scene in which she undresses him before they jump into bed. His cock appears in several frames, but there is a single frame where it seems "almost dramatically lighted for our specific attention."

Is this the real Tom Cruise or did director Michael Chapman use a body double?

Box Office Poison

Hollywood's Most Hated Actor

As *The New York Daily News*, among others, has demonstrated, Tom Cruise may be waging, in the words of reporter Christina Amoroso, "a war of his own world."

We conducted our own street survey in Manhattan. Here are some of the reactions:

Monica Corbett: "I would never go see another Tom Cruise movie. He's a total cliché anyway. A very bad actor. I hated him even before he jumped up and down on Oprah's sofa."

Jessica Williams: "If I hear Tom Cruise proclaim he's not gay one more time, I'll be forever convinced that he's a dedicated cocksucker. I saw him with his shirt off in a news photo. He's become a soft-bellied, middle-aged man. My daddy's more buffed than Cruise. What hot gay man would want him except one looking for a sugar daddy?"

Tom Bergen: "If a gay man goes to see another Tom Cruise or Mel Gibson movie, we'll confiscate his rainbow flag."

Robert Jonas: "If I hear another story about Tom Cruise pretending to be hot for Katie Holmes, I'll vomit. His displays of passion, as fed to the paparazzi, are sickening. Let's send this Scientology nut into orbit aboard one of L. Ron Hubbard's alien spacecraft. Or, better yet, throw him into a volcano and hit it with one of Hubbie's atomic bombs."

Johanna Revelson: "Who cares if he's gay or straight? We'd do the world a favor by boycotting his stupid movies. He's a freak--and a midget. He's destroyed whatever illusion of romance he ever had. Let him, in the privacy of his home, tongue Katie Holmes all he wants—that is, if he ever wanted that at all. I seriously doubt it."

Timony Arnold: "I'd go see a Tom Cruise movie, but only if it were a love story of two broken-down gay cowboys, Cruise himself and perhaps John Travolta, who'll ride off into the sunset together holding hands. Do you want to know who's a real heterosexual in films today? It sure ain't Cruise or that drag queen *Hairspray* guy. It's Colin Farrell. Judging from his sex video, I'm sure he packs more salami than Cruise and Travolta combined."

Farrell: "Compare it to a whiskey bottle"

Is Tom Cruise Really a Top Gun?

In Chuck Thompson's newsletter, originally published during the early 90s, an anonymous hospital intern in California filed this detailed report after a medical inspection of Tom Cruise after he was injured during the making of *Top Gun* in 1986.

"Cock is large, with a deep coronal ridge at the base of the glans, with a prominent circumcision scar halfway down the penis. One would call it a 'high and tight' circumcision with very little loose skin or 'give' on the shaft. Scrotum smooth, practically hairless, and generous sized. Relatively little pubic hair."

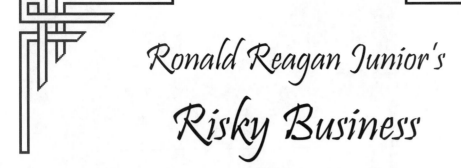

Ronald Reagan Junior's
Risky Business

Born May 20, 1958, in Los Angeles, **Ronald Prescott Reagan**, known as Ron Reagan, is the son of the late former president of the United States and his First Lady, Nancy.

A liberal and an atheist, Ron lives today in Seattle with his wife, Doria, a clinical psychologist whom he married in 1980. He attended Yale University for one semester, but dropped out in 1976 to join the Joffrey Ballet in pursuit of a lifelong dream.

The homosexual playwright, Larry Kramer, when interviewed on *The Larry King Show* in 1989 claimed, "I have no doubt that Ron Jr. is gay. He is always with a gang of men. Besides, we know our own." Ron Jr. later defined Kramer's remarks as an "unconscionable insult." and asked for an apology which he never received.

"What Risky Business!"

A Ballet Dancer for a Son

Nancy Davis Reagan always made it clear that Ron Jr. was her favorite child, often regarding the more rebellious Patti, his sister, as the black sheep of the family. She called her son "Skipper," and her love for him was so strong that she was accused of being overly protective as a mother.

There's a famous picture of Nancy as First Lady, kissing her son on the lips after witnessing one of his ballet performances. When he was still young, Ron Jr. told dear old Mum that he was not going into politics, denouncing the game as "corrupt and sleazy. There were too many unhealthy guys in wrinkled suits that smelled like cigars."

The script demanded that his parents retreat to Camp David, leaving their son to preside over The White House during their absence. Then, inspired by Tom Cruise in his hit film, *Risky Business,* the "high school senior" throws a wild party.

Some six million viewers of NBC's *Saturday Night Live* were subsequently stunned when the son of then-President Ronald Reagan, Ron Reagan, Jr., gyrated out in a pair of scanty undershorts. His "red panties dance" was even better than the one executed by Cruise himself in the film.

In one of the understatements of 1986, Ron, Jr., said, "I thought it would stir things up."

Watching at the White House in February of that year, Nancy was stunned to see her son on nationwide TV in his underpants. A member of the Secret Service had to explain to her that he was spoofing Cruise in *Risky Business,* a film she hadn't seen.

Ron had dropped out of Yale as a freshman in 1977, and he more or less failed as a performer at the Joffrey Ballet. But on *Saturday Night Live,* seizing the advantage afforded by his surname, the kid showed he could really

Ron Reagan Jr. has become known for his strong opinions He claimed that Jimmy Carter "has the morals of a snake," and that the institution of marriage was "nothing more than a $20 license fee and a clap test."

On the subject of outing, he once said, "I regard questions about a person's sexuality as invasive, anti-intellectual, and irrelevant."

dance. "If people insist I'm taking advantage of my position as the son of a sitting president, I say, 'Who cares?' Let's face it: It's a *Risky Business*."

When President Reagan faced the press about the ballet dancer thing, he claimed that, "We've checked it out, and Ron is all man." The president did not explain what method he had used in his verification that Ron Jr. was not a homosexual.

For the *Saturday Night Live* performance, Ron demanded a change in the script, which had originally instructed that the role he was playing was that of a gay hairdresser. "I also told them I didn't want them trashing my folks in a mean way."

The show's director, however, did include a catty reference to Reagan's first wife, the Oscar-winning actress, Jane Wyman. And Nancy (Ron's biological mother) was portrayed as a chain-smoking lush by an actor in Adolfo-inspired drag.

What did President Reagan, that "great communicator," think of Junior's television debut? "Like father, like son," he said.

"I got a little note from Tom Cruise afterward," Ron (Jr.) recalled. "just saying that he enjoyed the sketch and that he thought it was really funny…And yet, there were some people who were upset by it. I don't really understand why. I guess it was the jockey shorts. Every time we rehearsed, and right after the dress rehearsal, Standards and Practices would come back and say, "Could we put another pair on him?"

Sure enough by the time the sketch actually appeared on the air, Reagan, Jr., was wearing more than one pair of jockey shorts, perhaps as a safety device to avoid additional exposure.

California's most dysfunctional family *(left to right)* Ronald Sr., Ron Jr., Nancy, and Patti Davis, who even as a kid, places herself a slight distance away from her mother.

Nancy ruled her family on the advice of an astrologer. For example, she insisted that her husband be sworn in as governor of California in the middle of the night when the stars were in a favorable alignment.

Long before she even dreamed of becoming First Lady of America, Nancy Davis was an attractive and ambitious starlet known otherwise as "The Fellatio Queen of Hollywood." as described by Kitty Kelley in the First Lady's unauthorized biography.

As an aspiring starlet, Nancy's affairs included dalliances with Clark Gable, Peter Lawford, Spencer Tracy, and Frank Sinatra. Reagan himself was a handsome gay blade (in the old-fashioned sense of that word), seducing, among others, Lana Turner, Betty Grable, Doris Day, Ruth Roman, Ann Southern, and Marilyn Monroe.

(Above, left) During their moment of triumph, assuming the presidency of the United States, Ronald Sr. and Nancy were joined by their son, Ron Jr.--at the time in need of a haircut. "This would never have happened if Hollywood had given him better parts," said Lauren Bacall on the eve of Reagan's inauguration.

Gloria Grahame, who won an Academy Award for Best Supporting Actress in *The Bad and the Beautiful* (1952), said, "I can't stand the sight of Ronald Reagan. I'd like to stick my Oscar up his arse."

(Left), "Ronnie and Nancy" in the White House at the height of their imperial elegance, when they presided over the Free World and the collapse of the Soviet Union.

Despite having been the target of harsh criticism during his regime, Reagan is evolving into a beloved figure to Republicans.

Nancy, in her dotage, remembered the day when she was the most powerful and influential woman in the history of the United States.

(Above) Long before a lingering bout with Alzheimer's disease ended his life in 2004, Ronald Reagan was a handsome, strapping, lifeguard.

At California's Eureka College in 1929, he was the star of the swimming team.

Later, in Hollywood, he fell in love with Jane Wyman, who gave him a review: "He's about as good in bed as he is on the screen."

Reagan's first wife, Jane Wyman, was a much bigger star than either Ronald Reagan and most definitely Nancy Davis, who never rose above the rank of "starlet." Photos above show Reagan with Wyman during their engagement in 1940.

Below, in scenes from *Johnny Belinda* (1948), a "deglamorized" Wyman won an Oscar playing a deaf-mute who is raped by Stephen McNally (*left character in left-hand photo*).

In the right-hand photo below, Lew Ayres had an affair with Wyman during the filming. When Reagan learned about his wife's infidelity, he said, "Jane very much needs to have a fling and I intend to let her have it."

(Photo left) United at last in grief, Ron Jr. and Patti Davis (*on right side of photo*)) comfort their grief-stricken mother, Nancy. Before the funeral, Patti shared an "emotional reconciliation" with her mother.

(Below) Happier Times. Reagan family portrait (Ron and Nancy with Ron, Jr., and Patti) circa 1960.

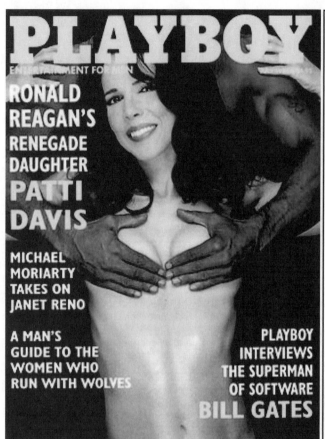

PLAYBOY

ENTERTAINMENT FOR MEN

RONALD
REAGAN'S
RENEGADE
DAUGHTER
PATTI
DAVIS

MICHAEL
MORIARTY
TAKES ON
JANET RENO

A MAN'S
GUIDE TO THE
WOMEN WHO
RUN WITH WOLVES

PLAYBOY
INTERVIEWS
THE SUPERMAN
OF SOFTWARE
BILL GATES

(Left) **Patti Davis**, daughter of Ronald and Nancy Reagan, was the prodigal daughter, dumping the Reagan name and using her mother's maiden name instead to symbolize her disgust with her father's right-wing political views.

As for her own politics, she was a pot-smoking liberal. At the age of 41, she posed for *Playboy,* appearing on the cover with the hands of a black man cupping her (otherwise naked) breasts. She also made a direct-to-video *Playboy Celebrity Centerfold,* the tape showing her cavorting in lesbian settings outdoors, followed by a solo masturbation scene.

Patti's first novel, *Homefront,* published in 1986, recorded fictionalized events inspired by her own childhood and teenaged years, an artistic choice which seriously pissed off her father's Republican friends.

Privately, Ronald Reagan expressed some dismay to his friend, Gene Kelly, when Ron Jr. told him that he wanted to be a ballet dancer. Kelly was supportive, urging that Ron be enrolled at the Stanley Holden Dance Center in Los Angeles. "I think the press was surprised by our reaction to Ron's new career," Nancy later said. "They thought we'd be embarrassed about Ron's decision to become a dancer, but we weren't. Some people expected us to distance ourselves from Ron, but that never entered our minds. We were surprised at his choice, but we were proud of his dedication and talent."

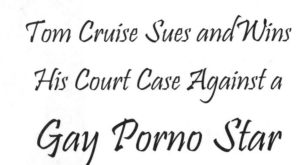

Tom Cruise Sues and Wins
His Court Case Against a
Gay Porno Star

Both **Tom Cruise** *(left in photo above)* and **Kyle Bradford** *(right)* display well-toned bodies that would qualify either of them for a role in pornographic films. So far, Cruise has resisted the temptation. At least to <u>our</u> knowledge, there's not even a Paris Hilton-style sex video out there with him as a member of the chorus.

But that's definitely not the case with Bradford. Appearing under the name of "Chad Slater," Bradford has become a major (gay) porn star.

When accusations surfaced in the media that Bradford had sustained an affair with Cruise, the megastar took him to court, hoping to dispel those rumors. Cruise won his case, but the judge's verdict only fanned charges of Cruise's alleged homosexuality by presenting it to a wider audience.

Like her husband, Katie Holmes has had her own troubles with the XXX-rated movie industry. She threatened legal action against a teenaged porn star who changed her name to "Katee Holmes" and subsequently announced plans to "lose my virginity on screen."

Gay Porn Star Rolls Over for Tom Cruise

The pulp sci-fi writer, L. Ron Hubbard, created the money-making "religion" of Scientology in 1950, calling it "Dianetics." In spite of Hubbard's notorious background, his cult has prospered and grown, attracting celebrity devotees who have included the very heterosexual Tom Cruise and even another very heterosexual worshipper, John Travolta. Significantly, these two stars don't follow totally in Hubbard's footsteps. After all, the man referred to by his disciples as "The Source" practiced "ritualistic sex magic" based on the tenets of Satanist Aleister Crowley, once referred to by the British press as "The Beast" or "The Wickedest Man in the World."

But when it comes to lawsuits, the very heterosexual Cruise at least does seem to follow religiously one of Hubbard's tenets. In 1976, the guru wrote: "The purpose of a lawsuit is to harass and discourage rather than to win. The law can be used very easily to harass, and enough harassment on somebody who is simply on the thin edge anyway, well knowing that he is not authorized, will generally be sufficient to cause his professional decease. If possible, of course, ruin him utterly."

On May 2, 2001, Harvard-educated Hollywood entertainment attorney Bertram Fields, purportedly safeguarding the interests of his very heterosexual client, Tom Cruise, filed a $100 million lawsuit against Chad Slater (aka Kyle Bradford), an actor who had appeared in pornographic films.

"Kyle Bradford" is the stage name used for the American gay porn star Chad Slater. His porn flicks feature nude wrestling, including submission matches where

Tom Cruise's suit against **Bradford** (*photos top and bottom*) was filed in Los Angeles Superior Court. It claimed that the erotic wrestler "concocted and spread the completely false story that he had a continuing homosexual affair with Tom Cruise, and that this affair was discovered by Mr. Cruise's wife, leading to their divorce."

When pressed, that wife at the time, Nicole Kidman, dismissed it. "I personally don't believe in doing huge lawsuits about that stuff. Tom does. That's what he wants to do. That's what he's going to do. You do not tell Tom what to do. That's it. Simple. He is a force to be reckoned with."

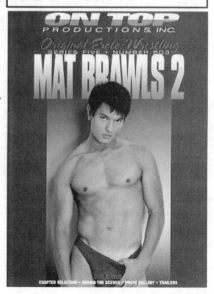

the loser is forced to masturbate or to engage in anal or oral sex. Bradford dominates his matches and in most cases performs sexually as a top.

In Fields' complaint for defamation, he claimed that "to promote his career as an actor in pornographic films, defendant Chad Slater, known professionally as Kyle Bradford, has concocted and spread the completely false story that he had a continuing homosexual affair with Tom Cruise and that this affair was discovered by Mr. Cruise's wife, Nicole Kidman, leading to their divorce."

The document filed in the Superior Court in Los Angeles stated that, "While Cruise thoroughly respects others' right to follow their own sexual preference, he is not a homosexual, and had no relationship of any kind with Kyle Bradford and does not even know him."

The complaint noted that even though Cruise respects gays' right to do what they wish, "vast numbers of the public throughout the world do not share that view, and, believing that he had a homosexual affair and did so during his marriage, they will be less inclined to patronize Cruise's films, particularly since he tends to play parts calling for heterosexual romance and action adventure."

In filing that suit, the very heterosexual Cruise lost millions of his gay fans and became a laughing joke and the subject of ridicule in gay bars in both the United States and Europe. Many respected members of the legal community offer the opinion that in years to come, the accusation of being a homosexual will not automatically be considered grounds for defamation.

Obviously at this stage of his life, this very heterosexual actor doesn't agree. Of course, where Cruise and Fields thought Chad Slater was going to suddenly generate $100 million in the event that he lost the case was never adequately determined.

The porno star's accusation first appeared in the French magazine, *Actustar*, which has an international circulation for unveiling secret peccadillos of celebrities. The article asserted that Kidman (married at the time to Cruise) walked in on Cruise and Slater, and it was this discovery of man-on-man sex that led to her divorce from the megastar. The French-language article was translated into Spanish and subsequently published in the magazine, *TV y Novelas*.

In his affidavit, Fields claimed, "Cruise is not and has never been a homosexual." But how could an attorney, or anybody for that matter, verify such a claim? Fields then charged that Slater had made the accusations against the superstar "for the purpose of publicizing himself at Cruise's

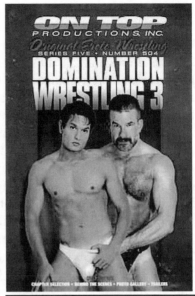

Kyle Bradford *(left-hand figure in the photo above)* learned the high price of crossing Cruise. The litiginous actor won a mega-judgment of $10 million in the wake of his defamation lawsuit against the gay porn star, who alleged that he had had a sexual affair with Cruise.

Attorney Bert Fields told the media, "Tom feels very strongly that he doesn't want his kids or his grandkids, for that matter, to read about the fact that he did things he never did, so whenever anybody says false things about Tom, he's going to go after them. He has the will and the means to do it."

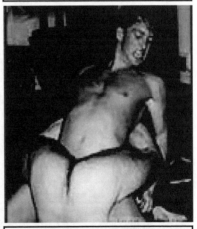

In porno flicks whose titles have included *Forced to Submit*, Bradford usually emerges on top. But during his legal tussle with Cruise, the superstar once again proved that at least legally speaking, he's still *Top Gun.*

expense."

A second $100 million suit was filed against Michael Davis, the magazine's publisher, after he claimed to have a videotape of Cruise engaging in sexual relations with another man. That suit was dropped after Davis "publicly asserted that Cruise was not gay," and admitted to not having a tape that would prove otherwise. It's totally believable that Davis did not have the tape. But, like Fields, he could not possibly know if Cruise were gay, straight, or somewhere in between.

Cruise also sued Kristina Slater, when she tried to sell a story to the *National Enquirer* about her husband's alleged gay fling with Cruise. But the judge then tossed the case out of court, awarding Kristina more than $27,000 in attorney's fees. Cruise at first appealed but later ended the suit against the woman in what was called "a mutual walkaway." Her lawyer, Charles Fester, said, "Cruise finally saw that it might be in his best interest to leave my poor client alone. He agreed to go get a life and sue other people."

To protect himself, Slater went public, claiming that he'd never made the statements that *Actustar* attributed to him. The magazine later printed a retraction.

The very heterosexual Cruise was undeterred and proceeded with his lawsuit, winning $10 million. As for collecting those millions, which do not exist in Slater's bank account, call that *Mission Impossible*.

As could have been predicted, Slater defaulted on the ten million dollar penalty imposed upon him by the court. Slater reportedly chose to default on the payment because, in his words, "the lawsuit has no merit" and because he wanted the "hurtful publicity" against him to end. "I hope by my defaulting, Mr. Cruise will finally get what he is after, and I can finally start to put my life back in order." However, as a result of Cruise's lawsuit, sales of Slater's films, including *Forced to Submit* and *The Cockpit Club*, skyrocketed.

What Slater should have done is to challenge the very heterosexual star into the "erotic ring" for a wrestling match—and may the best man win. That seems like a more reasonable approach than chasing rainbows for non-existent millions.

In case you want to see what the very heterosexual Cruise missed out on, order a copy of the Kyle Bradford video, *The Size of It*.

Lia Haberman, on E-Online, issued this warning: "Hustlers beware! It'll cost you $10 million just to claim you went to bed with Tom Cruise."

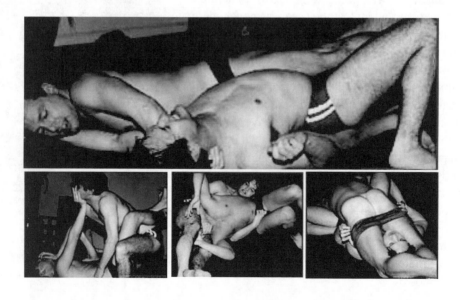

Penelope & Salma

Latina and Gorgeous, but Gay?

Lesbian rumors started flying when Penelope Cruz (left) grabbed Salma Hayek's ass during a photo shoot. "I was sick with the flu and a little delirious when I made a public show of affection toward Salma. I grabbed her ass just to keep things moving because everyone was a little slow.   And the energy changed when I did that."

Did Tom Cruise drive his former girlfriend Penelope Cruz into a gay relationship with her best pal Salma Hayek? Surely not. But these rumors became so prevalent that in 2007 they made the press and most definitely the Internet. Cruz laughs off these reports, claiming the two have been close friends for some six years.

Hayek posed for a series of pictures with Cruz which were recently published in *Interview* magazine. The pair also posed together for one provocative shot showing Cruz grabbing Hayek's ass. It was this shot, more than all the others, that started those rumors that the beautiful *latina* pair were romantically involved.

On *The Late Show with David Letterman*, Cruz defended the photo when the host showed it to the audience. "You know what they've been saying because of that picture?" Cruz asked. "We are like sisters, and we have some sense of humor. We did that in front of 100 photographers, and the story now is that apparently we are lovers. I'm sorry to say, that is not the case!"

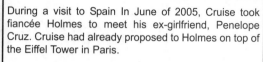

During a visit to Spain In June of 2005, Cruise took fiancée Holmes to meet his ex-girlfriend, Penelope Cruz. Cruise had already proposed to Holmes on top of the Eiffel Tower in Paris.

In Madrid, Holmes came face to face with Cruz who had split up with Tom in 2004 after an on-again, off-again romance that dragged on for three years.

The two rivals, Holmes and Cruz, had little to say to each other.

Originally a dancer, the Spanish-born **Penelope Cruz** *(on the left in all four pictures)* claims the equally sexy Salma Hayek is her best "gal pal."

After being dumped by Cruise, Penelope started dating Matthew McConaughey when the two finished filming *Sahara* in 2005. Both Cruise and McConaughey have been voted sexiest men on the planet at various times. Salma and Penelope also heated up the screen when the two south-of-the-border hotties costarred in the 2006 film, *Bandigas*.

Salma's most memorable film role was that of Frida Kahlo, the legendary Mexican painter, which won her a Best Actress nomination. FHM named her one of the "100 Sexiest Women in the World" in 2005.

Lesbian rumors aside, Salma asserts, "I keep waiting to meet a man who has more balls than I do."

Ewan McGregor

Letting It All Hang Out

Born in Crief, Scotland in 1971, actor Ewan McGregor stands 5'10 ½" but is impressive in other measurements.

A former roommate of Jude Law (if only those walls had a hidden camera), he was ranked eighth in the 2001 Orange Film Survey of Greatest British Actors.

Like a true Scotsman, McGregor wears nothing under his kilt. Often these Scotsmen leave us guessing, but in this young actor's case, movie audiences already know what's hidden under his kilt. Call it "Garb of the Gods."

Ewan McGregor Talks about His Full Monty

"I'm naked a lot of the time, and they don't try to frame planted pots in front of my dick like they do in most other films. It's all part of the story but they don't zoom in on it or anything and go, 'Cock shot!' I've been naked in almost everything I've been in, really. It's written in my contract."

"I'm doing my bit for the women's movement. The woman have always been naked in movies and now I'm just desperate to take my clothes off as much as possible. It's a great feeling of power to be naked in front of people. We're happy to watch actual incredible graphic violence and gore, but as soon as somebody's naked it seems like the public goes a bit bananas about the whole thing."

"I've been naked in a number of films. A friend of mine once joked that Richard Gere, who I think was the first name actor to do frontal nudity, was 'stiff competition' for me. I had to reply, 'Not from what I've seen!' I've done it in TRAINSPOTTING and BRASSED OFF. But when THE PILLOW BOOK opened in Scotland, where my parents live, I warned my dad he might not want to go see it. But they did, and my dad sent me a fax, said it was a great film and he added, 'I'm glad to see you've inherited one of my major assets.'"

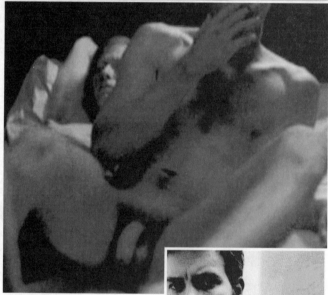

Ewan McGregor (right-hand figure in photo, left) not only will go naked, or dress up as a queen. He's also uninhibited about crawling naked into bed with a good-looking guy.

Since Ewan (two photos above, and right) has no trouble showing frontal nudity, going topless is the least of his inhibitions.

364

(Above) In film after film **Ewan McGregor** has flashed his pole in front of movie audiences, seemingly believing that pants are something you wear around your head – not to cover your ass.

(Left) **Ewan McGregor** is not only uninhibited about showing his Scottish cock and balls to the world, but he doesn't mind dressing up as a queen, complete with feather boa and limp wrist. As one gay blogger exclaimed, "If only Ewan was gay in real life. What fun the boys would have with this handsome top from the far north of Europe."

McGregor (above and above, right), on researching Moulin Rouge: "I needed to go and just find out exactly what it meant to be out and having fun in a kind of hedonistic and debauched environment. That's right, something I wasn't familiar with. The secret of my sex appeal is that I smoke a lot. I drink far too much, and I don't exercise. I torture small animals."

As for appearing with **Nicole Kidman** (right) in Moulin Rouge, "I called her Knickers. I would swear, burp, and fart in front of her."

In *Nora* (2001) **Ewan McGregor** liked to go in through the back door when seducing the star of the film, Susan Lynch, playing Nora Carnalce. The film opens in Dublin, 1904, and McGregor is surprisingly cast as James Joyce. Nora enchants Joyce with her frank, direct, and uninhibited manner.

"From *VELVET GOLDMINE* (1998), I got fond of wearing nail polish and eye makeup. I used to wear it quite a lot. We all wear makeup when we go to events – men and women alike. I've also had some good makeup artists, and I like to let them have a good time. I don't think we should pretend we're not wearing makeup when we are. I quite like the look of it."

Ewan McGregor *(photo above)*

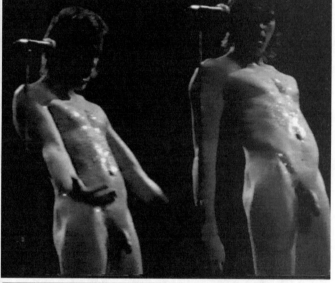

Fans not only got to see McGregor's cock in *Velvet Goldmine* (1998) *(photo above)* but even his rosebud *(photo left)*. The film was controversial to say the least. It found its devotees but was also venomously denounced.

The plot has British newspaper reporter Arthur Stuart (Christian Bale) in 1984 investigating the career of the 1970s glam rock star Brian Slade (Jonathan Rhys Meyers).

Slade was heavily influenced during his early years by American rock singer Curt Wild (as played by Ewan McGregor). Wild's show, as the scenes above illustrate, was by virtually anyone's standards, quite crazy for its era.

366

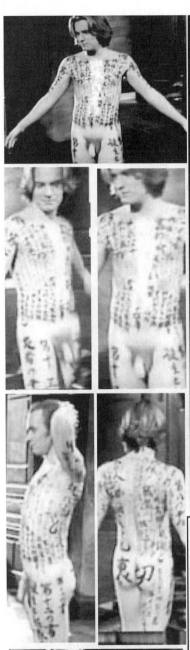

Let's face it. The reason gay men rented the DVD of *The Pillow Book* (1996) was to see the full monty of Ewan McGregor on ample display. There, of course, was a plot in British director Peter Greenaway's film, which starred **Vivian Wu** as Nagiko *(above)*.

According to critic Michael C. Berch, "As a young girl in Japan, Nagiko's father paints characters on her face, and her aunt reads to her from *The Pillow Book*, a diary of a 10th century lady-in-waiting. Nagiko grows up obsessed with books, papers, and writing on bodies, and her sexual odyssey is a *parfait mélangé* of classical Japanese, modern Chinese, and Western film images."

When Nagiko runs into British translator, Jerome (as played by **McGregor**, *above*), she is enchanted. He not only turns out to be a sensual lover, but he can do calligraphy with and upon her. (*Refer to the following page for more scenes from* The Pillow Book.)

Scenes with Ewan from "The Pillow Book"

368

Those Bisexual Rumors About
Jake Gyllenhaal

There has never been a Santa Claus like that played by Jake Gyllenhall in *Jarhead.* As a postmodern and very hip Santa, he's literally wearing two hats--one of them covering his genitals. (Movie audiences were left wondering what Santa was concealing.)

Unlike Tom Cruise, the handsome young actor is a very sophisticated young man. He grew up in Hollywood, where at an early age, he became familiar with the homosexual lifestyle, if not for himself, then for others around him. "In my family, many of our close friends were gay couples," Jake told the press. "And every man goes through a period of thinking they're attracted to another guy."

From Jarhead to Brokeback Cowboy

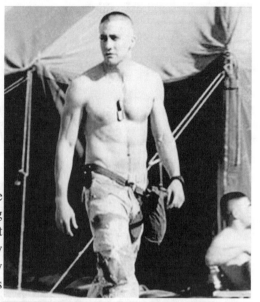

Unlike Tom Cruise, who goes ballistic at the mere suggestion he might be gay, and starts calling lawyers, handsome Jake Gyllenhaal is cool about rumors swirling about him. The co-star of "that gay cowboy movie" says he's actually "flattered" by rumors that he is bisexual, even though he insists he is not. He claims that he's never had a gay experience, but isn't afraid of the possibility. "I'm open to whatever people want to call me. I've never really been attracted to men sexually, but I don't think I would be afraid of it if it happened."

When he signed for *Brokeback Mountain*, a lot of his pals kidded the Hollywood heartthrob, who had to play love scenes with his pal, the Aussie hunk, Heath Ledger. "All my friends said, 'Dude, you're gonna kiss a guy?' But it's not about that for me. It's about how impossible love can be sometimes, and I can relate to that."

While shooting *Brokeback Mountain*, Jake confessed that it almost led to a broken nose. "He [Ledger] grabs me and he slams me up against the wall and kisses me, and then I grab him and I slam him up against the wall and I kiss him," he said. "The love scenes were the most violent I've ever done. We were doing take after take after take. I got the shit beat out of me."

At the close of the movie, Jake said, "I fooled around with Heath Ledger but it was Michelle Williams who got pregnant."

Before Jake and Ledger exchanged body fluids on the sets of *Brokeback*—and became great pals—they were rivals, at least for certain roles. Jake almost got the male lead in *Moulin Rouge*. His competition, or so it appeared, was Ledger himself. But in the final hour and after months of auditions, the director cast Ewan McGregor.

Looking lean, mean, and butch, Jake caused a sensation, at least among women and gay men, when he appeared as the handsome and buff marine, Swoff, in the film *Jarhead*.

When stills from that film were released, those posters of Johnny Depp came off toilet walls across America and were replaced by that of the shirtless jarhead, Jake.

The movie has barely begun before Jake is mockingly asked if he is gay, and if he is attracted to the film's brutal, sadistic sergeant. If only Duke Wayne had seen this movie, he'd surely roll over in his Green Beret coffin.

In *Jarhead*, we get to see Jake's ass, covered with a G-string so thin that it would shock a stripper. Above, at a Christmas party for fellow marines, he appears *sans* clothing. We get to see him in a simulated fellatio scene (he's the object of another marine's mock affection) and in yet another incident, he's masturbating in a toilet booth. And as if to prove that he really understands that in some circumstances, golden showers can be fun, in one scene, Jake pisses in his marine fatigues.

During the making of *Moulin Rouge*, certain scandalous rumors were spread about McGregor and his co-star, Nicole Kidman. Surely they weren't true? No, they couldn't be true. Right?

Jake also lost out on another role. Had he been given the part, he might today be one of the richest actors in Hollywood. When Tobey Maguire dropped out of *Spider Man 2* (2004), Jake was offered the role. As he was preparing for the part, Maguire was back again as Spiderman.

Even so, as some surveys have shown, gay men would infinitely prefer Jake to come in their "web," not unsexy Maguire. These diehard fans with the hots for Jake call themselves "Gyllenhaalics."

Jake is the son of director Stephen Gyllenhaal and screenwriter Naomi Foner. He is also the younger brother of Maggie Gyllenhaal, the actress.

His godmother is Jamie Lee Curtis (surely those hideous rumors about her are not true). His godfather is Paul Newman (let's hope all those rumors about him are true). Jake is of noble Swedish and Russian-Jewish descent.

Although Jake accepted the role of a gay cowboy, in 2003 he turned down the opportunity to work with Italian filmmaker, Bernardo Bertolucci in *The Dreamers*. The reason? He didn't want to take his clothes off. The star said, "I'll only agree to nudity in my roles when it plays a part in the story-telling of the movie. I'll show my dick if it helps the narrative. I'm not going to throw my dick around just because."

His sister Maggie didn't have such modesty. "My sister's naked in *Secretary*," Jake said, "and it was in *Playboy* later. But she made a great movie and it was part of the narrative and she said if it's in *Playboy* fuck it! More publicity for the movie. At least the movie told a great story."

Movie fans will have to wait to learn the answer to the all-important question on every fan's lips. Is Jake cut or uncut? After all, with a Swedish father his dick might have been left intact. But, what if his Jewish Mom prevailed?

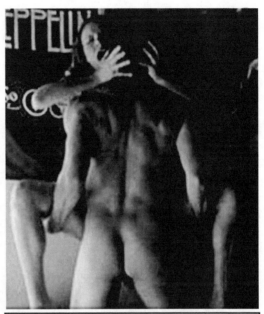

Jake Gyllenhaal can prove his credentials as a straight guy, at least on screen, if the part calls for it. "He can deliver the goods, and he seems to know his way around a woman," said one of the actor's former directors who didn't want his name used. "At least I didn't have to call in a sex therapist to teach him how it's done."

Instead of a crazed-looking **Ewan McGregor** in this shot from *Moulin Rouge* with **Nicole Kidman**, it might have been Jake positioned beside her. "I came *soooo close* to getting Ewan's part," Jake said. "It was a toss-up between Heath Ledger and myself, but Ewan won out. I sang and everything. I went through months of auditions. I think it came down to age. I was younger and less well-known at the time. I would hope it didn't have anything to do with my talent. Maybe it did."

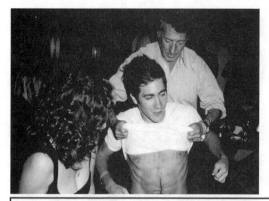 

For reasons understood perhaps only to himself, veteran actor **Dustin Hoffman** (on the right in both of the photos above) gleefully strips down Jake Gyllenhaal. But for what purpose? Could Dustin still be playing that gay character in *Midnight Cowboy?* Susan Sarandon blissfully looks on.

One of the screen's greatest love affairs played itself out between two men, Jake Gyllenhaal (left in both photos above, both from *Brokeback Mountain*) and Heath Ledger (right). Within the shadows of a claustrophobic little tent, Jack (Jake) makes sexual overtones to Ennis (Heath), who at first resents it. Then, in a rush of long-suppressed passion, he takes to gay sex like a duck to water. Jack/Jake quickly becomes his ever-loving bottom, as Ennis discovers an ecstacy he never thought possible. Once inside Jack's bowels, he wants to stay forever.

And What About Jake's Talented and Gorgeous Sister, Maggie?

Jake's older sister, **Maggie Gyllenhall**, isn't bashful about taking off her clothes and showing the full monty. She replaced supermodel Kate Moss as the newest piece of ass representing the lingerie giant Agent Provocateur. "Maggie is not an obvious sex symbol," said a company executive, Serena Rees. "She is interesting-looking, confident, and beautiful in a way that is non-threatening, which makes her appealing to men and women alike."

When a depiction of one of the A.P. ads appeared on the web, Maggie wore a black bra, a corset, and tiny panties as she sits open-legged and handcuffed to a chair. One of the first comments from the blogger community was posted on September 5, 2007. It expressed it this way: "Who the fuck is Maggie Gyllenhaal? I don't know who the whore is, but I'd love to cuff her to the bed and fuck the shit out of her! Hᴇʟʟ Yᴇᴀʜ!!"

McConaughey & Armstrong
Call It a "Bro-Mance"

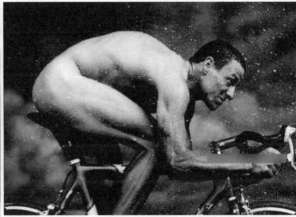

Best pals **Matthew McConaughey** *(left)* and cycling athlete **Lance Armstrong** *(above)* posed for two of the sexiest sports pictures on record.

Looking like a Greek God descended from Mount Olympus, young McConaughey presents some anonymous woman (we're referring to her hand on his crotch) with a handful of goodies. Usually Matthew doesn't show this much skin, and he's most often photographed shirtless even though he is technically middle-aged. (He was born in 1969 in Uvalde, Texas.)

When Tom Cruise dumped Penelope Cruz, McConaughey picked up the slack. Armstrong *(below, left)* broke off his engagement to rocker Sheryl Crow in 2006. The Tour de France champ decided he liked partying too much with his pals McConaughey *(below, right)* and occasionally Jake Gyllenhaal.

The Sexiest Men Alive

"We tried it (being gay) but it wasn't for us," the "Sexiest Man Alive" (Matthew McConaughey) told *Details* magazine in 2007. He was responding to rumors that he and Tour de France winner Lance Armstrong were having a torrid affair. Along with his pal, *Brokeback Mountain* star Jake Gyllenhaal, Armstrong and McConaughey are often photographed shirtless.

They like to bike, to party, whatever. In fact, it was McConaughey's partying that led to his arrest in 1999 after police responded to a noise complaint at his Austin home. They arrived to find him and a friend playing bongos in the nude, with marijuana in plain sight. WHERE WAS OUR VIDEO CAMERA? Charges were dropped. The nudity and marijuana escaped a fine, but he paid a $50 fine for loud music.

You can be sure that the hot, sweaty McConaughey smelled like a man that night. He never uses deodorant, preferring his natural smell.

After he broke up with Penelope Cruz, who had broken up with Tom Cruise, McConaughey, 36, started hanging with Armstrong, 35. Armstrong had called off his engagement to Sheryl Crow, 43.

"Our relationship just kind of developed," Armstrong said. "He got out of a relationship. I've just gotten out of a relationship. We all have those kind of relationships, and relationship isn't a bad word. I mean, we all have buds, we all take guy trips, but you take something very normal and you put it in a magazine and people start talking."

"A lot of people don't understand friendship and brotherhood," McConaughey added. "I have a great friend in Lance. It's fun going out and living life and

Lance Armstrong *(left)*, seen jogging with **Matthew McConaughey**, beat out Tom Cruise's beloved Katie Holmes in the New York Marathon race of November 2007. Among the 40,000 long-haul runners, the Tour de France cycling great finished within an impressive time slot of 2 hours and 46 minutes.

Fleet-footed Holmes ain't. Huffing and puffing, she finished in 5 hours, 29 minutes, and 58 seconds.

Three close amigos (at least at the moment) are **Matthew McConaughey** *(left)*, **Lance Armstrong** *(center)*, and **Jake Gyllenhaal** *(right)*. When People Magazine voted Matthew the sexiest man of the year – and not Jake – Jake was baited by the press. Newsweek asked him if he thought he should have been People's sexiest man. "You're pinning me against him?" Jake asked. "I have no hard feelings. But I'll challenge Matthew McConaughey in the kitchen anytime." But, Jake, what about moving that challenge into the boudoir?

doing thing at the drop of a hat."

Let those gay rumors fly. McConaughey doesn't seem to care. "He's truly carefree," said best buddy Armstrong.

We'll take these guys at their word unless sex tapes surface. Surely such a tape would outsell Paris Hilton's nocturnal adventures.

In 2005 McConaughey was named *People* magazine's Sexiest Man Alive, beating out James Denton, Matthew Fox, Brad Pitt, Matt Damon, Terrence Howard, and Vince Vaughn (Vince Vaughn?). "He's pretty much the perfect package," Julie Jordan, *People* spokesperson said. (We had already concluded that he was, but we'd have preferred more graphic evidence—and not just her word.)

It's been a long time since Tom Cruise was named *People*'s Sexiest Man Alive. It was way back in 1990. Does anybody in the world, except for Katie Holmes, think Cruise is sexy anymore?

In 2003 it was Sandra Bullock who was said to be in love with McConaughey, at least in August, but reportedly, in October she had found love with Armstrong. It's up to Bullock to tell us which of the two is the Sexiest Man Alive. So far, she hasn't written her memoirs.

Party boys above, **Lance Armstrong** *(left)* and **Matthew McConaughey** *(right),* launched a friendship in their hometown of Austin, Texas that caused much speculation in the press. "I've seen them partying late at night at Antone's, Austin's most popular music club, and it seems they always have a beer in their hands," said a patron. *(See evidence in bottom photo.)* "They were always surrounded by beautiful women."

In spite of speculation, they are very straight – in fact, woman crazy. McConaughey *(lower left)* is so assured of his masculinity that he'll even pose in his girlfriend's lingerie from Victoria's Secret.

375

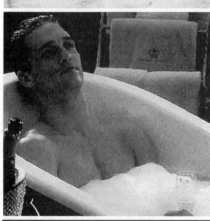

Is **Matthew McConaughey** *(above)* in the bathtub contemplating the end of his friendship with Lance Armstrong and Jake Gyllenhaal? Reports have it that Gyllenhaal has edged out the bathing beauty for the coveted role of Armstrong in an upcoming biopic on Armstrong. That's a bit hard to take since McConaughey has logged far more hours of friendship with the cycling legend than Gyllenhaal.

At last report, Armstrong and Gyllenhaal were spotted biking together in Malibu at sunset. The press speculated that Gyllenhaal has wooed Armstrong away from McConaughey, his wine-shopping, nightclubbing and intimate jogging partner on the beach.

Before he became a Hollywood movie star, **Jake Gyllenhaal** was a lifeguard. His only rescue was of a swimmer who had been stung on the leg by a jellyfish. Gyllenhaal pulled down his bathing trunks and pissed on the swimmer's leg to relieve the pain.

Believe it or not, urine is said to do just that. But since his days as a lifeguard, there are about 100,000 men in gay bars across America who claim to be his love. According to these bitchy queens, the actor's actual cock size ranges from five inches to twelve inches.

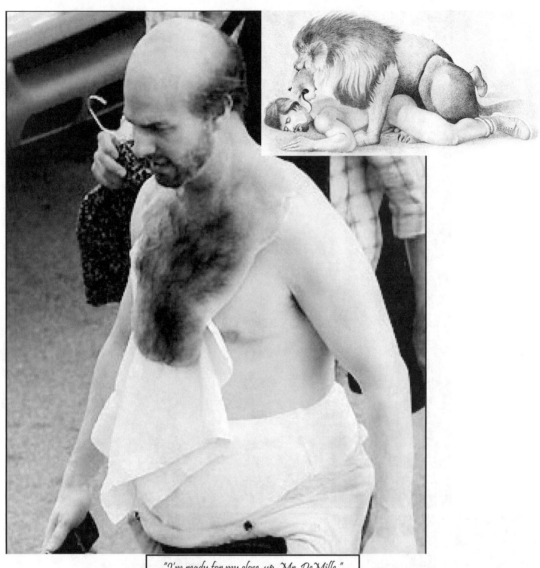

"I'm ready for my close-up, Mr. De Mille."

Index

BLOOD MOON PRODUCTIONS

Entertainment about How America interprets its celebrities.

Blood Moon is staffed with writers who otherwise devote their energies to *THE FROMMER GUIDES*, a trusted name in travel publishing.

It originated in 1997 as *The Georgia Literary Association*, a vehicle for the promotion of obscure writers from America's Deep South.

Today, Blood Moon Productions is based in New York City.

Four of Blood Moon's recent biographies have been extensively serialized (excerpted) by the largest-readership publications of the U.K., including *The Mail on Sunday* and *The Sunday Times*. Other serializations of Blood Moon's titles have appeared in Australia's *Women's Weekly* and *The Australian*.

Our releases have also generated literary and arts-industry reviews, tons of blogsite commentaries, and in some cases hate mail.

Thanks for your interest in Blood Moon. For more about us, click on **www.BloodMoonProductions.com,** or refer to the pages which immediately follow.

Salvaging the previously unrecorded
Oral Histories of Hollywood

The Georgia Literary Association

Entertainment You Wouldn't Necessarily Expect
from America's Deep South

THE SECRET LIFE OF
HUMPHREY BOGART

THE EARLY YEARS (1899-1931) BY DARWIN PORTER

The Secret Life of
Humphrey Bogart
The Early Years
(1899 - 1931)
Darwin Porter

This myth-shattering biography gives
a controversial CLOSEUP of a young,
hot and horny Bogart
pre-Casablanca, pre-Bacall, pre-African Queen
Revealing for the first time what was under the
trench coat of history's most famous movie star

Loaded with information once suppressed by the Hollywood studios, this is the most revealing book ever written about the undercover lives of movie stars during the 1930s. Learn what America's most visible male star was doing during his mysterious early years on Broadway and in Hollywood at the dawn of the Talkies--details that Bogie worked hard to suppress during his later years with Bacall.

The subject of more than 80 radio interviews by its author, and widely covered by both the tabloids and the mainstream press, it's based on never-before-published memoirs, letters, diaries, and interviews from men and women who either loved Bogie or who wanted him to burn in hell. No wonder Bogie, in later life, usually avoided talking about his early years.

Serialized in three parts by Britain's *Mail on Sunday*, with some of its revelations flashed around the world, it demonstrates that Hollywood's Golden Age stars were human, highly sexed, and at least when they were with other Hollywood insiders, remarkably indiscreet.

"This biography has had us pondering as to how to handle its revelations within a town so protective of its own...This biography of Bogart's early years is exceptionally well-written."

JOHN AUSTIN, *HOLLYWOOD INSIDE*

"In this new biography, we learn about how Bogart struggled for stardom in the anything goes era of the Roaring 20s."

THE GLOBE

"Porter's book uncovers scandals within the entertainment industry of the 1920s and 1930s, when publicists from the movie studios deliberately twisted and suppressed inconvenient details about the lives of their emerging stars."

TURNER CLASSIC MOVIE NEWS

"This biography brilliantly portrays a slice of time: In this case, the scandal-soaked days of Prohibition, when a frequently hung-over Bogie operated somwhat like a blank sheet of paper on which other actors, many of them infamous, were able to design their lives. The book is beautifully written."

LAURENCE HAZELL, PhD. University of Durham (UK)

From the Georgia Literary Association. 527 pages, with an index and at least 60 vintage photos.
Now in its third printing
ISBN 0-9668030-5-1 SOFTCOVER $16.95

HOWARD HUGHES: HELL'S ANGEL

AMERICA'S NOTORIOUS BISEXUAL BILLIONAIRE--THE SECRET LIFE OF THE U.S. EMPEROR

by Darwin Porter

A rigorously researched, highly entertaining hardcover about the Good Old Days in Hollywood from Blood Moon Productions **ISBN 0-9748118-1-5**. $26.95 814 pages, plus 175 vintage photos

As serialized by London's
Mail on Sunday,
this book is about the Hollywood intrigue,
and the Hollywood debauchery of
Howard Hughes
and the A-list legends
who participated.

Researched over a period of 40 years, it's
a stormingly good read about
Who and *What* money can buy.

**Outrageous
Fortune and
Tragic Greed**

"Thanks to Darwin Porter's biography of Howard Hughes, we'll never be able to look at the old pin-ups in quite the same way"

THE LONDON TIMES

"Darwin Porter grew up in the midst of Hollywood Royalty. his access to film industy insiders and other Hughes confidantes supplied him with the resources he needed to create a portrait that both corroborates what other Hughes biographies have divulged and go them one better."

FOREWORD MAGAZINE

"According to a new biography by Darwin Porter, Hughes's attitude toward sex, like the Emperor Caligula, was selfish at best and at its worst, sadistic. He was obsessed with controlling his lovers and, although he had a pathological fear of relationships and marriage, he proposed to countless women, often at the same time. Only three people successfully resisted Hughes's persistent advances: Elizabeth Taylor, Jean Simmons, and Joan Crawford. Of the three, it was Crawford who most succinctly revealed her reasons for refusing Hughes's advances, "I adore homosexuals, but not in my bed after midnight."

THE SUNDAY EXPRESS (LONDON)

Read about Hughes' complicated emotional and sexual entanglements with Katharine Hepburn, Cary Grant, Tallulah Bankhead, David Bacon, Jack Buetel, Bette Davis, and just about every other player, major and minor, in Hollywood.

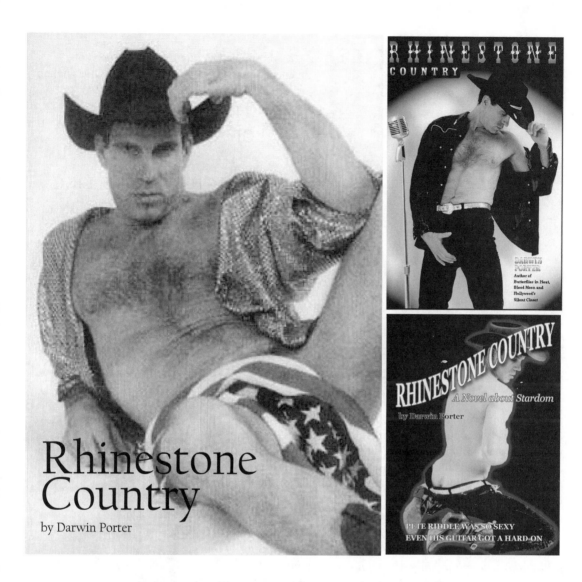

Rhinestone Country

by Darwin Porter

A provocative but tender portrait of a closeted superstar within Nashville's country-western music industry.   Sweeping across the sexual landscapes and racial barriers of the Deep South, it takes a hard look at hero-worship, fear, sacred icons, and loathing south of the Mason-Dixon line.

> *"A sexual kick in the groin. High-adrenaline love, violence, and betrayal.*
> *A riveting show-biz tale of fame and lust."*
> *-Tyrone Maxwell*

GEORGIA LITERARY ASSOCIATION

AN EROTIC NOVEL ABOUT BIG MONEY, COUNTRY-WESTERN MUSIC,
THE DEEP SOUTH, AND THE DESTRUCTIVE ASPECTS OF FAME.

FROM THE GEORGIA LITERARY ASSOCIATION
ISBN 0-9668030-3-5 PAPERBACK $15.95

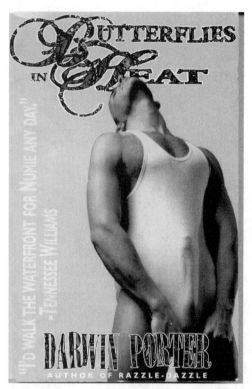

From the Georgia Literary Association,
in cooperation with the Florida Literary Association:

THE RENAISSANCE
OF A CULT CLASSIC

ONE OF THE BEST-SELLING
GLBT NOVELS OF ALL TIME

A study in malevolence, vendetta, morbid fascination, and redemption. One of the very few pop novels ever praised by Tennessee Williams ("I'd walk the waterfront for Numie any day...."), it was the inspiration for the original character of the male prostitute as portrayed by Jon Voight in *Midnight Cowboy*. Its hero is blond god Numie Chase, an unlucky hustler with flesh to sell.

"Darwin Porter writes with an incredible understanding of the milieu--hot enough to singe the wings off any butterfly."
James Kirkwood, co-author, *A Chorus Line*

"How does Darwin Porter's garden grow? Only in the moonlight, and only at midnight, when man-eating vegetation in any color but green bursts into full bloom to devour the latest offerings."
James Leo Herlihy, author of ***MIDNIGHT COWBOY***

"Not since I saw Tennessee Williams's first Broadway play have I experienced such a compelling American writer."
Greta Keller

Butterflies in Heat by **Darwin Porter** Now in its 18th printing.
**Originally published by Manor Books. Now available from the
Georgia Literary Association and Blood Moon Productions
Paperback $12.95 ISBN 1-877978-95-7**

The Erotic Thriller

BLOOD MOON

Learn what really happens
when the moon turns to blood

BLOOD MOON

A novel about power, money, religious
fanaticism, sexual obsession, and love

"*Blood Moon* is like reading Anaïs Nin on Viagra with a bump of crystal meth."

Eugene Raymond

"In your face thrills. Forget morality. Forget redemption. Hide it from your children and by all means, don't let your wife know you're reading it. She's always suspected you. This will convince her."

Queer Biz

Set within the glittery and sometimes tawdry context of South Florida, this is about love, sexual obsession, power, and religious fanaticism in America today. And because of recent revelations about the links between the regime of George W. Bush and the Saudi oil empire, many of its then-shocking premises seem almost clairvoyant.

"Rose Phillips, *Blood Moon*'s charismatic and deviant evangelist, and her uncontrollable gay son, Shelley, were surely written in hell."   **Buddy Hamilton**

"*Blood Moon* reads like *Dynasty* on steroids. A compelling psycho-sexual adventure of three beautiful men meeting on the fast road to hell."   **Kathryn Cobb**

FROM THE GEORGIA LITERARY ASSOCIATION AND BLOOD MOON PRODUCTIONS
ISBN 0-9668030-4-3   ABRIDGED EDITION PAPERBACK, 514 PAGES $10.99

This is the book
that satirized THE BOOK
that changed the face of tourism in Savannah
for all time.

MIDNIGHT IN SAVANNAH

BY DARWIN PORTER   ISBN 09668030-1-9   Paperback   **$14.95**

This is the more explicit and more entertaining alternative to John Berendt's Savannah-based *Midnight in the Garden of Good and Evil*. Decadent but insightful, it's a saga of corruption, greed, sexual tension, and murder that gets down and dirty in the Deep Old South.

For more than a year after its publication in 2000, this was was the best-selling GLBT novel in Georgia and the Carolinas.   If you're gay and southern, or if you've ever felt either traumatized or eroticized south of the Mason-Dixon Line, you should probably read this book.

"In Darwin Porter's <u>Midnight</u>, both Lavender Morgan ("At 72, the world's oldest courtesan") and Tipper Zelda ("an obese, fading chanteuse taunted as "the black widow,") purchase lust from sexually conflicted young men with drop-dead faces, chiseled bodies, and genetically gifted crotches.   These women once relied on their physicality to steal the hearts and fortunes of the world's richest and most powerful men.   Now, as they slide closer every day to joining the corpses of their former husbands,   these once-beautiful women must depend, in a perverse twist of fate, on sexual outlaws for <u>le petit mort.</u>   And to survive, the hustlers must idle their personal dreams while struggling to cajole what they need from a sexual liaison they detest.   Mendacity reigns, Perversity in extremis.   Physical beauty as living hell.   CAT ON A HOT TIN ROOF'S Big Daddy must be spinning in his grave right now."

EUGENE RAYMOND

404

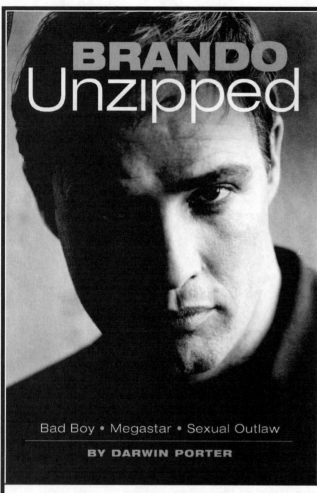

BRANDO
Unzipped

Bad Boy • Megastar • Sexual Outlaw

BY DARWIN PORTER

"Lurid, raunchy, perceptive, and definitely worth reading... One of the best show-biz biographies of the year"
The Sunday Times (London)

"*Brando Unzipped* is the definitive gossip guide to the late, great actor's life"
The New York Daily News

"Entertainingly Outrageous"
Frontiers

Winner of an honorable mention from Foreword Magazine, a silver medal from the IPPY Awards, and the subject of LOTS of critical debate.

Yummy!...Practically every page discloses a fascinating tidbit --about Liberace successfully seducing Dean, for example. This is an irresistibly flamboyant romp of a read."
Books to Watch Out For

"This shocking new book is sparking a major reassessment of Brando's legacy as one of Hollywood's most macho lotharios."

Daily Express (London)

"As author Darwin Porter finds, it wasn't just the acting world Marlon Brando conquered. It was the actors, too."

Gay Times (London)

From Blood Moon   *Brando like you've never seen him before*

BRANDO UNZIPPED, by Darwin Porter
ISBN 978-0-0748118-2-6   Now in its fourth printing
Hardcover. 625 pages with 300 photos. $26.95

407

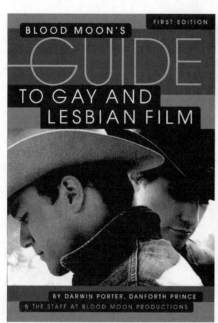

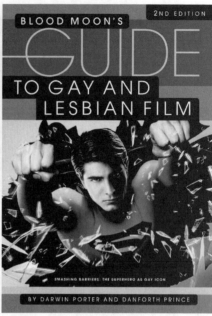

"Authoritative, exhaustive, and essential, it's the queer girl's and queer boy's one-stop resource for what to add to their feature-film queues . The film synopses and the snippets of critic's reviews are reason enough to keep this annual compendium of cinematic information close to the DVD player. But the extras--including the special features and the Blood Moon Awards--are butter on the popcorn."

Richard LaBonte, Books to Watch Out For

"Blood Moon's Guide to Gay and Lesbian Film is like having access to a feverishly compiled queer film fan's private scrapbook. Each edition is a snapshot of where we are in Hollywood now. It's also a lot of fun..."

Gay Times (London)

"Startling. It documents everything from the mainstream to the obscure, detailing dozens of queer films from the last few years."

HX (New York)

"Includes everything fabu in the previous years' movies. An essential guide for both the casual viewer and the hard-core movie watching homo."

Bay Windows (Boston)

"From feisty Blood Moon Productions, this big, lively guidebook of (mostly) recent gay and gayish films is not meant to be a dust-collecting reference book covering the history of GLBT films. Instead, it's an annual running commentary on what's new and what's going on in gay filmmaking.

Mandate

First Edition (published 2006)
ISBN 978-0-9748118-4-0 $19.95

Second Edition (published 2007)
ISBN 978-0-9748118-7-1 $21.95

Third Edition available October, 2008